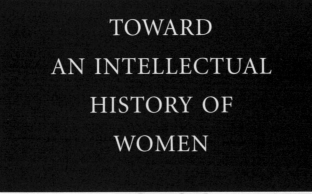

TOWARD
AN INTELLECTUAL
HISTORY OF
WOMEN

TOWARD
AN INTELLECTUAL
HISTORY OF
WOMEN

ESSAYS BY LINDA K. KERBER

THE UNIVERSITY OF NORTH CAROLINA PRESS

CHAPEL HILL & LONDON

© 1997

The University of North Carolina Press

All rights reserved

Manufactured in the United States of America

The paper in this book meets the guidelines for

permanence and durability of the Committee on Production Guidelines

for Book Longevity of the Council on Library Resources.

Acknowledgments of permission to reprint previously published material

appear at the end of the book, following the index.

Library of Congress Cataloging-in-Publication Data

Kerber, Linda K.

Toward an intellectual history of women : essays / by Linda K. Kerber.

p.   cm. — (Gender and American culture)

Includes index.

ISBN 0-8078-2348-1 (cloth : alk. paper).

— ISBN 0-8078-4654-6 (pbk. : alk. paper)

1. Women—United States—Intellectual life.   2. Women in politics—

United States—History.   3. Feminism—United States—History.

I. Title.   II. Series: Gender & American culture.

HQ1410.K47   1997

305.4'0973—dc21   96-45138

CIP

01   00   99   98   97   5   4   3   2   1

FOR DICK,

an anniversary present

CONTENTS

Acknowledgments *xi*

Introduction *1*

I. FINDING WOMEN IN THE REVOLUTIONARY ERA

Daughters of Columbia:
Educating Women for the Republic, 1787–1805 (1973) *23*

The Republican Mother:
Women and the Enlightenment—An American Perspective (1976) *41*

"History Can Do It No Justice":
Women and the Reinterpretation of the American Revolution (1989) *63*

"I Have Don . . . much to Carrey on the Warr":
Women and the Shaping of Republican Ideology after the
American Revolution (1990) *100*

The Republican Ideology of the Revolutionary Generation (1985) *131*

II. TOWARD AN INTELLECTUAL HISTORY OF WOMEN

Separate Spheres, Female Worlds, Woman's Place:
The Rhetoric of Women's History (1988) *159*

Can a Woman Be an Individual?:
The Discourse of Self-Reliance (1991) *200*

"Why Should Girls Be Learn'd and Wise?":
The Unfinished Work of Alice Mary Baldwin (1993) *224*

III. FINDING GENDER IN AMERICAN CULTURE

The Paradox of Women's Citizenship in the Early Republic:
The Case of *Martin vs. Massachusetts*, 1805 (1992) *261*

Women and Men:
Boredom, Violence and Political Power (1993) *303*

Index *319*

Permissions *335*

ILLUSTRATIONS

Sarah Franklin Bache *82*

Esther De Berdt Reed *83*

Petition of Rachel Wells *101*

Frontispiece for Philadelphia *Ladys Magazine* *114*

Patience Wright *126*

A Happy Family *181*

Switchboards, Cortland Exchange, c. 1890 *186*

Jane Addams in Hull House dining room, c. 1930 *191*

Halsted Street view of Hull House, c. 1915 *193*

Plan of the Hull House buildings, c. 1963 *194*

Physics lecture room at the University of Michigan, c. 1890 *197*

Alice Mary Baldwin *226*

James Sullivan *283*

Dorothy Kenyon *304*

ACKNOWLEDGMENTS

Barbara Hanrahan, now director of the Ohio State University Press, had faith in this project from the beginning, and her wise counsel gave the book its shape.

The visible college of students and colleagues in the Department of History at the University of Iowa has sustained my work for more than twenty-five years. At a time when many who wished to initiate courses in women's history had to fight hard battles with curriculum committees, the department only wanted to know whether I wished to teach on Monday-Wednesday-Friday or Tuesday-Thursday. By the rigorous standards it sets and the supportive conversations it sustains, the department has provided the conditions for much of this work. The May Brodbeck Chair in the Liberal Arts offered precious gifts of time and research funds; Jay Semel and Lorna Olson make the Obermann Center for Advanced Studies a congenial retreat.

I am deeply grateful for support received over the years from the National Endowment for the Humanities. I have been fortunate to work at a time when a national system of financial support and peer review for scholarship funded not only my own research and writing but also the invigorating work of many others on which my own depends. Fellowships from the John Simon Guggenheim Memorial Foundation, the Rockefeller Foundation, and the National Humanities Center came at crucial moments and made possible much that appears here.

In the invisible college, colleagues taught by example. They also taught by scribbling in my margins, by raising challenging questions, by urging me on. When it came time to conceptualize the Introduction, Robert Gross helped in very important ways; so did Alfred F. Young and Alice Kessler-Harris. I am grateful for the advice of Suzanne Lebsock, Jeanne Boydston, Cindy Aron, and Nell Irvin Painter.

At the University of North Carolina Press, Kate Torrey nudged gently, making sure that this book did not get pushed aside by my commitments as president of the Organization of American Historians. Ron Maner managed the steps toward publication with skill. I feel very lucky and very grateful that Richard Hendel has designed this book.

Chance brought Jane De Hart and me together on the first American Historical Association Committee on Women Historians in 1971. There we found ourselves part of an extraordinary national community of feminist historians; there we learned that the learned societies—the American Historical Association, the Organization of American Historians, the American Studies Association—could be havens for historians who were striking out in new directions and also forces for professional change. Working on the committee, we wrote reports and proposals and manifestos; when our terms were up, we had learned to finish each other's sentences and often each other's thoughts. Ever since then Jane has scrutinized my arguments and my prose, including much that has gone into this book. She is the best of colleagues, best of friends.

And for all my adult life Dick has been there, companion through the distractions that these essays have brought with them, colleague who reads every word that I write. Once again, this book is for him.

TOWARD
AN INTELLECTUAL
HISTORY OF
WOMEN

INTRODUCTION

In the invisible college that students do not see, academics educate each other. Term papers do not stop when Ph.D.s are awarded. With varying mixtures of loyalty, pride, curiosity, and energy, we accept each other's assignments. We submit our work to each other's review. Sometimes we know our critics, sometimes we don't. Masquerading as flattery, as opportunity, as obligation, commissions pour in.

When I look at the table of contents of this book, each title resonates simultaneously with a friend's voice and a colleague's will power, urging me to reschedule what I had thought was my own research agenda. Sometimes it is a matter of honor: Eric McKitrick and Stanley Elkins are gathering essays by Richard Hofstadter's former students to honor his memory after his untimely death; it is itself an honor to be part of that project. Sometimes it is an assignment. An old and dear friend, arranging a conference on the theme "Defining Our Terms," calls to say that she's certain that I am the appropriate person to reflect on the changing uses of the term "separate spheres"; the exercise will be strenuous, she admits, but it will be good for my intellectual health. Sometimes it is opportunity: travel now, pay later in manuscript. Ron is organizing a conference and needs a keynote speaker; Darline is organizing an international conference and needs an Americanist. Each time I accepted an assignment, I wondered if it were deflecting me from my "real" work on a longer project, but my own research agenda has been enriched by what I have learned in the invisible college about my capacities as a historian and as a writer.

In the early 1970s, when the first of the essays in this book was published, a friendly but unadventurous colleague tried to warn me off. "Women's history is a topic, not a subject," he said gently. I knew he was wrong: Mary Beard's *Woman as Force in History* (1946) and Eleanor Flexner's *Century of Struggle* (1959) sat rock-solid on our shelves; Gerda Lerner had already begun a series of major interpretative essays in 1969. But I also knew he was right: gender was not yet understood to be, in Joan Scott's felicitous phrase, "a useful tool of historical analysis." Throughout my graduate student years

1

at Columbia University, my colleagues and I had read virtually no books by women historians, no biographies of women activists, and, with the exception of works by abolitionists, no primary source materials testifying to women's experience. This would have been less true had we been medievalists. Columbia historians took great pride in public speaking, and during my years there, from 1961 to 1968, I heard many dazzling lectures. But none were by women faculty members. There were, in fact, no women faculty members among the Americanists at Columbia, although I had been taught by women at Barnard, the women's college of the university, whose faculty had courtesy privileges at Columbia and occasionally served as graduate examiners or as members of dissertation committees. No lecture in graduate school that I remember focused clearly on women's historical experience—as workers, teachers, educators, politicians, criminals. None of the books that I was expected to read in preparation for examinations were written by women.

I am no longer surprised. I was in school during the Cold War, in the long 1950s that stretched until 1967. The constraining politics of the time was accompanied by an ideology that undermined the ambitions of women to shape careers outside the home and that rewrote history to deny that they had ever done so. When women figured in historical narratives they were an odd and disruptive force, from the witches of Salem in the eighteenth century to Communist sympathizers in the present. My parents held progressive political views, but they had been too frightened by the witch-hunts of the 1950s—which in New York City had reached into classrooms, humiliating teachers sometimes literally before the eyes of their astonished students—to permit their daughter to explore the left publications where some concern for women's history still flourished. I was thirteen years old when Ethel Rosenberg was executed, and I can still remember the ominous emptiness of the Manhattan streets that day, as if Yom Kippur were being observed. When Judith Coplon, a bright Jewish graduate of Barnard College, was arrested as a spy, my mother was shocked enough to worry about the risks of sending her daughter to one of the few elite colleges that no longer had a Jewish quota.

There are three sorts of academic occasional essays: leftovers from one's last book, warning signals for one's new book, and experiments. The first essay in this collection "Daughters of Columbia," is of the first sort. An invitation to contribute to *The Hofstadter Aegis* elicited in me a very traditional response: here was a place to use the outtakes from my dissertation, which had recently been published as *Federalists in Dissent*. But if I had learned no women's history in the Cold War years, why had I taken all those unused notes—on Mary Wollstonecraft, on women's fashions—in that era before photocopiers when notes were laboriously copied by hand and retyped? While I had been writing what I thought was a history of political thought, my subconscious had been playing identity politics. Perhaps more precisely, my subconscious was driven by the academic feminism it had absorbed in the 1950s as an undergraduate at Barnard College, where the feminism of the 1930s persisted, where my teachers made sure that the women's march on Versailles in 1789 was part of what we learned about the French Revolution, and where Edith Wharton was central to the American literature survey course. In my freshman English class, the obligatory Shakespearean play we read was neither *Hamlet* nor *Julius Caesar* but *Antony and Cleopatra*; the complexities of a woman's choices were central to our introduction to the Western literary tradition.

That English class was taught by John Kouwenhoven, a man of patrician bearing and sly wit, who taught first-year students with great dedication—he was fond of saying that he wanted to get hold of students *first*—and who had initiated Barnard's American Civilization program. He had recently published *The Columbia Historical Portrait of New York*, a book that remains unusual for its construction of a narrative history in which images—prints, maps, portraits—are used as visual evidence for the substantive arguments, not merely as illustration. (Years later, when I used visuals in a similar spirit in *Women of the Republic*, his influence was surely at work.)

In the 1950s there was an inchoate but pervasive sense that American Civilization—which I chose for my major—was an exciting place to be. Nowadays as global studies, African American studies, women's studies, and other interdisciplinary programs flourish, it is useful to remember that it was the American Civilization programs of the 1940s and 1950s which challenged departmental boundaries by juxtaposing literature and politics, art and social history, architecture and foreign relations (one friend wrote a memorable senior thesis on the ideologies of design that informed American embassies abroad). American Studies programs at least suggested—as did virtually no other element in the standard college curriculum of the 1950s—that African Americans and women were central to understanding American culture. By the variety of cross-disciplinary choices they offered, it was American Studies programs that first surrendered to undergraduates substantial power for innovation in the planning of a personal academic career.

I could not tell that the intellectual excitement of American Civilization in those days was greatly facilitated by the substantial amounts of federal and foundation money going into it. I did not then understand that I was living in a postwar, Cold War world, where American Civilization was one way among many of making a defensive claim for Our Side against theirs. The American Civilization curriculum involved a strident validation of American exceptionalism. The organizing analytical question of the 1950s was "What's American about America?" The answer, brilliantly framed in an essay by John Kouwenhoven with that subtitle, published in *Harper's* only two months before I met him, stressed interchangeable and endlessly extendable structures of the sort found in an infinitely amendable Constitution, an expandable grid town plan, the poetic forms of Walt Whitman (as contrasted to the sonnet), or the musical forms of jazz (as compared to the sonata). To approach American culture in this way, however, was necessarily to drain it of political content and political responsibility. To search for American culture in processes that had shape but not closure was necessarily *not* to search for power, for hierarchy, or for structure. I have been greatly indebted to what I learned at Barnard, but I did not learn much about the exercise of power.

I have often wondered whether had I been a history major I would have focused more clearly on those issues. On the other hand, had I not chosen an interdisciplinary major I would have written books of a different character. In *Federalists in Dissent* I wrote chapters juxtaposing political and scientific thought, political and literary satire, ideas about education and ideas about government, the language of legislation and the language of the polemic: all juxtapositions that had been common to our discussions in Barnard seminars and that drove major books in American Studies like John William Ward's *Andrew Jackson: Symbol for an Age* and Henry Nash Smith's *Virgin Land* but that never, to my recollection, filtered into graduate work in history at Columbia. By the late 1960s, there was wide recognition that the term "Civilization" itself made a polemical claim to authority and distinctiveness. The learned society in the field had always been called the "American Studies Association," and by the 1970s most college and university programs had been renamed to reflect their goal of engaging in critical inquiry rather than mere celebration—which, of course, the best work in the field always had done.

I graduated from Barnard in 1960, at a commencement in which the college president assured our parents that over half the class was married or engaged. (Since I was to be married the following week, the words seemed to me at the time only the common sense of the matter, but decades later there remain dozens, maybe hundreds, of my classmates who have never forgiven her for intruding this reminder of what was perceived to be their inadequacy into a day which was supposed to be dedicated to a celebration of their academic accomplishments.) We emerged into a world in which most women who worked outside the home did so in occupations that were traditionally female, and the average woman earned sixty-one cents for every dollar earned by a man. I would learn from bitter experience not to convey at fellowship interviews that my plans for graduate school would be adjusted to my plans for marriage. Women were regularly asked openly why they were taking up a space that could be held by a man. Professional schools generally maintained informal quotas on race, gender, and ethnicity. Although Jewish quotas were eroding, no one denied that they still existed. As David Hollinger has lucidly explained, if by the 1990s Jews have "long since come to be perceived as part of an empowered white, or European-American demographic bloc," that had not been true in 1940, or 1950, or 1960.

But there were in 1960 competing understandings of what women were and might become. My parents—my mother was a public school teacher in New York City; my father, trained as a lawyer, was the manager of a camera store and a superb amateur photographer—were unambivalently committed to supporting professional aspirations. They never needed persuasion. I landed luckily in a college full of women like myself—only years later did I learn that Barnard administrators had for generations felt uneasy about their necessary hospitality to the Jewish and Italian girls of New York City—where we were simultaneously instructed that we were to marry and that we were to put our educations to serious, preferably professional, use. Our models were Eleanor Roosevelt, who had five children, and our distinguished college president, Millicent McIntosh, who had four. At the first freshman luncheon, Mrs. McIntosh was introduced with a brief biographical sketch that made a point of telling us that she had had all her babies in the summer. I was sixteen years old and thought that was a curious point to make so publicly. Only many years later, when my friends and I found it not so easy to accomplish a pregnancy while simultaneously maintaining a career, did we realize what the message had been. So long as a woman accepted her role as the center of home and family life there was much that she might attempt; problems came when professional identity competed with the demands of the nuclear family. (At that point, even powerful minds confessed themselves at a loss.)

After a year at New York University, I returned to Columbia, then one of the very few elite universities reasonably hospitable to women students and authentically hospitable to Jewish men. The first generation of Jewish men to receive tenure were among its most distinguished faculty—Lionel Trilling, Richard B. Morris, Richard Hofstadter—although, naif that I was, I could not read the signs of ethnicity if they were unaccompanied by a New York accent, and I was surprised and moved to tears when the *Kaddish* was recited at Richard Hofstadter's memorial service in 1970.

In the years when I was in his seminar, Richard Hofstadter was publishing a substantial book roughly every three years. He taught by the dazzling example of his own work that ideas as well as economic relations matter and are often deeply intertwined, that historical knowledge can link to political understanding, and that historians should be confident that if they can write simultaneously sharply and gracefully, their work will claim its audience. I am not sure what drew me to the inquiry that shaped my dissertation, Federalist opposition to Jefferson, but I now think it was compounded in roughly equal measure of an urge on the part of a descendant of immigrants to say something original about the founding generation and of an authentic admiration, in the early stages of the Vietnam War, for a political faction that had resisted the War of 1812.

I did not find it particularly difficult to be a graduate student; it seemed not very different from the life my husband Dick was living as medical student—we worked equally long hours, although I had much more flexibility—and when we decided to have a child, it was not impossible to mold the final stages of dissertation writing around the last months of pregnancy and the first months of our son Ross's life.

I was lucky to find a teaching appointment while working on my dissertation; the women's college of Yeshiva University accepted me although I was not an observant Jew. The dean asked only for assurance that I respected what his students believed. The intensely serious environment of Stern College was the safest of spaces; only when I went outside of it, onto the coed, secular job market, would I find that I was virtually unemployable.

Of the next few years I find it still almost impossible to write. Dick was drafted into the army after his second year of residency. Anxious anticipation of my dissertation defense evaporated in the face of the authentic panic I felt during the year he was in Vietnam. I still cannot remember a single question I was asked at that defense in the early spring of 1968. Not long after, the Columbia campus erupted in resistance to university authority and a generalized opposition to the war; we joked that I was sending photographs to Vietnam from the New York battlefront. When Dick returned in the summer we moved to California, where our second son, Justin, was born in 1969; we lived through the next few intensely political years in Palo Alto, then the most intensely political of places.

If I somehow had known that it was wise to take notes about women in the mid-1960s, I had not known what to do with the notes I had taken. In *Federalists in Dissent* I wrote three paragraphs—of which I am still very proud—on the women and children who served as the first American proletariat in the primitive cotton mills of the early republic. I had a hunch that there was more to be said, but I could not think how or where to push the research. My advisers never prompted me; I didn't know how to ask for help. Not until the revitalized feminist movement of the late 1960s and early 1970s could I see what I already had done, could I muster the courage (I take no credit; stronger spirits than mine had done this long before) to intrude into a manuscript library to ask what women's collections they had without feeling like a fool. In 1968 that was a dumb question, revealing that the asker was on a fishing expedition and need not be taken seriously; in any event a woman's manuscripts were generally absorbed into her father's or husband's papers and many curators had no idea what their own collections held. But in 1972 the same question was, in many libraries, a welcome one, which could be counted on to elicit sparkles in curatorial eyes, compliments on one's perspicacity, and not infrequently an invitation to ramble in closed stacks. Women's history has regularly flourished in times of progressive and feminist politics and regularly declined in periods of repression; activists are hungry for their history. Elizabeth Cady Stanton and Susan B. Anthony saved the records of the suffrage movement and regularly commissioned historical essays recording the work that was done, decade by decade, state after state, country after country, until they and their successors had filled six indispensable volumes with their *History of Woman Suffrage*. The revitalized feminist movement of 1969 and thereafter sustained its own demand and its own audience for women's history, and my own work has been done in response to and sustained by the feminism of my own time.

By 1971 we were in Iowa City. Dick was appointed to the faculty of the medical school and I was made welcome by the history department. After the years at Stern there had been a year without a job, then a part-time appointment at San Jose State College, then a temporary but glorious year at Stanford, replacing a professor on sabbatical leave, and then Iowa. But there had been absolutely no options in each transition; there had been lots of rejection letters, and had the single job not appeared—and had Dick, who as a smart young cardiologist had many choices, not also seen opportunity in the University of Iowa faculty—I would have been unemployed.

Women of my graduate school cohort at Columbia had much the same experience, different only in the details. One of my fellow students, who is now a senior professor at a major university, holds the record for our cohort of nine consecutive temporary appointments. Another, who currently holds a chaired professorship, spent nearly a decade marginally employed or dependent on grant money. Looking back from the perspective of the 1990s, comparing our experiences to what graduate students in the humanities now face, the rickety early years of finding a job don't seem so outrageous. But those were years of enormous growth in the size of colleges and universities, and the men of our cohort were likely to emerge from graduate school into tenure-track positions. We knew we were as smart—or smarter—than they.

What I could not see was that I was one of the lucky ones. My gender and ethnicity may have made me marginal, but my skin color did not. When I received my Ph.D., only 2 percent of the nation's university, college, and community college faculty and staff members were African American. Columbia was almost as segregated as if it had been in the Deep South. Had I been born ten years earlier, the professions would have been even less merciful. My generation mostly escaped the political tragedies of the McCarthy era. Supreme Court Justice Ruth Bader Ginsburg has not forgotten the petty humiliations to which she and her women colleagues were subjected at Harvard Law School in 1956. Janet Wilson James, who completed a brilliant dissertation on women in the early republic at Harvard in 1954, could not find a stable job until 1971, when she was fifty-three years old. Her dissertation went unpublished until 1981. When I wrote *Women of the Republic*, I had no idea that it had a predecessor in Janet's dissertation until my own book was nearly complete. Scores, hundreds, thousands—no one has counted—of women started graduate school in the 1940s and 1950s and were deflected. I have lived my professional life in an academic world from which women ten and twenty years older than I have been virtually absent. The very few who seem to fit the category—Gerda Lerner, Anne Firor Scott—often had interrupted careers and took their Ph.D.s or entered the job market only a few years earlier than my own generation did. They only appear to be significantly older than we. The few of us who managed to hang on into the transitional years of 1971–75 were those whose timing was right, although, in the exhaustion of our struggle, we rarely appreciated it.

In 1970, an unemployed historian and new mother—our younger son, Justin, had been born eight months before—I watched in awe as Professor Willie Lee Rose of Johns Hopkins University told the business meeting of the American Historical Association that women historians faced discrimination because of their sex. In effect she was explaining why there were no older women historians. In the 1980s it would be common for patronizing men to observe that the new generation of women academics was sui generis; ever since the generation of the 1930s women just hadn't had the smarts and the gumption of the liberated women they knew. But that was false history. Rose presented a modest statistical report that revealed the severe underrepresentation of women historians in all history departments in 1970 except those in women's colleges (where, nevertheless, their proportion had declined in the previous twenty years). On behalf of a distinguished committee of historians—which included Carl Schorske, Page Smith, Hanna Holborn Gray (who some years later would serve as president of the University of Chicago), and Patricia Albjerg Graham (who would a decade later be dean of the Harvard School of Education and subsequently president of the Spencer Foundation)—Rose called upon the American Historical Association to establish a permanent committee charged with working actively to enlarge the number of women in the profession and deal with cases of discrimination against them, to ensure greater representation of women on the programs and in the committees of the AHA, to work with history departments to eliminate nepotism rules, to support more flexible part-time employment, and to develop policies of maternity leaves. They called the situation "urgent" and in need of "prompt action."

To acknowledge that women historians faced "discrimination" from their own mentors and colleagues was to name publicly a situation that had theretofore been understood to be "normal," "natural," and permanent. The Rose Report spoke directly to my own confusion as a woman who claimed a professional life that was intellectual at its core and to which many thought no woman was entitled. The atmosphere in the Boston hotel ballroom—standing room only, some five hundred historians—was almost as charged as it had been in Washington, D.C., the year before, when radical historians had demanded that the AHA take a position against the Vietnam War.

The Rose Committee had its own history. It had been formed in response to a petition signed by twenty-two women who shortly thereafter would organize themselves as the Coordinating Committee on Women in the Historical Profession (CCWHP—still flourishing as the Coordinating Committee of Women Historians). The signers were themselves involved on their own campuses in demands for reports on the status of women modeled on the pioneering report produced at Berkeley in 1969, which showed, among other things, that in some departments no woman had been appointed since the 1920s and that seven departments had never had a woman member.

Instead of the permanent committee that the petitioners demanded, the AHA had established a temporary one, instructed to "commission studies and collect statistics," to gather information about discrimination, and to publish what they had learned. The temporary committee was given no money to spend. But it could be clever, and the brilliance of the Rose Committee lay in its decision to collect rapidly a set of statistics that everyone could understand. The Rose Report focused on the previous ten years— that is, the decade of my own graduate work—in three strategic groups of ten institutions each: ten major public and private research universities, ten selective coeducational colleges, and ten women's colleges. They found that only in women's colleges did women account for nearly half the faculty, and in those colleges the proportion of women in the history faculties had declined in the decade of the 1960s. Although some 15 percent of the Ph.D.s in history awarded in the decade of the 1950s had gone to women, not a single woman was a full professor in the ten most distinguished graduate departments of history in the early 1960s. By the end of the 1960s, a decade in which the size of these departments roughly doubled and the number of full professors went from 160 to 274, only *two* women became full professors in those ten large departments, which numbered forty to sixty men each. When Willie Lee Rose called upon the AHA to establish a permanent committee on the status of women, the ten history departments at major research universities which had been awarding between 10 and 15 percent of their Ph.D.s in history to women for decades, employed a total of seven women in tenure-track or tenured positions. There were no women in *any* rank at Cornell, Stanford, or Wisconsin between 1959 and 1967.

The Rose Report frankly and explicitly said that these statistics were no accident, that they were the result of intention, and that intentions were shaped by prejudice, misjudgment, and perverse ideology. The report concluded:

One factor militating against the advancement of women Ph.D.s is the widely-held assumption that women prefer to marry and devote themselves to domestic life. This assumption is belied by the evidence . . . [which] shows that 91 percent of the women receiving doctorates in all fields in the mid-fifties were employed in some type of work seven years later. Moreover, married women PhDs who are employed full-time show a higher publication rate than either unmarried women PhDs or men PhDs. . . . The discrepancy between women's professional status and performance is thus not grounded in any lack of commitment to the life of learning. . . . Those who practice discrimination against women in academic employment also hold general views concerning female inferiority.

As luck would have it, I had already been drawn into the circle of feminist historians organized as the Berkshire Conference of Women Historians. The Conference had originally been organized in 1929 by Jeannette Nicols and Mary Beard at a time when women historians were unwelcome at the "smokers" to which male historians repaired in the evenings at conventions. In the late 1960s the "Berks," at which attendance had declined in the 1950s and 1960s—perhaps a dozen historians actually came to the annual informal meetings in the Berkshires or at country inns elsewhere—was greatly invigorated by a younger generation that found it to be, in effect, a profession-specific consciousness-raising group. Along with the CCWHP, Berks people were mobilized to make sure that the Rose Report passed. We were prepared to take to the floor microphones ourselves to speak in its favor. But without our prompting, historians crowded the floor to speak in support of it, including—much to our surprise but as the report itself had predicted—elderly men who rose to address the meeting on the barriers faced by their granddaughters. And the following year I found myself appointed to the first permanent Committee on Women Historians, which Patricia Albjerg Graham, who had drafted much of the Rose Report, chaired. A year after that I served as the committee's chair. I would thus be given a ringside seat for the controversies and changes that were to come and a crash course in the sociology, politics, and academic culture of the historical profession.

The most significant sentence of the Rose Report, I have always thought, read, "The discrepancy between women's professional status and performance is thus not grounded in any lack of commitment to the life of learning." Its description of the demography of the profession was shocking but also reassuring: we were not unemployed because our scholarship was weak or because we had made fools of ourselves at interviews. We were unemployed because a profession that prided itself on its commitment to the life of the mind measured its colleagues by nonintellectual criteria. (Long before, in 1947, John Hope Franklin had made much the same point regarding the bar against black men in academia.) In the interludes between the working sessions of the permanent committee, we talked endlessly about whether it would be possible to improve the status of women as professional historians without simultaneously constructing for women a history that professional historians would have to respect.

As we talked, political change was undercutting historical narratives that had once been credible. The history of medicine, for example, had seemed unproblematic: a narrative composed of campaigns for antiseptic conditions in hospitals, discoveries of miracle drugs, biographies of heroes. But, in 1969, after bitter and very public debates, therapeutic abortion was made legal in several states. The margin in favor of this action was often very narrow—a single vote in one house of the New York legislature, for example—and even to obtain legal abortions women had to demonstrate that their physical or mental health was in grave danger. Suddenly it became clear that a distinctive, gendered history of health care was crying to be written. In 1971, persuaded by a brief written by Ruth Bader Ginsburg on behalf of the Women's Rights Project of the American Civil Liberties Union, the Supreme Court ruled for the first time in American history that discrimination on the basis of sex could be a violation of the Fourteenth Amendment's promise of equal treatment to all citizens. This ruling meant that virtually the entire history of citizenship as it had been written needed to be rewritten. In 1973 the Supreme Court ruled that the army could not provide benefits to male soldiers that it did not provide to their female counterparts; their opinion in the case of *Frontiero v. Richardson* was a long history lesson in how protective labor law had changed over three-quarters of a century. Labor history was in desperate need of rewriting. Historians had for the most part been complicit in explaining away different treatment of men and women as mere convenience, or as women's privilege, or as based in biology and nature. The generic "he" that had been alleged to encompass women's experience as well as men's turned out to be a fraud.

Now miles of shelves of books were outdated. In colleges across the country, feminist students perceived that their courses were conceptually old-fashioned and that their classes may have been coed but their faculties most definitely were not. Coalitions—often composed of women students and liberal male faculty—shamed administrators into changing the configurations of faculties and classes. The women's movement of the 1970s was many things, and among them was an invigorating agenda for feminist historians.

In that context I returned to the unused dissertation notes—responding to a new sense that not only was I myself newly situated but that the professional situation in which I lived had long been politicized had I only had the wit to see it. By 1972 I was not only chairing the AHA committee but was also teaching my first course in the history of women in the United States. In those days junior faculty rarely invented new courses; they taught the standard ones—the American Revolution, the Progressive Era, the New Deal—and the changes they made were relatively minor. But the demands of women students for women's history courses opened the curriculum to us. For me, as for my colleagues across the country, this experience came as a revelation. There turned out to be no dearth of material to teach. Even in those early years there was more than enough available in paperback to sustain many different courses—emphasizing work, or culture, or politics, or family life. Once we attacked the archives, looking for documents, they sprang out at us as if alive. There were diaries, there were letters, there were acts of legislation and public reports. There were artifacts of women's making, like quilts. There were institutions women had populated: girls' schools and colleges, women's prisons, textile factories, and garment shops. In this embarrassment of riches, my colleagues and I made our choices for our next research projects.

We also found ourselves shaping new spaces in coeducational institutions. Courses with the word "women" in the title were heavily enrolled by women students, often to the surprise and sometimes to the dismay of male faculty who had not been troubled when the reverse gender imbalance obtained in courses marked "the Civil War." My own courses in women's history were cross-listed with American Studies and later with Women's Studies. Against those who insisted that women's history was a topic within family history, we insisted that if it were a subfield, it was a subfield of everything: social history, legal history, intellectual history. Indeed, whatever topics we were drawn to, everyone who taught women's history became perforce an intellectual historian. We had to ask what different generations had meant by the terms they used: how they had conceptualized the categories of male and female, man and woman, or how the meaning of the term "feminism" itself had changed over the course of the century. When people in the nineteenth century spoke of "The Woman Question," what did they mean? Does "woman suffrage" mean the same as "women suffrage"? Over the decades, the conceptual questions grew in complexity. To what extent have concepts like "feminism" been implicitly located in racialized standpoints? What is the difference between sex and gender? To what extent is gender a social construction? To teach even the most basic narratives, we had to engage these questions. That was true in the early 1970s and it is even more true now; feminist scholars cannot ignore theorists of language or historians of ideas.

I teach graduate students now, and I am always conscious of urging them to be aware of how they are themselves located in time and in relationship to social movements and of encouraging them to enter into argument with their major predecessors in the field. In 1972 it was long past time to engage the implicit argument of virtually every historical study that women had not been intellectually consequential. It now strikes me as strange that the Columbia historians did so little along these lines, given their own progressive politics and the presence among them of the sociologist C. Wright Mills—a close friend of Richard Hofstadter—and the anthropologist Margaret Mead, both of whom had already published their pathbreaking work on the ways in which knowledge itself is located in the social context from which it emerges.

There was a continuity in my own work. I had once insisted that the Federalist objection to the Jeffersonians was not fully explained by different economic self-interest, as traditional progressive historians would have had it, and had taken the position that Federalist *ideas* deserved to be taken seriously and evaluated on their own terms. Now I took the position that the founding generation, which had such complex ideas about so many other things—the relation between ruler and ruled, the appropriate power of masters over servants, the natural history of the continent—must also have had ideas about women and the social order. Wherever I looked, that turned out to be so. The first essays in this book were the result of this inquiry.

"Daughters of Columbia" and "The Republican Mother" made—as publishers like to say—a splash. They were reprinted, cited extensively, included in lists of required reading for graduate and undergraduate students; they formed the foundation for my next book. The essays began serendipitously. In 1974 or 1975, Joseph Ellis, then and now a professor of history at Mount Holyoke, had undertaken to edit a special issue of the *American Quarterly* scheduled to appear for the bicentennial of the Declaration of Independence.

When Joe's invitation flattered me into the project, I was fresh from writing "Daughters of Columbia" as a memorial tribute to Richard Hofstadter. I had a hunch that I had not exhausted the subject, and indeed was already committed to a book, but I had not yet thought through how I would develop and extend the ideas in the original essay. Joe was not in a hurry for his essay, but because of the bicentennial, the special issue was going to be advertised well in advance of its appearance. Long before the essay was due, Joe needed a title. Like many writing people, I usually write titles last, after everything else is in shape. I put Joe off. He wrote pleading notes. I didn't answer. Finally he tracked me down on the phone, and refused to hang up until we had come up with a title for the preliminary table of contents. Desperate, I offered Joe "The Republican Mother" more in the hope of bringing the conversation to closure than because I was certain of the theme of the essay. Yet nothing I have written, before or since, has been so instantly useful for my own thinking or, it turned out, to other historians, as the essay that I developed on that theme. I have been reflecting on why this should be so.

While I was writing "Daughters of Columbia" and "The Republican Mother," I was less conscious of actively seeking a new interpretation—whereas years later, writing "The Paradox of Women's Citizenship" I was consciously trying for a new interpretation—than I was desperately trying to make sense out of a confused mass of note cards. There were few interpretative schemes with which I could connect. Everyone knew that Abigail Adams had written to John "Remember the ladies" and thought they knew—inaccurately—that Betsy Ross had sewn a flag. When I found women's verses against drinking tea, or Rachel Wells bringing food to soldiers under fire on the battlefield at Yorktown, or Judith Sargent Murray calling for "a new era in female history," what was I to make of them except a few more anecdotes?

In "The Republican Mother" I tried to move from anecdote to meaning, and to argue that those who thought about the future stability of the new republic *necessarily* considered the role of women in it. A few of the shrewdest members of the founding generation understood that the status of married women gave the lie to claims of government by the consent of the governed. In a culture that solidly associated intellect with masculinity—"women of masculine minds have generally masculine manners" one Federalist minister confidently asserted—some who did not have the stomach for radical disruption found a compromise position by envisioning mothers as playing a political role in the socializing role they played in their own families. By refusing to marry unpatriotic men, by raising their sons to be the next generation of virtuous citizens, women could play a meaningful political role, assuring the future stability of the fragile republic. Political virtue, a revolutionary concept that has troubled writers from Edmund Burke to Hannah Arendt, could be safely domesticated in eighteenth-century America; the mother, and not the masses, could be the custodian of civic morality.

By politicizing private behavior, the concept of "republican motherhood" pulled women's agency and the relations of men and women into the narrative of the American Revolution, suggested further questions about the transmission of republican ideology to the next generation, and challenged other historians to ground it more firmly in social experience. It supported the understanding that even when women were absent from legislatures and had not yet organized large-scale political movements, gender was of central significance to the great questions of the relationship between law and liberty. *Women of the Republic* carried the subtitle *Intellect and Ideology in Revolutionary America* because everywhere I turned, ideas about what women were, what relations between men and women should be, seemed to infuse contemporary understanding of major problems: in political theory, in the new law for an independent nation, in educational institutions, and in the substance of what men and women should study and should write. To search for the revolutionary generation's own understanding of women meant to work toward a new narrative of intellectual history grounded in gender as well as in other elements of American political and cultural life.

But if the concept of "republican motherhood" is deployed without the ironic, double-sided implications I meant to convey, if it is taken to mean unambivalent progress—from the Revolution white men get a more democratic polity and white women get republican motherhood—then it is silly and misleading. In this unnuanced sense, the term started turning up in textbooks (and, no doubt, in student examination papers) making me edgier and edgier over the years.

After the publication of *Women of the Republic* in 1980, I continued to be asked to speak or to write on the themes of the book. I accepted these invitations as occasions to restate what I thought in different contexts than my own book had provided. This work, in turn, kept me pondering what I had once said, re-examining the notes and documents I had once used, until, turning them around and around like crystals before the light, I disengaged from the irony and decided that republican motherhood was the ideological result of the gendered deployment of the old law of social relations. It had been a strategy middle-class women adopted to enter political conversation despite the bitter laws of coverture, which when they married denied to them power over their bodies, their property, and their children. "The Paradox of Women's Citizenship in the Early Republic" describes less a paradox than a hard fact of hierarchical relations. I would now say—as I would not have said in 1972 when I was pondering the problem of women in American revolutionary thought—that the founding generation understood clearly that they were sustaining the power of husbands over wives, parents over children, masters over servants and slaves while simultaneously undermining the power of the king over his subjects. American revolutionaries stabilized the radical changes they were making in conceptions of sovereignty by keeping the hierarchies of domestic relations intact. The subordination of women was not unintentional; it was an essential ingredient of the Revolution and the republican polity that followed. That is why it has taken more than two centuries and much bitter struggle to change it.

By the mid-1980s women's history was firmly established as a field of inquiry. Virtually every history department supported at least one course (although most history majors still graduate without having taken even one), prizewinning books had been written, and the scope of investigations continued to expand. Distinctive to the revitalized women's history of the 1970s—as contrasted to that written by previous generations, which had tended to focus on women's own experiences—was the confidence that "the social relations of the sexes," in Joan Kelley's graceful term, had a history as well as a sociology. The effort transformed the field of social history.

But the field of intellectual history was less resilient. Survey texts were still appearing in which, except for a nod in the direction of Jane Addams or Margaret Mead, women did not think serious thoughts. What intellectual difference might the feminist perspective make, applied to the life of the mind?

One difference it made, I think, was to energize the pursuit of evidence for women's engagement with complex ideas. The usual hunting grounds for intellectual historians—sermons, lectures, pamphlets, treatises on law, history, philosophy—revealed little or nothing of women's thoughts. Most historians gave up. But as I read women's diaries, I found more than I had expected by way of their own reflections on what they read and why they read it. I also found that advice—by both men and women—about what women should read was accompanied by urgent warnings of what they should not read. "We own that Ladies sometimes read," wrote the poet John Trumbull at the end of the eighteenth century, "And grieve that reading is confined / To books that poison all the mind." In a cultural context in which working-class women were often illiterate and middle-class women were warned against the dangers of reading, the practices of reading became actions of resistance rather than passive amusement, keys to women's own claims for freedom of imagination. The history of women's reading turned out to be a route to a better understanding of the relationship of women to intellectual communities. Chapter 8 of *Women of the Republic* set reading as a subject for historical inquiry, a concern that I have continued to explore—especially in the essays on individualism and on Alice Mary Baldwin that appear in this book—and that many other scholars—notably Mary Kelley, Barbara Sicherman, Jan Radway, Cathy Davidson, and Helen Horowitz—have subsequently pursued, so that the historian Robert Gross, recently summarizing the state of the field, has observed: "If we are to assay the history of readers and reading in America . . . we must look to women's lives. For a rare change in U.S. historiography, reading history is women's history."

Another difference the feminist perspective, applied to the life of the mind, has made, I think, is that it prompted us to isolate and interrogate ideas that had not been examined attentively. The metaphor that men and women live in "separate spheres" had been commonly used in the nineteenth century and had been seized upon in the twentieth as an interpretative device by women's historians. (Gerda Lerner was one of the few who remained skeptical.) By the early 1980s the term had become indispensable. Like most people who employed the concept of the "frontier" before Frederick Jackson Turner wrote his famous lecture in 1893, most of those who used the term "separate spheres" assumed its meaning was simple and obvious. They did not suspect it had a history of its own.

The task of the historiographer is to unsettle such assumptions, to place historians themselves in historical perspective, to demonstrate that what had been assumed to be solidly grounded is in fact historically contingent. That is what I tried to do in the essay on separate spheres that appears in this collection, which I began to write in 1984 and which finally reached print, after many revisions, four years later. The essay on individualism has a similar historiographical agenda. Ideas are grounded in social context. The construction of higher education and of opportunities to be, as one historian has described intellectuals, "people whose chief business it was to argue" has been a gendered construction; the history of ideas is also a history of changing social relations. As I write, I am completing a book on Americans' changing understanding of the obligations that citizens owe the state. Although these obligations—the obligation to refrain from treason, to refrain from being a vagrant, to pay taxes, to serve on juries, to risk one's life for the defense of the republic—are invariably framed in generic terms, all have distinctive histories for men and for women (and for men and women of different racial identifications). Historians who have trusted the generic, who have treated each of these obligations as unproblematic and ungendered, have neglected, I believe, a major dimension of citizenship. The concept of citizenship is yet another basic idea that has been gendered in ways we have only begun to appreciate.

The invisible college is an international one, challenging participants to pose old questions in new ways, to look at familiar evidence from unfamiliar angles. The feminist community of scholars and activists is also an international one—I cherish the thrill of seeing, for the first time, a book that I wrote reviewed in Italian. The final essay in this book is centered in U.S. materials but, in its focus on the League of Nations and matters of international importance, is a down payment on a research agenda in which I hope to be increasingly attentive to international and comparative matters.

I hope that these essays, focused as they are on core legal ideas and some key concepts that have undergirded our systems of gender relations, will point toward the next revision of our understanding of the major themes in U.S. intellectual history. I hope to have contributed to the next generation of revision, in which we will understand that both men and women think seriously about large matters, that *who* is given the time and opportunity to think and to argue is a matter not only of personal intelligence but of social history and social situation, and that when women are absent from the narrative histories of ideas, it is not because they are truly absent, but because the historian did not seek energetically enough to find them. I use "Toward" in the title of this collection of essays as a clue that the project is not yet accomplished, and I hope that these essays will be a contribution toward a goal that many share.

I

FINDING WOMEN IN

THE REVOLUTIONARY

ERA

DAUGHTERS
OF COLUMBIA
EDUCATING WOMEN
FOR THE REPUBLIC,
1787–1805

"I expect to see our young women forming a new era in female history," wrote Judith Sargent Murray in 1798.[1] Her optimism was part of a general sense that all possibilities were open in the post-Revolutionary world; as Benjamin Rush put it, the first act of the republican drama had only begun. The experience of war had given words like "independence" and "self-reliance" personal as well as political overtones; among the things that ordinary folk had learned from wartime had been that the world could, as the song had it, turn upside down. The rich could quickly become poor, wives might suddenly have to manage family businesses; women might even, as the famous Deborah Gannett had done, shoulder a gun. Political theory taught that republics rested on the virtue of their citizens; revolutionary experience taught that it was useful to be prepared for a wide range of unusual possibilities.[2]

A desire to explore the possibilities republicanism now opened to women was expressed by a handful of articulate, urban, middle-class men and women. While only a very few writers—Charles Brockden Brown, Judith Sargent Murray, Benjamin Rush—devoted extensive attention to women and what they might become, many essayists explored the subject in the periodical literature. In the fashion of the day, they concealed their

1. *The Gleaner*, III (Boston, 1798), 189.
2. Montesquieu's comment that republics differed from other political systems by the reliance they placed on virtue is explored in Howard Mumford Jones, *O Strange New World* (New York, 1964), p. 431.

identity under pseudonyms like "Cordelia," "Constantia," or, simply, "A Lady." These expressions came largely from Boston, New York, and Philadelphia: cities which were the centers of publishing. The vitality of Philadelphia, as political and social capital, is well known; the presence of so many national legislators in the city, turning up as they did at dances and dinner parties, was no doubt intellectually invigorating, and not least for the women of Philadelphia. In an informal way, women shared many of the political excitements of the city. Philadelphia was the home of the Young Ladies' Academy, founded in 1786, with explicitly fresh ideas about women's education, and an enrollment of more than a hundred within two years; Benjamin Rush would deliver his "Thoughts upon Female Education" there. The first attempt at a magazine expressly addressed to women was made by the Philadelphia *Lady's Magazine and Repository*. Two of the most intense anonymous writers—"Sophia" and "Nitidia"—wrote for Philadelphia newspapers. And after the government moved to Washington, Joseph Dennie's *Port Folio* solicited "the assistance of the ladies," and published essays by Gertrude Meredith, Sarah Hall, and Emily Hopkinson. Boston and New York were not far behind in displaying similar interests: in New York, Noah Webster's *American Magazine* included in its prospectus a specific appeal for female contributors; the *Boston Weekly Magazine* was careful to publish the speeches at the annual "Exhibition" of Susanna Rowson's Young Ladies' Academy.

Most journalists' comments on the role and functions of women in the republic merged, almost imperceptibly, into discussions of the sort of education proper for young girls. A pervasive Lockean environmentalism was displayed; what people were was assumed to be dependent on how they were educated. "Train up the child in the way he should grow, and when he is old he will not depart from it"; the biblical injunction was repeatedly quoted, and not quoted idly. When Americans spoke of what was best for the child they were also speaking—implicitly or explicitly—of their hopes for the adult. Charles Brockden Brown, for example, is careful to provide his readers with brief accounts of his heroines' early education. When we seek to learn the recipe for Murray's "new era in female history" we find ourselves reading comments on two related themes: how young women are to be "trained up," and what is to be expected of them when they are old.

If the republic were to fulfill the generous claims it made for the liberty and competence of its citizens, the education of young women would have to be an education for independence rather than for an upwardly mobile marriage. The periodicals are full of attacks on fashion, taking it for an emblem of superficiality and dependence. The Philadelphia *Lady's Magazine* criticized a father who prepared his daughters for the marriage market: "You boast of having given your daughters an education which will enable them 'to shine in the first circles.' . . . They sing indifferently; they play the harpsichord indifferently; they are mistresses of every common game at cards . . . they . . . have just as much knowledge of dress as to deform their persons by an awkward imitation of every new fashion which appears. . . . Placed in a situation of difficulty, they have neither a head to dictate, nor a hand to help in any domestic concern."[3] Teaching young girls to dress well was part of the larger message that their primary lifetime goal must be marriage; in this context, fashion became a feature of sexual politics. "I have sometimes been led," remarked Benjamin Rush, "to ascribe the invention of ridiculous and expensive fashions in female dress entirely to the gentlemen in order to divert the ladies from improving their minds and thereby to secure a more arbitrary and unlimited authority over them."[4] In the marriage market, beauty, flirtatiousness, and charm were at a premium; intelligence, good judgment, and competence (in short, the republican virtues) were at a discount. The republic did not need fashion plates; it needed citizens—women as well as men—of self-discipline and of strong mind. The contradiction between the counsel given to young women and their own self-interest, as well as the best interests of the republic, seemed obvious. The marriage market undercut the republic.[5]

Those who addressed themselves to the problem of the proper education

3. August 1792, pp. 121–123.

4. "Thoughts upon Female Education, Accommodated to the Present State of Society, Manners, and Government in the United States of America" (Philadelphia and Boston, 1787). Reprinted in Frederick Rudolph, ed., *Essays on Education in the Early Republic* (Cambridge, Mass., 1965), p. 39.

5. "The greater proportion of young women are trained up by thoughtless parents, in ease and luxury, with no other dependence for their future support than the precarious chance of establishing themselves by marriage: for this purpose (the men best know why) elaborate attention is paid to external attractions and accomplishments, to the neglect of more useful and solid acquirements. . . . [Marriage is the] *sole* method of procuring for themselves an establishment." *New York Magazine*, August 1797, p. 406. For comment on the marriage market, see letter signed, "A Matrimonial Republican" in Philadelphia *Lady's Magazine*, July 1792, pp. 64–67; "Legal Prostitution, Or Modern Marriage," Boston *Independent Chronicle*, October 28, 1793. For criticism of fashion, see *American Magazine*, December 1787, p. 39; July 1788, p. 594; *American Museum*, August 1788, p. 119; *Massachusetts Mercury*, August 16, 1793; January 16, 1795.

for young women used the word "independence" frequently. Sometimes it was used in a theoretical fashion: How, it was asked, can women's minds be free if they are taught that their sphere is limited to clothing, music, and needlework? Often the context of independence is economic and political: it seemed appropriate that in a republic women should have greater control over their own lives. "The *dependence* for which women are uniformly educated" was deplored; it was pointed out that the unhappily married woman would quickly discover that she had "neither liberty nor property."[6]

The idea that political independence should be echoed by a self-reliance which would make women as well as men economically independent appears in its most developed form in a series of essays Judith Sargent Murray published in the *Massachusetts Magazine* between 1792 and 1794, and collected under the title *The Gleaner* in 1798. Murray insisted that instruction in a manual trade was especially appropriate in a republic, and decried the antiegalitarian habit of assuming that a genteel and impractical education was superior to a vocational one. She was critical of fathers who permitted their sons to grow up without knowing a useful skill; she was even more critical of parents who "pointed their daughters" toward marriage and dependence. This made girls' education contingent on a single event; it offered them a single image of the future. "I would give my daughters every accomplishment which I thought proper," Murray wrote, "and to crown all, I would early accustom them to habits of industry and order. They should be taught with precision the art economical; they should be enabled to procure for themselves the necessaries of life; independence should be placed within their grasp." Repeatedly Murray counseled that women should be made to feel competent at something: "A woman *should reverence herself.*"[7]

Murray scattered through the *Gleaner* essays brief fictional versions of self-respecting women, in the characters of Margaretta, Mrs. Virgilius, and Penelope Airy. In his full-length novel *Ormond*, published in 1799, Charles Brockden Brown imagined a considerably more developed version of a competent woman. Constantia Dudley is eminently rational. When her father is embezzled of his fortune she, "her cheerfulness unimpaired," sells "every superfluous garb and trinket," her music and her books; she supports the family by needlework. Constantia never flinches; she can take

6. *New York Magazine*, August 1797, p. 406; Philadelphia *Universal Asylum and Columbian Magazine*, July 1791, p. 11.

7. Murray, *Gleaner*, I, 168, 193.

whatever ill fortune brings, whether it is yellow fever or the poverty that forces her to conclude that the only alternative to starvation is cornmeal mush three times a day for three months. Through it all, she resists proposals of marriage, because even in adversity she scorns to become emotionally dependent without love.[8]

Everything Constantia does places her in sharp contrast to Helena Cleves, who also "was endowed with every feminine and fascinating quality." Helena has had a genteel education; she can paint, and sing, and play the clavichord, but it is all fashionable gloss to camouflage a lack of real mental accomplishment and self-discipline. What Brown called "exterior accomplishments" were acceptable so long as life held no surprises, but when Helena meets disaster, she is unprepared to maintain her independence and her self-respect. She falls into economic dependence upon a "kinswoman"; she succumbs to the "specious but delusive" reasoning of Ormond, and becomes his mistress. He takes advantage of her dependence, all the while seeking in Constantia a rational woman worthy of his intelligence; eventually, in despair, Helena kills herself.[9]

The argument that an appropriate education would steel girls to face adversity is related to the conviction that all citizens of a republic should be self-reliant. But the argument can be made independent of explicit republican ideology. It may well represent the common sense of a revolutionary era in which the unexpected was very likely to happen; in which large numbers of people had lived through reversals of fortune, encounters with strangers, physical dislocation. Constantia's friend Martinette de Beauvais has lived in Marseilles, Verona, Vienna, and Philadelphia; she had dressed like a man and fought in the American Revolution; after that she was one of the "hundreds" of women who took up arms for the French.[10] Constantia admires and sympathizes with her friend; nothing in the novel is clearer than that women who are not ready to maintain their independence in a crisis, as Constantia and Martinette do, risk sinking, like Helena, into prostitution and death.

8. Charles Brockden Brown, *Ormond; Or the Secret Witness*, ed. by Ernest Marchand (New York, 1799; reprinted 1937, 1962), p. 19.

9. *Ibid.*, pp. 98–99.

10. "It was obvious to suppose that a woman thus fearless and sagacious had not been inactive at a period like the present, which called forth talents and courage without distinction of sex, and had been particularly distinguished by female enterprise and heroism." *Ibid.*, p. 170.

The model republican woman was competent and confident. She could ignore the vagaries of fashion; she was rational, benevolent, independent, self-reliant. Writers who spoke to this point prepared lists of what we would now call role models: heroines of the past offered as assurance that women could indeed be people of accomplishment. There were women of the ancient world, like Cornelia, the mother of the Gracchi; rulers like Elizabeth of England and the Empress Catherine of Russia; a handful of Frenchwomen: Mme. de Genlis, Mme. Maintenon, and Mme. Dacier; and a long list of British intellectuals: Lady Mary Wortley Montagu, Hannah More, Elizabeth Carter, Mrs. Knowles (the Quaker who had bested Dr. Johnson in debate), Mary Wollstonecraft, and the Whig historian Catharine Macaulay.[11] Such women were rumored to exist in America; they were given fictional embodiment by Murray and Brown. Those who believed in these republican models demanded that their presence be recognized and endorsed, and that a new generation of young women be urged to make them patterns for their own behavior. To create more such women became a major educational challenge.

Writers were fond of pointing out that the inadequacies of American women could be ascribed to early upbringing and environmental influences. "Will it be said that the judgment of a male of two years old, is more sage than that of a female of the same age?" asked Judith Sargent Murray. "But . . . as their years increased, the sister must be wholly domesticated, while the brother is led by the hand through all the flowery paths of science." The *Universal Asylum* published a long and thoughtful essay by "A Lady" which argued that "in the nursery, strength is equal in the male and female." When a boy went to school, he immediately met both intellectual and physical challenge; his teachers instructed him in science and language, his friends dared him to fight, to run after a hoop, to jump a rope. Girls, on the other hand, were "committed to illiterate teachers, . . . cooped up in a room, confined to needlework, deprived of exercise." Thomas Cooper de-

11. For examples of such lists, see: Murray, *Gleaner*, III, 200–219; John Blair Linn, *The Powers of Genius: A Poem in Three Parts* (Philadelphia, 1802); Philadelphia *Weekly Magazine*, August 4, 11, 1798; *Port Folio*, February 12, 1803; September 27, 1806; Philadelphia *Minerva*, March 14, 1795. For the admiration expressed by Abigail Adams and Mercy Otis Warren for Catharine Macaulay, see Abigail Adams to Isaac Smith, Jr., April 20, 1771; Abigail Adams to Catharine Sawbridge Macaulay, n.d., 1774; Mercy Otis Warren to Abigail Adams, January 28, 1775; in L. H. Butterfield, ed., *Adams Family Correspondence*, I (Cambridge, Mass., 1963), 76–77, 177–179, 181–183. For the circle of English "bluestockings," in the 1780s, see M. G. Jones, *Hannah More* (Cambridge, 1952), pp. 41–76.

fined the problem clearly: "We first keep their minds and then their persons in subjection," he wrote. "We educate women from infancy to marriage, in such a way as to debilitate both their corporeal and their mental powers. All the accomplishments we teach them are directed not to their future benefit in life but to the amusement of the male sex; and having for a series of years, with much assiduity, and sometimes at much expense, incapacitated them for any serious occupation, we say they are not fit to govern themselves."[12]

Schemes for the education of the "rising generation" proliferated in the early republic, including a number of projects for the education of women. Some, like those discussed in the well-known essays of Benjamin Rush and Noah Webster, were theoretical; others took the form of admitting girls to boys' academies or establishing new schools for girls. There were not as many as Judith Sargent Murray implied when she said: "Female academies are everywhere establishing," but she was not alone in seeing schools like Susanna Rowson's Young Ladies' Academy and the Young Ladies' Academy of Philadelphia as harbingers of a trend. One pamphlet address, written in support of the Philadelphia Academy, expressed the hope that it would become "a great national seminary" and insisted that although "stubborn prejudices still exist . . . we must (if open to conviction) be convinced that *females* are fully capable of sounding the most profound depths, and of attaining to the most sublime excellence in every part of science."[13]

Certainly there was a wide range of opinion on the content and scope of female education in the early republic. Samuel Harrison Smith's essay on the subject, which won the American Philosophical Society's 1797 prize for the best plan for a national system of education, began by proposing "that every male child, without exception, be educated."[14] At the other extreme

12. *Massachusetts Magazine*, II (March 1790), 133; *Universal Asylum* and *Columbian Magazine*, July 1791, p. 9; Thomas Cooper, "Propositions Respecting the Foundation of Civil Government," in *Political Arithmetic* (Philadelphia [?], 1798), p. 27. See also *Boston Weekly Magazine*, May 21, 1803, pp. 121–122; *American Museum*, January 1787, p. 59; Philadelphia *Lady's Magazine*, June 1792.

13. J. A. Neale, "An Essay on the Genius and Education of the Fair Sex," Philadelphia *Minerva*, April 4, March 21, 1795.

14. *Remarks on Education: Illustrating the Close Connection between Virtue and Wisdom* (Philadelphia, 1798), reprinted in Rudolph, *Essays on Education*, p. 211. Smith did acknowledge that female instruction was important, but commented that concepts of what it should be were so varied that he feared to make any proposals, and despaired of including women in the scheme he was then devising. "It is sufficient, perhaps, for

was Timothy Dwight, the future president of Yale, who opened his academy at Greenfield Hill to girls and taught them the same subjects he taught to boys, at the same time and in the same rooms.[15] But Dwight was the exception. Most proposals for the education of young women agreed that the curriculum should be more advanced than that of the primary schools but somewhat less than that offered by colleges and even conventional boys' academies. Noah Webster thought women should learn speaking and writing, arithmetic, geography, belles-lettres; "A Reformer" in the *Weekly Magazine* advocated a similar program, to which practical instruction in nursing and cooking were added. Judith Sargent Murray thought women should be able to converse elegantly and correctly, pronounce French, read history (as a narrative substitute for novels, rather than for its own interest or value), and learn some simple geography and astronomy.[16] The best-known proposal was Benjamin Rush's; he too prescribed reading, grammar, penmanship, "figures and bookkeeping," geography. He added "the first principles of natural philosophy," vocal music (because it soothed cares and was good for the lungs) but not instrumental music (because, except for the most talented, it seemed a waste of valuable time), and history (again, as an antidote to novel reading).

Rush offered his model curriculum in a speech to the Board of Visitors of the Young Ladies' Academy of Philadelphia, later published and widely reprinted under the title "Thoughts upon Female Education Accommodated to the Present State of Society, Manners and Government in the United States of America." The academy claimed to be the first female academy chartered in the United States; when Rush spoke, on July 28, 1787, he was offering practical advice to a new school. Rush linked the academy to the greater cause of demonstrating the possibilities of women's minds. Those who were skeptical of education for women, Rush declared, were the

---

the present, that the improvement of women is marked by a rapid progress and that a prospect opens equal to their most ambitious desires" (p. 217). The other prizewinner, Samuel Knox, proposed to admit girls to the primary schools in his system, but not to the academies or colleges. Knox's essay, "An Essay on the Best System of Liberal Education," may be found in Rudolph, *Essays on Education*, pp. 271–372.

15. Charles E. Cunningham, *Timothy Dwight: 1752–1817: A Biography* (New York, 1942), pp. 154–163.

16. Noah Webster, "Importance of Female Education," in *American Magazine*, May 1788, pp. 368, 369. This essay was part of his pamphlet *On the Education of Youth in America* (Boston, 1790), conveniently reprinted in Rudolph, *Essays on Education*, pp. 41–78. *Weekly Magazine*, April 7, 1798; Murray, *The Gleaner*, I, 70–71.

same who opposed "the general diffusion of knowledge among the citizens of our republics." Rush argued that "female education should be accommodated to the state of society, manners, and government of the country in which it is conducted." An appropriate education for American women would be condensed, because they married earlier than their European counterparts; it would include bookkeeping, because American women could expect to be "the stewards and guardians of their husbands' property," and executrices of their husbands' wills. It would qualify them for "a general intercourse with the world" by an acquaintance with geography and chronology. If education is preparation for life, then the life styles of American women required a newly tailored educational program.[17]

The curriculum of the Young Ladies' Academy (which one of the Board of Visitors called "abundantly sufficient to complete the female mind") included reading, writing, arithmetic, English grammar, composition, rhetoric, and geography. It did not include the natural philosophy Rush hoped for (although Rush did deliver a dozen lectures on "The Application of the Principles of Natural Philosophy, and Chemistry, to Domestic and Culinary Purposes"); it did not include advanced mathematics or the classics.[18]

In 1794 the Young Ladies' Academy published a collection of its graduation addresses; one is struck by the scattered observations of valedictorians and salutatorians that reading, writing, and arithmetic were not enough. Priscilla Mason remarked in her 1793 graduation address that while it was

17. Benjamin Rush, "Thoughts upon Female Education," in Rudolph, *Essays on Education*, pp. 25–40. See also the comments of the Reverend James Sproat, a member of the Board of Visitors, June 10, 1789, in *The Rise and Progress of the Young Ladies' Academy of Philadelphia; Containing an Account of a Number of Public Examinations and Commencements; the Charter and Bye-Laws; Likewise, a Number of Orations delivered by the Young Ladies, and several by the Trustees of Said Institution* (Philadelphia, 1794), p. 24.

18. Benjamin Say, "Address," December 4, 1789, in *Rise and Progress of the Young Ladies' Academy*, p. 33; Benjamin Rush, *Syllabus of Lectures, Containing the Application of the Principles of Natural Philosophy . . .* (Philadelphia, 1787). Rush, of course, was waging his own crusade against the classics as inappropriate in a republic; he argued elsewhere that to omit Latin and Greek would have the beneficial effect of diminishing "the present immense disparity which subsists between the sexes, in the degrees of their education and knowledge." When his contemporaries omitted the classics from the female curriculum it was usually because they thought women's minds were not up to it. Rush, "Observations upon the Study of the Latin and Greek Languages," in *Essays, Literary, Moral and Philosophical* (Philadelphia, 1798), p. 44.

unusual for a woman to address "a promiscuous assembly," there was no impropriety in women's becoming accomplished orators. What had prevented them, she argued, was that "our high and mighty Lords . . . have denied us the means of knowledge, and then reproached us for the want of it. . . . They doom'd the sex to servile or frivolous employments, on purpose to degrade their minds, that they themselves might hold unrivall'd, the power and pre-eminence they had usurped." Academies like hers enabled women to increase their knowledge, but the forums in which they might use it were still unavailable: "The Church, the Bar, and the Senate are shut against us."[19]

So long as the propriety of cultivating women's minds remained a matter for argument, it was hard to press a claim to public competence; Priscilla Mason was an exception. Rush had concluded his advice to the Young Ladies' Academy by challenging his audience to demonstrate "that the cultivation of reason in women is alike friendly to the order of nature and the private as well as the public happiness." But meeting even so mild a challenge was difficult; "bluestocking" was not a term of praise in the early republic. "Tell me," wrote the Philadelphian Gertrude Meredith angrily, ". . . do you imagine, from your knowledge of the young men in this city, that ladies are valued according to their mental acquirements? I can assure you that they are not, and I am very confident that they never will be, while men indulge themselves in expressions of contempt for one because she has a *bare elbow*, for another because she . . . never made a *good pun, nor smart repartee*. . . . [Would they] not titter . . . at her expense, if a woman made a Latin quotation, or spoke with enthusiasm of Classical learning?"[20] When Gertrude Meredith visited Baltimore, she found that her mildly satirical essays for the *Port Folio* had transformed her into a formidable figure: "Mrs. Cole says she should not have been more distressed at visiting Mrs. Macaulay the authoress than myself as she had heard I *was so sensible*, but she was very glad to find I was so free and easy. You must allow," she concluded dryly, "that this compliment was elegantly turned." A similar complaint was made by an essayist whom we know only as "Sophia":

> A woman who is conscious of possessing, more intellectual power than is requisite in superintending the pantry, and in adjusting the ceremoni-

19. Priscilla Mason, "Oration," May 15, 1793, in *Rise and Progress of the Young Ladies' Academy*, pp. 90–95. See also the valedictory oration by Molly Wallace, June 12, 1792, *ibid.*, pp. 73–79.

20. Letter signed M.G., "American Lounger," *Port Folio*, April 7, 1804.

als of a feast, and who believes she, in conforming to the will of the giver, in improving the gift, is by the wits of the other sex denominated a learned lady. She is represented as disgustingly slovenly in her person, indecent in her habits, imperious to her husband, and negligent of her children. And the odious scarecrow is employed, exactly as the farmer employs his unsightly bundle of rags and straw, to terrify the simple birds, from picking up the precious grain, which he wishes to monopolize. After all this, what man in his sober senses can be astonished, to find the majority of women as they really are, frivolous and volatile; incapable of estimating their own dignity, and indifferent to the best interests of society. . . ?"[21]

These women were not creating their own paranoid images of discouragement. The same newspapers for which they wrote often printed other articles insisting that intellectual accomplishment is inappropriate in a woman, that the intellectual woman is not only invading a male province, but must herself somehow be masculine. "Women of masculine minds," wrote the Boston minister John Sylvester John Gardiner, "have generally masculine manners, and a robustness of person ill calculated to inspire the tender passion." Noah Webster's *American Magazine*, which in its prospectus had made a special appeal to women writers and readers, published the unsigned comment: "If we picture to ourselves a woman . . . firm in resolve, unshaken in conduct, unmoved by the delicacies of situation, by the fashions of the times, . . . we immediately change the idea of the sex, and . . . we see under the form of a woman the virtues and qualities of a man." Even the *Lady's Magazine*, which had promised to demonstrate that "the FEMALES of Philadelphia are by no means deficient in *those talents*, which have immortalized the names of a *Montagu*, a *Craven*, a *More*, and a *Seward*, in their inimitable writings," published a cautionary tale, whose moral was that although "learning in men was the road to preferment . . . consequences very opposite were the result of the same quality in women." Amelia is a clergyman's only daughter; she is taught Latin and Greek, with the result that she becomes "negligent of her dress," and "pride and pedantry grew up with learning in her breast." Eventually she is avoided by both sexes, and becomes emblematic of the fabled "white-washed jackdaw (who, aiming at a station from which nature had placed him at a distance, found

21. Gertrude Meredith to David Meredith, May 3, 1804, Meredith Papers, Historical Society of Pennsylvania; Philadelphia *Evening Fireside*, April 6, 1805.

himself deserted by his own species, and driven out of every society)." For conclusion there was an explicit moral: "This story was intended (at a time when the press overflows with the productions of female pens) . . . to admonish them, that . . . because a few have gained applause by studying the dead languages, all womankind should [not] assume their Dictionaries and Lexicons; else . . . (as the Ladies made rapid advances towards manhood) we might in a few years behold a sweepstakes rode by women, or a second battle at Odiham, fought with superior skill, by Mesdames Humphries and Mendoza."[22]

The prediction that accomplishment would unsex women was coupled with the warning that educated women would abandon their proper sphere; the female pedant and the careful housekeeper were never found in the same person. The most usable cautionary emblem for this seems to have been Mary Wollstonecraft, whose life and work linked criticism of women's status with free love and political radicalism. Mary Wollstonecraft's *Vindication of the Rights of Woman* was her generation's most coherent statement of what women deserved and what they might become. The influence of any book is difficult to trace, and although we know that her book was reprinted in Philadelphia shortly after its publication in 1792, it would be inaccurate to credit Wollstonecraft with responsibility for raising in America questions relating to the status of women. It seems far more likely that she verbalized effectively what a larger public was already thinking or was willing to hear; "In very many of her sentiments," remarked the

22. *New-England Palladium*, September 18, 1801; *American Magazine*, February 1788, p. 134; *Lady's Magazine*, January 1793, pp. 68–72. (The "battle at Odiham" refers to a famous bare-knuckle prize fight, one of the earliest major events in the history of boxing, fought in 1788 by Daniel Mendoza and Richard Humphries in Hampshire, England.) Other attacks on female pedantry, which express the fear that intellectual women will be masculine, are found in the *American Magazine*, March 1788, pp. 244–245 ("To be lovely you must be content to be women . . . and leave the masculine virtues, and the profound researches of study to the province of the other sex"); *New-England Palladium*, September 4, 18, December 4, 1801, March 5, 9, 1802; Benjamin Silliman, *Letters of Shahcoolen, a Hindu Philosopher, Residing in Philadelphia; To His Friend El Hassan, an Inhabitant of Delhi* (Boston, 1802), pp. 23–24, 62; *American Museum*, December 1788, p. 491; *Boston Weekly Magazine*, March 24, 1804, p. 86 ("Warlike women, learned women, and women who are politicians, equally abandon the circle which nature and institutions have traced round their sex; they convert themselves into men").

Philadelphia Quaker Elizabeth Drinker, "she, as some of our friends say, *speaks my mind*."[23]

Wollstonecraft's primary target was Rousseau, whose definition of woman's sphere was a limited one: "The empire of women," Rousseau had written, "is the empire of softness, of address, of complacency; her commands are caresses; her menaces are tears." Wollstonecraft perceived that to define women in this way was to condemn them to "a state of perpetual childhood"; she deplored the "false system of education" which made women "only anxious to inspire love, when they ought to cherish a nobler ambition, and by their abilities and virtues exact respect." Women's duties were different from those of men, but they similarly demanded the exercise of virtue and reason; women would be better wives and mothers if they were taught that they need not depend on frivolity and ignorance. Wollstonecraft ventured the suggestion that women might study medicine, politics, and business, but whatever they did, they should not be denied civil and political rights, they should not have to rely on marriage for assurance of economic support, they should not "remain immured in their families groping in the dark."[24]

If, in some quarters, Mary Wollstonecraft's work was greeted as the common sense of the matter, in others it was met with hostility. The *Vindication* was a popular subject of satire, especially when, after the author's death in childbirth in 1797, William Godwin published a *Memoir* revealing that she had lived with other men, and with Godwin himself before her pregnancy and their marriage. Critics were then freed to discount her call for reform as the self-serving demand of a woman of easy virtue, as Benjamin Silliman did throughout his *Letters of Shahcoolen*. Timothy Dwight, who had taken the lead in offering young women education on a par with young men, shuddered at Wollstonecraft and held "the female philosopher" up to ridicule in "Morpheus," a political satire which ran for eight installments in the *New-England Palladium*.[25] Dwight called

23. *Extracts from the Journal of Elizabeth Drinker, from 1759 to 1807, A.D.*, ed. by Henry D. Biddle (Philadelphia, 1889), p. 285. The entry is dated April 22, 1796.

24. Mary Wollstonecraft, *A Vindication of the Rights of Woman, With Strictures on Political and Moral Subjects* (New York, 1891), pp. 23, 149–156.

25. *New-England Palladium*, November 24, 27, December 8, 11, 15, 1801; March 2, 5, 9, 1802. Identification of Dwight as author is made by Robert Edson Lee, "Timothy Dwight and the Boston *Palladium*," *New England Quarterly*, XXXV (1962), 229–239.

Wollstonecraft "an unchaste woman," "a sentimental lover," "a strumpet"; as Silliman had done, he linked her radical politics to free love. " 'Away with all monopolies,' " Dwight has her say. " 'I hate these exclusive rights; these privileged orders. I am for having everything free, and open to all; like the air which we breathe. . . .' "

" 'Love, particularly, I suppose, Madam [?]' "

" 'Yes, brute, love, if you please, and everything else.' "[26] Even Charles Brockden Brown's feminist tract *Alcuin* concluded with a long gloss on the same theme: to permit any change in women's status was to imply the acceptance of free love. Alcuin, who has been playing the conservative skeptic, concludes that once it is established that marriage "has no other criterion than custom," it becomes simply "a mode of sexual intercourse." His friend Mrs. Carter protests energetically that free love is not at all what she wanted; " 'because I demand an equality of conditions among beings that equally partake of the same divine reason, would you rashly infer that I was an enemy to the institution of marriage itself?' " Brown lets her have the last word, but he does not make Alcuin change his mind.[27]

Dwight had one final charge to make against Wollstonecraft; he attacked her plea that women emerge from the confines of their families. " 'Who will make our puddings, Madam?' " his protagonist asks. When she responds: " 'Make them yourself,' " he presses harder: " 'Who shall nurse us when we are sick?' " and, finally, " 'Who shall nurse our children?' " The last question reduces the fictional Mary to blushes and silence.[28]

It would not, however, reduce Rush, or Murray, or Brown, to blushes and silence. (Nor, I think, would it have so affected the real Mary Wollstonecraft.) They had neither predicted that women would cease their housewifely duties nor demanded that women should. Priscilla Mason's demand that hitherto male professions be opened to women was highly unusual, and even she apologized for it before she left the podium. There were, it is true, some other hints that women might claim the privileges and duties of male citizens of the republic. In *Alcuin*, Mrs. Carter explains her intense political disappointment through the first two chapters, arguing that Americans had been false to their own revolutionary promises in denying political status to women. "If a stranger questions me concerning

26. *New-England Palladium*, March 9, 1802.

27. Charles Brockden Brown and Lee R. Edwards, *Alcuin: A Dialogue* (New York, 1971), pp. 44–88.

28. *New-England Palladium*, March 9, 1802.

the nature of our government, I answer, that in this happy climate all men are free: the people are the source of all authority; from them it flows, and to them, in due season, it returns . . . our liberty consists in the choice of our governors: all, as reason requires, have a part in this choice, yet not without a few exceptions . . . females . . . minors . . . the poor . . . slaves. . . . I am tired of explaining this charming system of equality and independence." St. George Tucker, commenting on Blackstone, acknowledged that women were taxed without representation, like "aliens . . . children under the age of discretion, idiots, and lunatics," American women had neither political nor civil rights. "I fear there is little reason for a compliment to our laws for their respect and favour to the female sex," Tucker concluded. As did Tucker, John Adams acknowledged that women's experience of the republic was different from men's; he hesitantly admitted that the republic claimed the right "to govern women without their consent." For a brief period from 1790 to 1807, New Jersey law granted the franchise to "all free inhabitants," and on occasion women exercised that right; it is conceivable that New Jersey might have stood as a precedent for other states. Instead, New Jersey's legislature rewrote its election law; the argument for political competence was taken no further.[29]

All of these were hesitant suggestions introduced into a hostile intellectual milieu in which female learning was equated with pedantry and masculinity. To resist those assumptions was to undertake a great deal; it was a task for which no one was ready; indeed, it is impossible to say that anyone really wanted to try. Instead, the reformers would have been quick to reply, with Brown's Mrs. Carter, that they had no intention of abandoning marriage; that they had every intention of making puddings and nursing babies; that the education they demanded was primarily to enable women to function more effectively within their traditional sphere, and only secondarily to fulfill demands like Priscilla Mason's that they emerge from it. People were complaining that American women were boring,

29. Brown, *Alcuin*, pp. 32–33; St. George Tucker, *Blackstone's Commentaries: With Notes of Reference, to the Constitution and Laws, of the Federal Government of the United States, and of the Commonwealth of Virginia*, II (Philadelphia, 1803), 145, 445; John Adams to James Sullivan, May 26, 1776, in *The Works of John Adams*, ed. by Charles Francis Adams, IX (1856), 375–379; Edward Raymond Turner, "Women's Suffrage in New Jersey: 1790–1807," *Smith College Studies in History*, I (1916), 165–187. Opposition to woman suffrage apparently surfaced after women voted as a bloc in an unsuccessful attempt to influence the outcome of an Essex County election in 1797.

frivolous, spending excessive amounts of money for impractical fashions; very well, a vigorously educated woman would be less likely to bore her husband, less likely to be a spendthrift, better able to cope with adverse fortune. Judith Sargent Murray versified an equation:

> *Where'er the maiden* Industry *appears,*
> *A thrifty contour every object wears;*
> *And when fair* order *with the nymph combines,*
> *Adjusts, directs, and every plan designs,*
> *Then* Independence *fills her peerless seat,*
> *And lo! the matchless trio is complete.*

Murray repeatedly made the point that the happiness of the nation depended on the happiness of families; and that the "felicity of families" is dependent on the presence of women who are "properly methodical, and economical in their distributions and expenditures of time." She denied that "the present enlarged plan of female education" was incompatible with traditional notions of women's duties: she predicted that the "daughters of Columbia" would be free of "*invidious and rancorous passions*" and "even the semblance of pedantry"; "when they become wives and mothers, they will fill with honour the parts allotted them."[30]

Rarely, in the literature of the early Republic, do we find any objection to the notion that women belong in the home; what emerges is the argument that the Revolution had enlarged the significance of what women did in their homes. Benjamin Rush's phrasing of this point is instructive; when he defined the goals of republican women, he was careful not to include a claim to political power: "The equal share that every citizen has in the liberty and the possible share he may have in the government of our country make it necessary that our ladies should be qualified to a certain degree by a peculiar and suitable education, *to concur in instructing their sons in the principles of liberty and government.*" The Young Ladies' Academy promised "not wholly to engross the mind" of each pupil, "but to allow her to prepare for the duties in life to which she may be destined." Miss P. W. Jackson, graduating from Mrs. Rowson's Academy, explained what she had learned of the goals of the educated woman: "A woman who is skilled in every useful art, who practices every domestic virtue . . . may, by her precept and example, inspire her brothers, her husband, or her sons, with such a love of virtue, such just ideas of the true value of civil liberty . . .

30. *Gleaner,* I, 161, 12, 29, 191, 190.

that future heroes and statesmen, who arrive at the summit of military or political fame, shall *exaltingly declare, it is to my mother I owe this elevation.*" By their household management, by their refusal to countenance vice, crime, or cruelty in their suitors and husbands, women had the power to direct the moral development of the male citizens of the republic. The influence women had on children, especially on their sons, gave them ultimate responsibility for the future of the new nation.[31]

This constellation of ideas, and the republican rhetoric which made it convincing, appears at great length in the Columbia College commencement oration of 1795. Its title was "Female Influence"; behind the flowery rhetoric lurks a social and political message:

> Let us then figure to ourselves the accomplished woman, surrounded by a sprightly band, from the babe that imbibes the nutritive fluid, to the generous youth just ripening into manhood, and the lovely virgin. . . . Let us contemplate the mother distributing the mental nourishment to the fond smiling circle, by means proportionate to their different powers of reception, watching the gradual openings of their minds, and studying their various turns of temper. . . . Religion, fairest offspring of the skies, smiles auspicious on her endeavours; the Genius of Liberty hovers triumphant over the glorious scene. . . . Yes, ye fair, the reformation of a world is in your power. . . . Reflect on the result of your efforts. Contemplate the rising glory of confederated America. Consider that your exertions can best secure, increase, and perpetuate it. The solidity and stability of the liberties of your country rest with you; since Liberty is never sure, 'till Virtue reigns triumphant. . . . Already may we see the lovely daughters of Columbia asserting the importance and the honour of their sex. It rests with you to make this retreat [from the corruptions of Europe] doubly peaceful, doubly happy, by banishing from it those crimes and corruptions, which have never yet failed of giving rise to tyranny, or anarchy. While you thus keep our country virtuous, you maintain its independence. . . .[32]

Defined this way, the educated woman ceased to threaten the sanctity of marriage; the bluestocking need not be masculine. In this awkward—and

31. Rush, "Thoughts upon Female Education," in Rudolph, *Essays on Education*, p. 28 (my italics); "On Female Education," *Port Folio*, May 1809, p. 388; *Boston Weekly Magazine*, October 29, 1803.

32. *New York Magazine*, May 1795, pp. 301–305.

in the 1790s still only vaguely expressed—fashion, the traditional womanly virtues were endowed with political purpose. A pivotal political role was assigned to the least political inhabitants of the Republic. Ironically, the same women who were denied political identity were counted on to maintain the republican quality of the new nation. "Let the ladies of a country be educated properly," Rush said, "and they will not only make and administer its laws, but form its manners and character."[33]

When Americans addressed themselves to the matter of the role of women, they found that those who admired bluestockings and those who feared them could agree on one thing: in a world where moral influences were fast dissipating, women as a group seemed to represent moral stability. Few in the early republic demanded, in a sustained way, substantial revisions in women's political or legal status; few spoke to the nascent class of unskilled women workers. But many took pride in the assertion that properly educated republican women would stay in the home and, from that vantage point, would shape the characters of their sons and husbands in the direction of benevolence, self-restraint, and responsible independence. They refuted charges of free love and masculinization; in doing so they created a justification for woman as household goddess so deeply felt that one must be permitted to suspect that many women of their generation were *refusing* to be household goddesses.[34] They began to make the argument for intelligent household management that Catharine Beecher, a generation later, would enshrine in her *Treatise on Domestic Economy* as woman's highest goal. The Daughters of Columbia became, in effect, the Mothers of the Victorians. Whether Judith Sargent Murray, Charles Brockden Brown, or Benjamin Rush would have approved the ultimate results of their work is hard to say.

33. Rush, "Thoughts upon Female Education," in Rudolph, *Essays on Education*, p. 36.

34. See, for example, *Boston Weekly Magazine*, December 18, 1802; *Weekly Magazine*, March 3, 1798; *Port Folio*, February 12, 1803, March 3, 1804, April 20, 1805.

THE REPUBLICAN MOTHER
WOMEN AND THE ENLIGHTENMENT—AN AMERICAN PERSPECTIVE

The great questions of political liberty and civic freedom, of the relationship between law and liberty, the subjects of so many ideological struggles in the eighteenth century, are questions which have no gender. Philosophes habitually indulged in vast generalizations about humanity: Montesquieu contemplated the nature of society, Rousseau formulated a scheme for the revitalized education of children, Lord Kames wrote four volumes on the history of mankind. The broad sweep of their generalizations has permitted the conclusion that they indeed meant to include all people in their observations; if they habitually used the generic "he" two centuries before our own generation began to be discomfited by it, then it is a matter of syntax and usage, and without historical significance.

Yet Rousseau permitted himself to wonder whether women were capable of serious reasoning. If the Enlightenment represented, as Peter Gay has remarked, "man's claim to be recognized as an adult, responsible being" who would "take the risk of discovery, exercise the right of unfettered criticism, accept the loneliness of autonomy," it may be worth asking whether it was assumed that women were also to recognize themselves as responsible beings. Is it possible, by definition, for women to be enlightened? The answers to that question have important implications for historians of

An earlier version of this essay was read at the Annual Meeting of the Southern Historical Association in November, 1975. The author is grateful to Anne Firor Scott and Linda Grant De Pauw for comments offered on that occasion.

political thought and for those who seek to write women's intellectual history.

We should be skeptical of the generous assumption that the Enlightenment *man* was generic. Philosophe is a male noun: it describes Kant, Adam Smith, Diderot, Lessing, Franklin, Locke, Rousseau. With the conspicuous exceptions of Catharine Macaulay and Mary Wollstonecraft, women are absent even from the second and third ranks. They hover on the fringes, creating a milieu for discussions in their salons, offering their personal and moral support to male friends and lovers, but making only minor intellectual contributions. Mme. Helvetius and Mme. Brillon, Mme. Condorcet, even Catherine of Russia, are consumers, not creators of Enlightenment ideas. Is it by accident or design that the Molly Stevensons, the Sophie Vollands, the Maria Cosways figure primarily as the address*ees* of letters by Franklin, Diderot, Jefferson?

A careful reading of the main texts of the Enlightenment in France, England and the colonies reveals that the nature of the relationship between women and the state remained largely unexamined; the use of *man* was in fact literal, not generic. Only by implication did the writers say anything of substance about the function and responsibilities of women in the monarchies they knew and the ideal communities they invented. Just as their inadvertent comments on the mob revealed the limits of their democracy, their comments on women reveal the limits of their definition of civic virtue.

Perhaps the most striking feature of Enlightenment literature is that the more abstract and theoretical his intention the more likely it is that the writer would consider the function of women in the polity. Because a standard way of reinventing natural law was to posit the first family in a state of nature and derive political relationships from its situation, philosophes were virtually forced by the form in which they had chosen to work to contemplate women's political role—even if, with Rousseau, they did so in an antifeminist mode. By contrast, the more the writer's intention was specific criticism of contemporary affairs, as it was apt to be among the Whig Opposition, the less the likelihood of serious consideration of women as political beings. But both groups shared the unspoken assumption that women acted in a political capacity only in special and unusual circumstances.

In the face of a denial that women might properly participate in the political community at all, there was invented a definition of women's relationship to the state that sought to fill the inadequacies of inherited political theory. The republican ideology that Americans developed included—hesitantly—a political role for women. It made use of the classic formulation of the Spartan Mother who raised sons prepared to sacrifice themselves to the good of the *polis*. It provided an apparent integration of domestic and political behavior, in a formula that masked political purpose by promise of domestic service. The terms provided were ambivalent and in many ways intellectually unsatisfying; the intellectual history of women is not a whiggish progression, ever onward and ever upward, toward autonomy and liberation. The tangled and complex role of the Republican Mother offered one among many structures and contexts in which women might define the civic culture and their responsibilities to the state; radical feminist political movements would develop in dialectical opposition to it. This essay seeks to describe the elements of that republican role, and the gaps in available political theory it was intended to fill.

To what extent was there room for women in the philosophe's vision of the political order? Let us begin with Locke, whose consideration of the relationship of women to public order was extensive, and who was read and generally admired by the philosophes of the eighteenth century.[1] Locke's *Two Treatises on Government* are a direct attack on Robert Filmer's *Patriarcha*, which spins a justification for absolute monarchy by divine right out of the biblical injunction to honor thy father. But the commandment, after all, is to "Honor thy father *and mother*"; Filmer's defense of absolutism in government conveniently forgot mothers; it imagined a power structure that was masculine, that was absolute, and that descended through primogeniture. To create this structure and defend it as he did, Filmer had to ignore a large network of other relationships and impose a hierarchical subordination on all those he did acknowledge. Locke needed for *his* purposes only a reader who would concede that the biblical commandment was to "Honor thy father and mother"; grant him that, and Locke could proceed to race through Filmer, restoring mothers as he went, and by that device undercutting Filmer's analogy between parental power and royal authority. If familial power is shared with women and limited by mutual responsibilities, the nature of royal authority must also be shared and

1. See Peter Gay, *The Enlightenment: An Interpretation—The Science of Freedom* (New York: Knopf, 1969), 189 et passim.

limited. What Locke accomplished in the *First Treatise* was the integration of women into social theory.[2]

"The first society was between man and wife," Locke wrote in the *Second Treatise*, "which gave beginning to that between parents and children; to which, in time, that between master and servant came to be added." But these relationships are not all hierarchical: "conjugal society is made by a voluntary compact between men and women."[3] The grant of dominion made to Adam in *Genesis* is not, as Filmer would have it, over people in general and Eve in particular; it is to human beings over animals. If Adam is lord of the world, Eve is lady. The curse of Eve, Locke thought, could not justify women's permanent and universal submission to men; the curse was part of her punishment for sin, but it was a sin which Adam had shared and for which he too was punished, not rewarded. Husbands reigned over wives, wives suffered the pains of childbirth; but these were descriptions of reality and reality might be changed by human intention. Labor might be medically eased; a woman who was queen in her own right did not become, when she married, her husband's subject.[4]

Locke came closer than most of his contemporaries and successors to defining a political role for women. He underlined the rights and powers women ought to have in their domestic capacity: mothers have a right to the respect of their children that is not dependent on the husband's will; mothers have their own responsibilities to their children; women ought to control their own property. There is not even a hint in his work that women unsex themselves when they step into the political domain.[5] But once Filmer had been disposed of, and Locke could generalize more broadly about civic powers and responsibilities, his insistence on defining the role of women in the social order diminished. He did, however, phrase his most

2. John Locke, *Two Treatises of Government*, Peter Laslett, ed. (London: Cambridge Univ. Press, 1967); see especially *First Treatise*, §§62–65. Robert Filmer, *Patriarcha: or the Natural Power of Kings*, Thomas I. Cook, ed. (New York: Hafner Pub. Co., 1947).

3. Locke, *Second Treatise*, §§77, 78.

4. *First Treatise*, §§30, 47.

5. *First Treatise*, §§61, 63; *Second Treatise*, §§52, 65, 183. In the *Second Treatise*, §§80–83, Locke argues that the primary justification for marriage is the lengthy dependence and vulnerability of the child, and he permits himself to "enquire, why this Compact, when Procreation and Education are secured, and Inheritance taken care for, may not be made determinable, either by consent, or at a certain time, or upon certain conditions, as well as any other voluntary compacts, there being no necessity in the nature of the thing, . . . that it should always be for Life . . . ."

significant generalizations in the *Second Treatise* in terms of *persons*: the legislative body is composed of persons, the supreme power is placed in them by the people, "using Force upon the People without Authority . . . is a state of War with the People."[6] Women were included, presumably, among "the people," but they had no clear mechanism for expressing their own wills.[7] Locke obviously assumed that women contributed in some way to the civic culture, but he was not very clear about what they might do were they to find themselves under a king who had forfeited their confidence. One ends by wishing he had written a *Third Treatise*.

Montesquieu also returned to first principles: "I have first of all considered mankind."[8] The principles by which governments are regulated— virtue in a republic, honor in a monarchy, fear in a despotism—are abstractions apparently devoid of gender. The virtue that buttresses the republic is transmitted by parents (not only fathers) who are responsible for raising virtuous children (not only sons).

Sensitive as he was to the implications of private manners for public style, Montesquieu argued that "The slavery of women is perfectly conformable to the genius of a despotic government, which delights in treating all with severity. . . . In a government which requires, above all things, that a particular regard be paid to its tranquillity, it is absolutely necessary to shut up the women." On the other hand, "In a republic, the condition of citizens is moderate, equal, mild and agreeable . . . an empire over women cannot . . . be so well exerted."[9]

Although women did not play, for Montesquieu, a central role in shaping the civic character of the government under which they lived, the form that

6. *Second Treatise*, §§124, 153, 154, 155.

7. For women as a special case of relatively minor significance, see *Second Treatise*, §§180–83, 233.

8. Charles Louis de Secondat, Baron de Montesquieu, *The Spirit of the Laws*, Thomas Nugent, tr. (New York: Hafner Pub. Co., 1949), lxvii–lxix.

9. Montesquieu, 255–56. Book VII includes a curious pair of paragraphs headed "Of Female Administration" which offer the paradox that "It is contrary to reason and nature that women should reign in families . . . but not that they should govern an empire." In families women's natural weakness "does not permit them to have the pre-eminence"; but in governments that same weakness means that they administer their governments with "more lenity and moderation." It is the classic double bind, and applies, in any event, only to women who inherit their thrones. Despite Montesquieu's defense of women's political ability, he suggests no devices which would increase the likelihood that they will use these abilities.

government ultimately took *did* have crucial implications for their private lives. By his description of the "connection between domestic and political government," Montesquieu provided strong support for the conclusion that it is in women's self-interest to live in a republic. He offered no mechanism by which a woman unfortunate enough not to be born into a republic might change her condition, but the message that it was of crucial importance for women to live under certain forms of government and not under others was there, strongly phrased, available if anyone wished to use it.

Condorcet came closest to inventing procedure for as well as justification for including women in politics. His feminist comments emerge naturally from his general vision of the social order; they appear most extensively in his essay "Sur l'admission des Femmes au Droit de Cité," and in his "Lettres d'un Bourgeois de New-Heaven" (an appealing typographical error).[10]

Condorcet argued that although it was true that women had not exercised the right of citizenship in any "constitution called free," the right to political voice in a republic is claimed by men on the grounds that they are "sensible beings, capable of reason, having moral ideas," qualities which can be equally well claimed by women. "Men have . . . interests strongly different from those of women," Condorcet said in an unusual and forceful statement (although he did not specify what those differences were), and have used their power to make laws that establish "a great inequality between the sexes." Once it were admitted that people cannot legitimately be taxed without representation, "it follows from this principle that all women are in their rights to refuse to pay parliamentary taxes." Condorcet proceeded to argue that except in matters requiring brute strength, women were obviously men's equals; the brightest women were already superior to men of limited talents, and improvements in education would readily narrow what gaps there were. He concluded what was perhaps his generation's most detailed statement of the political rights and responsibilities of women:

> Perhaps you will find this discussion too long; but think that it is about the rights of half of human beings, rights forgotten by all the legislators; that it is not useless even for the liberty of men to indicate the means of

10. The essay, "Sur l'admission des Femmes," originally appeared July 3, 1790, in the *Journal de la Société de 1789*; it is reprinted in *Oeuvres de Condorcet* (Paris: Firmin Didot Frères, 1847), X, 119–30. The letters were published as pages 267–71 in Vol. I of Filippo Mazzei, *Recherches Historiques et Politiques Sur les États-Unis . . . avec Quatre Lettres d'un Bourgeois de New-Heaven sur l'unité de la Législation* (Paris: A. Colle, 1788).

destroying the single objection which could be made to republics, and to make between them and states which are not free a real difference.[11]

Condorcet is best remembered, of course, for his *Esquisse d'un tableau historique des progrès de l'esprit humain*, sometimes for the book's own sake, more often for the bravery of his authorship of a testament to the human spirit at the very moment when that same spirit was hounding him to a premature death. In the *Esquisse*, he imagined that women had been an integral part of prehistoric society and important contributors to the social order. The original society consisted of a family, "formed at first by the want that children have of their parents, and by the affection of the mother as well as that of the father." Children gradually extend the affection they naturally have for their parents to other members of their family and then to their clan. But before the first stage of primitive society has been outgrown, women have lost their central position. Condorcet suggests that the origins of governmental institutions resided in the meetings of men who planned hunting trips and wars. It seemed obvious to him that "the weakness of the females, which exempted them from the distant chase, and from war, the usual subjects of debate, excluded them alike from these consultations"; women were thus excluded at the outset from "the first political institutions" and consigned to "a sort of slavery." Their slavery is modified in the second, or pastoral epoch, and manners are "softened" and modified still more in the third epoch, which also sees the invention of alphabetical writing. "A more sedentary mode of life had introduced a greater equality between the sexes. . . . Men looked upon them as companions, . . . [but] even in countries where they were treated with most respect . . . neither reason nor justice extended so far as to an entire reciprocity as to the right of divorce. . . . The history of this class of prejudices, and of their influence on the lot of the human species . . . [evinces] how closely man's happiness is connected with the progress of reason."[12]

The more rational the government, the more improved will be the status of women. It is an important formulation, but Condorcet, oddly enough, does not develop it further. In its omission of women from the fourth

11. *Lettres d'un Bourgeois . . .*, 281–87, translation mine.

12. Marie Antoine Nicolas Caritat, Marquis de Condorcet, title usually translated as *Sketch for a Historical Picture of the Progress of the Human Mind* (Philadelphia: M. Carey, 1794), 24, 26, 28, 32, 43. In his list of tasks that remained unaccomplished, Condorcet specifically listed the improvement of the status of women: his words on this point have frequently been reprinted (p. 280).

through ninth epochs of one of the very few histories that begins as in fact a history of mankind in the generic sense, the *Esquisse* falls into traditionalism: "he" lapses into literal usage, and the assumption that men represent the general case, women the rare and insignificant exception, is reinforced. Those who wish to find in Condorcet reiteration of the rule that the world is a man's world will find it in the *Esquisse*.[13]

Condorcet offered his comments on women in politics in direct challenge to those of Rousseau. Although much that Rousseau wrote implied sharp criticism of contemporary society and envisaged drastic change, what he said about women usually reinforced the existing order. This conservatism about women may well have served to make his radical comments about men's behavior more palatable; if the world were to be changed into a new one, characterized by a new style of men's behavior as demonstrated by Émile, governed by a General Will in accordance with a new Social Contract, it was surely reassuring to know that the women of that world, exemplified by Émile's wife Sophie, would not change—that they would remain deferential to their men, clean in their household habits, complaisant in their conversation.

The key to Rousseau's understanding of women's political function is in his discussion of the origins of government in *The Social Contract*. The General Will, after all, is a concept without gender; the freedom of the social contract comes from the paradoxical identification of the ruler with

13. See Keith Michael Baker's magisterial *Condorcet: From Natural Philosophy to Social Mathematics* (Chicago: Univ. of Chicago Press, 1975). Baker does not, however, comment on Condorcet's treatment of women's role in political society or on the essay "Sur l'admission des Femmes au droit de cité" or the "Lettres d'un Bourgeois. . . ." In 1785 Condorcet's careful analysis of "the calculus of consent" was published as "Essai sur l'application de l'analyse à la probabilité des decisions rendues à la pluralité des voix"; as Baker phrases it, the essay attempts to deal with the problem of "Under what conditions will the probability that the majority decision of an assembly or tribunal is true be high enough to justify the obligation of the rest of society to accept that decision." Condorcet viewed "the process of political decision-making . . . not as a means of ascertaining the strongest among a number of opposing parties—not, that is, as a mere expression of will—but as a method for the collective discovery of truth." Like Turgot, Condorcet rejected the claim that "monarchical government" could "impose a just order in a constant war of corporate claims and counterclaims" in favor of "the doctrine of a nation of individuals united by the common, reciprocal bond of citizenship" (Baker, 228–29). This reasoning has something in common with Rousseau's General Will, in which all individuals choose to submit to the community. But even in Condorcet's formulation, women are not explicitly part of the community.

the ruled. If it is obvious that women are among the ruled, ought they not also be among the legislators?

There is a hidden paradox in this generally paradoxical essay: the women who are ruled are, at the same time, not ruled; because they are not ruled they need not participate in the General Will. They are invisible. As Rousseau explained in *Émile*, they lived in another world. Theirs is "the empire of softness, of address, of complacency; her commands are caresses; her menaces are tears."[14] This is not hyperbole; women have moral and physical relationships to men, but not political ones; nor do they relate to any women other than their mothers. Rousseau is explicit. The shift from the generic to the literal "he" occurs before *The Social Contract* has scarcely begun: the most ancient and only natural society is the family, Rousseau remarks, but children soon outgrow their dependence on their *fathers*.[15] After that the specific terms in which the General Will is explained are masculine ones; it is only men, taken literally, whom Rousseau expects to display disinterested civic spirit. In *Émile* he takes it as self-evident that it is "the good son, the good father, the good husband, that constitute the good citizen."[16]

Émile is a book about the task of forming a citizen for an idealized society. Émile is a body at ease with its mind, a sophisticated innocent, a person as paradoxical as the society for which he is educated. But Rousseau did not rethink the terms on which women ought to be educated for his new social order. He did not posit, for Sophie, as he did for Émile, a *tabula rasa* on which a rational mentor writes only what is necessary and natural; he did not end for Sophie, as he did for Émile, with a personality radically different from the one that standard systems of education were geared to create. Sophie is as traditional a woman as it is possible to imagine, reformed only in the sense that she does not dote on fashion or read novels.

Rousseau's refusal to rethink the terms of Sophie's education was intentional. Due to his own private sexual tastes he had, after all, a substantial personal stake in the submissiveness of women. He was not loath to make the broadest generalizations: "To oblige us, to do us service, to gain our love and esteem . . . these are the duties of the sex at all times, and what

14. Jean-Jacques Rousseau, *Emilius, Or, a Treatise of Education* (Edinburgh: A. Donaldson, 1768), III, 10.

15. Jean-Jacques Rousseau, *The Social Contract*, G. D. H. Cole, ed. (London: Dent, 1913), Book I, ch. II, p. 6.

16. *Emilius*, III, 14.

they ought to learn from their infancy."[17] Relationships between men and women are always sexual, and always verge on the uncontrollable: "Woman is framed particularly for the delight and pleasure of man. . . . Her violence consists in her charms . . . [her modesty masks her] unbounded desires."[18]

Nor did Rousseau need to rethink the bases of Sophie's mental development. As men's education became more highly developed it had strayed further from the natural into bookish abstraction. Rousseau needed a revolution to arrange for Émile to grow up among things rather than books, to postpone learning to read, to postpone foreign languages until he traveled to countries where they were used. But girls were already barred from books, rarely taught foreign languages, already limited to physical tasks relating to household chores. Only erase excessive attention to fashion, and women's education needed no renovation. Émile thanks his mentor for having been "restored to my liberty, by teaching me to yield to necessity." But Sophie's life is at all times largely directed by necessity; the more that women's lives were shaped by repeated cycles of pregnancy, lying-in, nursing, and childrearing, the closer they were to nature; the less the need to reform their education.[19]

17. Ibid., III, 74–75.
18. Ibid., III, 5–6.
19. Ibid., III, 229. In Book V of *The Wealth of Nations*, Adam Smith expresses similar admiration for the practical aspects of women's education. "There are no public institutions for the education of women, and there is accordingly nothing useless, absurd, or fantastical in the common course of their education. They are taught what their parents or guardians judge it necessary or useful for them to learn; and they are taught nothing else. Every part of their education tends evidently to some useful purpose; either to improve the natural attractions of their person, or to form their mind to reserve, to modesty, to chastity, and to economy; to render them both likely to become the mistresses of a family, and to behave properly when they have become such. In every part of her life a woman feels some conveniency or advantage from every part of her education. It seldom happens that a man, in any part of his life, derives any conveniency or advantage from some of the most laborious and troublesome parts of his education" (*The Wealth of Nations* [New York: Modern Library, 1937], Book V, ch. I, part II, article II, pp. 720, 734). When Smith comes to reform the educational system, women continue to be excluded from it. Men are to envy women the practicality of their education, and the direct relationship between women's education and their adult roles; it is harder to predict what skills boys will ultimately find most useful. That women's education can be directly related to women's adult roles precisely because these roles are so limited and so predictable does not seem to Smith to be a cause for concern.

Rousseau's most substantial target was Plato, who had offered, in Book V of *The Republic*, the classic attack on assigning social roles by gender. Rousseau defended Plato against the charge of encouraging promiscuity by inventing a community of women, but he was horrified by the "civil promiscuousness" implied by the assigning of the same employments to men and women. It represented, Rousseau sneered, the conversion of women into men.[20]

The argument that women ought not be part of the political community (as they are in Plato) was reinforced by Rousseau's insistence that women who seek to do so deny their sexual identity. The woman who seeks to be a politician or philosopher does violence to her own character: "A witty [i.e. articulate] woman is a scourge to her husband, to her children, to her friends, her servants, and to all the world. Elated by the sublimity of her genius, she scorns to stoop to the duties of a woman, and is sure to commence a man. . . ." Rousseau was sure his readers would share his scorn of "a female genius, scribbling of verses in her toilette, and surrounded by pamphlets"; although if she were scribbling emotional effusions, as Julie does throughout all six books of *La Nouvelle Héloïse*, he apparently had no objection. "The art of thinking is not foreign to women," Rousseau conceded, "but they ought only to skim the surface of abstruse sciences."[21] Attacks on masculine, articulate women are one of the more common themes of English literature (both British and American) in the late eighteenth and early nineteenth centuries. The image would prove to be a formidable obstacle to feminists throughout the nineteenth and twentieth centuries; if the concept is not original with Rousseau, surely he did much to strengthen it in precisely those liberal and reformist circles where it would be logically predicted to die out.

Rousseau's impact on American thought is difficult to measure. There was no American edition of *Émile*, but it was available in translation in even more editions than Locke's *Two Treatises*. Much more widely circulated than either was Lord Kames' *Sketches of the History of Man*, which occasionally cites Rousseau and whose comments on women's place in society are in rough congruence with Rousseau's. For Lord Kames, women's history was "a capital branch of the history of man." It demonstrated a crude progress from women's debased condition among savages to "their

20. *The Republic*, H. D. P. Lee, tr. (London: Penguin, 1955), 209–10. Rousseau's comments appear in *Emilius*, III, 14.

21. *Emilius*, III, 104–05, 139.

elevated state in civilized nations." He explicitly denied that women have a direct responsibility to their nation; their relationship to their country is secondhand, experienced through husbands and sons, and they therefore have "less patriotism than men." Like Rousseau, Kames feared masculinization: "Remove a female out of her proper sphere, and it is easy to convert her into a male." He agreed that women's education ought to fit them to be sensible companions and mothers; the great danger to be guarded against was frivolity and disorderly manners. Having disposed of women in 97 pages, he was free to ignore them in the remaining 1,770 pages of his four-volume treatise; his final conclusion was merciless: "Cultivation of the female mind, is not of great importance in a republic, where men pass little of their time with women."[22]

We are left with an intellectual gap. The great treatises of the Enlightenment, which provided so changed a framework for attitudes toward the state, offered no guidance on how women might think about their own relationship to liberty or civic virtue. Even Rousseau, one of the most radical political theorists of an age famous for its ability to examine the assumptions it had inherited, failed to examine his own assumptions about women. Ought a woman dare to think? Might a woman accept "the loneliness of autonomy"? To be alone, in fact, was to be male; women were invariably described, even by Locke, in relationship to others. Only Condorcet occasionally imagined an autonomous woman: for Locke, Montesquieu, Rousseau, Kames, women existed only in their roles as mothers and wives. If Fred Weinstein and Gerald M. Platt are right in defining the Enlightenment as the expression of "a desire to end the commitments to passivity and dependence in the area of politics," women were not a part of it.[23]

Of all branches of Enlightenment thought, Americans were most attracted to the literature of the Commonwealth and Radical Whig opposition in England. As Bernard Bailyn and Gordon Wood have shown, eighteenth-century Americans were familiar with the work of Trenchard and Gordon, Sidney, Harrington, James Burgh, Catharine Macaulay. American political theorists made much use of it. But this literature is largely concerned with specific issues of opposition to crown policy; it

22. Henry Home, Lord Kames, *Sketches of the History of Man* (Edinburgh: W. Strahan & T. Cadell, 1778), II, 1–2, 5, 85, 97.

23. *The Wish to be Free: Society, Psyche and Value Change* (Berkeley: Univ. of California Press, 1969), 49.

rarely needed a presocial family to make its argument. One result of the overwhelming influence of the Whig tradition in America was that American political theory was rooted in assumptions that never gave explicit attention to basic questions about women. It was the good fortune of male Whigs that they did not need to begin at the beginning, but that same good fortune inhibited the likelihood that they would include women in their contemplations of the good society.

As Edwin Burrows and Michael Wallace have brilliantly shown, Whigs had a major ideological concern for parent-child relationships, but their discussions faded into the specific case of sons and fathers, or the limits of the obligations of sons to mothers.[24] Other variants of familial relationships were less thoroughly explored. John Trenchard, for example, addressed himself only to the evils of marrying women for money. In all four volumes of vigorously egalitarian rhetoric which rang the changes on the theme of the relationship between the state and the individual, *Cato* always contemplates political man, narrowly defined.[25] Not even so articulate a feminist as Catharine Macaulay felt the need to discuss women in her histories and essays, though she did discuss women's education elsewhere. She attacked Rousseau, and wrote in the seven small pages of her twenty-second "Letter on Education" most of what it took Wollstonecraft hundreds of pages to argue in the *Vindication*. But Macaulay, who was confident enough to plunge directly into public political debate and to criticize a Hobbes or a Burke without even a passing apology for the frailties of her sex, apparently felt no need to address the responsibilities of women to political society. Perhaps she believed she had made her position clear by implication and in practice. But her direct comments speak of the private responsibilities of women—even reformed, chaste, nonfrivolous women—to individual men. In this she was more in agreement with Rousseau than she thought.[26]

24. Edwin G. Burrows and Michael Wallace, "The American Revolution: The Ideology and Psychology of National Liberation," in *Perspectives in American History*, VI (1972), 167–306. See especially parts II and III.

25. John Trenchard, *Cato's Letters, or, Essays on Liberty, Civil and Religious and Other Important Subjects* (London: J. Wilkins, T. Woodward, et al., 1733), II, 201–12. There are no comments on women in Trenchard and Thomas Gordon's *The Independent Whig* (London: J. Peele, 1721).

26. Catharine Macaulay, *Letters on Education with Observations on Religious and Metaphysical Subjects* (London: C. Dilly, 1790); *An Address to the People of England,*

American Whigs were as unlikely as their British counterparts to integrate into political theory a concept of the proper relationship between women and the body politic. It may even be that Americans ignored the problem because the British did. Any body of theory that addresses basic issues of sex role must reach back to presocial or psychological sources of human behavior. The issues are so basic that they demand probing to the deepest and most mythological layers of human experience. Americans felt little need to do this; James Otis was one of the few to try, in the opening pages of the 1764 pamphlet, *The Rights of the British Colonies Asserted and Proved*:

> The original of *government* has in all ages no less perplexed the heads of lawyers and politicians than the origin of *evil* has embarrassed divines . . . the gentlemen in favor of [the theory that government is based on] the *original compact* have often been told that *their* system is chimerical and unsupported by reason or experience. Questions like the following have been frequently asked them. . . . Who were present and parties to such compact? Who acted for infants and women, or who appointed guardians for them? Had these guardians power to bind both infants and women during life and their posterity after them? . . . What will there be to distinguish the next generation of men from their forefathers, that they should not have the same right to make original compacts as their ancestors had? If every man has such right, may there not be as many original compacts as there are men and women born or to be born? Are not women born as free as men? Would it not be infamous to assert that the ladies are all slaves by nature? If every man and woman born or to be born has and will have a right to be consulted and must accede to the original compact before they can with any kind of justice be said to be bound by it, will not the compact be ever forming and never finished?

Otis raised embarrassing questions about women's political role:

> If upon abdication all were reduced to a state of nature, had not apple women and orange girls as good a right to give their respectable suf-

---

Ireland and Scotland, on the Present Crisis of Affairs, 3d ed. (New York: n.p., 1775); *Observations on the Reflections of Edmund Burke . . .* (Boston: Thomas and Andrews, 1791); *Loose Remarks on Certain Positions to be Found in Mr. Hobbes . . .* (London: T. Davies, 1767).

frages for a new King as the philosopher, courtier, and politician? Were these and ten millions of other such . . . consulted?[27]

Although Otis could ask embarrassing questions and imply their answers, on this as on so many points of theory, his developing mental illness prevented him from suggesting constitutional devices for implementing them. Nor did his sister, the vigorous Mercy Otis Warren, deal with the questions he had opened. She was certainly intelligent and a fluent writer. She could viciously criticize men for their private treatment of women and counsel friends that flirting and deference were "a little game" by which one charmed male admirers into doing what one wished, but even she avoided the theoretical questions: what responsibility does the state have to women? what responsibility do women have to the state? The closest she came was to describe the political woman as observer and commentator, not participant. If the ideas were valid, she wrote, "I think it very immaterial if they flow from a female lip in the soft whispers of private friendship or are thundered in the Senate in the bolder language of the other sex."[28] But it must be said that her belief that private recognition of woman's political potential is more important than public recognition loses some of its force when held up against the fact of her own publication of her history of the Revolution, and the fact that the "soft whispers" of the sister of James Otis and the wife of James Warren were more likely than those of most women to be heard by politically influential men. Warren's comments supported the notion that the family circle is a woman's state.

It was left to postrevolutionary ideology in America to justify and popularize a political role for women, accomplishing what the English and French Enlightenment had not. Montesquieu had implied that if women had the choice they ought to choose to live in republics; Condorcet had said explicitly that republics were imperfect until they took account of the political claims of half of their people. But Americans did not move directly to the definition of women as citizens and voters. The only reference to women in *The Federalist* is to the dangers to the safety of the state posed by

27. Reprinted in Bernard Bailyn, ed., *Pamphlets of the American Revolution, 1750–1776* (Cambridge: Harvard Univ. Press, 1965), I, 419–22.

28. Mercy Otis Warren to Catharine Macaulay, 29 Dec. 1774, Mercy Otis Warren Letterbook, Massachusetts Historical Society.

the private intrigues of courtesans and mistresses.[29] Instead, Americans offered an ironic compromise, one which merged Rousseau and Condorcet. It represented both an elaboration of the image of Sophie and a response to attacks like Rousseau's on the mental capacity of women. In this, as in so many other cases, Rousseau provided his own oxymoron.

The path *not* taken was suggested by one of the rare direct attacks on Rousseau that appeared in America, a pamphlet that contemplated the details of the integration of women into the political community. It came in 1801 from the pen of an "aged matron" from Connecticut who signed herself "The Female Advocate." She bristled at the arrogance of those who would deride "masculine women": if by

> the word "Masculine" be meant a person of reading and letters, a person of science and information, one who can properly answer a question, without fear and trembling, or one who is capable of doing business, with a suitable command over self, this I believe to be a glory to the one sex, equally with the other . . . custom, which is not infallible, has gradually introduced the habits of seeing an imaginary impropriety, that all science, all public utility, all superiority, all that is intellectually great and astonishing, should be engrossed exclusively by the male half of mankind.

The Female Advocate wished to function primarily as a citizen, only secondarily as a subject. She attacked contemporary refusals to include women in matters of church and public governance. She complained that "men engross all the emoluments, offices, honors and merits of church and state." She would grant that St. Paul had counseled women to be silent in public, and "learn from their husbands at home," but she pointed by contrast to St. Paul's own willingness to appoint women deaconesses. Women were not unsexed by taking part in community decisions:

> What if they have no husbands, or what if their husbands . . . are not of the church, or what if, as is very common, the husband knows less of the scriptures than the wife? . . . the point . . . is carried much too far, in the exclusive male prerogative to teach, to censure, to govern without the voice of women, or the least regard to the judgment or assent of the other sex. If a woman may not vote, or speak, on any occasion whatever, even tho' she have no husband, if she may not take any active part, by

29. Edward Meade Earle, ed., *The Federalist* (New York: Modern Library, 1941), 28–29.

approbation or disapprobation, no not even in a silent vote, and that too when perhaps one of her sex is the subject of discipline or controversy, yea, when, farther, as is generally the case, the great majority of the church is female—how, pray you, is the sex to be viewed? Are they mere cyphers . . . ?

The proper model for females, she thought, was the biblical Deborah, who lived actively in both the religious and the secular worlds: "Behold her wielding the sword with one hand, and the pen of wisdom with the other: her sitting at the council board, and there, by her superior talents, conducting the arduous affairs of military enterprise! Say now, shall woman be forever destined solely to the distaff and the needle, and never expand an idea beyond the walls of her house?"[30]

Other Americans had also made demands for the direct participation of women in public affairs: there is the well-known comment by Abigail Adams, which her husband jokingly turned away, that women required the right to participate in the new system of government, arguing pointedly that "all men would be tyrants if they could." All her life Abigail Adams would be a shrewd private commentator on the political scene, assuming as active an obligation to judge good and evil as though she were called on annually to vote on it. But she was known, of course, only in a circle which, though relatively large, remained private. Charles Brockden Brown sneered at the "charming system of equality and independence" that denied women a part in the choice of their governors, but the circulation of *Alcuin* was small; St. George Tucker conceded that laws neither respected nor favored females, but he made the concession in a minor aside in a three-volume work.[31] The women whom Esther de Berdt Reed and Sarah Bache led through Philadelphia collecting contributions for the American soldiers in 1780 encountered many who thought, with Anna Rawle, that "of all absurdities the ladies going about for money exceeded everything." The campaign, as we know, was a success: they collected some 300,000 paper dollars, managed to keep Washington from merging it into the general funds "contributed by the gentlemen"; and they saw to it that the soldiers knew to whom they were indebted for their new and much-needed shirts. The effort formed the model for a score of postwar women's philanthropic

30. *The Female Advocate* (New Haven, Conn.: T. Green, 1801), 22, 10.

31. *Alcuin; A Dialogue* (New York: Grossman, 1971), 32–33; St. George Tucker, ed., *Blackstone's Commentaries* (Philadelphia: n.p., 1803), II, 145, 445.

groups, but it did not, it has to be said, provide a model of political action except by sacrifice.[32]

Direct political participation and influence require voting and office-holding. American intellectuals who sought to create a vehicle by which women might demonstrate their political competence shrank from that solution, hesitating to join the Female Advocate in the wish that women be admitted to active participation and leadership in civic government. To do so would have required a conceptual and political leap for which they were apparently not prepared. Instead of insisting that competence has no sex, an alternate model was proposed in the 1790s. It contained many traditional elements of the woman's role, but it also had a measure of critical bite.

The theorists of this alternate position were Judith Sargent Murray, Susannah Rowson, and Benjamin Rush.[33] They deplored the "dependence for which women are uniformly educated"; they argued that political independence in the nation should be echoed by self-reliance on the part of women. The model republican woman was to be self-reliant (within limits), literate, untempted by the frivolities of fashion. She had a responsibility to the political scene, though not to act on it. As one fictional woman put it, "If the community flourish and enjoy health and freedom, shall we not share in the happy effect? If it be oppressed and disturbed, shall we not endure our proportion of evil? Why then should the love of our country be a masculine passion only?"[34] But her competence did not extend to the making of political decisions. Her political task was accomplished within the confines of her family. The model republican woman was a mother.

The Republican Mother's life was dedicated to the service of civic virtue; she educated her sons for it; she condemned and corrected her husband's lapses from it. If, as Montesquieu had maintained and as it was commonly assumed, the stability of the nation rested on the persistence of virtue

32. Anna Rawle to Rebecca Rawle Shoemaker, June 30, 1780, *Pennsylvania Magazine of History and Biography*, 35 (1911), 398; *The Sentiments of an American Woman* [broadside], Philadelphia, June 10, 1780.

33. See especially Judith Sargent Murray, *The Gleaner* (Boston: I. Thomas, 1798), III, 188–224, 260–65; Benjamin Rush, "Thoughts upon Female Education, Accommodated to the Present State of Society, Manners and Government in the United States of America" (Philadelphia: Prichard and Hall, 1787), reprinted in Frederick Rudolph, ed., *Essays on Education in the Early Republic* (Cambridge: Harvard Univ. Press, 1965); Susannah Rowson, *Reuben and Rachel* (Boston: Hanning and Loring, 1798).

34. Hannah Foster, *The Coquette* (Charlestown, Mass.: E. and S. Larkin, 1802), 62.

among its citizens, then the creation of virtuous citizens was dependent on the presence of wives and mothers who were well informed, "properly methodical," and free of "invidious and rancorous passions." As one commencement speaker put it, "Liberty is never sure, 'till Virtue reigns triumphant. . . . While you [women] thus keep our country virtuous, you maintain its independence." It was perhaps more than mere coincidence that *virtù* was derived from the Latin for man, with its connotations of virility; political action seemed somehow inherently masculine. Virtue in a woman seemed to require another theater for its display. To that end the theorists created a mother who had a political purpose, and argued that her domestic behavior had a direct political function in the republic.[35]

Western political theory, even during the Enlightenment, had only occasionally contemplated the role of women in the civic culture. It had habitually considered women only in domestic relationships, only as wives and mothers. It had not devised any mode by which women might have a political impact on government or fulfill their obligations to it. The Republican Mother was a device which attempted to integrate domesticity and politics.

The ideology of Republican Motherhood also represented a stage in the process of women's political socialization. In recent years, we have become accustomed to thinking of political socialization as a *process* in which an individual develops a definition of self as related to the state.[36] One of the intermediate stages in that process might be called the deferential citizen: the person who expects to influence the political system, but only to a limited extent. Deference represents not the negation of citizenship, but an approach to full participation in the civic culture. The best description of

35. *New York Magazine*, May 1795, pp. 301–05. I have discussed this in greater detail in "Daughters of Columbia: Educating Women for the Republic, 1787–1805," in *The Hofstadter Aegis: A Memorial*, Stanley Elkins and Eric McKitrick, eds. (New York: Knopf, 1974), 36–59 [which is reproduced as the first essay in the present volume]. For the idealization of the Spartan mother, see Elizabeth Rowson, *The Spartan Tradition in European Thought* (Oxford: Oxford Univ. Press, 1969).

36. See Gabriel Almond and Sidney Verba, *The Civic Culture: Political Attitudes and Democracy in Five Nations* (Princeton: Princeton Univ. Press, 1963). Almond and Verba view politicization as a gradual process by which individuals cease to think of themselves as invariably acted *on* by the state, and end by thinking of themselves as *actors*, who force governments to respond to them. There are many stages along this continuum, and there is room for internal contradictions.

the genre is Charles Sydnor's of the voters of Jefferson's Virginia, who freely chose their social superiors to office rather than exercise a claim on office themselves.

Deference was an attitude that many women adopted and displayed at a time when it was gradually being abandoned by men; the politicization of women and men, in America as elsewhere, was out of phase. Women were still thinking of themselves as subjects while men were deferential citizens; as the restrained, deferential democracy of the republic gave way to an aggressive, egalitarian democracy of a modern sort among men, women invented a restrained, deferential but nonetheless political role. The voters of colonial Virginia did not think themselves good enough to stand for election but they chose legislators; the deferential women whom Judith Sargent Murray prescribed for the republic did not vote, but they took pride in their ability to mold citizens who would. This hesitancy of American women to become political actors would persist. Are not the women of the postsuffrage twentieth century who had the vote but did not use it to elect people like themselves to office similar to the deferential males of Sydnor's Virginia?

There was a direct relationship between developing egalitarian democracy among men and the expectation of continued deferential behavior among women. Émile needs Sophie; the society in which he functions cannot exist without her. Just as white democracy in the antebellum South rested on the economic base of slavery, so egalitarian society similarly rested on a moral base of continuing deferential behavior among a class of people—women—who would devote their efforts to service: raising sons and disciplining husbands to be virtuous citizens of the republic. The learned woman, who might very well wish to make choices as well as influence attitudes, was a visible threat to this arrangement.[37] A political community that accepted women as political actors would have to eliminate the Rousseauean assumption that the world in which women live is separate from the empire of men. The political traditions on which Ameri-

37. It is hard to find objective grounds for a fear of learned ladies; as Kenneth Lockridge has shown, literacy among women lagged substantially behind literacy among men in the colonial years. The subject has been insufficiently studied, but it appears that women's literacy rates do not catch up with men's until well into the nineteenth century. See Kenneth Lockridge, *Literacy in Colonial New England* (New York: Norton, 1974), 38–42; Daniel Calhoun, *The Intelligence of a People* (Princeton: Princeton Univ. Press, 1974), Appendix A.

can politics were built offered little assistance in defining the point at which the woman's private domain intersected with the public one. The Republican Mother seemed to offer a solution.

The notion that mothers perform a political function is not silly; it represents the recognition that political socialization takes place at an early age, and that the patterns of authority experienced in families are important factors in the general political culture. The willingness of American women to discuss politics at home is apparently more characteristic than in other western democracies; so is the rate of women's interaction in their communities, their rate of office holding in voluntary associations.[38] Americans live—and have long lived—in a political culture in which the family is a basic part of the system of political communication. This did not "just happen." It is a behavior pattern that challenges far older ones. The separation of male and female domains within a community is a very ancient practice, maintained by a wide range of often unarticulated but nevertheless very firm social restrictions.[39] There are nations today—even fairly modern democracies—in which these separate domains and premodern patterns still shape the political community: where women are much less likely than their American counterparts to discuss politics; where men are much more likely to carry on their political discussions among men, outside the home. In premodern political cultures mothers do not assume a clear political function. In this sense, Republican Motherhood was a very important—even revolutionary—invention. It altered the female domain in which most women had always lived out their lives; it justified an extension of women's absorption and participation in the civic culture.

In the years of the early republic there developed the consensus that a mother could not be a citizen but that she might serve a political purpose. Those who said that women ought to play no political role at all had to meet the proposal that women might play a deferential political role through the raising of a patriotic child. The concept of Republican Motherhood began to fill the gap left by the political theorists of the Enlightenment. It would continue to be used by women well into the twentieth century; one thinks of the insistence of Progressive women reformers that

38. Almond and Verba, 377–401.

39. On female spheres, see Carroll Smith-Rosenberg, "The Female World of Love and Ritual: Relations Between Women in Nineteenth-Century America," *Signs: A Journal of Women in Culture and Society*, 1 (1975), 1–30; Rayna Reiter, ed., *Toward an Anthropology of Women* (New York: Monthly Review Press, 1975).

the obligations of women to ensure honesty in politics, efficient urban sanitation, pure food and drug laws were extensions of their responsibilities as mothers. But the ideology of Republican Motherhood had limitations; it provided a context in which skeptics could easily maintain that women should be content to perform this limited political role permanently and ought not to wish fuller participation. For one woman, Republican Motherhood might mean an extension of vistas; for another it could be stifling. The ambivalent relationship between motherhood and citizenship would be one of the most lasting, and most paradoxical, legacies of the revolutionary generation.

"HISTORY CAN DO IT NO JUSTICE"
WOMEN AND THE REINTERPRETATION OF THE AMERICAN REVOLUTION

My title comes from a rueful observation of Elizabeth Ellet, the first historian to address extensively the relationship of women to the American Revolution. Ellet was a writer for popular periodicals; her grandfather had fought in the Revolution. In 1848 she published two volumes of biographical sketches of some sixty women who lived through the Revolution. In her preface Ellet addressed the practical problem of recovering their lives.

> In offering this work to the public, it is due to the reader no less than the writer, to say something of the extreme difficulty which has been found in obtaining materials sufficiently reliable for a record designed to be strictly authentic. . . . Inasmuch as political history says but little—and that vaguely and incidentally—of the Women who bore their part in the Revolution, the materials for a work treating of them and their actions and sufferings, must be derived in great part from private sources. The apparent dearth of information was at first almost disheartening. . . . Of the little that was written, too, how small a portion remains in this . . . manuscript-destroying generation?[1]

Ellet interviewed and corresponded with elderly survivors and with the children and relatives of her subjects. After a while her problem ceased to be one of finding information—she had enough to fill many volumes—but

1. Elizabeth F. Ellet, *The Women of the American Revolution*, 2 vols. (1848–50; reprint ed., Philadelphia, 1900) 1:15–17.

was instead the analytical one of arranging and interpreting it. She did not solve this analytical problem, but she did begin to sneak up on the solution.

Ellet deduced that there had been at least two sets of equally authentic wartime experiences, documented in different ways. Attested to by public records, "the actions of men stand out in prominent relief," she wrote. But the actions and influence of women occurred in the private "women's sphere," and for these activities documentation was deficient.[2] Thus there were two perspectives on the Revolution, as there were on any great event, waiting to be written about; of the two, retrieving the women's perspective was the more challenging and difficult. Retrieval was difficult for technical reasons: the paucity of official and personal records, the inattention with which women's behavior was regarded, and the scorn with which records of that behavior were treated by a "manuscript-destroying generation." But retrieval was especially difficult, Ellet suspected, because women's history necessarily had a distinctive psychological component. She thought that women shaped the history of their generation by personal influence, by the force of "sentiment," by *feeling*. This second factor, inchoate, ill-defined, which represented the difference women made, could not be measured and was not easily described. "History can do it no justice."

Ellet wrote in the now dated language of nineteenth-century romanticism, and it is easy to read her work in a way that stresses its naive celebration of domesticity and service, its simplistic narrative strategies, and its implicit racism. (She thought it was generous when a slave who had saved his master's plantation was rewarded by easier work and, only many years later, by the purchase of his wife from a neighboring plantation so they could end their lives together.) I would not agree with her that sentiment and feeling are a female monopoly. But I do believe that it was an analytical improvement to recognize that there were at least two wars, a men's war and a women's war (just as there was a soldier's war and a civilian's war), that the two merged and often interacted, and that one might serve the other but was not necessarily subsumed by it. As Justice William O. Douglas observed many years later, "The two sexes are not fungible."

Ellet began by recovering the stories, mostly of patriot women but some of loyalists, and getting them into the record before time ran out. Among them are the stories of prominent women like Abigail Adams, Mercy Otis Warren, and Martha Washington, but there were also sixteen-year-old Dicey Langston of backcountry South Carolina, who forded a river at night

2. Ibid., p. 18.

to bring news of loyalist troop movements to her brother's patriot camp; Lydia Darragh of Philadelphia, who managed to communicate with Washington's scouts despite the occupation of her house by British officers; and the women of Groton, Massachusetts, who, after their minutemen husbands had left with Col. Job Prescott, guarded the bridge on the road to the town border "clothed in their absent husbands' apparel, and armed with muskets, pitchforks, and such other weapons as they could find," arrested, unhorsed, and searched a loyalist messenger carrying dispatches.[3]

Then Ellet went further. She had written a distinctive women's history and in the process discovered a large audience for her work (two years after its publication *Women of the American Revolution* was in its fourth edition). In 1850 she tried to write a different book, one which placed gender at the narrative center of the Revolutionary experience and which would tell the history of the American Revolution from the perspective of both men and women. That book bears the wimpy title *Domestic History of the American Revolution*, but it turns out to be a surprising volume.[4] Ellet really does do a measure of justice to the women whose life experiences she had uncovered for the 1848 series of biographical sketches. *Domestic History* is the only history of the Revolution—perhaps of any war—I have read that devotes as much space to women as to men. The book is not distinctly a "women's history"; it seeks to be holistic. It offers a narrative of the war years, arranged by standard political set pieces: the great battles—of Long Island, of Saratoga, of King's Mountain, and so forth, all the way to Yorktown; the winter at Valley Forge, the treason of General Arnold, the mutiny of the Pennsylvania troops. But Ellet's text treats these episodes briskly, and in that way makes room for women's boycotts of British goods, women who contributed massive quantities of food to armies on the march, women who collected substantial contributions of money and supplies. As the war proceeds, clashes of armies alternate with accounts of women's activity and response.

3. Ibid., 2:296. This episode has been described in detail in Linda Grant De Pauw, "Women in Combat: The Revolutionary War Experience," *Armed Forces and Society* 7 (1981): 221–22. The women apparently numbered thirty or forty and were led by Prudence Wright and Sarah Shattuck. The latter was married to Job Shattuck, who had marched with the militia to Lexington; in 1787 he would be sentenced to be hanged for his leading role in Shays's Rebellion but would ultimately be pardoned (Caleb Butler, *History of the Town of Groton, Including Pepperell and Shirley* . . . [Boston, 1848], pp. 336–37).

4. Elizabeth F. Ellet, *Domestic History of the American Revolution* (New York, 1850). Subsequent printings appeared in 1851, 1854, and 1856; there were new editions in 1876 and 1879.

Sometimes the women are victims: the confrontation at Lexington and Concord is followed by a woman's memoir of her flight from Cambridge, "the road filled with frightened women and children, some in carts with their tattered furniture, others on foot fleeing into the woods."[5]

Sometimes women's presence is ceremonial: "On the third day after the battle [in which the British were repulsed from Sullivans Island in Charleston Harbor] . . . the wife of Col. Barnard Elliott presented to the second regiment, commanded by Col. Moultrie, a pair of richly embroidered colors, wrought by herself. They were planted, three years afterwards, on the British lines at Savannah, by Sergeant Jasper, who in planting them received his death wound."[6]

Always it is women who maintain elementary decency when it is dissolving around them. They talk back to uppity loyalists; they stand up for their property rights. Thus an innkeeper to whose hostelry a boisterous British scouting party brings a wounded American officer stays up to guard him through the night. She cares for him without fee, but charges the British outrageous prices. In South Carolina the daughters of General Gaston care for wounded and dying American soldiers when "men dared not come to minister to their wants."[7] And a steady stream of women brings food and blankets to prisoners; among these women is the mother of Andrew Jackson, who dies of a fever caught on one of these expeditions.[8]

In Ellet's hands the actions of individual women often shape the occasion or the outcome of a particular battle. Thus the loyalist Mrs. Rapalje is only narrowly thwarted in her attempt to warn the British of American troop movements; had she succeeded, the outcome of the battle of New York might have been different.[9] Mrs. Robert Murray detains Governor Tryon at her tea table long enough to give the Americans under Putnam time to retreat.[10] And always women ride through the woods—at night, in dead of winter—to bring word to American detachments of British plans.

This riding through the woods is worth attention. Ellet's accounts are as much literary vision as historical reporting. They are a folk history, gleaned from the stories she heard. If we add anecdotes from the two-volume

5. Ibid., p. 31.
6. Ibid., p. 45.
7. Ibid., p. 179.
8. Ibid., pp. 213, 223, 225.
9. Ibid., p. 56.
10. Ibid., p. 57.

Women of the Revolution to the ones in *Domestic History* we are left with American forests as peopled as those of the Brothers Grimm, in which instead of orphaned children and witches we have lone women hastening breathlessly on errands of mercy or information. There is, for example, Mary Slocumb of North Carolina, who dreamed that her husband was lying dead in battle. She "rose in the night, saddled her horse and rode at full gallop." When she gets to the battlefield she finds a wounded man wrapped in her husband's cloak, but it turns out to be another man, whom she nurses; she later discovers her husband unharmed. After working with the wounded for a day, "in the middle of the night she again mounted and started for home, declining the offer to send an escort with her. . . . This resolute woman thus rode alone, in the night, through a wild, unsettled country, a distance—going and returning—of a hundred and twenty-five miles, and that in less than forty hours, and without any interval of rest!"[11]

Or there is the tale of Dicey Langston, who, in order to give warning of British troop movements to her brother's detachment, leaves

> her home alone, by stealth, and at the dead hour of night. Many miles were to be traversed, and the road lay through woods, and crossed marshes and creeks where the conveniences of bridges and foot-logs were wanting. She walked rapidly on, heedless of slight difficulties; but her heart almost failed her when she came to the banks of the Tyger—a deep and rapid stream, rendered more dangerous by the rains that had lately fallen. But the thought of personal danger weighed not with her; she resolved to accomplish her purpose, or perish in the attempt. She entered the water; but when in the middle of the ford, became bewildered, and knew not which direction to take. The hoarse rush of the waters, which were up to her neck—the blackness of the night—the utter solitude around her—the uncertainty lest the next step should ingulph her past help, confused her, and she wandered some time in the channel without knowing whither to turn her steps. But the energy of a resolute will, under the care of Providence, sustained her.[12]

These tales demand deconstruction. Of course we need to proceed with caution, recognizing that they are nineteenth-century tales, not eighteenth-century artifacts. The analogy to the Grimm tales may not be accidental; as Peter Taylor and Hermann Rebel have recently pointed out, the Grimm

11. Ibid., p. 47.
12. Ibid., p. 234.

tales come from the same region that furnished the Hessian soldiers and were developed at the same time. The Grimm tales—especially those that focus on impoverished children thrust out prematurely to seek their fortunes, and on some deprived of their birthright—resonate with themes that link them to the American Revolution.[13] Ellet's versions were constructed in the 1840s, and the manner of their retelling expresses nineteenth-century romanticism and the limitations of professional historians of her generation at least as much as it does eighteenth-century experience. Still, the themes that her informants kept transmitting to her are rich ones for our understanding of how ordinary women perceived their experience. These women understood that they had been victims; they claimed for themselves fortitude, decency, and heroism. Ellet's informants located their action in the interstices of the great public set pieces of the historical drama, but they did not underestimate their value.

Ellet's revision of the narrative of the Revolution will not satisfy the twentieth-century historian seeking an account of the Revolution that embeds women's roles and experiences deeply into both narrative and analysis. Ellet ignored themes that we now find indispensable: major questions of strategy and tactics, of internal and international politics, of class relations, of the social dynamics of the army. The actors on Ellet's stage are an assortment of American officers, who are made to stand for the entire armed forces, and individual civilian women, who stand only for themselves.

But if we cannot rely on Ellet, neither can we rely on currently popular narratives of the war to tell us about the experiences of both men and women, whether they were black or white. Although the last decade has seen an outpouring of new specialized scholarship on the distinctive experiences of women, the main lines of general analysis have not changed recognizably. The women of the Revolutionary era remain becalmed in the E208 section of our libraries, wringing their hands like the White Queen in *Through the Looking Glass*, suffering gracefully in otherwise admirable books of otherwise distinguished historians.

For example, virtually the only woman we meet in Robert Middlekauff's magisterial *The Glorious Cause* is Sarah Hodgkins of Ipswich, Massachusetts, who assures her husband of her love through the strenuous years of

13. Peter Taylor and Hermann Rebel, "Hessian Peasant Women, Their Families, and the Draft: A Social-Historical Interpretation of Four Tales from the Grimm Collection," *Journal of Family History* 6 (1981): 347–78. "Trees and forests turn up in all of the tales as elements of shelter and as locales where magical transformations take place."

war, and when his battlefield is close enough, takes in his washing and sends his clean clothes back in a packet. In Charles Royster's prize-winning *A Revolutionary People at War*, we encounter only two women—Janet Montgomery, who spends the years after her husband's death in battle burnishing his reputation to a fine gloss, and poor Faithy Trumbull Huntington, who is so unhinged by her view of the battlefield at Bunker Hill (as well she might have been) that she is driven to suicide.

Yet the ingredients—both material and theoretical—for an analysis that recognizes the role of gender in the Revolutionary war are now available. We know better than to discount the female experience as inherently marginal or trivial. We have gathered a considerable amount of information and know where to get more about the actions and responses of women in the pre-Revolutionary political crises and in the war itself. Although sex remains a biological given, gender—the learned sense of self, the social relations between the sexes—is now well understood to be a social construction. We understand better the paradoxical quality of Western ideas about women, which, at least since the Middle Ages, have stressed both that women were weak and should be ruled by men and that women were more disorderly, more lustful, and yet less predictable than men. We are ready to ask whether and how the social relations of the sexes were renegotiated in the crucible of Revolution.

Like all revolutions, the American Revolution had a double agenda. Patriots sought to exclude the British from power: this task was essentially physical and military. Patriots also sought to accomplish a radical psychological and intellectual transformation: "Our principles, opinions, and manners," Benjamin Rush argued, would need to change to be congruent with "the forms of government we have adopted."[14] As Cynthia Enloe has remarked, a successful revolutionary movement establishes new definitions of "what is valued, what is scorned, what is feared, and what is believed to enhance safety and security."[15]

In America this transformation involved a sharp attack on social hierarchies and a reconstruction of family relationships, especially between

14. Benjamin Rush to Richard Price, May 25, 1786, Lyman H. Butterfield, ed., *Letters of Benjamin Rush*, 2 vols. (Princeton, 1951), 1:388.

15. Cynthia Enloe, "Beyond the Battlefield: A Feminist Approach to 'Pre-War' and 'Post-War' Military Politics" (Paper presented at the Conference on Gender and War, Princeton University, 1984).

husbands and wives and between parents and children. Military resistance was enough for rebellion; it was the transformation of values—which received classic expression in Thomas Paine's *Common Sense*—that defined the Revolution. Both tasks were intertwined, and both tasks—resistance and redefinition—involved women as supporters and as adversaries far more than we have understood.

If the army is described and analyzed solely from the vantage point of central command, the women and children will be invisible. To view it from the vantage point of the foot soldier and the thousands of women who followed the troops is to emphasize the marginality of support services for both armies, and the penetrability of the armies by civilians, especially women and children. From the women's perspective, the American army looks far less professional, far more disorganized, than it appears to be in most scholarly studies of the war of the Revolution.

Women were drawn into the task of direct military resistance to a far greater extent than we have appreciated. Along with the French Revolution, the American Revolution was the last of the early modern wars. As they had since the sixteenth century, thousands of women and children traveled with the armies, functioning as nurses, laundresses, and cooks. Like the emblematic Molly Pitcher, they made themselves useful where they could— hauling water for teams that fired cannon, bringing food to men under fire. In British practice, with which the colonists had become familiar during the Seven Years' War, each company had its own allocation of women, usually but not always soldiers' wives and occasionally mothers; when the British sailed, their women sailed with them. This role remains unstudied; we still depend on Walter Hart Blumenthal's 1952 account. He reports that in the original complement of eight regiments that the British sent to put down the American rebellion, each regiment had 677 men and 60 women, a ratio of approximately 10 to 1. Blumenthal suggests that as the war continued the number of women attached to British troops *increased*. Burgoyne's army of 7,200 troops was followed by 2,000 women. Native-born women attached themselves to the troops and followed the armies because they feared to lose track of men with whom they had developed relationships or by whom they were pregnant, or because they feared to stay on in a loyalist area after it had returned to patriot control.[16]

16. Blumenthal reports a return of March 1779 which shows that the British forces in New York numbered 4,000 soldiers, 1,550 women, and 968 children; a report on the total British army in America as of May 1777 shows 23,101 men, 2,776 women, and 1,901

Patriots were skeptical about giving women official status in the army; Washington objected to a fixed quota of women. But the women followed nevertheless, apparently for much the same reasons as the British and German women did. By the end of the war, Washington's General Orders established a ratio of one woman for every fifteen men in a regiment. Extrapolating from this figure, Linda Grant De Pauw estimates that in the course of the war some "20,000 individual women served as women of the army on the American side."[17] Some, no doubt, came for a taste of adventure. Generals' wives, like Martha Washington and Catherine Greene, took their right to follow as a matter of course, and spent the winters of Valley Forge and Morristown with their husbands. But by far most women who followed the armies were impoverished.[18] Wives and children who had no

---

children. In the Twenty-sixth Regiment alone there were 305 men, 82 women, and 144 children (*Women Camp Followers of the American Revolution* [Philadelphia, 1952], pp. 38–39, 18). Other reports appear in "Return of the Number of Men, Women and Children of the British and Foreign Regiments, New Levies and Civil Departments, Victualled at New York and the Out Posts the 20th August 1781," in "Proceedings of a Board of General Officers of the British Army at New York, 1781," New-York Historical Society *Collections* 49 (1916): 84–89. This return shows totals of 2,173 women and 9,686 men (a ratio of approximately 1:4). In the "civil departments" the ratio was more like 1:5 (763 women, 3,512 men) with the numbers of women and children particularly high among engineers (perhaps because a high proportion of officers brought their families with them). Among refugees there were more women (196) than men (166) and more children than either (390). The ratios were considerably lower for the German troops: 679 women and 10,251 men.

Women are shown in Louis Van Blarenberghe's great panorama of the surrender at Yorktown, located at the Yorktown Historical Park. See also the illustrations in Richard M. Ketchum, ed., *The American Heritage Book of the Revolution* (New York, 1958), pp. 170–71, 255. The Van Blarenberghe panorama appears on pp. 372–73 of Ketchum's book.

17. De Pauw, "Women in Combat," p. 210. For size of American regiments, see Worthington C. Ford, ed., *Journals of the Continental Congress, 1774–1789*, 34 vols. (Washington, D.C., 1904–37), 3:322, which sets size of regiments at 728 men and officers. See also General Orders, Dec. 28, 1782, in John C. Fitzpatrick, ed., *The Writings of George Washington*, 39 vols. (Washington, D.C., 1931–44), 25:480. For requests for counts of women belonging to a camp, see General Orders, June 4, 1777, ibid., 8:181; for counts of women belonging to regiments, ibid., 25:496.

18. Billy Smith shows that two-income families, dependent on the labor of all their members, were the norm among working people in cities ("The Material Lives in Laboring Philadelphians, 1750–1800," *William and Mary Quarterly*, 3d ser. 38 [1981]:

means of support when their husbands and fathers were drawn into service—whether by enthusiasm or in the expectation of bounties—followed after and cared for their own men, earning their subsistence by nursing, cooking, and washing for the troops in an era when hospitals were marginal and the offices of quartermaster and commissary were inadequately run. Perhaps the most mythologized of these women is Mary Hays, of Carlisle, Pennsylvania, who followed her husband when he enlisted as an infantryman. She seems to have spent the winter of 1777–78 at Valley Forge; at the Battle of Monmouth she not only carried water for his gun crew (apparently a standard task for women) but joined the crew and continued the firing when he was disabled. Both stayed on with the army until the end of the war, although he died shortly thereafter. After a brief second marriage, "Molly Pitcher" lived out her life in Carlisle, "doing nursing and menial work" until her death in 1832. "In this last month of her life," writes her memorist, "Pennsylvania recognized her as a veteran" and gave her a pension, which she did not live to enjoy.[19]

The women of the army made Washington uncomfortable. He had good reason to regard them with skepticism. Although they processed food and supplies by cooking and cleaning, they were also a drain on these supplies in an army that never had enough. Even the most respectable women represented something of a moral challenge; by embodying an alternate loyalty to family or lover, they could discourage reenlistment or even encourage desertion in order to respond to private emotional claims. They were a steady reminder to men of a world other than the controlled one of the camp; desertion was high throughout the war, and no general needed anyone who might encourage it further. Most importantly, perhaps, the women of the army were disorderly women who could not be controlled by the usual military devices and who were inevitably suspected of theft and spying for the enemy.[20] As a result, Washington was constantly issuing

---

163–202). Gary B. Nash's work suggests that in northern urban societies women were especially likely to be the objects of poor relief, a conclusion confirmed by virtually every examination of the records of almshouses and "out-of-door" relief efforts (*The Urban Crucible: Social Change, Political Consciousness, and the Origins of the American Revolution* [Cambridge, Mass., 1979], pp. 332–37).

19. Robert Secor et al., *Pennsylvania: 1776* (University Park, Pa., 1975), p. 344.

20. Occasionally (probably less often than they deserved) they were accused of theft; in April 1781, women who traveled with Nathanael Greene's army were suspects of involvement in the burning of civilian homes (Robert Middlekauff, *The Glorious*

contradictory orders. Sometimes the women of the army were to ride in the wagons so as not to slow down the troops; at other times they were to walk so as not to take up valuable space in the wagons. But always they were there, and Washington knew they could not be expelled. These women drew rations in the American army; they brought children with them, who drew half rations. American regulations took care to insist that "sucking babes" could draw no rations at all, since obviously they couldn't eat. "The very rules that denied a place in the army to all women sanctioned a place for some," remarks Barton Hacker. However useful the women of the army might be, they certainly were neither orderly nor professional.[21]

It is true that cooking, laundering, and nursing were female skills; the women of the army were doing in a military context what they had once done in a domestic one. But we ought not discount these services for that reason, or visualize them as taking place in a context of softness and luxury. "One observer of American troops . . . attributed their ragged and unkempt bearing to the lack of enough women to do their washing and mending; the Americans, not being used to doing things of this sort, choose rather to let their linen, etc., rot upon their backs than to be at the trouble of cleaning 'em themselves." Washington was particularly shocked at the appearance of the troops at Bunker Hill, some of whom apparently were so sure that washing clothes was women's work that "they wore what they had until it crusted over and fell apart."[22] A friend of Mercy Otis Warren's described the women who followed the Hessians after the surrender of Burgoyne: "Great numbers of women, who seemd to be the beasts of burthen, having a bushel basket on their back, by which they were bent double, the contents seemd to be Pots and Kettles, various sorts of Furniture, children peeping thro' gridirons and other utensils, some very young Infants who were born on the road, the women bare feet, cloathd in dirty raggs, such effluvia filld the air while they were passing, had they not been smoking all the time, I should have been apprehensive of being contaminated by them." Susanna Rowson's fictional Charlotte Temple, at the end of her rope, is bitterly ad-

Cause: The American Revolution, 1763–1789, Oxford History of the United States, vol. 2 [New York, 1982], p. 539, citing Nathanael Greene, General Orders, Apr. 1–July 25, 1781 [Apr. 27, 1781]).

21. Barton Hacker, "Women and Military Institutions in Early Modern Europe: A Reconnaissance," *Signs* 6 (1981): 643–71.

22. Charles Royster, *A Revolutionary People at War: The Continental Army and American Character, 1775–1783* (Chapel Hill, 1979), p. 59.

vised to "go to the barracks and work for a morsel of bread; wash and mend the soldiers' cloaths, and cook their victuals . . . work hard and eat little."[23]

Women who served such troops were performing tasks of the utmost necessity if the army were to continue functioning. John Shy has remarked that the relative *absence* of women among American troops put Americans at a disadvantage in relation to the British; women maintained "some semblance of cleanliness."[24] They did not live in gentle surroundings in either army, and the conditions of their lives were not pleasant. Although they were impoverished, they were not inarticulate. The most touching account of Yorktown I know is furnished by Sarah Osborn, who cooked for Washington's troops and delivered food to them under fire because, as she told Washington himself, "it would not do for the men to fight and starve too." At the end she watched the British soldiers stack their arms and then return "into town again to await their destiny."[25]

It is not at all clear why these women should have been so ignored in so many general accounts of the Revolution, even granting the scattered nature of the documentary record. The historian, despite the justifiable complaints of quantifiers, often works by synecdoche, making a few well-documented cases stand for the whole. But the habit among historians of the Revolution has rather been to treat the well-documented cases of women among the army as oddities who stand only for themselves. Thus we have the requisite mentions of Deborah Sampson and Mary Hays, but little more. It is true that searching for them is very difficult; the American army was not as effective in record keeping as was the British; nor did it have a vested interest in keeping good records on the women, whose presence was already regarded as a sign of unprofessionalism. But we need not take Washington's embarrassment for our own.

In 1786 Benjamin Rush made a famous distinction between the "first act" of the "great drama" of the Revolution, a war accomplished by armies, and the revolution in "principles, opinions and manners so as to accommodate

23. Hannah Winthrop to Mercy Otis Warren, Nov. 11, 1777, "Warren-Adams Letters," Massachusetts Historical Society *Collections* 73 (1925): 451–53; Susanna Rowson, *Charlotte Temple*, ed. Cathy Davidson (New York, 1986), pp. 103–4.

24. John Shy, *A People Numerous and Armed: Reflections on the Military Struggle for American Independence* (New York, 1976), p. 32.

25. John C. Dann, ed., *The Revolution Remembered: Eyewitness Accounts of the War for Independence* (Chicago, 1980), p. 245.

them to the forms of government we have adopted."[26] The dichotomy applies to women's roles as well as the more general aspects of life that he had in mind. Women had been embedded in the military aspects of the war against Britain, but their roles were politically invisible. Americans literally lacked a language to describe what was before their eyes. On the other hand, women were visible, even central, to the Revolution and to the patriot effort to transform political culture. That transformation was crucial if the Americans were to sustain the claim that they were doing more than refusing to pay their fair share of taxes. Americans claimed both implicitly and explicitly that they were creating a new kind of politics, a democracy in which the people acted as constituent power, in which every adult citizen had an obligation to play an intelligent and thoughtful role in shaping the nation's destiny. They were inventing a political mobilization that relied on reason and cultural transformation, not mob and riot. It was this cultural transformation that entitled Americans to claim they had accomplished a revolution which, in the words of the English radical Richard Price, "opens a new prospect in human affairs."[27] It was this cultural transformation that Americans had in mind when they referred, as they frequently did, to the "new era" that political mobilization would usher in.[28]

26. "There is nothing more common, than to confound the terms of the *American Revolution* with those of the *late American war*. The American war is over: but this is far from being the case with the American Revolution" (Benjamin Rush, "Address to the People of the United States" [1787], in Hezekiah Niles, ed., *Principles and Acts of the Revolution in America* [Baltimore, 1822], p. 402).

27. Richard Price, "Observations on the Importance of the American Revolution" [1784], conveniently reprinted in part in Jack P. Greene, ed., *Colonies to Nation: 1763–1789* (New York, 1967), pp. 422–25. Robert R. Palmer, *The Age of the Democratic Revolution: A Political History of Europe and America, 1760–1800*, 2 vols. (Princeton, 1959), 1:255.

28. Judith Sargent Murray expected "to see our young women forming a new era in female history" (*The Gleaner*, 3 vols. [Boston, 1798], 3:189). Rush promised a new "golden age" once the implications of the Revolution were embodied in systems of education for the rising generation ("Thoughts upon the Mode of Education Proper in a Republic" [1786], reprinted in Frederick Rudolph, ed., *Essays on Education in the Early Republic* [Cambridge, Mass., 1965], pp. 9–23). The minister Samuel Williams of Massachusetts predicted that America would lead the way to a "new era" that would "promote *the perfection and happiness of mankind*" by demonstrating behaviors which had not been seen since the Roman republic: officers and soldiers returning "to their fields and farms, to cultivate the more useful arts of peace" (Greene, *Colonies to Nation*, pp. 382–83).

A dramatic feature of pre-Revolutionary political mobilization was the consumer boycott. The boycott was central to the effort to change values, to undermine psychological as well as economic ties to England, and to draw apolitical people into political dialogue. Although consumer boycotts seem to have been devised by men, they were predicated on the support of women, both as consumers—who would make distinctions on what they purchased as between British imports and goods of domestic origin—and as manufacturers, who would voluntarily increase their level of household production. Without the assistance of "our wives," conceded Christopher Gadsden, "'tis impossible to succeed."[29]

Women who had thought themselves excused from making political choices now found that they had to align themselves politically, even behind the walls of their own homes. The loyalist Peter Oliver complained that "Mr. Otis's black Regiment, the dissenting Clergy, were also set to Work, to preach up Manufactures instead of Gospel." Many middle-class women spun in the context of service to the church, presenting their skeins to ministers, and leaving blurred the distinction between what they did politically and what they did in the name of religion. As Gary Nash has argued, the most important association of spinning and patriotism was to be found in schemes "to turn spinning into a patriotic activity and a symbol of defiance against England," which used spinning and cloth manufacture as a political expression and also as out-of-doors poor relief.[30] As they decided how much spinning to do, whether to set their slaves to weaving homespun, or whether to drink tea or coffee, men and women devised a political ritual congruent with women's understanding of their

29. For extensive discussion of this issue, see Linda K. Kerber, *Women of the Republic: Intellect and Ideology in Revolutionary America* (Chapel Hill, 1980), chap. 2, and Mary Beth Norton, *Liberty's Daughters: The Revolutionary Experience of American Women, 1750–1800* (Boston, 1980).

30. For Laurel Thatcher Ulrich's caution that spinning parties may not have represented collective support for the consumer boycotts and the war, see " 'Daughters of Liberty': Religious Women in Revolutionary New England," in Ronald Hoffman and Peter J. Albert, eds., *Women in the Age of the American Revolution* (Charlottesville: University Press of Virginia, 1989). For the encouragement of spinning by radical leaders, see Nash, *The Urban Crucible*, pp. 333–37. See also Alfred F. Young, " 'Daughters of Liberty' in the Cradle of the Revolution: The Women of Boston, 1765–1776" (Paper presented at the Conference on Gender and Political Culture in the Age of Democratic Revolution, Bellagio, Italy, July 1985).

domestic roles and readily incorporated into their daily routines. (Peter Oliver suspected that undermining the boycott was *also* easily incorporated into daily routine: "The Ladies too were so zealous for the Good of their Country, that they agreed to drink no Tea, except the Stock of it which they had by them; or in the Case of Sickness. Indeed, they were cautious enough to lay in large Stocks before they promised; & they could be sick just as suited their Convenience or Inclination.")[31]

The boycotts were an occasion for instruction in collective political behavior, formalized by the signing of petitions and manifestos. In 1767 both men and women signed the Association, promising not to import duty items. Five years later, when the Boston Committee of Correspondence circulated the Solemn League and Covenant establishing another boycott of British goods, they demanded that both men and women sign.[32] The manifesto of the women of Edenton, North Carolina, against imported tea is perhaps the best known of these collective statements. Collective petitions would serve women as their most usable political device deep into the nineteenth century.

After the war, control of their consumption patterns would remain the most effective weapon in women's small political arsenal. In 1786, for example, the Patriotic and Economic Association of Ladies of Hartford announced that they would eschew conspicuous consumption as a patriotic gesture against the national debt. An anonymous columnist (it is impossible to tell whether male or female), offered their reasoning: "The sheep's wool that grows in this state is, I believe, not sufficient for stockings for its inhabitants; what then must be the wretched situation, particularly of the poor of this town, [during] the approaching winter, when the wool, which might cover the legs of hundreds, is diverted from that use" to form fashionable dresses and petticoats and "bustlers" which deform the shape.[33] Consumption boycotts were used during the Quasi War in the 1790s and persisted into the nineteenth century; when women's abolitionist soci-

---

31. Douglass Adair and John A. Schutz, eds., *Peter Oliver's Origin & Progress of the American Rebellion: A Tory View* (San Marino, 1961), p. 73.

32. Peter Oliver saw hypocrisy in this effort as well. Of the Townshend duty boycott he observed: "Among the various prohibited Articles, were *Silks, Velvets, Clocks, Watches, Coaches & Chariots*; & it was highly diverting, to see the names & marks, to the Subscription, of Porters and Washing Women" (ibid., p. 61).

33. Broadside, Nov. 6, 1786.

eties searched in the 1830s and 1840s for a strategy to bring pressure on the slave economy, a boycott of slave-made goods seemed to them an obvious answer.

Nowhere can the dependence of rebellion on the transformation of values be seen more clearly than in the continuing struggle for recruitment into the army or militia. The draft never worked automatically; ways had to be devised to co-opt men, and this co-optation had to overcome men's own inertia and lack of enthusiasm for placing themselves at risk. One explicit mode of deflecting resistance was the offering of bounties in money or in land. Others, as John Shy has suggested, were the psychological and legal pressures of militia training. In every state except Pennsylvania, militias inscribed every able-bodied free white man in their rolls, and drew those men together in the public exercises of training day.[34] There was no counterpart for women of a training day as a bonding experience that simultaneously linked men to each other, to the local community, and at the same time to the state.

Training day underscore men's and women's different political roles; military training was a male ritual that excluded women.[35] Women, in turn, castigated it as an arena for antisocial behavior. When peacetime drill turned into actual war, women logically complained that they had been placed at risk without their consent. No one asked women if they thought the war worth the cost, yet women faced intrusion, violence, and rape. Furthermore, religiously believing women were deeply skeptical of a military culture that encouraged drink as indispensable to the display of courage and was unperturbed by those who broke the third commandment.[36]

In this context patriots needed to find an alternative to women's traditional skepticism and resistance of mobilization. It is not yet clear whether the primary energy for this alternative came from men seeking to deflect women's resistance or from those women who wished to define for themselves a modern political role in which they could demonstrate their own voluntary commitment to the Revolution. In either case, the alternative role involved sending sons and husbands to battle. The *Pennsylvania Eve-*

34. See Shy, *A People Numerous and Armed*, pp. 163–80, for an insightful analysis of how the militias forced conformity and how the armies enlisted those men with no other options.

35. For shrewd comments on this point, see John Keegan, *The Face of Battle* (New York, 1976).

36. Ulrich, " 'Daughters of Liberty.' "

ning Post offered the model of "an elderly grandmother of Elizabethtown, New Jersey" in 1776: "My children, I have a few words to say to you, you are going out in a just cause, to fight for the rights and liberties of your country; you have my blessings. . . . Let me beg of you . . . that if you fall, it may be like men; and that your wounds may not be in your back parts."[37] Ellet's books were replete with examples equally hard to take literally. "A lady of New Jersey" calls after her parting husband: "Remember to do your duty! I would rather hear that you were left a corpse on the field than that you had played the part of a coward!"[38] Mrs. Draper of Dedham, Massachusetts, "with her own hands bound knapsack and blanket on the shoulders of her only son, a stripling of sixteen, bidding him depart and do his duty."[39]

Women who thrust their men to battle were displaying a distinctive form of patriotism. They had been mobilized by the state to mobilize their men; they were part of the moral resources of the total society. Sending men to war was in part their expression of surrogate enlistment in a society in which women did not fight. This was their way of shaping the construction of the military community. They were *shaming* their men into serving the interests of the state; indeed shaming would become in the future the standard role of civilian women in time of war. The pattern is far older than the American Revolution, but it was strengthened during that war and further enlarged during the French Revolution.[40] It would reach its apogee in England during World War I, when women handed out white feathers to men who walked the streets of London in civilian dress, and when a modern state maintained a mass war with volunteers alone for two long years.[41]

The third way in which women transformed what was valued and what was scorned involved crowd behavior that was both disorderly and ritual-

37. *Pennsylvania Evening Post*, Aug. 10, 1776, cited in *Documents Relating to the Revolutionary History of New Jersey*, New Jersey Archives, 2d ser. (1901), 1:161–62.

38. Ellet, *Domestic History*, p. 70.

39. Ibid., p. 32.

40. See Peter Paret, "The Relationship between the Revolutionary War and European Military Thought and Practice," in Don Higginbotham, ed., *Reconsiderations on the Revolutionary War* (Westport, Conn., 1976), p. 148: "Nothing similar can be found in Europe in the hundred years preceding Lexington: A revolutionary struggle which involved an armed insurgent population was unique in the memory of the age."

41. Sandra Gilbert, "Soldier's Heart: Literary Men, Literary Women, and the Great War," *Signs* 8 (1983): 422–50.

ized—sometimes at one and the same time.[42] Working-class women, who spent much of their lives on the streets as market women or shopkeepers, surely were part of these crowds; occasionally someone thought it worthwhile to highlight their presence, as Peter Oliver did when he sneered at a woman who threw her feather pillows out a Boston window in 1772 to help in the work of tarring and feathering.[43]

The organizers of the Revolutionary crowds were male, and the bulk of the participants seem to have been young artisans. The rhetorical devices of the great Pope's Day crowds, with their violent battles centered on the effigies of Pope, Devil, and Pretender, were couched in male emblem and male language.[44] In these tableaux, women seem to have been marginal. But women devised their own roles in public ritual. They formed part of funeral processions; Alfred F. Young has emphasized their presence in the great public funerals for the victims of the Boston Massacre and for the martyred child Christopher Seider. (Mercy Otis Warren helped solidify Seider's martyred status by her play *The Adulateur*.)[45]

Women also invented their own public rituals. Most noteworthy of these was the effort of Hannah Bostwick McDougall in New York in April 1770. When her patriot husband, Alexander McDougall, was arrested for publishing a seditious broadside, his wife "led a parade of ladies from Chapel Street to the jail, entertaining them later at her home." As part of the campaign to make him into the American Wilkes, "45 virgins of this city,

42. The classic fictional portrayal of the crowd is Nathaniel Hawthorne's "My Kinsman, Major Molineux." See also Pauline Maier, *From Resistance to Revolution: Colonial Radicals and the Development of American Opposition to Britain, 1765–1776* (New York, 1972), Dirk Hoerder, *Crowd Action in Revolutionary Massachusetts, 1765–1780* (New York, 1977), and Edward Countryman, "The Problem of the Early American Crowd," *Journal of American Studies* 7 (1973): 77–90. The understanding of crowd behavior as ritual owes much to the arguments of Natalie Zemon Davis, *Society and Culture in Early Modern France* (Stanford, 1975), esp. chaps. 5 and 6, Alfred F. Young, "English Plebeian Culture and Eighteenth-Century American Radicalism," in Margaret Jacob et al., eds., *Origins of Anglo-American Radicalism* (London, 1983), and Peter Shaw, *American Patriots and the Rituals of Revolution* (Cambridge, Mass., 1981), esp. chaps. 1 and 9.

43. Adair and Schutz, eds., *Origin & Progress*, pp. 97–98.

44. See Young, " 'Daughters of Liberty,' " and Shaw, *American Patriots*, esp. parts 1 and 3.

45. Young, " 'Daughters of Liberty,' " pp. 31–33. Mercy Otis Warren, *The Adulateur: A Tragedy, As It Is Now Acted in Upper Servia* [1772], reprinted in the *Magazine of History* (1918). For comment, see Shaw, *American Patriots*, p. 194.

went in procession to pay their respects," and McDougall "entertained them with tea, cakes, chocolate and conversation."[46]

Better known is the house-to-house campaign of the patriot women of Philadelphia, led by Esther Reed and Sarah Franklin Bache, to raise money for Washington's soldiers and to get women of other states to do the same, accompanied by an explicit political broadside and by intimidating fund raising. "I fancy they raised a considerable sum by this extorted contribution," sneered Quaker loyalist Anna Rawle, "some giving solely against their inclinations thro' fear of what might happen if they refused."[47]

Bringing ritual resistance to Britain out of the household and into the streets shaded into violence. During the war, boycotts occasionally escalated into what the French would call *taxation populaire*, such as the intimidation of the "eminent, wealthy, stingy" Thomas Boylston in Boston for hoarding coffee, or of Westchester's Peter Mesier for hoarding tea.[48] Perhaps the most violent act of resistance we know is that of the New York woman who was accused of incendiarism in the Great Fire when the British entered the city in 1776. She received her eulogy from Edmund Burke on the floor of the House of Commons:

> Still is not that continent conquered; witness the behaviour of one miserable woman, who with her single arm did that, which an army of a hundred thousand men could not do—arrested your progress, in the moment of your success. This miserable being was found in a cellar, with her visage besmeared and smutted over, with every mark of rage, despair, resolution, and the most exalted heroism, buried in combustibles, in order to fire New-York, and perish in its ashes;—she was brought

46. Roger J. Champagne, *Alexander McDougall and the Revolution in New York* (Schenectady, 1975), p. 28. *New-York Journal*, Feb. 15, Mar. 22, 1770; *New York Mercury*, Apr. 2, 1770. McDougall was jailed for distributing a broadside castigating the legislature for failing to resist the Quartering Act effectively. Quartering soldiers in private homes was an issue to which women were particularly sensitive; it was a practice understood to put the women of the family particularly at risk.

47. Anna Rawle to Rebecca Rawle Shoemaker, June 30, 1780, Shoemaker Papers, Historical Society of Pennsylvania, Philadelphia.

48. Abigail Adams to John Adams, July 31, 1777, Lyman H. Butterfield, ed., *Adams Family Correspondence*, 4 vols. (Cambridge, Mass., 1963–73), 2:295; for Mesier, see *Minutes of the Committee and of the First Commission for Detecting and Defeating Conspiracies in the State of New-York* (New York, 1924), 1:301–3.

John Hoppner, *Sarah Franklin Bache* (1797).
Courtesy Metropolitan Museum of Art, Catharine Lorillard Wolfe Collection,
Wolfe Fund, 1901 (01.20).

Charles Willson Peale, *Esther De Berdt Reed*.
Courtesy Frick Art Reference Library. In the collection of Mrs. David Middleton.

forth, and knowing that she would be condemned to die, upon being asked her purpose, said, "to fire the city!" and was determined to omit no opportunity of doing what her country called for. Her train was laid and fired; and it is worthy of your attention, how Providence was pleased to make use of those humble means to serve the American cause, when open force was used in vain.[49]

When Elizabeth Ellet created the first history of women during the American Revolution, she recorded the way middle-class survivors and their descendants remembered their experience; her work was congruent with the conservative use of the Revolutionary tradition characteristic of historians of the 1840s and 1850s, George Bancroft among them.[50] Writing of women, Ellet confirmed their victimization, their decency, and their respect for ceremony and propriety in the midst of horror. She did not want to hear, nor did her informants wish to recover for her, the record of women's presence in violent crowds, their thefts, their spying. She offered posterity women of sensitivity and the sentiment that her own romantic culture required of females; she blotted disorderly women from memory.[51]

Boycotting imports, shaming men into service, disorderly demonstration— all were ways in which women obviously entered the new political community created by the Revolution. It was less apparent what that entrance might mean. There followed a struggle to define women's political role in a modern republic. The classic roles of women in wartime were two: both had been named by the Greeks, both positioned women as critics of war. Antigone and Cassandra are both outsiders and therefore less subject than men to ambivalence about doing their share or abandoning their comrades;

49. Edmund Burke, in William Cobbett, ed., *Parliamentary History of England*, vol. 18, 14th Parliament, 3d sess., Nov. 6, 1776, Debate in Commons on a Motion for the Revisal of All the Laws by which the Americans Think Themselves Aggrieved (London, 1813?), p. 1443. See also Isaac Newton Phelps Stokes, *The Iconography of Manhattan Island, 1498–1909*, 6 vols. (New York, 1915–28), 5:1023.

50. See Michael Kammen, *A Season of Youth: The American Revolution and the Historical Imagination* (New York, 1978), chap. 2, esp. p. 51, and Alfred F. Young, "George Robert Twelves Hewes (1742–1840): A Boston Shoemaker and the Memory of the American Revolution," *William and Mary Quarterly*, 3d ser. 38 (1981): 561–623.

51. My use of the term *disorderly women* owes much to Davis, *Society and Culture in Early Modern France*, chaps. 4–6, and Jacquelyn Dowd Hall, "Disorderly Women: Gender and Labor Militancy in the Appalachian South," *Journal of American History* 73 (1986): 354–82, who in turn draws on Davis.

they are free to concentrate on the price rather than the promise of war. While understanding that she cannot affect the outcome of battle, Antigone, who confronts Creon with the demand that her brother's body be buried, claims the power to set ethical limits on what men do in war.[52] Like Ellet's heroines, Antigone upholds decency. Cassandra, who foresees the tragic end of the Trojan War, expresses generalized anxiety and criticism.[53]

In America an evangelical version of Cassandra flourished. Many, perhaps most, women were unambivalently critical of the war and offered their criticism in religious terms. In 1787, when the delegates to the Philadelphia Convention were stabilizing a Revolutionary government and embodying their understanding of what the Revolution had meant in the Federal Constitution, there appeared the classic text of the alternative perspective: an anonymous pamphlet called *Women Invited to War*.[54] The author defined herself as a "Daughter of America" and addressed herself to the "worthy women, and honourable daughters of America." She acknowledged that the war had been a "valiant . . . defense of life and liberty," but discounted its ultimate significance. The *real* war, she argued, was not against Great Britain, or Shaysites, but against the Devil. Satan was "an enemy who has done more harm already, than all the armies of Britain ever will be able to do. . . . we shall all be destroyed or brought into captivity, if the women as well as the men, do not oppose, resist, and fight against this destructive enemy."[55]

As she wrote, her voice shifted and the argument became exhortation:

52. Jean Bethke Elshtain recommends one of these roles in "Antigone's Daughters," *Democracy* 2 (1982): 46–59, but neglects to take into consideration Antigone's ultimate powerlessness or to mention that in the end she must hang herself to escape a death even more cruel. An example of a woman in such a role is Elizabeth Drinker, crossing the American lines to plead with George Washington to release her Quaker husband from quarantine in Winchester, Virginia, in 1778.

53. Contemporary examples are Faith Trumbull Huntington, in Royster, *A Revolutionary People at War*, pp. 54–58, and Margaret Livingston (Margaret Livingston to [Catherine Livingston], Oct. 20, 1776, Ridley Papers, Massachusetts Historical Society, Boston).

54. Published anonymously, but ascribed to Hannah Adams by Charles Evans. Authorship of this pamphlet has recently been questioned by curators at the Huntington Library. It seems to me that the prose rhythms are quite different from those characteristic of Hannah Adams's signed works.

55. *Women Invited to War. Or a Friendly Address to the Honourable Women of the United States. By a Daughter of America* (Boston, 1787), p. 3.

"Are there not many in America, unto whom the Lord is speaking, as to his people of old, saying, The spoil of the poor is in your houses. . . . Thou hast despised mine holy things, and hath profaned my sabbaths. . . . Because of swearing the land mourneth. . . . The people of the land have used oppression, and exercised robbery, and have vexed the poor and needy. . . . Hath not almost every sin which brought destruction upon Jerusalem, been committed in America?"[56] Then the "Daughter of America" assumed an unusual voice, the voice of the minister, speaking to the special responsibilities of women and articulating the murmur that men were more prone to sin than were women: "But perhaps some of you may say, there are some very heinous sins, which our sex are not so commonly guilty of, as the men are; in particular the vile sin of drinking to excess, and also prophane swearing and cursing, and taking the great and holy name of God in vain, are practiced more by men than by women." There was a paradox; the same men who were particularly guilty of sin were generally thought to be the leaders in religious affairs; she suspected her audience would assert, "Therefore let them rise up first." To this she responded that all were equal in Christ; that Eve had been made from Adam's rib to walk by his side, not from his foot, to be trampled underneath, and that "in the rights of religion and conscience . . . is neither male nor female, but all are one in Christ."[57]

In a few pages the author had moved from the contemplation of women in war emergencies to the argument that women ought to conduct their wars according to definitions that were different from men's; that the main tasks that faced the republic were spiritual rather than political, and that in these spiritual tasks women could take the lead; indeed that they had a special responsibility to display "mourning and lamentation."[58]

In the aftermath of the Revolutionary war, many women continued to define their civic obligations in religious terms. The way to save the city, argued the "Daughter of America," was to purify one's behavior and pray for the sins of the community. By the early nineteenth century, women flooded into the dissenting churches of the Second Great Awakening, bringing their husbands and children with them and asserting that their

56. Ibid., pp. 7–9.
57. Ibid., pp. 10–12. This is a fairly common image for eighteenth- and nineteenth-century feminists to use (see, for example, *The Female Advocate* [New Haven, Conn., 1801], pp. 30, 19–20).
58. Ibid., p. 13.

claim to religious salvation made possible new forms of assertive behavior—criticizing sinful conduct of their friends and neighbors, sometimes traveling to new communities and establishing new schools, sometimes widening in a major way the scope of the books they read.[59] Churches also provided the context for women's benevolent activity. Despairing that secular politics would clear up the shattered debris of the war, religious women organized societies for the support of widows and orphans in a heretofore unparalleled collective endeavor. If women were to be invited to war, they would join their own war and on their own terms.

To define the woman citizen as Cassandra is to constrain her permanently to the role of outsider as well as critic; at her worst Cassandra simply whines. The traditional role was clearly not enough to meet the rising expectations generated by war. The role of Antigone, with its claim that women might judge men, was perhaps more appealing, but it was best suited to exhausting moments of dramatic moral confrontation, and Antigone cannot make her claim effective until she is dead. Moreover, neither solution (certainly not Cassandra in her updated evangelical form) entered directly into dialogue with the problem of bringing the Revolution to political closure. Both maintained the classic dichotomy in which men were the defenders of the state and women were the protected.[60] Neither addressed the task of devising a new relationship between the individual and the state or of forcing the state to be responsive to public opinion in a rigorous and regular way. Neither addressed the role of the woman as citizen of a republic; for that a secular political solution was required.

Between 1775 and 1777 statutory language moved from the term *subject* to *inhabitant, member*, and, finally, *citizen*. By 1776 patriots were prepared to say that all loyal inhabitants, men and women, were citizens of the new republic, no longer subjects of the king. But the word *citizen* still carried

59. For the career of one woman whose life was changed in this way, see Samuel Worcester, *The Christian Mourning with Hope: A Sermon . . . on the Occasion of the Death of Mrs. Eleanor [Read] Emerson . . . to Which Are Annexed Writings of Mrs. Emerson* (Boston, 1809). I have discussed this episode more extensively in "Can a Woman Be an Individual? The Limits of Puritan Tradition in the Early Republic," *Texas Studies in Literature and Language* 25 (1983): 165–78 [reprinted in the present volume]. See also Mary P. Ryan, *Cradle of the Middle Class: The Family in Oneida County, New York, 1790–1865* (Cambridge, 1981), esp. chap. 2.

60. See Judith Hicks Stiehm, "The Protected, the Protector, the Defender," *Women's Studies International Forum* 5 (1982): 367–76.

overtones inherited from antiquity and the Renaissance, when the citizen made the city possible by taking up arms on its behalf. In this way of reasoning, the male citizen "exposes his life in defense of the state and at the same time ensures that the decision to expose it can not be taken without him; it is the possession of arms which makes a man a full citizen."[61] This mode of thinking, this way of relating men to the state, had no room in it for women except as something to be avoided. (The principal section on women and the state in Machiavelli's *Discourses* is entitled "How a State Falls because of Women.")[62] Thus, as Charles Royster reports, "the first anniversary of the Declaration of Independence was celebrated with the toast 'May only those Americans enjoy freedom who are ready to die for its defence.'" To be free required a man to risk death.[63] In a formulation like this one, the connection to the republic of male patriots—who could enlist—was immediate. The connection of women, however patriotic they might feel themselves to be, was remote.

Many aspects of American political culture reinforced the gender-specific character of citizenship. First, and most obvious, men were linked to the republic by military service. Military service performed by the women of the army was not understood to have a political component. Second, men were linked to the republic by the political ritual of suffrage, itself an expression of the traditional link between political voice and ownership of property deeply embedded in Lockean political theory. By the late eighteenth century most jurisdictions permitted male owners of land, of movable property of a set value, or men who paid taxes to exercise the franchise; in each case it was understood that control of property was connected with independence of judgment. "Such is the frailty of the human heart," John Adams observed, "that very few men who have no property, have any judgment of their own. They talk and vote as they are directed by some man of property, who has attached their minds to his interest."[64] The feme covert, who normally did not control the disposition of family property, was equally if not more vulnerable to direction and

61. J. G. A. Pocock, *The Machiavellian Moment: Florentine Political Thought and the Atlantic Republican Tradition* (Princeton, 1975), p. 90.

62. *Discourses*, trans. Leslie J. Walker, rev. Brian Richardson, ed. Bernard Crick (Harmondsworth, 1970), 3:26.

63. Royster, *A Revolutionary People at War*, p. 32.

64. John Adams to James Sullivan, May 26, 1776, in Charles Francis Adams, ed., *The Works of John Adams: With the Life of the Author*, 10 vols. (Boston, 1850–56), 9:376.

manipulation by her husband or guardian. If the ownership of property was requisite to political independence, very few women—even in wealthy families—could make that claim. As Sally Mason remarks of the women of the Carroll family, "The wealth accumulated and controlled by the men to whom they were connected determined the material aspects of their existences."[65] Women of the laboring poor were of course particularly vulnerable. Like all married women, they were legally dependent on their husbands; as working people the range of economic opportunities open to them was severely restricted. Apprenticeship contracts, for example, reveal that cities often offered a wide range of artisanal occupations to boys but limited girls to housekeeping and occasional training as a skilled seamstress. Almshouse records display a steady pattern: most residents were women and their children; most "outwork" was taken by women. Their lack of marketable skills must have smoothed the path to prostitution for the destitute. The material dependency of women was well established in the early republic.[66] Indeed, the assumption that women as a class were dependent was so well established that individual women who were *not* materially dependent (for example, wealthy widows or unmarried women) were treated as though they were dependent in political theory and in practice.[67]

Finally, men were linked to the Revolutionary republic psychologically, by their understanding of self, honor, and shame. These psychological connections were gender-specific and therefore unavailable to women. Thus in his shrewd analysis of the psychological prerequisite for rebellion, Tom Paine linked independence from the empire to the natural independence of the grown son. The image captured the common sense of the matter for a wide range of American men, who made *Common Sense* their

65. See also David E. Narrett, "Men's Wills and Women's Property Rights in Colonial New York," in Hoffman and Albert, eds., *Women in the Age of the American Revolution*, for the erosion of Dutch women's financial autonomy under English law after 1689.

66. Smith, "Lives of Philadelphians." Although she acknowledges the opportunities that a prosperous mercantile community could offer skilled women who sold household crafts, the economic dependency of poor women is stressed by Elaine F. Crane, "Struggle for Survival: Women in Eighteenth-Century American Seaports" (Paper presented at the Seventy-sixth Annual Meeting of the Organization of American Historians, Cincinnati, April 1983).

67. For an argument for the necessity of treating women this way, see John Adams to Sullivan, May 26, 1776, Adams, ed., *Works of John Adams*, 9:375–78.

manifesto.[68] Charles Royster has described the psychological tension experienced by army officers caught in the web of idealistic expectations for fame and honor that were embedded in the "ideals of 1775." Although ambition was still a pejorative word, the "search for fame . . . was the proper accompaniment and reward of military virtue."[69] And again: "The extravagant rhetoric of the revolution, which celebrated native courage, pure patriotic selflessness, and quick victorious freedom . . . tested the boundaries of glory to which the . . . [young officers, like] the revolution [itself] could aspire."[70]

The promise of fame was positive reinforcement for physical courage. The army had negative reinforcements as well. For cowardice there were courts-martial and dismissal from service. There was also humiliation, which might take the form of "being marched out of camp wearing a dress, with soldiers throwing dung at him."[71] Manliness and honor were thus sharply and ritually contrasted with effeminacy and dishonor. It is not accidental that dueling entered American practice during the Revolution. Usually "British and French aristocrats" are blamed for its introduction, but that does not explain American receptivity; Royster's analysis implies that the duel fit well with officers' needs to define their valor and to respond to their anxieties about shame.[72]

All these formulations of citizenship and civic relations in a republic were tightly linked to men and manhood: it was men who offered military service, men who sought honor, men who dueled in its defense. In a triumphant feat of circular definition, it was understood by all that women could not offer military service—not even the women of the army were understood to do so. Nor could women pledge their honor in defense of the republic, since honor, like fame, was psychologically male. The language of citizenship for women had to be freshly devised.

With virtually no aid from political theory, the Revolutionary genera-

68. See Edwin G. Burrows and Michael Wallace, "The American Revolution: The Ideology and Psychology of National Liberation," *Perspectives in American History*, 1st ser. 6 (1972): 167–308.

69. Royster, *A Revolutionary People at War*, p. 205. For more on fame, see Gerald Stourzh, *Alexander Hamilton and the Idea of Republican Government* (Stanford, 1970), pp. 98–99; Douglass Adair, *Fame and the Founding Fathers* (Chapel Hill, 1974), pp. 8–21.

70. Royster, *A Revolutionary People at War*, p. 206.

71. Ibid., p. 205.

72. See Bertram Wyatt-Brown, *Southern Honor* (New York, 1982), p. 354; Royster, *A Revolutionary People at War*, pp. 204–10.

tion addressed the conundrum. Mary Wollstonecraft was of only belated help to them: her *Vindication of the Rights of Woman* was not published until 1792 and then directed at an English audience. Wollstonecraft was dazzling in her use (probably for the first time in modern history) of the term *oppression* to describe the denial to women of political privilege and civil rights, and in her demand that women have "a civil existence in the State" not only for their own good but for the health and vitality of the community as a whole.[73] But she did not write programmatically. Although she stressed that economic independence was a precondition of political independence, she did not provide a political blueprint for defining or achieving citizenship. The first American theorist of female citizenship, Elizabeth Cady Stanton, would not be born until 1815.[74]

For the earliest extended American attempt to locate women in the larger political community, we must turn to the fund-raising broadside that Bache and Reed devised for their campaign and sent to Washington along with their contributions. That revealing document is an ambivalently worded expression of their political self-concept, meandering from third person to first person and back again. Sometimes its authors speak in emphatic collective voice, claiming that only relatively trivial "opinions & manners" forbade them "to march to glory by the same paths as the Men." Otherwise, "we should at least equal, and sometimes surpass them in our love for the public good." Sometimes they offered only the humble viewpoint of an individual excluded from the center of action: "The situation of our soldiery has been represented to me." Their ambiguity reflects the oxymoronic quality of the conception of the woman citizen in the early republic.[75]

Women were assisted in their effort to refine the idea of the woman citizen by changes in male understanding of the role. "The people" of Revolutionary broadsides had clearly been meant to include a broader sector of the population than had been meant by the citizenry of Renaissance Florence; how much more inclusive American citizenship ought to be was under negotiation. It seemed obvious that it had to include more than those who actually took up arms. Gradually, as James H. Kettner has ex-

---

73. Mary Wollstonecraft, *A Vindication of the Rights of Woman*, ed. Miriam Brody Kramnick (1792; reprint ed., London, 1975), pp. 306, 262.

74. I have discussed the problem of the absence of theory in *Women of the Republic*, chap. 1.

75. I have discussed this episode at length ibid., pp. 99–105.

plained, allegiance (as demonstrated by one's physical presence and emotional commitment) came to be given equal weight with military service.[76] An allegiance defined by location and volition was an allegiance in which women could join. As this latter sort of citizen, women could be part of the political community, unambivalently joining in boycotts, fund raising, street demonstrations, and the signing of collective statements.

But the nature of citizenship remained gendered. Behind it still lurked old republican assumptions, beginning with the obvious one that men's citizenship included a military component and women's did not. The classical republican view of the world had been bipolar at its core, setting reason against the passions, virtue against a yielding to the vagaries of fortune, restraint against indulgence, manliness against effeminacy. The first item in each of these pairs was understood to be a male attribute. The second was understood to be characteristic of women's nature; when displayed by men it was evidence of defeat and failure. The new language of independence and individual choice (which would be termed *liberal*) welcomed women's citizenship; the old language of republicanism deeply distrusted it.[77]

Between 1770 and 1800 many writers, both male and female, articulated a new understanding of the civic role of women in a republic. This understanding drew on some old ingredients but rearranged them and added new ones to create a gendered definition of citizenship that attempted (with partial success) to resolve these polarities. The new formulation also sought to provide an image of female citizenship alternative to the passivity of Cassandra or the crisis-specificity of Antigone. The new formulation had two major—and related—elements. The first, expressed with extraordinary clarity by Judith Sargent Murray in America and Mary Wollstonecraft in England, stressed women's native capability and competence and offered these as preconditions of citizenship. "How can a being be generous who has nothing of its own? or virtuous who is not free?" asked Wollstonecraft. Murray offered model women who sustained themselves by their own efforts, including one who ran her own farm.[78]

76. James H. Kettner, *The Development of American Citizenship* (Chapel Hill, 1978), chaps. 6, 7.

77. I have discussed this point in "The Republican Ideology of the Revolutionary Generation," *American Quarterly* 37 (1985): 474–95; see esp. pp. 483–85, 487–88 [which is included in the present volume].

78. Wollstonecraft, *Vindication*, p. 259; Murray, *The Gleaner*, 3:217.

With women understood to be competent, rational, and independent beings, it finally became possible to attack directly the classical allocation of civic virtue to men and of unsteadiness, complaisance toward *fortuna*, to women. The mode of attack implicitly undermined yet another ingredient of the classical republican view of the world: its cyclical vision of historical time.[79]

Theorists of the Revolution were sharply aware of the danger of the epigone: the generation that cannot replicate the high accomplishments of its fathers.[80] Both political theory and common sense taught that history was an endless cycle of accomplishment and degeneration; the Revolution had been intended to stop time and break the traditional historical cycle. But the Revolutionary generation had been specific to its own time; it had developed out of experience with British tyranny and the exigencies of war. When the war was over, the leading loyalists gone with the British, what was to prevent history from repeating itself? The problem was one every revolution and every successful social movement faces, made even more urgent by inherited political theory that seemed to assure disaster.

By claiming civic virtue for themselves, women undermined the classical polarities. Their new formulation of citizenship reconstructed general relations, politicizing women's traditional roles and turning women into monitors of the political behavior of their lovers, husbands, and children. The formulation claimed for women the task of stopping the historical cycle of achievement followed by inevitable degeneration; women would keep the republic virtuous by maintaining the boundaries of the political community. Women undertook to monitor the political behavior of their lovers: "Notwithstanding your worth," wrote Cornelia Clinton to Citizen Edmond Genet (whom she would later marry) during his troubled mission to persuade Washington to abandon neutrality, "I do not think I could have been attached to you had you been anything but a Republican— support that character to the end as you have begun, and let what may happen."[81] Mercy Otis Warren adamantly cautioned her son Winslow against

79. Stow Persons, "The Cyclical Interpretation of History in Eighteenth-Century America," *American Quarterly* 6 (1954): 147–63; see also J. G. A. Pocock, *Politics, Language, and Time: Essays on Political Thought and History* (New York, 1971).

80. I have commented on this point in *Federalists in Dissent: Imagery and Ideology in Jeffersonian America* (Ithaca, 1970), chap. 1.

81. Cornelia Clinton to Edmond Genet, Dec. 18, 1793, De Witt Clinton Family Papers, New-York Historical Society, New York City.

reading Lord Chesterfield, advice congruent with her steady belief that "luxurious vices . . . have frequently corrupted, distracted and ruined the best constituted republics."[82] Thus Lockean childrearing was given a political twist; the bourgeois virtues of autonomy and self-reliance were given extra resonance by the Revolutionary experience.[83]

Men, even young men, seem to have recognized, even encouraged, this new woman's role. "Yes, ye fair, the reformation of a world is in your power," conceded a Columbia College commencement speaker. Considering women in the "dignified character of patriots and philanthropists" who aim at "the glory of their country and the happiness of the human race," he maintained that women displayed their patriotism and philanthropy in the context of courtship, marriage, and motherhood. In courtship, they can exclude "libertines and coxcombs" from their society, influencing suitors "to a sacred regard for truth, honour, candour, and a manly sincerity in their intercourse with her sex." In marriage, the wife could "confirm virtuous habits" in her husband, and "excite his perseverance in the paths of rectitude."[84]

But it was when he reached the role of mother that his paean to the republican woman waxed most enthusiastic. It was, after all, in her role as mother that the republican woman entered historical time and republican political theory, implicitly promising to arrest the cycle of inevitable decay by guaranteeing the virtue of subsequent generations, that virtue which alone could sustain the republic, guarding the Revolutionary generation against the epigone.

> Let us then figure to ourselves the accomplished woman, surrounded by a sprightly band, from the babe that imbibes the nutritive fluid, to the generous youth just ripening into manhood, and the lovely virgin, blest with a miniature of maternal excellence. Let us contemplate the mother distributing the mental nourishment to the fond smiling circle. . . . See, under her cultivating hand, reason assuming the reins of government,

82. Mercy Otis Warren to Winslow Warren, Dec. 27, 1779, Mercy Otis Warren Letterbooks, Mass. Hist. Soc.; Mercy Otis Warren, "The Sack of Rome," *Poems, Dramatic and Miscellaneous* (Boston, 1790), p. 10.

83. For further reflections, see Jacqueline Reinier, "Rearing the Republican Child," *William and Mary Quarterly*, 3d ser. 39 (1982): 150–63, and the manual referred to in that article, *The Maternal Physician* (Philadelphia, 1811).

84. *New York Magazine*, May 1795, pp. 298–300.

and knowledge increasing gradually to her beloved pupils. . . . the Genius of Liberty hovers triumphant over the glorious scene; Fame, with her golden trump, spreads wide the well-earned honours of the fair.[85]

He concluded by welcoming women's new political responsibilities: "Contemplate the rising glory of confederated America. Consider that your exertions can best secure, increase, and perpetuate it. The solidity and stability of the liberties of your country rest with you, since Liberty is never sure, till Virtue reigns triumphant. . . . While you thus keep our country virtuous, you maintain its independence and ensure its prosperity."[86]

As the comments of the Columbia commencement speaker suggest, the construction of the role of the woman of the republic marked a significant moment in the history of gender relations. What it *felt* like to be a man and what it *felt* like to be a woman had been placed under considerable stress by war and revolution; when the war was over, it was easy to see that it had set in motion a revised construction of gender roles. Wars that are not fought by professional armies almost always force a renegotiation of sex roles, if only because when one sex changes its patterns of behavior the other sex cannot help but respond. In this the American Revolution was not distinctive. The Revolution does seem to have been distinctive, however, in the permanence of the newly negotiated roles, which took on lives of their own, infusing themselves into Americans' understanding of appropriate behavior for men and for women deep into the nineteenth and even twentieth centuries.

Some of the change in men's roles was intentional: republicans had in mind an explicit revision of the relationship of individual men to the state. Furthermore, the independence that the state had claimed for itself against Great Britain was understood to be appropriately echoed in the self-assertiveness of individual men; it would not be many more steps to Emerson's "Self-Reliance." Some of the change in men's roles was unexpected: the spirit of independence, observed John Adams, "spread where it was not intended." Hierarchical relationships were disrupted. Thousands who had intimidated stamp tax collectors, or invaded the homes of loyalist elite like Gov. Thomas Hutchinson, or mutinied within the army for back pay would never be deferential again. College students rebelled against

85. Ibid., pp. 301–2.
86. Ibid., pp. 303–5.

ancient restrictions, slaves ran away with the British, or, as in the case of Quock Walker, successfully claimed their natural rights under the new constitutions.

Revolutionary ideology had no place in it for the reconstruction of women's roles. But these roles could not help but change under the stress of necessity and in response to changes in men's behavior. Dependence and independence were connected in disconcerting ways. For example, the men of the army were dependent on the services of the women of the army, much as the former would have liked to deny the existence of the latter. And, paradoxically, although men were "defenders" and women "protected" in wartime, the man who left his wife or mother to "protect" her by joining the army might actually place her at greater physical risk. Even those most resistant to changed roles could not help but respond to the changed reality of a community in which troops were quartered or from which supplies were commandeered. Women's survival strategies were necessarily different from those of men. It ought not surprise us that women would also develop different understandings of their relationship to the state. In the years of the early republic, middle- and upper-class women gradually asserted a role for themselves in the republic that stressed their worthiness of the lives that had been risked for their safety, their service in maintaining morals and ethical values, and their claim to judge fathers, husbands, and sons by the extent to which these men lived up to the standards of republican virtue they professed. Seizing the idea of civic virtue, women made it their own, claiming for themselves the responsibility of committing the next generation to republicanism and civic virtue, and succeeding so well that by the antebellum years it would be thought to be distinctively female and its older association with men largely forgotten. Virtue would become for women what honor was for men: a private psychological stance laden with political overtones.[87]

Those who did most to construct the ideology of republican womanhood—like Judith Sargent Murray and Benjamin Rush—had reflected Revolutionary experience authentically, but also selectively. They drew on Revolutionary ideology and experience, emphasizing victimization, pride, decency, and the maintenance of ritual and self-respect. But they denied

87. John M. Murrin makes this suggestion in his unpublished essay "Can Liberals Be Patriots? Natural Rights, Virtue, and Moral Sense in the America of George Mason and Thomas Jefferson."

the most frightening elements of that experience. There was no room in the new construction for the disorderly women who had emptied their piss-pots on stamp tax agents, intimidated hoarders, or marched with Washington and Greene. There was no room for the women who had explicitly denied the decency and appropriateness of the war itself. There was no room for the women who had despaired and who had contributed to a war-weary desire for peace at any price in 1779–81. There was no room for the women who had fled with the loyalists; no room, in short, for women who did not fit the reconstructed expectations. Denial of disorder was probably connected to the institutionalization of the Revolution in the federal republic. The women of the army were denied as the Shaysites were denied; to honor and mythologize them would have been to honor and to mythologize the most disconcerting and threatening aspects of rebellion.

In announcing her certainty that the essential differences between the sexes lay in the realm of feeling and sentiment, Elizabeth Ellet had offered not only a distinctive memory of the Revolution but a selective one that reflected the selective memories of her informants. Yet Elizabeth Ellet was no naïf. Perhaps in recognition that her contemporaries linked military service with citizenship, Ellet was at great pains to move her women close to the army camps, to place them on horses, cloaked like men, undergoing physical risks associated with heroes: the wild ride through the night, the passage of dangerous rivers. She wrote for a political generation that needed to make this claim. She understood that to place gender at the narrative center of the Revolutionary experience would require a major shift of perspective and would introduce complexity and ambivalence into issues previously assumed to be one-dimensional. In painting, an analogy would be to shift from the directness and simplicity of John Trumbull's great depiction of the signing of the Declaration of Independence that hangs in the Capitol Rotunda—a painting that must be seen in the same way by each pair of eyes, depicting one species, using one vanishing point—to the doubled vision of modern painting like Henri Rousseau's *Sleeping Gypsy*, an unsettling painting in which, as Arthur Danto has explained, we see at the same moment the gypsy from the perspective of the lion and the lion, foreshortened, looking down, from the perspective of the gypsy.[88] When we write, at last, an authentic, holistic history of the Revolution it

88. For a brilliant comment to this effect, see Arthur Danto, *The Nation*, Mar. 23, 1985, p. 345.

will be no easier to read than Rousseau or Picasso are to view. The new narrative will be disconcerting; its author will have to have the ability to render multiple perspectives simultaneously.

The new narrative will provide a more rigorous investigation of the sexual division of labor prevalent in America in the second half of the eighteenth century; it will provide a more rigorous investigation of the impact of civil unrest, war, and a changing global economy on that labor system. The new narrative will make room for the women who lived in the interstices of institutions that we once understood as wholly segregated by gender: the women tavernkeepers who provided the locales for political meetings, the thousands of orderly and disorderly women on whom the army was dependent for essentials of life. The new narrative will imply a more precise account of the social relations of the sexes in the early republic, a precision that in turn will make it possible for us to develop a more nuanced understanding of the extent to which Victorian social relations were a response to what had preceded them.

In the new narrative the Revolution will be understood to be more deeply radical than we have heretofore perceived it because its shock reached into the deepest and most private human relations, jarring not only the hierarchical relationships between ruler and ruled, between elite and yeoman, between slave and free, but also between men and women, husbands and wives, mothers and children. But the Revolution will also be understood to be more deeply conservative than we have understood, purchasing political stability at the price of backing away from the implications of the sexual politics implied in its own manifestos, just as it backed away from the implications of its principles for changed race relations. The price of stabilizing the Revolution was an adamant refusal to pursue its implications for race relations and for the relations of gender, leaving to subsequent generations to accomplish what the Revolutionary generation had not. By contrast, French Revolutionaries did admit to debate the possibility of major change in the social relations of the sexes, as shown in working-class women's seizure of power in the October Days, in divorce legislation, in admission of women to the oath of loyalty and citizenship, and in the programs of Jacobin societies of Revolutionary Republican Women; but it could also be argued that thus entertaining the woman question was severely destabilizing and contributed to the disruption of the Republic in 1793–95.

In the end, most men and women were probably less conscious of changed relationships than of simple relief that they had survived. Yet even simple survival seemed to call for a transformation in women's political role. When the war was over, Mercy Otis Warren wrote a play about two women in revolutionary times in which she placed herself as heroine.[89] Her message was framed in terms of the contrasting experience of two women, but its burden surely was meant to apply to both sexes. *The Ladies of Castile* is about two women of contrasting temperaments caught up in a revolutionary civil war; it provided the heroic imagery in which Americans would prefer, from that day to this, to embed their Revolution. The soft and delicate Louisa, who introduces herself with the words "I wander wilder'd and alone / Like some poor banish'd fugitive. . . . I yield to grief" is contrasted with the determined Maria, who announces in her opening that she scorns to live "upon ignoble terms." The message of *The Ladies of Castile* is simple and obvious: the Louisas of the world—who ignore politics—do not survive revolutions; the Marias—who take political positions, make their own judgment of the contending sides, risk their own lives—emerge stronger and in control. It is the Marias, whose souls grow strong by resistance and who take gritty political positions, who survive and flourish. "A soul, inspir'd by freedom's genial warmth," says Maria, "Expands—grows firm, and by resistance, strong."[90]

89. At least Judith Sargent Murray thought so; see *The Gleaner*, 3:263.
90. Mercy Otis Warren, *Poems, Dramatic and Miscellaneous* (Boston: I. Thomas, 1790), pp. 97–178.

"I HAVE DON . . . MUCH TO CARREY ON THE WARR"
WOMEN AND THE SHAPING OF REPUBLICAN IDEOLOGY AFTER THE AMERICAN REVOLUTION

I take my title from what I think is the most moving witness to the American Revolution left to us by a woman: the petition of Rachel Wells of Bordentown, New Jersey, to the Continental Congress.[1] Wells faced the loss of the repayment of her war bonds due to a technicality.

> To the Honnorabell Congress I Rachel do make this Complaint, Who am a Widow far advancd in years & dearly have ocasion of ye Intrust for that Cash I Lent the Stats. I was a Sitisen in ye Jearsey when I Lent ye Stats a Considerable Sum of Moneys & had I justice don me it mite be Suficant to Suporte me in ye Contrey whear I am now . . . Now gentelmen is this Liberty, had it bin advertisd that he or She that moved out of the Stats should Louse his or her Intrust you mite have sum plea against me. But I am Innocent. Suspectd no Trick. I have Don as much to Carrey on the warr as Maney that Sett Now at ye healm of goverment. . . . God has Spred a plentifull Tabel for us & you gentelmen are ye Carvers for us pray forgit not the poor weaklings . . . Why Not Rachel Wells have a Littel intrust if She did not fight She Threw in all her mite which bought ye Sogers food & Clothing & Let them have Blankets . . .

Rachel Wells could not spell, but she had a high level of political consciousness. She had been deeply engaged in the war. She knew where her money had gone and what it had been used for. She had a clear sense of

1. May 18, 1786, *Papers of the Continental Congress*, Microfilm 247, Roll 56, Item 42, 8:354–55. National Archives.

To the Honnorabell Congrefs I Rachel do make this
Complaint Who am a widow far advancd in years & dearely have
ocasion of y Intruſt for that Cafh I lent the State
I was a Sitiſen in y jearſey when I Lent y State a Confidrealde Sum
of money & had I juſtice don me it mite be Suficant to Suporte me in y
Contrey wheaſ I am now near burdenton I lived hear then when m—
Joſeph burden Capt y office for the State but being torn to peaſe & fo
Robd by the Britans & others I went to Phia to try to git a Living as
I Could dee nothing in burdentown in my way fo afte y Englifh left
their I went to phia & was their in the year 1785 when our afembley
was pleaſ to paſ a Law that No one should have aney Intruſt that Lived
out of jearſey State I have Lent in a petition to y afembley they fay
it dies in your breſt as the Cafh was Lent to you they give me a form
of an oath which Runs this that I was a Refidentor when I put y Cafh
into the office & was in y year 83 & am Still I Can fwair that I was then
& am now but in 83 I was Not Now gentlemen is this Liberty had it bin
advertiſd that he or She that moved out of the State should Louſe
his or her Intruſt you mite have Sum plea againſt me But I am
Innpeſent fuſpecte no trick I have don as much to Carrey on the ware
as money that Sett Now at y healm of goverment & no notice taken
of me befides this one of your afembley borrowed 300 in gould of me
felt as the ware Comenſd & Now I Can nither git Intruſt nor
principell nor even Secureſty why) becauſe they have paſd a Law
that No officer Shall be troubled under five years after peace Comenſd
Not onley fo but one of our Chaplens to our armey I beleve has told me
of one hundred & Eighty Six pounds) & my acount was prood
& Carid into y office opinted for that Purpoſe of what I had Suffered by y
Englifh which Came to two thouſend Eight hundred & five pounds hard Cafh
But this I Can bair but to be Robd by my Contrey men is verey trying
to nature my d Sifter wright wrote to me to be thankfull that I had it in
my Power to Help on the ware which is well a nough but then this is to be
Confiderd that athers gits their Intruſt & why then a poor old widow to be put
of who am thus Stript I offlen think of a tex in Scripture Ecclefiaftes
y 9 & 15th their was in the City a poor man that by his wifdom
delivered the City yet No one Remembred that Same poor man
had their bin given to Sifter wright onley one quarter of an acker of groui
to have Laid her bone in I should not have thought I beleve of it. I

Petition of Rachel Wells, Bordentown, New Jersey, May 18, 1786.
Papers of the Continental Congress.
Courtesy National Archives and Records Administration, Washington, D.C.

what was due her. But the position she was forced to assume was that of a supplicant.

The political community that was fashioned by the American war was a deeply gendered community, one in which all white adults were citizens but in which men's voices were politically privileged. For men, political institutions—the army, the militia, the state legislatures, the Continental Congress, organizations of artisans—facilitated collective experience. A notable male elite—its patriarchal character encoded in its identification as the Founding Fathers—articulated political republicanism and embedded it in successive manifestos and institutions, acting in the name, they said, of all Americans, though they certainly did not formally consult women of any race or class, any black men, and only rarely propertyless white men. There was no female counterpart of the Founding Fathers. American women shared many experiences but only occasionally formalized their collective response or articulated their reactions as a group or on behalf of more than one. It has not been easy for historians to say much that is reliable about American women in the revolutionary era—either about their behavior or about their understanding of what that behavior meant. Reading the history of the American Revolution from the perspective of women is a little like entering the world of Tom Stoppard's *Rosenkrantz and Guildenstern Are Dead*: a world that has been turned inside out so that we can pay attention to voices that were present in the original telling but overpowered by the narrator's choice of central characters.

There is much merit to thinking of the era as an "age of the democratic revolution," and to melding the French and American upheavals into a single set of shared events on a large scale. Lafayette's career alone may furnish all the proof we need of the merits of that approach. But there were also enormous differences between the political cultures of the two revolutions, a difference that is underscored by the sharp differences in women's behavior. French women were early to claim their political tongues, beginning with the cahiers of the flower sellers of Paris and proceeding through Olympe de Gouges' "Declaration of the Rights of Woman" and the activities of the Society of Revolutionary Republican Women.[2] For these collective activities we have no direct counterparts in America. When Rachel Wells petitioned the Continental Congress, she petitioned alone.

2. Reprinted in Darline Gay Levy, Harriet Branson Applewhite, and Mary Durham Johnson, eds., *Women in Revolutionary Paris, 1789–1795* (Urbana: University of Illinois Press, 1979), 22–26.

Indeed, virtually the only mechanism the American republic made available to Rachel Wells was the traditional mechanism of the individual petition, which forces deference and subservience on the claimant. The music of her words is in the counterpoint: there is the tone of the forceful demand ("Now gentelmen is this Liberty") in which she addresses her readers as an equal; against it rings the tone of the mendicant ("God has spread a plentifull tabel for us & you gentelmen are ye Carvers"). Reading her petition, we learn something about her social status (poor), her role during the revolutionary war (contributor and supporter), and finally her hesitant articulation of the meaning and significance of that experience.

Rachel Wells faced the Revolution on her own, as an individual, with only her family for her support. It is this absence of a collective dimension to most of their activities that marks the greatest difference between the experiences of American women and their brothers and between the female experience of the French and American Revolutions. Historians of France emphasize the collective behavior of French women, especially urban women, in the great *journées* that mark the major turning points of the French Revolution.

Two factors seem of particular significance. The first is the comparative scale of events. Paris was an urban place of more than 650,000 inhabitants; Philadelphia, the largest American city, was home to 40,000. Calling both places "urban" masks real differences in social dynamics. Second, Paris was a city with two important institutions that had long been engaged in providing at least the preconditions for women's consciousness of themselves as engaged in shared collective enterprise; neither institution existed in America. One was the established Roman Catholic Church. I am thinking here not only of religious orders, which would become part of the mobilization *against* the Revolution, but the theatre that the Church provided for ritual behavior by otherwise secular women. Darline G. Levy and Harriet Applewhite have drawn attention to the women's processions to the Eglise St. Geneviève in Paris. Originally acts of supplication, the processions were gradually transformed during the summer of 1789 into the antecedents for the secular, political, and violent women's march on Versailles. Second were the women's guilds or guild-like organizations, which existed only in Paris and a few major cities, but that provided an institutional tradition in which women shared a collective experience and collective responsibilities. Thus the Fishwives of Paris had a responsibility to be present at the birth of the royal heir and to certify that the child had in fact been born of the body of the Queen. These groups—flower sellers, fishwives—seem to have been core groups that served, like the grains of sand in the oyster, to facilitate the formation of politicized women's groups.[3]

In America the Catholic Church was marginal. The only religious group that gave women space of their own and accustomed them to making institutional decisions was the Quakers, and they were deeply disaffected during the war.[4] There was no tradition of women's guilds. (In New York midwives were licensed, but apparently as individuals.) We have as yet been unable to identify the specific women who gathered in the few well-documented women's collective displays—the destruction of the stores of Peter Mesier in Westchester in 1777, the intimidation of the Boston merchant Thomas Boylston in 1778—or to ascertain what experiences these women had in common. The absence of a collective dimension makes the reconstruction of the gendered dimensions of the American experience a subtle challenge. But it is nonetheless an important challenge. Having established that events had an impact on women and also that women participated in events, historians must move on to examine political process, social experience, and the ways in which political discourse reflected relations between the sexes of which contemporaries were only dimly aware. Societies at war are societies engaged in a renegotiation of gender relations, usually in such a way as to emphasize and sometimes redefine the meaning of masculinity. An ideology that takes enormous pains to *exclude* women is, by that very fact, an ideology that is interactive *with* women. There is, as Joan Wallach Scott has suggested, "a politics of gender . . . [embedded] in the politics of war."[5] Republican ideology was a creation of the revolutionary generation, and in its shaping we can discern the subtle ways in which it reflected the gender dynamics of the generation that created it.

3. On women's processions to the Eglise Sainte-Geneviève, see Darline G. Levy and Harriet B. Applewhite, "Women and Political Revolution in Paris," in *Becoming Visible: Women in European History*, ed. Renate Bridenthal et al., 2d ed. (Boston: Houghton Mifflin, 1987), 285–86. See also their essay "Women, Radicalization, and the Fall of the French Monarchy," in *Women and Politics in the Age of the Democratic Revolution*, ed. Levy and Applewhite (Ann Arbor: University of Michigan Press, 1990), 81–107.

4. On Quaker women, see Mary Maples Dunn, "Saints and Sinners: Congregational and Quaker Women in the Early Colonial Period," *American Quarterly* 30 (1978): 582–601.

5. "Rewriting History," in *Behind the Lines: Gender and the Two World Wars*, ed. Margaret Randolph Higonnet, Jane Jenson, Sonya Michel, Margaret Collins Weitz (New Haven: Yale University Press, 1987), 25–26.

Thomas Paine's *Common Sense*, published in January, 1776, occupies a special place in the literature of the Revolution; it lucidly expressed a developing ideology and was widely quoted as a tract that gave words to what a large political community was ready to hear. In the informal language of ordinary people, *Common Sense* challenged reliance on authority, and promised that together the people of America could create a society without oppression. At a time when 4,000 copies was an impressive circulation for a pamphlet, 150,000 copies of *Common Sense* were published in its first year.[6] Usually treated simply as a public political text, we have come to understand, thanks to the work of Michael Wallace and Edwin Burrows, that along with Paine's series *The Crisis*, it also offers an interpretation of private family dynamics that permeated the political discourse of both Patriots and Tories.[7] From Burrows and Wallace, it is a short step to appreciating what *Common Sense* suggests about the social relations of the sexes.

Paine addresses himself explicitly to the male reader; Paine's use of the male pronoun is emphatically not generic.

> In the following pages I offer nothing more than simple facts, plain arguments, and common sense; and have no other preliminaries to settle with the reader, than that he will divest himself of prejudice and prepossession, . . . that he will not put *off* the true character of a man . . .[8]

Paine wrote in the language of Enlightenment political discourse, in which the "state of nature" was well established as a standard trope in political literature. It was common for political philosophers to begin by visualizing a pre-political world and to draw on this *tabula rasa* what seemed to them to be a logical political community. In the classic state of nature as concep-

6. See the useful introductory comments of Jack P. Greene, ed., *Colonies to Nation, 1763–1789: A Documentary History of American Life* (New York: McGraw-Hill, 1967), 268–70. But also see Cecelia M. Kenyon, "Where Paine Went Wrong," *American Political Science Review* 41 (1951): 1086–99.

7. Edwin G. Burrows and Michael Wallace, "The American Revolution: The Ideology and Psychology of National Liberation," *Perspectives in American History*, 1st ser., 6 (1972): 167–308.

8. *Thomas Paine Reader*, ed. Michael Foot and Isaac Kramnick (Harmondsworth, England: Penguin Books, 1987), 79.

tualized by Locke, Hobbes, and Condorcet, the beginning point was usually a man and a woman who, by their creation of children, initiated the social relations of the community. As Locke and Hobbes warmed to their task the woman slipped out of their constructions. Although Paine acknowledges that "Male and female are the distinctions of nature," women do not figure in the original social community at all.

> In order to gain a clear and just idea of the design and end of government, let us suppose a small number of persons settled in some sequestred part of the earth, unconnected with the rest: they will then represent the first peopling of any country, or of the world. In this state of natural liberty, society will be their first thought. A thousand motives will excite them thereto, the strength of one man is so unequal to his wants, and his mind so unfitten for perpetual solitude, that he is soon obliged to seek assistance and relief of another, who in his turn requires the same. . . . Four or five united would be able to raise a tolerable dwelling in the midst of a wilderness; but *one* man might labour out of the common period of life without accomplishing any thing; when he had felled his timber he could not remove it, nor erect it after it was removed . . .

After men have built their homes, they were likely to find themselves to have different opinions, and they would gather themselves into a distinctly male political community:

> Some convenient tree will afford them a statehouse, under the branches of which the whole colony may assemble to deliberate on public matters. . . . In this first parliament every man by natural right will have a seat.

Eligibility for membership is measured by their relations to good women:

> . . . as a man, who is attached to a prostitute, is unfitted to choose or judge of a wife, so any prepossession in favour of a rotten constitution of government will disable us from discerning a good one.

The reciprocal is absent: women do not prove their eligibility for membership in the political community by their marriage to a good man. Addressing the reader as "husband, father, friend or lover," Paine writes "to awaken us from fatal and unmanly slumbers." Later he observes, "As well can the lover forgive the ravisher of his mistress, as the continent forgive the murders of Britain," suggesting by his language that those inclined to negotiate, despite the Boston Massacre and other Patriot martyrs, are men who would not defend their private honor.[9]

The language of American resistance, not only Paine's, was suffused with an image of Britain as an unnatural mother and of Americans as vigorous youths ready to assume the responsibilities of manhood.[10] Burrows and Wallace found in Paine the culmination of this expression: "To know whether it be the interest of the continent to be independent, we need only ask this easy, simple question: Is it the interest of a man to be a boy all his life?"[11]

Increasingly republican ideology envisioned the single male individual, standing independently against the encroachments of royal power, joining as an individual with other men to form an intentional political community.[12] The more republicans reasoned in this way, the more gender-specific their ideology became, even when they did not say so explicitly. Patriarchalism, under attack at least since the English Civil Wars, was eroding,

9. It is important, perhaps, to point out that despite the gendered subtext, Paine's work appealed to women as well as to men. We know, for example, that Abigail Adams (AA) admired his pamphlets and circulated them to her friends. She referred to *Common Sense* as "a Book [which] . . . carries conviction wherever it is read. I have spread it as much as it lay in my power, every one assents to the weighty truths it contains. I wish it could . . . be carried speadily into Execution." AA to John Adams (JA), 21 February 1776, *Adams Family Correspondence* (hereafter *AFC*), ed. L. H. Butterfield (Cambridge, Mass.: Harvard University Press, 1963), 1:350. See also AA to JA, 2 March 1776, *AFC* 1:352 and AA to JA, 7 March 1776, *AFC* 1:354. She was considerably more enthusiastic than was her husband, whose response was ambivalent: "Sensible Men think there are some Whims, some Sophisms, some artfull Addresses to superstitious Notions, some keen attempts upon the Passions, in this Pamphlet. But all agree there is a great deal of good sense, delivered in a clear, simple, concise and nervous Style. . . . Indeed this Writer has a better Hand at pulling down than building." JA to AA, 19 March 1776, *AFC* 1:363. In 1780, when the *American Crisis* essays were reprinted in Boston newspapers, AA quoted from them in her letters; see AA to JA, 5 July and 16 July 1780, *AFC* 3:371, 376.

10. Burrows and Wallace, "American Revolution," 206–13.

11. Burrows and Wallace, "American Revolution," 215, citing *The Crisis, III.*

12. For an important review of recent argumentation about the tensions implicit in early American political ideology—a review that does not, however, include considerations of gender—see James T. Kloppenberg, "The Virtues of Liberalism: Christianity, Republicanism, and Ethics in Early American Political Discourse," *Journal of American History* 74 (1987): 9–33, especially 30–33. See also Ruth Bloch, "The Gendered Meanings of Virtue in Revolutionary America," *Signs: Journal of Women in Culture and Society* 13 (1987): 98–120.

but its erosion was more swift in the public realm than in the private, and more swift in the relations among men than between men and women. Indeed, there may even have been a heightened insistence during the years of the early republic that men validated their own claims to independence by, as Joan Gundersen has phrased it, "stressing the dependence of others (including women) on them. . . . Much of the discussion of independence during the Revolutionary period used a system of negative reference to define independence. Independence was a condition arrived at by exclusion . . . by *not* being dependent or enslaved."[13] As there gradually developed a political community that empowered the independent male citizen who controlled his own property, women remained marginalized as the objects of conflict and achievement; indeed women embodied all that was vulnerable. "The people," observed John Adams, "are Clarissa."

In the society of the early republic, the elements of political independence were denied to women by custom and by practice. This political marginality was sustained by the traditional inequality of property rights. In Anglo-American law, married women had little control over the property they earned or inherited. Although women were often defined in terms of their domestic duties, households and their property were controlled by men; only the dower "thirds" were assured to women after the death of their husband.[14] Marginality remained despite the hard fact that the work of women was central to the maintenance of the family economy, especially in laboring and artisan classes, as it is in every known society. It seems a reasonable generalization that the wages of laboring women approximated half of the wages of laboring men, even when performing similar work.[15] Families of the laboring class usually needed the work of

13. Joan R. Gundersen, "Independence, Citizenship, and the American Revolution," *Signs: Journal of Women in Culture and Society* 13 (1987): 75, 77. See also Elaine F. Crane, "Dependence in the Era of Independence: The Role of Women in a Republican Society," in *The American Revolution: Its Character and Limits*, ed. Jack P. Greene (New York: New York University Press, 1987), 253–75.

14. I have discussed the implications of this in chapters 4 and 5 of *Women of the Republic: Intellect and Ideology in Republican America* (Chapel Hill: University of North Carolina Press, 1980); see also Marylynn Salmon, *Women and the Law of Property in Early America* (Chapel Hill: University of North Carolina Press, 1986) and Michael Grossberg, *Governing the Hearth: Law and the Family in Nineteenth Century America* (Chapel Hill: University of North Carolina Press, 1985).

15. See Billy G. Smith, "The Material Lives of Laboring Philadelphians, 1750 to 1800," *William and Mary Quarterly*, 3d ser., 38 (1981): 163–202; Carole Shammas, "The Female

women and children to meet the costs of simple necessities.[16] Widows had a high probability of continuing in their husband's craft or trade. Deserted women became heads of households and required their own income. In towns and cities, women worked as market women, seamstresses, laundresses, and as domestic servants. What we now call "the feminization of poverty" was already well underway. Women seem to have been more likely than men to have had to accept "indoor relief"—residence in almshouses— rather than "outdoor relief"—aid offered outside of institutions.[17]

The fact that women had to work was buttressed by a pervasive assumption that women ought constantly to be at work. The pathetic phrase "women's work is never done" described the steady round of domestic labor within middle-class households. Poor women could demonstrate their worthiness for public assistance only by constant labor. Philadelphia vagrancy records show women confined to brief jail sentences on vague charges of "idleness" or "for following no employment."[18] Literacy, a skill

---

Social Structure of Philadelphia in 1775," *Pennsylvania Magazine of History and Biography* 107 (1983): 69–84.

16. "Unskilled workers and their families in Philadelphia generally lived on the edge of, or occasionally slightly above, the subsistence level; simply to maintain that level both spouses had to work." Smith, "Material Lives," 189.

17. On the basis of the poorhouse list for Salem, Massachusetts, Elaine Crane argues that the Revolutionary War years saw a massive increase in the number of women unable to provide for themselves. "Dependence in the Era of Independence: The Role of Women in a Republican Society." Sharon Salinger finds that two-thirds of the residents of the Philadelphia poorhouse between 1787 and 1790 were women. "Female Servants in Eighteenth Century Philadelphia," *Pennsylvania Magazine of History and Biography* 107 (1983): 45. Robert E. Cray is less impressed by gender disparities among poor New Yorkers in the eighteenth century; see *Paupers and Poor Relief in New York City and Its Rural Environs, 1700–1830* (Philadelphia: Temple University Press, 1988), esp. 59.

18. E.g., Eleanor Garvin, "an Idle disorderly person not following any employment for an honest livelihood." 8 June 1797, Prison Vagrancy Docket, 1790–1797, Philadelphia City Archives, RG 38.44. Nowhere does the occupational segregation by sex that prevailed in the early republic show up more sharply than in apprenticeship contracts, which indicate that boys and girls were apprenticed to different crafts, and which reveal substantial distinctions in the amount of schooling offered. As Alfred Young has shown for Boston, the ways in which a woman could be self-supporting were severely limited. A sharp contrast in apprenticeship records in all cities and towns is the disparity in skills that prospective masters offered male and female apprentices. A standard feature of apprenticeship contracts for boys was that by the completion of

that facilitated the acquisition of other skills, was substantially weaker among women than among men. Our best estimates suggest that women's literacy rates on the eve of the Revolution were half that of their male counterparts, whether the area studied is rural or urban.

Jürgen Habermas has urged us to understand the concept of the "public sphere" as something distinct from an antique distinction between the simply public and the private; by "public sphere" he means, as his translator Peter Hohendahl has put it, "the sphere of non-governmental opinion making." This realm is distinguished from legislative debate on the one hand and private conversation on the other; Habermas locates its emergence in a particular historical moment, the emergence of bourgeois society in the eighteenth century and particularly in the era of the democratic revolution. Its characteristic site is the political newspaper, "the mediator and intensifier of public discussion." By their published expressions of opinion, private individuals in effect assemble themselves into a "public body" which positions itself "against the public authority itself." "In those newspapers, and in moralistic and critical journals, they debated that public authority on the general rules of social intercourse."[19] In a society in which men controlled the press and were using it to explain to each other how good republicans could retain their manhood while eschewing the patriarchal role, women faced the challenge of making space for themselves in the public sphere and participating in the task of opinion-making. Judith Sargent Murray, who later published her "Gleaner" essays as a book

---

their term they were to have been taught a trade and have had some schooling; girls' contracts rarely promised to teach more than housework. See, for example, the apprenticeship list reprinted in the Pennsylvania German Society, *Proceedings and Addresses* 16 (1905); Philadelphia City Archives, Guardians of the Poor: Memorandum Book, Indentures 1751–1797.

19. Jürgen Habermas, "The Public Sphere: An Encyclopedia Article (1964)," *New German Critique*, no. 3 (Fall, 1974): 49–55, and Jürgen Habermas, *The Structural Transformation of the Public Sphere: An Inquiry into a Category of Bourgeois Society*, trans. Thomas Burger (Cambridge, Mass.: MIT Press, 1989), esp. 27–56. I am indebted to Michael Warner's formulations of this development in an American context. See "The Letters of the Republic: Literature and Print in Republican America" (Ph.D. diss., Johns Hopkins University, 1985), and "Printing, 'The People' and the Transformation of the Public Sphere," unpublished paper, Organization of American Historians, Annual Meeting, 1988. For an effort to apply Habermas's conceptualizations to the era of the French Revolution, see Joan B. Landes, *Women and the Public Sphere in the Age of the French Revolution* (Ithaca: Cornell University Press, 1988), esp. Introduction and chap. 2.

sold by subscription, was one of the very few women who claimed regular newspaper space.[20] A few women found funds to publish pamphlets; a handful wrote occasional letters of opinion to newspapers or to journals that announced themselves receptive to women's contributions. Americans concluded from the Revolution that dependence was to be deplored. It is not surprising that women would seek space to articulate a vision of the sort of independence that they would find most pleasing. Their efforts to do so marks the deeply gendered nature of republican ideology after the American Revolution.

In short, American women, not unlike their French counterparts, were in a position of limited resilience when subjected to the added stress of the war, which would make thousands of them widows and leave others abandoned. An older patriarchal tradition had offered a rationale for women's dependence by linking it to other dependent relationships in society. But the more patriarchalism came under attack from republican ideology, the less "republican" adult married women seemed to be. If they were to enter the republic, they would have to devise their own, gendered variant of republicanism; they would have to explain how women could enter the political community.

II

For men and women alike, participation in some aspects of the Revolution could be empowering, making it possible to make claims on the republic. We find evidence of men's claims on the postwar republic everywhere: in artisans' parades and rallies, in voting on the ratification of the Constitution, in political positions articulated orally in legislatures, and in writing in the newspapers. Evidence of women's claims on the republic is more scattered, since women controlled virtually none of the usual fora in which politics were expressed. As one graduate of a girls' school explained in a graduation speech, "The Bench and the Bar are closed to us." Even in newspapers owned and published by women, it was assumed that men's words filled the columns. But evidence there is, in larger quantities and far richer than we have assumed, and this evidence increases substantially in quantity in the 1780s and 1790s. When governments stabilized, women

20. Another was Gertrude Meredith of Philadelphia, who published in the *Portfolio* in the first decade of the nineteenth century.

turned to them with petitions for redress for griefs and wrongs experienced during the Revolution. The growing strength of dissenting churches meant audiences for accounts of religious experiences. And the successful demands for improved education meant an increase in literacy, complemented by more female writers to write and by more female readers to read; by the 1790s it was the unusual newspaper that did not print at least occasional letters signed with a female *nom de plume*. Female audiences for fiction—self-conscious but persistent—provided opportunities for women writers to claim a relationship with the public sphere. And in the absence of legislative action, what we might call women's support groups undertook to save the most desperate and "deserving" of the female and youthful poor shipwrecked by revolutionary dislocations, testifying to what they were doing in handwritten minutes and published reports.

We will rarely find men initiating discussions of women's concerns or of women's relationship to the state; as Edward Countryman has remarked, white men of at least modest property thought of themselves as the makers of the Revolution, and it was to them—as voters, as soldiers, as citizens— that legislators, in turn, felt themselves responsible.[21] But if we turn to texts written by women, we can find women developing their own distinctive agendas, a politics congruent with their own understanding of reality. No single individual gathered all the elements of women's political perspectives into a single vision or text. But the elements of a female consciousness and the beginnings of a female agenda can be discerned in the writings of several women who "carried on the war" into the postwar years, articulating the issues that meant most to them. An authentic intellectual history of the founding generation will make room for these women's texts on bookshelves and in anthologies already crowded with the work of the men of their age.

The earliest Americans to encounter Mary Wollstonecraft's *Vindication of the Rights of Woman* were the readers of the Philadelphia *Ladys Magazine*, which published extensive extracts—nearly 5,000 words—in September, 1792. They appeared in the same issue that reported the introduction into the French National Assembly of a resolution to the effect that Louis XVI had forfeited his crown. The *Ladys Magazine* was edited by men, who aimed at a female audience characterized by "virtue and prudence." Woll-

---

21. Edward Countryman, *A People in Revolution: The American Revolution and Political Society in New York 1760–1790* (Baltimore: Johns Hopkins University Press, 1981), 288–89.

stonecraft's message was packaged in a form that both contained and endorsed its radical import. The frontispiece of the issue included an engraving, by the Philadelphia artists James Thackara and John Vallance, of three women dressed in vaguely Grecian garb and framed by a classical temple. "The Genius of the Ladies Magazine, accompanied by the Genius of Emulation, who carries in her hand a laurel crown, approaches Liberty, and kneeling, presents her with a copy of the Rights of Woman." The Spirit of the *Ladys Magazine*, who kneels to present her text, is traditionally deferential, but the Spirit of Ambition who accompanies her bears the torch and laurel crown normally reserved for male heroes, and Liberty had long since absorbed from Minerva the Phrygian cap, the pole, and the shield. By associating traditional republican imagery with Wollstonecraft's claims for women, Thackara and Vallance enfolded her radicalism in familiar and powerful imagery.[22]

What the artists did visually, the editors did verbally, introducing selected passages as the common sense of the matter for a postrevolutionary republic. Nowhere was this strategy clearer than in their approval of Wollstonecraft's attacks on standing armies and her analogies between soldiers, who are trained to deference, and women of fashion. ". . . military men . . . are, like [women], sent into the world before their minds have been stored with knowledge, or fortified by principles. The consequences are similar; soldiers acquire a little superficial knowledge, snatched from the muddy current of conversation, and, from continually mixing with society, they gain [an] acquaintance with manners and customs [which] has frequently been confounded with a knowledge of the human heart."[23] The editors included in their selection only snippets of Wollstonecraft's attacks on Rousseau and other writers, but extensive selections from her call for practical education for women. They ended with her broadest claims, including her radical argument that women's status was itself a measure of the authenticity of men's civic virtue: "Moralists have unanimously agreed, that unless virtue be nourished by liberty, it will never attain due strength— and what they say of man, I extend to mankind . . . Let women share the rights, and she will emulate the virtues of man; for she must grow more perfect when emancipated, or justify the authority that chains such a weak being to her duty.—If the latter, it will be expedient to open a fresh trade with Russia for whips; a present which a father should always make to his

22. I am grateful to Gary Nash for his suggestions on this point.
23. *Ladys Magazine* (Philadelphia) 1 (1792): 192–93.

James Thackara and John Vallance,
frontispiece for Philadelphia *Ladys Magazine*, September, 1792.
Courtesy Library Company of Philadelphia.

son in-law, on his wedding-day, that a husband may keep his whole family in order. . . ."[24]

Judith Sargent Murray provides the most extensive and most fully developed texts in the history of women's thinking about American public issues in the revolutionary era; in that sense she is something of an American counterpart to Mary Wollstonecraft. Murray's "Gleaner" essays, published in serial form in 1792–94 and as a three-volume set of books in 1798, are nearly 700 pages in length and touch on issues of education, manners, fashion, religion, and politics. After a long period in which little attention was paid to them (the full work, for example, has only recently been reprinted[25]), the essays in which she addresses women's education and need for independence have received fresh attention. But the entire work is more ambivalent than most who have quoted it have recognized. If there was much on which Murray and Mary Wollstonecraft would have agreed, there was also a great deal of Murray's work of which Wollstonecraft would have been bitterly skeptical. Set next to Murray, Wollstonecraft's liberal formulations look stridently radical. The conservative context of Murray's liberal message requires attention.

Judith Sargent was born in 1751 into a prominent mercantile family in Gloucester, Massachusetts. Her family sent its sons to Harvard and encouraged her to study along with her brothers while they prepared for college with local tutors; when she was married, at the age of 18, to John Stevens, a sea captain and trader, her portrait was painted by John Singleton Copley. She was twenty-five in 1776. The years of the Revolution were intense ones for her. Although the fighting itself rarely touched Gloucester, her husband served on the Committee of Safety. The seagoing trade was badly affected; one historian estimates that a sixth of the population was living on charity. During the war years, Judith Sargent Stevens, her father, and her husband were also caught up in a liberal religious revival brought to Gloucester by John Murray, an itinerant Universalist preacher. Murray was English; he had been a follower of John Wesley before coming to America in 1770 to preach a doctrine of universal salvation. Finding a warm welcome among the Sargents and their friends in Gloucester's First Parish Church, Murray remained there, but his presence and the challenge of his message split the congregation. In September, 1778, fifteen dissidents (eleven women and

24. *Ladys Magazine* 1 (1792): 197.

25. Judith Sargent Murray, *The Gleaner* (Schenectady, N.Y.: Union College Press, 1992).

four men), including Judith Stevens, her parents, and her brother (though not her husband), were suspended from the First Parish Church. She and her husband signed an "Appeal to the Impartial Public by the Society of Christian Independents, Gloucester," and were part of the community that formed the first Universalist meetinghouse in America in December, 1780.[26] Thus the years of the war were years of religious as well as political dissidence for Judith Stevens.

Judith Sargent Stevens's marriage fell victim to the financial dislocations of the post-war years. In the hope of avoiding creditors and bankruptcy, John Stevens apparently fled to the West Indies in 1786; soon after word came of his death. In 1779, while caught up in the religious struggles, she was "seized with a violent desire to become a writer." She had drafted an essay titled "Desultory Thoughts upon the Utility of Encouraging a Degree of Self-Complacency, Especially in Female Bosoms," that would not be published until 1784.[27] In 1792, Murray began to publish a series of essays, under the heading "The Gleaner," in the newly established *Massachusetts Magazine*; she signed them with the pseudonym "Constantia." These essays continued to run for two years. In 1798, one year after her marriage to John Murray, she published them in three volumes. Some seven hundred people subscribed; the subscription list was headed, alphabetically, by John Adams, President of the United States, who ordered two copies. The list was dotted with distinguished male subscribers—George Washington, the governors of Massachusetts and New Hampshire. There were 121 women on the list, also an impressive assortment, including the novelist and playwright Susannah Rowson, "Mary" (Mercy?) Warren of Plymouth, Martha Washington, and the poet Sarah Morton. Although heavily from New England, there were strong contingents from New York and Philadelphia, and scat-

26. Vera Bernadette Field, *Constantia: A Study of the Life and Works of Judith Sargent Murray, 1751–1820*, University of Maine Studies, 2d ser., no. 17 (Orono, Me.: 1931), 17–21. On John Murray's Universalism, see Richard Eddy, *Universalism in America: A History* (Boston: Universalist Publishing House, 1891); Russell E. Miller, *The Larger Hope: The First Century of the Universalist Church in America 1770–1870* (Boston: Unitarian Universalist Association, 1979), 34–51. On the continuing and distinctive appeal of Universalism to women, see Judy Nolte Lensink, ed., *"A Secret to Be Burried": The Diaries of Emily Hawley Gillespie* (Iowa City: University of Iowa Press, 1989).

27. The phrase is quoted in Janet Wilson James, "Judith Sargent Murray," in *Notable American Women*, ed. Edward T. James and Janet Wilson James (Cambridge, Mass.: Harvard University Press, 1971), 2:603–5.

tered subscribers from Virginia and Georgia. The volumes were published in Boston by the distinguished firm of Isaiah Thomas and E. T. Andrews.

Thus *The Gleaner* essays are a product of the intense years of the new republic. While they were written, the precedent-making First and Second Congresses met, the first presidential election was held, and the French guillotined a king and queen. The format of an essay series permitted Murray to experiment with a variety of genres without committing herself to any single one. She could attempt a novel, a chapter at a time, without bringing it to closure; she could insert the texts of two dramatic plays that received single performances on the Boston stage and supplement them by a defense of theatre-going (*Gleaner*, 1:224). She could write about the Universalist perspective on life (1:182ff), comment on politics, and develop an elaborate defense of female education and intellectual development. When she wrote on this last topic she was at her least derivative, her most forthright and original; her essays on this theme are the most vigorous and fresh. It is an easy guess that they came out of her own experience and frustrations.

The most succinct way of summarizing Murray's extended comments on women and intellect is to say that she wanted men to recognize that women were capable of substantial intellectual achievement, and that she wanted women to understand that a serious education would make authentic independence possible. In support of the first point she wrote a series of essays that amounted to a brief history of women, in a form that dated back to Christine de Pisan's *City of Ladies*, which was a discursive and anecdotal, but roughly chronological, overview that rambled through the centuries identifying women of accomplishment from Semiramis to Mary Wollstonecraft. Like Wollstonecraft, Murray often seems to write without an outline, pouring her ideas out as they came to her, and badly in need of formal editing. But she is very clear as to her intentions: she wants her reader to share her conclusion that women are

First, alike capable of enduring hardships.
Secondly, Equally ingenious, and fruitful in resources.
Thirdly, Their fortitude and heroism cannot be surpassed.
Fourthly, They are equally brave.
Fifthly, They are as patriotic
Sixthly, As influential
Seventhly, As energetic, and as eloquent

Eighthly, As faithful, and as persevering in their attachments
Ninthly, As capable of supporting, with honour, the toils of
   government. And
Tenthly, and Lastly, They are equally susceptible of every literary
   acquirement. (*Gleaner*, 3:198)

"*The idea of the incapability* of women is, we conceive, in this *enlightened age*, totally *inadmissible*." (3:191).

Murray was as insistent as Wollstonecraft on the point that women should be educated for independence and psychological integrity. Although she did not refer directly to the political claims of the Revolution, the implicit message of much that she wrote was that the new republic required a new woman: "I expect to see our young women forming a new era in female history." (3:189). The new woman of the republic would be forthright and practical; she would not be attracted by passing fashion or by frivolity. She would be prepared for a world that might literally turn upside down, a world in which violent changes of fortune (like those John Stevens experienced) would be the rule rather than the exception. She did not shape her life around the marriage market; she did not consider an "old maid" a "contemptible object" (1:167–68). As a model, Murray provided a fictional Penelope (named, obviously enough, for a woman who had had to find a way to sustain herself without a husband), who sought to cultivate her own talents and in that way sustain her own "noble ardour of independence" (1:176). To that end, Penelope rises every morning at sunrise to study reading, music, drawing, and geography because they "polish my mind; and when I have made sufficient progress therein, they will open to me, should there be occasion, new sources of emolument as well as pleasure" (1:177). The rhetoric of republican virtue and independence provided the language for her insistence on the need for women to avoid subservience and docility, the need for women to be self-supporting and self-respecting. When Murray wrote that a serious education would put women in an independent stance in the world, she could well have been thinking of the adversity that she herself had faced in marriages to men with far less financial security than her father had provided, and to her own situation when her husband was driven to desperate flight and then left her a young widow.

Murray urged a constitutional provision or congressional legislation to provide an award for "*real genius*, whether it be found in the male or female world" (*Gleaner*, 1:52). She satirized the man who announced that "subordination . . . is so essential to the character of a woman . . . I shall expect *obedience from my wife*; that she must not only be very well taught, *industrious*, and uniformly economical, but also extremely docile" (1:66). And over and over again she defended the "learned lady" from the charge that she was sexually unappealing, or neglected her duties.

The advantage of the periodical essay form was the permission it gave to inconsistency. Murray's stance, forthright and demanding when she addressed the theme of women's education, changed abruptly when she turned to politics. Her dedication of the *Gleaner* volumes to John Adams was sycophantic, her vision of the American political order anything but relativist. The arrangements made by the American Constitution were not for her political solutions to political problems; they were the "*lineaments of nature—the lineaments of liberty*" (1:271). When Washington became Commander in Chief, "Confusion fled at his approach; discipline ranged itself under his banners . . . simple untrained villagers became a regular army of brave, patient and effective soldiers!" (3:92).

Her view of political parties echoed a crude, high Federalist line; in April, 1794, she joined high Federalist hysteria: "Faction hath introduced its cloven foot among us . . . and, drawing the sword of discord, it is preparing to sheath it in the vitals of that infant constitution, whose budding life expands so fair to view . . . Is not the idea of murdering in the very cradle so promising an offspring, a conception which can have received a form only in the maddening pericranium of hell-born monarchy?" (1:256–57). Entering the debate on whether American treaties with France were still valid after the change in government, she was sure that American obligations had evaporated in the face of the reign of terror, and she moved easily from criticism of Robespierre (1:256) to the assertion that liberty is not licentiousness and that "sacred and genuine Liberty . . . is fond of the necessary arrangement of civil subordination . . ." (1:266). She illustrated her point by a brief tale of the mess her fictional household is thrown into when a brief attempt is made to conduct it on the rule of equality (1:264–65). Her dismay at the French example apparently was so great that she could not see the contradictions into which she had been drawn.

When *The Gleaner* was published in book form in 1798, it was signed forthrightly as "Constantia." But that signature was a shift from the original voice, which had been explicitly male. When the essays first appeared, the author introduced "himself": "I am *rather* a plain man, who, after spending the day in making provision for my little family, sit myself comfortably down by a clean hearth, and a good fire . . ." (1:13). Not until the final installment, "The Gleaner Unmasked," did Judith Sargent Murray identify herself as the Constantia who had "filled some pages" in the *Boston Magazine* and the *Massachusetts Magazine*. Her readers were owed, she acknowledged, an explanation of "why I have endeavoured to pass myself upon them in the masculine character. . . ." Her response to her own rhetorical question was straightforward: "ambitious of being considered *independent as a writer*; if I possessed any merit, I was solicitous it should remain undiminished . . ." (3:314). Recognizing that she had no chance of being taken seriously if she wrote as a woman—"Rousseau had said, that although a female may *ostensibly* wield the pen, yet it is certain some man of letter sits behind the curtain to guide its movements"—she was anxious to assure her readers that she kept her secret even from her own husband (3:314). She had taken to heart the advice of "a celebrated writer of the present century" who had observed that "a *woman* ought never to suffer a *man* to add a *single word* to her writings; if she does, the man she consults, let him be who he may, will always pass for the original inventor, while she will be accused of putting her name to the works of others" (3:315). In so misogynist a culture, "observing, in a variety of instances, the indifference, not to say contempt, with which female productions are regarded . . ." she even now feared that "it will be affirmed, that the *effeminacy* and *tinsel glitter* of my style could not fail of betraying me at every sentence which I uttered" (3:313). She wanted her readers to know that she had done all her work alone, even, she observed ruefully, "To the toil of writing letters to myself, I have been condemned . . ." (3:316).

Murray sought an authoritative authorial voice. "I confess I love the paths of fame / And ardent wish to glean a brightening name," she wrote in the opening epigraph. She hoped to find her model in the British classical journalists; she envied "the smoothness of Addison's page, the purity, strength and correctness of Swift. . . ." Eventually she "took shelter" in the more modest promise of *The Gleaner*: "With diligence then, I shall ransack the fields, the meadows, and the groves [of literature] . . . deeming myself privileged to crop with impunity a hint from one, an idea from another, and to aim at improvement upon a sentence from a third. . . . in this expressive name I shall take shelter . . ." (1:13–16).

The political voice was so deeply understood to be specific to men, that a woman who wished to enter into the dialogue needed, as it were, to dress in men's clothes. The secret, however, was soon out, and Murray's columns were known to an increasingly wide audience as those of a woman (3:316).

Judith Sargent Murray remains a lucid exponent—perhaps the most vigorous single voice—of the ideology I have called republican motherhood:

the position that women have an obligation, both to themselves and to the political society in which they live, to educate themselves for economic competence and intellectual growth. This venture was assumed by Murray and her contemporaries to represent a departure from traditional practice ("a new era in female history") and one that promised to strengthen family relationships as well as to satisfy female ambition. For perhaps the first time in western culture, members of Murray's generation acknowledged and even welcomed female ambition, offering it support *if* ambition developed in a context that also involved companionable relationships with husbands and tutorial relationships with children. The model republican mother would raise her children to be decent and public-spirited citizens, and thus by her private decisions strengthen the civic order in which she lived.[28] In the intensity of her insistence that a woman be trained to respect herself, to take pride in her own competence, and to be prepared to support herself, Murray reveals herself a member of a generation of survivors who found in her faith and her own ambition the strength to persevere.

When Judith Sargent Stevens committed herself to the support of the itinerant minister John Murray and the new Universalist Church, she acted with a group that was disproportionately female. This disproportion was not uncommon in Protestant churches; indeed Cotton Mather had long since commented that the ratio established at the Cross ("three Marys to one Christ") persisted in modern churches. Demographers have confirmed the pattern that Mather saw; Richard Shiels reports that the percentage of women among the new members of Congregational churches in Massachusetts increased sharply in the early stages of the war, rising from a low of 54 percent in 1768 to a high of 72 percent in 1777.[29] Women seem to have been particularly receptive to other forms of religious revival and recruitment; they made up large numbers of new Methodists, for example. Methodism had a particular appeal to women because its rhetoric of method and system was congruent with the practical lives of housekeepers, and also

---

28. Kerber, *Women of the Republic*, and "The Republican Mother: Women and the Enlightenment—An American Perspective," *American Quarterly* 28 (1976): 187–205 [reprinted in the present volume]. See also Jan Lewis, "The Republican Wife: Virtue and Seduction in the Early Republic," *William and Mary Quarterly*, 3d ser., 44 (1987): 689–721.

29. Richard D. Shiels, "The Feminization of American Congregationalism," *American Quarterly* 33 (1981): 46–62.

because of the important place it gave to John Wesley's mother, Susannah, as a teacher and founder of the sect. Mother Ann Lee, founder of the Shakers, arrived in America on the eve of the Revolution with a message that included equal rights for women and an equal role for them in the Shaker community; her audiences were heavily female, as were those of Jemima Wilkinson, the "Publick Universal Friend."[30] For many women, excluded from formal schooling and with limited access to reading material, intellectual development took the form of religious contemplation. Evidence of this remains in diaries that are primarily summaries of religious pamphlets and the Bible; a major example of this genre are the diaries of Mary Moody Emerson, who filled thousands of pages with religious speculation and meditation.[31]

In this context, a pamphlet bearing the title *Women Invited to War*, published in Boston in 1787, is less idiosyncratic than appears at first glance.[32] The author identified herself as a "Daughter of America" and addressed herself to the "worthy women, and honourable daughters of America." She observed that "it is our lot to live in a time of remarkable difficulty, trouble, and danger . . . yet blessed be God, we have had the honour and favour of seeing our friends and brethren exert themselves valiantly in defense of life and liberty" (3). While the author wrote, the Constitution was being prepared and ratified; the pamphlet begins as a predictable political exercise.

But the author quickly moved away from politics and war to another enemy, Satan, "who has done more harm already, than all the armies of Britain have done or ever will be able to do . . . we shall all be destroyed or

---

30. See the thoughtful discussions of Ann Lee and Jemima Wilkinson in Ruth H. Bloch, *Visionary Republic: Millennial Themes in American Thought, 1756–1800* (Cambridge: Cambridge University Press, 1985), 88–91, and in Stephen A. Marini, *Radical Sects of Revolutionary New England* (Cambridge, Mass.: Harvard University Press, 1982), *passim.*

31. Her extensive diaries, almanacs, and commonplace books are in the collection of the Emerson Family Papers, Houghton Library, Harvard University. See particularly Phyllis Cole, "The Advantage of Loneliness: Mary Moody Emerson's Almanacks, 1802–1855," in *Emerson: Retrospect and Prospect*, ed. Joel Porte (Cambridge, Mass.: Harvard University Press, 1983), 1–32. See also the extended diaries of Elizabeth Drinker, Historical Society of Pennsylvania.

32. This pamphlet had traditionally, but unreliably, been ascribed to the historian Hannah Adams.

brought into captivity, if the women as well as the men, do not oppose, resist, and fight against this destructive enemy" (3).

As she wrote, her voice shifted and the argument became exhortation:

> Are there not many in America, unto whom the Lord is speaking, as to his people of old, saying, The spoil of the poor is in our houses . . . Thou hast despised mine holy things, and hath profaned my sabbaths . . . Because of swearing the land mourneth . . . The people of the land have used oppression, and exercised robbery, and have vexed the poor and needy . . . Hath not almost every sin which brought destruction upon Jerusalem, been committed in America? (7–9)

Then the "Daughter of America" assumed an unusual voice—the voice of the minister, speaking to the special responsibilities of women and articulating the murmur that men were more prone to sin than were women:

> But perhaps some of you may say, there are some very heinous sins, which our sex are not so commonly guilty of, as the men are; in particular the vile sin of drinking to excess, and also prophane swearing and cursing, and taking the great and holy name of God in vain, are practiced more by men than by women . . .

There was a paradox: the same men who were particularly guilty of sin were generally thought to be the leaders in religious affairs. She suspected her audience would assert "therefore let them rise up first . . ." (10). To this she responded that all were equal in Christ, that Eve had been made from Adam's rib to walk by his side—not from his foot, to be trampled underneath—and that "in the rights of religion and conscience . . . There is neither male nor female, but all are one in Christ." (12).[33]

In a few pages the author had moved from the contemplation of women in war emergencies to the argument that women ought to conduct their wars according to definitions that were different from men's; that the main tasks that faced the republic were spiritual rather than political; and that in these spiritual tasks women could take the lead, indeed that they had a special responsibility to display "mourning and lamentation" (13).

"Daughter of America" can be located in a long Christian pacifist tradition of opposition to war. This tradition competed with religiously

33. This is a common image for eighteenth- and nineteenth-century feminists to use; see, for example, [A Lady], *Female Advocate* (New Haven, 1801), 30; see also 19–20.

grounded claims for "just wars." In the era of the American Revolution conscientious objectors often found it hard to distinguish themselves from Loyalists, for the practical outcome of both positions was the same: failure to resist British rule. Philadelphia Quakers sometimes crossed the line from pacifist neutrality into Loyalism; in New York and Massachusetts Mother Ann Lee's supporters were explicitly accused of Loyalism. John Murray apparently volunteered for a stint as minister to Nathanael Greene's troops in order to dispel suspicions that Universalists were Loyalist. But within the traditional denominations, even those whose ministers made up the "black regiment" of the patriot cause, there were many skeptics who saw the Revolution not as an occasion for patriotic enthusiasm, but as a sign of human depravity. Laurel Thatcher Ulrich has called our attention to the 1779 broadside "A New Touch on the Times . . . By a Daughter of Liberty, living in Marblehead." Molly Gutridge refused to make distinctions between Patriot and Tory. "For sin is all the cause of this, / We must not take it then amiss, / Wan't it for our polluted tongues / This cruel war would ne'er begun." Tongues polluted by swearing and a society permeated by sin were the natural breeding grounds of war.[34]

The roles and functions of Protestant churches in revolutionary America were sharply different from the roles and functions of the Catholic Church in revolutionary France. The rejection of the Church meant that French revolutionaries needed to invent their own alternate public spaces and their own public ritual. In doing so they developed dramatic formulations: parades, mass oath-takings on the Champ de Mars, armed processions—in all of which women participated in a structured and dramatic fashion. This need for mass public creation of new rituals was muted in America, where churches were more likely to be prorevolutionary and where patriotic clergy voluntarily offered ritual dramatization in support of the Revolution.

In the aftermath of the war, many women continued to define their civic obligations in this religious way; the way to save the city, argued the "Daughter of America," was to purify one's behavior and pray for the sins

34. For clerical support of the Revolution, see Patricia U. Bonomi, *Under the Cope of Heaven: Religion, Society, and Politics in Colonial America* (New York: Oxford University Press, 1986), 209–16; Laurel Thatcher Ulrich, " 'Daughters of Liberty': Religious Women in Revolutionary New England," in *Women in the Age of the American Revolution*, ed. Ronald Hoffman and Peter J. Albert (Charlottesville: University Press of Virginia, 1989), 228–35.

of the community. By the early nineteenth century, women flooded into the dissenting churches of the Second Great Awakening, bringing their husbands and children with them, and asserting that their claim to religious salvation made possible new forms of assertive behavior—criticizing sinful conduct of their friends and neighbors, sometimes traveling to new communities and establishing new schools, sometimes widening in a major way the scope of the books they read. Churches also provided the context for women's benevolent activity. Despairing perhaps of the hope that secular politics would clear up the shattered debris of the war, religious women organized societies for the support of widows and orphans in a heretofore unparalleled collective endeavor.[35] If women were to be invited to war, they would join their own war and on their own terms.

In her galaxy of women worthies, Murray mentioned the unusual career of Patience Lovell Wright. Patience Wright enjoyed minor fame as a wax portraitist, a medium that now lingers on in the guise of garish "Madame Tussaud" tourist ventures but that was in the eighteenth century a fashionable and reasonably inexpensive way of creating a likeness. In 1772, possibly with the encouragement of Benjamin Franklin, she established her trade in London. She was, wrote Murray, "a profound politician," and eventually ruined her business by her too-obvious sympathies with the rebel cause.[36]

Murray only knew the rudiments of Wright's story, but if any life could have demonstrated the proof of Murray's warning that women should be prepared to make their own way in the world, it was the lives of Wright and her sister, Rachel Wells. Wells is one of the rare members of the artisan class whose life it is possible to reconstruct with some degree of detail, and who left us reasonably clear testimony about her commitment to the Revolution and what she expected from it.

An important clue to Wells's identity is embedded in her petition, in a

35. For the career of one woman whose life was changed in this way, see Samuel Worcester, *The Christian Mourning with Hope: A Sermon . . . on the Occasion of the Death of Mrs. Eleanor [Read] Emerson . . . to which are Annexed Writings of Mrs. Emerson* (Boston: Lincoln and Edmonds, 1809). I discussed this episode more extensively in "Can a Woman Be an Individual? The Limits of Puritan Tradition in the Early Republic," *Texas Studies in Literature and Language* 25 (1983): 165–78. See also Anne M. Boylan, "Life Cycle Patterns Among Organized Women in New York and Boston, 1797–1840," *American Quarterly* 38 (1986): 779–97.

36. Constantia [pseud.], *The Gleaner: A Miscellaneous Production* (Boston: I. Thomas and E. T. Andrews, 1798), 2:284–88.

A determined Patience Wright carries a liberty pole and cap
in this drawing by John Downman.
Courtesy Trustees of the British Museum.

paragraph in which she mentioned her "Sister Wright" and Wright's activities as a spy in London in the years before the war. Rachel Lovell Wells
seems to have assisted her sister in exhibitions in Philadelphia, Charleston,
and New York. In 1772, encouraged by a meeting with Benjamin Franklin's
sister, Jane Mecom, Patience Lovell Wright set out for England to seek fame
as a portraitist. Arriving at a time when tension with the colonies was high,

and entering houses of the upper class for portrait sittings, Wright apparently was in a good position to overhear comments that would be useful to Benjamin Franklin, in his role as colonial agent. As might be expected, her sister overestimated Wright's contributions. ". . . how did she make her Cuntry her whole atention," Wells wrote in 1786. "her Letters gave us ye first alarm . . . She sent Letters in buttons & picturs heads to me, ye first in Congress atended Constantly to me for them in that perilous hour. . . ."

Included in the papers of Benjamin Franklin and John Adams are indeed a letter to each from Patience Wright, and she does appear to have done some smuggling of information. But her spying appears to have been of the most minor sort, and it is of interest to us primarily in that it clearly encouraged Rachel Wells to believe that her own claims on the republic could be made with special force because another member of her family had also served the Revolution.[37] "I think gentelmen that I can ask for my Intrust as an individual on Her account Now She is no more I oneley want my one."

The story of Rachel Wells does not have a happy ending. Her letter to Franklin asking for funds for a burial plot in America for Wright seems to have gotten no response. Her petitions to the legislature of New Jersey were read but apparently no action was taken. Still unsatisfied, she petitioned the Continental Congress; there too her petition was tabled.[38] When she came to draw up her will in 1795 she had only a modest amount of property to dispose of; her furniture and her "waring apriall" was divided among her sisters. Her share in a building in Bordentown went to her sisters and perhaps nieces. But she did not forget her claim: "if there be any moneys Left on bonds Standing out my will is that it be kept out for the Intrust & use of it for Sarah Wright and Rachel Finkings. . . ."[39]

37. Charles Coleman Sellers, *Patience Wright: American Artist and Spy in George III's London* (Middletown, Conn.: Wesleyan University Press, 1976), chaps. 5, 6, *et passim*; [Rachel Wells] to Benjamin Franklin, 16 December 1785, American Philosophical Society. I am grateful to *The Papers of Benjamin Franklin*, Yale University, for this reference.

38. See "Votes and Proceedings," 10th General Assembly, New Jersey Legislature, New Jersey Archives, Trenton.

39. Will of Rachel Wells, item 11709C, New Jersey Archives, Trenton. A "List of Ratables" for Chesterfield Township, Burlington County, the same year includes Rachel Wells as an individual householder with a house and lot valued at 12 pounds; her tax was 4 shillings 3 pence, which ranked her modestly in the town but not at the very bottom. She had no horses, cattle, nor slaves.

III

It is the common sense of the matter that no group can expect specific benefits from a revolution unless it has, as a collective body, been a force in making that revolution happen. Women had indeed served in and supported the American Revolution—as individuals, not as groups—but in 1787 were not in a strong position to make collective demands as a group. Political republicanism in America rested heavily on a definition of citizenship that privileged men for qualities that distinguished them from women; "luxury, effeminacy and corruption" was as much a revolutionary-era triad as "life, liberty and happiness."[40] If there were opportunities in the republican order that women would find useful, they would have to seize their opportunities and transform them into reality. Rachel Wells was not the only woman who could claim, "I did my Posabels every way . . . Ive Don as much to help on this war as Though I had bin a good Soger."[41] But as an individual she had only the most marginal hope of influencing the government to grant her petition. The petition itself remained in the archives of the Continental Congress and the New Jersey legislature; it never received a form in which it could hope to shape public opinion.

Republican ideology was antipatriarchal in the sense that it voiced, as Tom Paine had accurately sensed, the claim of adult men to be freed from the control of male governors who had defined themselves as rulers and political "fathers" in an antique monarchical system. But republican ideology did not eliminate the political father immediately and completely; rather it held a liberal ideology of individualism in ambivalent tension with the old ideology of patriarchy.[42] The men who remodeled the American polity after the war remodeled it in their own image. Their anxieties for the stability of their construction led them, in emphasizing its reasonableness, its solidity, its link to classical models, also to emphasize its manliness, its freedom from effeminacy. The construction of the autonomous, patriotic,

40. See, for one among many examples, George Washington to James Warren, 7 October 1785, *Writings of Washington, From the Original Manuscript Sources, 1745–1799*, ed. John C. Fitzpatrick (Washington, D.C.: U.S. Government Printing Office, 1931–44), 28:290.

41. "Rachel Wells Petition for Relief," 15 November 1785, New Jersey Archives, Trenton.

42. Thus George Washington quickly became the "father of his country"; at the Governor's Palace in Williamsburg, Virginia, the life-size portrait of George III was quickly replaced by a life-size portrait of Washington in the same pose.

male citizen required that the traditional relationship of women with unreliability, unpredictability, and lust be emphasized. Women's weakness became a rhetorical foil for republican manliness.[43]

When we encounter women of the American revolutionary generation articulating the conclusions they had drawn from that experience, we find them saying that what women needed was psychological independence, personal self-respect, a decent self-sufficiency, and a life over which they exercised some measure of control. Rachel Wells believed she had a right not to be ignored and to have her debts paid; the author of *Women Invited to War* asserted that women could pray without waiting for men to lead them; and Judith Sargent Murray called for "self-complacency," for psychological and economic self-sufficiency. These were precisely the grounds on which Tom Paine in 1776 had expressed men's views of the common sense of the matter.

Men who developed the new republican formulations developed them out of extended negotiations and struggle with other men; they assumed that women's part in the equation would remain constant. For all the emphasis on the need of the republican citizen to control his own property, for example, it does not seem to have occurred to any male patriot to attack coverture. "Put it out of the power of our husbands to use us with impunity," wrote Abigail Adams, suggesting that domestic violence should be on the republican agenda, but John Adams did not place it there.[44] Pensions were provided for retired officers, not for their widows.

If women were to devise a republican ideology that provided for autonomy, they first would have to destabilize and then renegotiate their relationships with men. We can follow the course of this effort in the newly formulated understanding of courtship and marriage that appeared explicitly in advice literature and implicitly in fiction. Advice literature counseled "friendship" and mutual respect between husbands and wives; it became a point of pride for republican spouses to address each other as "friend."[45] Fiction portrayed a world in which virtue was female, and must

43. See Christine Stansell, *City of Women: Sex and Class in New York 1789–1860* (New York: Knopf, 1986), 20–26, and Kerber, *Women of the Republic*, 31.

44. Nancy F. Cott, "Passionlessness: An Interpretation of Victorian Sexual Ideology, 1790–1850," *Signs: Journal of Women in Culture and Society* 4 (1978): 219–36.

45. See, for example, the comments in Lynne Withey, *Dearest Friend: A Life of Abigail Adams* (New York: Free Press, 1981). The transition from "My dearest girl" to "My friend" can be traced in the correspondence of Albert and Hannah Nicolson Gallatin, *Papers of Albert Gallatin*, Microfilm Reel 3, New-York Historical Society.

always be on guard against trickery and seduction; Judith Sargent Murray was one among many writers who counseled young women to take control of their choices in the major life decisions open to them.[46] Only in fiction was a language developed that made it possible to hint at the idea that women might have *interests* that were different than those of men. Extensively published and widely read, fiction reached more minds than theoretical political pamphlets, and was used by its readers to shape their understanding of the world in which they lived.

In short, women could not leave it to men to express what women thought of republican politics. It is interesting but frustrating to speculate on the course of affairs had Quaker women been part of the republican community from the beginning. Quakers were the single group of women already explicitly socialized to conducting their own institutions, negotiating with men on terms of at least rhetorical equality, and to speaking out loud in public to audiences of both sexes. But the pacifism of Quaker women meant that they remained outside the republic during the war years, aligned, for the most part, with Tories. With the rest of their fellow believers, it would take time for them to regain credibility. The role that Lucretia Mott and others of her generation played in the 1840s in articulating the claims of women on the republic and in educating the next generation to a women's criticism of the Constitution and the law suggests that republican ideology was ambivalent from the beginning, but in ways that only the trained eye could see, and the voice that might have articulated a criticism lacked political credibility. Not even Tom Paine, though he came close, could comprehend that "common sense" was gendered.

46. I have developed this point in chapter 8 of *Women of the Republic*. See also Jay Fliegelman, *Prodigals and Pilgrims: The American Revolution Against Patriarchal Authority 1750–1800* (New York: Cambridge University Press, 1982); Cathy Davidson, *Revolution and the Word: The Rise of the Novel in America* (New York: Oxford University Press, 1987); and Jan Lewis, "The Republican Wife: Virtue and Seduction in the Early Republic," *William and Mary Quarterly* 44 (1987): 689–721; and Carroll Smith-Rosenberg, "Engendering Virtue," in *Literature and the Body: Essays on Populations and Persons*, ed. Elaine Scarry (Baltimore: Johns Hopkins University Press, 1988), 160–84.

THE REPUBLICAN IDEOLOGY OF THE REVOLUTIONARY GENERATION

Fraud lurks in generals. There is not a more unintelligible word in the English language than republicanism.

JOHN ADAMS to Mercy Otis Warren, 8 August 1807

Not so long ago, as we reckon academic styles, American historians used the ungainly term "early national period" to describe the years between the adoption of the Constitution and the inauguration of Andrew Jackson. The phrase was so vague as to be of little use except to underline a general sense that nationalism was central to American life. A new label has been devised in the last decade: the modest phrase "early republic" is not much more descriptive, but it is richer in nuance. Aggressive nationalism has come to seem somewhat less important to an understanding of the early American political system than does the widely shared sense that Americans were engaged in a republican experiment. Substitution of "republican" for "national" in the historians' lexicon may have had some relationship to a growing distaste, among people writing in the midst of the Vietnam conflict, for nationalism as a nonpejorative explanatory device. But it also owes much to an enlarged sensitivity to and respect for words as carriers of culture, and to a respect for ideology as an authentic expression of political situation and cultural condition. It also represents historians' response to a growing

I am grateful for the careful readings Dorothy Ross, Lewis Perry, John Murrin, Sydney V. James and Richard Beeman gave to earlier drafts of this essay. The usual reminders that they are not responsible for my failures apply with special force.

body of work that seeks to place the concepts of republicanism in a practical political context, a context large enough, in the hands of Bernard Bailyn and his students: to include the opposition politics of eighteenth-century Britain; and stretching even further back, in the hands of J. G. A. Pocock, to the Florentine Renaissance.

As more and more historians swelled the crowd who came to recognize the achievement of a republic as a legitimate goal of the Revolutionary generation, Robert Shalhope thoughtfully provided an umbrella for them in his essay, "Toward a Republican Synthesis." Like Moliere's gentleman who was delighted to discover he was speaking prose, thanks to Shalhope a collection of rather disparate historians have discovered that they were part of a school. Shalhope's use of the tentative "toward" in his title suggests that agreement on the use of the concept of republicanism in explaining American political culture had not yet been reached in 1972, as indeed it still is not. But it is certainly possible to identify some of its main features and to suggest some of the ways in which our understanding of early American society and culture is being reshaped.[1]

Republicanism was once thought to be a simple, even self-evident, matter. It does not appear at all in Randolph G. Adams' magisterial *Political Ideas of the American Revolution*, nor did Carl Becker need it to explain *The Declaration of Independence*. The only place where the word republican appears in the Constitution is Article IV, section 4: "The United States shall guarantee to every state in this union a Republican form of government, and shall protect each of them against invasion; and, on application of the

---

1. Robert Shalhope, "Toward a Republican Synthesis: The Emergence of an Understanding of Republicanism in American Historiography," *William and Mary Quarterly* (hereafter cited as *WMQ*), 3d ser., 29 (1972), 49–80, and idem, "Republicanism and Early American Historiography," ibid., 39 (1982), 334–56. The latter historiographical article deals with the work that appeared in the intervening decade. Other recent historiographical essays include J. G. A. Pocock, "*The Machiavellian Moment* Revisited: A Study in History and Ideology," *Journal of World History*, 53 (1981), 49–72; Isaac Kramnick, "Republican Revisionism Revisited," *American Historical Review*, 87 (1982), 629–64. Other important essays include Gordon W. Wood, "Conspiracy and the Paranoid Style: Causality and Deceit in the Eighteenth Century," *WMQ*, 39 (1982), 401–41; and Rowland Berthoff, "Peasants and Artisans, Puritans and Republicans: Personal Liberty and Communal Equality in American History," *Journal of American History*, 69 (1982), 579–98.

legislature, or of the executive, (when the legislature can not be convened), against domestic violence."[2]

Usually republicanism was simply what monarchism was not; the usage was vague, and in *The Federalist* no. 39, James Madison kept it general: "we may define a republic to be, or at least may bestow that name on, a government which derives all its powers directly or indirectly from the body of the people; and is administered by persons holding their offices during pleasure, for an unlimited period, or during good behavior." Often, the argument between Federalist and Anti-Federalist had to do with the sort of republic each had in mind, rather than whether to have a republic at all. Madison was at some pains to assure his readers that all existing state constitutions fit the broad definition of "republican form" in the federal constitution. Each state had a wide range of options, and the federal government did not need to take a position on each one. For example, in the Constitutional Convention Gouverneur Morris could be reassured that the guarantee of a republican form of government would not require the federal government to guarantee the paper money laws of Rhode Island. (Madison should be pardoned if he could not foresee that the issue would be raised again in the debates over the admission of Utah to the Union, when it would be alleged that a community that countenanced polygamy could not possibly have a republican form of government.)[3]

In *The Federalist*, Madison also separated the matter of guaranteeing republican forms from the assurance that rebellion would be put down. He

2. Randolph G. Adams, *Political Ideas of the American Revolution* (Durham: Trinity College Press, 1922); Carl Becker, *The Declaration of Independence* (New York: Knopf, 1922, 1942).

3. *The Federalist* no. 39. See also *The Federalist* no. 14 and *The Federalist* no. 10: "a Government in which the scheme of representation takes place." [Also implied is majority rule and an absence of hereditary office.] Herbert Storing makes the point that the word *democracy* "is ambiguous, containing a range of ideas from simple, direct popular rule to a regulated, checked, mitigated rule of the people. Generally, especially when aiming at precision of expression, both the Federalists and the Anti-Federalists used the term 'popular government' to contain this whole range of ideas, reserving 'democracy' for the former end of the scale and 'republic' for the latter." See "What the Anti-Federalists Were *For*," in *The Complete Anti-Federalist* (Chicago: Univ. of Chicago Press, 1981), 1:90, n. 19. For polygamy, see Frederick Merk, *The History of the Westward Movement* (New York: Knopf, 1978), 111. I am grateful to Lewis Perry for providing this reference.

assumed that rebellion would come from antirepublicans, seeking "aristo-cratic or monarchical innovations." Despite Shays' Rebellion, which he regarded as "commotions" rather than a coherent challenge to the princi-ples of republicanism, he did not in *The Federalist* explore alternative responses to future rebellions which might seek to increase the degree of republicanism. The states had the right to expect "that the forms of govern-ment under which the compact was entered into, should be substantially maintained."[4]

As it turned out, little recourse has been had to the constitutional clause guaranteeing a republican form of government. It was not used to settle the issues in Rhode Island's Dorr War in 1841, even though the popular tumult was explicitly about whether the state's government was authentically re-publican. In *Luther v. Borden* (1849) the Supreme Court left it to the Presi-dent to decide which of two contending governors was the lawful executive rather than rule on the proper degree of republicanism.[5] In the antebellum years there was no attempt to force the judiciary to any determination that slavery was unrepublican; indeed after the Dred Scott case the Court surely would have said that slavery was republican, just as it told Virginia Minor in 1875 that it was republican to exclude women from the suffrage. The definition was an operational one even if it risked being circular; what had been acceptable in 1789 was in good faith to be respected subsequently as authentically republican.

But critics of the Court—abolitionists and suffragists—complained that the Court's definition was too narrow, a choice of form over substance. "The will of the entire people is the true basis of republican government," asserted Victoria Woodhull in 1871.[6] To insist on the "essence" of republi-

---

4. *The Federalist* no. 43. Madison's reluctance to define Shays' as a rebellion challeng-ing the foundations of the republic may be due to the fact that his criticism of the Shaysites was balanced by his reluctance to use excessive force to silence a majority. He was particularly troubled by efforts to disguise anti-Shaysite recruiting by the fiction that enlistments were needed to put down a nonexistent Indian uprising. See Irving Brant, *James Madison: The Nationalist* (Indianapolis: Bobbs-Merrill Co., 1948), 391, 401.

5. Arthur E. Bonfield, "The Guarantee Clause of Article IV, Section 4: A Study in Constitutional Desuetude," *Minnesota Law Review*, 46 (1962), 533–34.

6. Ibid., 537, 548; Victoria Woodhull, "Address to the Judiciary Committee of the House of Representatives," 11 January 1871, reprinted in Anne Firor Scott and Andrew McKay Scott, *One Half the People: The Fight for Woman Suffrage* (Urbana: Univ. of Illinois Press, 1982), 78. See also Arthur E. Bonfield, "*Baker v. Carr*: New Light on

canism had the effect of driving the term *republican* into the realm of metaphor and uncertainty, making it vulnerable to a host of alternate and conflicting definitions. It would be available to signify almost anything so long as it was nonmonarchical. It would become rich in overtones, useable in alternate contexts; we find ourselves speaking of republican religion, republican children, republican motherhood.

I suspect these varying definitions may help to explain why so little attention was paid to republicanism as ideology by otherwise sensitive and intelligent historians for so long. They naturally expected to find a political term accompanied by political analysis; instead "republicanism" was more likely, when it appeared, to be accompanied by hyperbole. A political term not used in a disciplined way was naturally taken to be a screen for self-interest, probably economic; the task of the historical analyst seemed to be to penetrate behind the metaphor to economic and political reality. When historians of the Progressive generation—who were already inclined to expect reality to lurk behind a screen of self-interest—came upon politicians arguing about the qualities of a republic they hastily concluded that the argument must *really* be about something else.

In the 1950s, however, there was a fresh sense of the importance of metaphor. J. H. Hexter has ascribed this interest simply to "a common sense, accessible to everybody in the craft, of the impropriety of anachronism."[7] Common sense surely did have something to do with renewed respect for rhetoric and willingness to take words and their overtones seriously. But so too did the reaction of a generation of historians, for whom Edmund Morgan spoke in his 1957 essay, "The American Revolution: Revisions in Need of Revising," who admired the Progressive historians but began to suspect that the case had been overstated and oversimplified. "In the study of history," Morgan would write a few years later, "it is always dangerous to assume that men do not mean what they say, that

---

the Constitutional Guarantee of Republican Government," *California Law Review*, 50 (1962), 245–63; J. R. Pole, *The Pursuit of Equality in American History* (Berkeley: Univ. of California Press, 1978), 113ff; William M. Wiecek, *The Guarantee Clause of the United States Constitution* (Ithaca: Cornell Univ. Press, 1972).

7. J. H. Hexter, "Republic, Virtue, Liberty, and the Political Universe of J. G. A. Pocock," in J. H. Hexter, ed., *On Historians: Reappraisals of Some of the Makers of Modern History* (Cambridge: Harvard Univ. Press, 1974), 267, n. 5. See also the chapter entitled, "Languages and Their Implications," in J. G. A. Pocock, *Politics, Language and Time* (New York: Atheneum, 1971), 3–41.

words are a facade which must be penetrated in order to arrive at some fundamental but hidden reality."[8]

This shift was contemporaneous with the development of studies of culture in the 1950s, the establishment of programs that were then called American Civilization, and the popularity of books like Henry Nash Smith's *Virgin Land* or John William Ward's *Andrew Jackson: Symbol for an Age*, which demonstrated how profitable it could be to read second- and third-rate literature and political pamphlets with the critical care usually given to literary texts. This development in turn was also dependent on a technological revolution in the accessibility of research materials. Thanks to microfilm and Readex microprint, every major university library could hold virtually every item in standard bibliographies of rare books and pamphlets. From the late 1950s on, graduate students had ready access to resources which an older generation of senior scholars had sought out at substantial expense.[9] As a result, historians began to argue, with Marshall Smelser, that the Federalist period had been "an Age of Passion." John Howe linked the passion to republicanism, and, from the 1960s on, historians were apt to pay careful attention to the revolutionary generation's choice of words—especially when that generation appeared to be saying that republicanism was at the core of their actions.[10]

"Republicanism," wrote Gordon Wood, "meant more for Americans than simply the elimination of a king and the institution of an elective system. It added a moral dimension, a utopian depth, to the political separation from England—a depth that involved the very character of their society." The major themes of republicanism, as Wood outlined them, included the inspiration of classical antiquity, self-disciplined civic virtue, and equality of opportunity. In this context, Montesquieu was particularly useful; indeed he had been cited in the Constitutional Convention more than Locke. One way or another, Montesquieu had said, all governments

8. Edmund S. Morgan, "The Revolution Considered as an Intellectual Movement," originally published in 1963, reprinted in *The Challenge of the American Revolution* (New York: Norton, 1976), 60. For Morgan's comments on his generation of historians, see his introductory notes to "Revisions in Need of Revising," originally published 1957, in *Challenge*, 43–59.

9. Henry Nash Smith, *Virgin Land* (Cambridge: Harvard Univ. Press, 1950); John William Ward, *Andrew Jackson: Symbol for an Age* (New York: Oxford Univ. Press, 1955).

10. Marshall Smelser, "The Federalist Period as an Age of Passion," *American Quarterly* (hereafter cited as *AQ*), 10 (1958), 391–419; John R. Howe, "Republican Thought and the Political Violence of the 1790's," ibid., 19 (1967), 147–65.

rested on their subjects; what makes the law effective in despotic governments is fear; what makes law effective in a republic is virtue. When post-Revolutionary Americans worried whether a virtuous citizenry would continue to sustain the republic, their words were less likely to be seen by historians as hyperbole and more likely to be understood as expressions of concern rooted in their culture and their education.[11]

Meanwhile, historians of Britain were doing their own variety of listening with care. The answers to the old question—why did the least-taxed people in the western world make a revolution about taxes?—seemed to be found in an ever more complex British-American social and political interaction. Setting the American Revolution in its eighteenth-century context, hearing the language of British political rivalry transplanted to America, we understand better the sources of the complaint that British policies were infected by hypocrisy and corruption. Indeed, thanks to J. G. A. Pocock's *The Machiavellian Moment*, we now understand the legacy of early modern republican theory to be a far more complex and ambivalent inheritance than we once thought it to be. In the antique balance between "the one, the few, and the many," the cards were stacked in favor of the few. In the Venetian Republic, even the Great Council, ostensibly the forum of "the many," was strictly confined to representatives of a severely limited list of old aristocratic families; in Florence its counterpart was more accessible but still closed to the *hoi polloi*. Republicanism could be comfortably congruent with aristocracy; it certainly was expected that the citizen had enough property to free himself to find his fulfillment in serving the public good. Republicanism was, in Pocock's words, "a civic and patriot ideal" which did not necessarily imply that all people, or even all men, were part of the political scheme. The ideal *did* imply that male citizens were made independent by their control of property. Moreover, it was understood that the integrity of republicans was perpetually threatened by corruption.[12]

Republicanism in America thus claimed a complex political heritage. It

11. Gordon S. Wood, *The Creation of the American Republic 1776–1787* (Chapel Hill: Univ. of North Carolina Press, 1969), 47–53; see also Linda K. Kerber, *Federalists in Dissent: Imagery and Ideology in Jeffersonian America* (Ithaca: Cornell Univ. Press, 1970), ch. 7.

12. J. G. A. Pocock, *The Machiavellian Moment: Florentine Political Thought and the Atlantic Republican Tradition* (Princeton: Princeton Univ. Press, 1975), 507. For an important and fresh reading of the theme of corruption, see Gordon S. Wood, "Conspiracy and the Paranoid Style: Causality and Deceit in the Eighteenth Century," *WMQ*, 39 (1982), 401–41.

had traveled from Renaissance Italy and early modern France into the political language of the eighteenth-century British Opposition, located solidly among country gentry who looked with suspicion on the patronage and the commercialism of metropolitan politics in London. Following Pocock's suggestion, John Murrin, Lance Banning and A. G. Roeber had traced Country habits of thought as carriers of civic republicanism into the American eighteenth and nineteenth centuries. They have shown that it is often easier to line up Americans of the Revolutionary era in terms of their congruity with British Court and Country political alignments than in terms of how well they anticipated nineteenth-century categories of Left and Right. Murrin observed astutely:

> The Court-Country paradigm heavily colored nearly all participants' perceptions of the issues and personalities of the era. The political rhetoric of the age implicitly assumed a spectrum of possibilities from an extreme Court position on the right, through Hamiltonism, then various stages of moderation in the middle, then a pure Country position on the left, and on to radical jacobinism. . . . Wherever one stood in this spectrum, he was likely to suspect anyone to his right of sinister conspiracies against liberty. . . . Conversely, everybody to one's left had to be flirting with disorder and anarchy.[13]

Court and Country are not neatly analogous to our modern Left and Right, because both were variants of elite politics, and because Country was itself a complex political amalgam which included Tory gentry as well as radical Whigs; Bolingbroke as well as Trenchard and Gordon. Banning has found an uncanny persistence of Country habits of thought in post-Revolutionary America, encouraging ambivalence about any policy which seemed to have elements of patronage (understood to be corruption) and forceful exercise of national power. Roeber has carefully traced the way in which leading patriot lawyers in revolutionary Virginia successfully fended off charges that they had deferred to Court interests. Although men like Jefferson, Madison and George Mason, in their desire for a more sophisti-

13. John G. Murrin, "The Great Inversion, or Court versus Country: A Comparison of the Revolution Settlements in England (1688–1721) and America (1776–1816)," in J. G. A. Pocock, ed., *Three British Revolutions: 1641, 1688, 1776* (Princeton: Princeton Univ. Press, 1980), 421. A related argument, to the effect that Court-Country polarity emerges in Federalist-Anti-Federalist debate of the 1780s, is found in James H. Hutson, "Country, Court and Constitution: Antifederalism and the Historians," *WMQ*, 38 (1981), 337–68.

cated legal system which would also be responsive to the needs of a commercial society, had something in common with Court habits, they positioned themselves as republicans and discredited the old-line Country gentry (whose spokesmen in the years of the early republic were John Taylor of Caroline and John Randolph of Roanoke). J. G. A. Pocock, Dorothy Ross, and Robert Kelley have in various ways been impressed by the persistence of classical republican patterns of reasoning long after the early republic had receded into history, and have suggested that utopian thought in nineteenth-century America ought to be understood as an effort to cling to a Country vision which in Ross's words, "would counter the corrupting effects of industrial growth with the moral strength of an agrarian yeomanry and fend off the decadence of increasing civilization with the dynamic energies bred in the conquest of nature." The old dream of the pure republic had a static quality; fear for the survival of the republic encouraged the skepticism about partisanship for which the postwar years were famous. This skepticism was also inherited from the Whig Opposition. Reading American political polemic from the other side of the ocean enormously enlarges our perspective; in this context the American was, as the title of a recent collection of essays has it, the third in a triad of *British* revolutions.[14]

But as republicanism has widened greatly in usage it is in danger of coming to signify too much and therefore to mean too little. Rowland Berthoff has recently used it to stand for the communal values of traditional peasantry; following Pocock, it has also often been taken to imply the presence of urban humanism. "Republicanism" has become so all-embracing as to absorb comfortably its own contradictions.

Yet the overtones of the term *republicanism* have not been fully identified; its possibilities as a guide—and also as a cautionary signal—for the historian are not fully played out. If it is in danger of becoming merely trendy, it has not yet become so. Historians continue to find it of use for complex pur-

14. Lance Banning, *The Jeffersonian Persuasion: Evolution of a Party Ideology* (Ithaca: Cornell Univ. Press, 1978); A. G. Roeber, *Faithful Magistrates and Republican Lawyers: Creators of Virginia Legal Culture, 1680–1810* (Chapel Hill: Univ. of North Carolina Press, 1981), ch. 7. Dorothy Ross, "The Liberal Tradition Revisited and the Republican Tradition Addressed," in John Higham and Paul K. Conkin, eds., *New Directions in American Intellectual History* (Baltimore: Johns Hopkins Univ. Press, 1979), 118. See also Robert Kelley, "Ideology and Political Culture from Jefferson to Nixon," *American Historical Review*, 82 (1977), 531–62, and J. G. A. Pocock, "Virtue and Commerce in the Eighteenth Century," *Journal of Interdisciplinary History*, 3 (1972), 119–34.

poses. But if they are to continue to use it, they will need to display increased precision in identifying its nuances. Paul Conkin has recently complained that just as the founders "had no accepted semantic convention governing their use of the word *republic*, so contemporary historians do not have a firm convention for either *republican* or ideology."[15] Perhaps it is enough to say that the appearance of "republican" is a market signifying that there is, somewhere, a political dimension to what is to be read; a warning that the critic will have to deal with metaphoric prose, will be drawn into what has been called the "hermeneutics of suspicion." As Gerald Bruns explains, "what appears to go on, whether in a mind or in any of its cognates (a text, language, society, and so on), is taken to be a problematic that needs to be penetrated by analysis in order to lay bare the structures or dynamic principles, the forces or illusions, the ideologies or systematic dispositions of desire that form the content of what *really* goes on."[16] Thus drawn in, we are perhaps not so far removed from the Progressive historians who were also sure that reality stalked somewhere *behind* the text.

Historians of the United States have displayed relatively little taste for complex theoretical analysis of how best to treat ideological terms; recently they have relied heavily on Clifford Geertz's essay "Ideology as a Cultural System." A double definition of ideology is offered there. Geertz speaks of ideology in the sense of system imposed on reality; system against received tradition. He calls attention to Edmund Burke's famous contrast between unexamined tradition and systematic ideological formulations: "The function of ideology is to make an autonomous politics possible by providing the authoritative concepts that render it meaningful." But Geertz also offers the contrasting definition that ideology is *embedded* in every culture, where it provides "maps of problematic social reality." If republicanism is thought of as the first sort of ideology then it did indeed make "autonomous politics possible" by providing the justification for revolution; but if it is of the second sort, an ideology embedded in the psychosocial map of its culture, then the American Revolution and subsequent political behavior will seem more emergent and less clearly intentional.[17] Ronald Walters has

15. Paul Conkin, review of Drew R. McCoy, *The Elusive Republic, WMQ*, 38 (1981), 301–05, quotation 304.

16. Gerald L. Bruns, *Inventions: Writing, Textuality, and Understanding in Literary History* (New Haven: Yale Univ. Press, 1982), x, xiii.

17. Clifford Geertz, "Ideology as a Cultural System," in *The Interpretation of Cultures* (New York: Basic Books, 1973), 218, 220.

warned, "Geertz's semiotics, so exciting a tool of explication, can . . . tend to freeze theory at a middle level [and] . . . ironically, has the potential to divorce itself from the gritty experiences of the common folk it intends to study . . . by elevating them to literature."[18]

Geertz has written another essay, "Common Sense as a Cultural System," which strengthens the case for the second of his two definitions, and which argues that ideology is to be located in those ideas people take so for granted that they assume no definition is needed. "In short," Geertz writes, "given the given, not everything else follows. Common sense is not what the mind cleared of cant spontaneously apprehends; it is what the mind filled with presuppositions . . . concludes."[19] For example, as Dorothy Ross, following Pocock, argues, the civic humanist legacy of republicanism "stimulated its adherents to begin to think analytically about historical conditions that could maintain virtue and about the historical changes that bred corruption; in effect, they began to develop a 'sociology of virtue.' "[20] Not only in Renaissance Florence, but in Revolutionary America, it became the common sense of the matter that social change can be controlled and directed. In fact, history itself, which had been thought to be composed of ceaselessly recurring cycles of advance, corruption, and decay, was by the late eighteenth century understood to be interruptible and vulnerable to direction toward improvement and progress. When the term *republican* creeps into Americans' discourse, especially when it is not associated with political forms, we do well to take it as a mark of an effort to systematize an understanding of the world—an effort to connect two concepts which are not obviously connected—and so to make sense of what is experienced.

Republicanism may therefore be used as a theme which helps us understand not only particular political arrangements, but the complexity of a culture. It has been used that way recently by many historians, among them John Kasson, who, in *Civilizing the Machine*, has described early nineteenth-century efforts to justify industrial change in the hope that it would strengthen republicanism. In "Raising the Republican Child," Jac-

18. Ronald G. Walters, "Signs of the Times: Clifford Geertz and Historians," *Social Research*, 47 (1980), 537–56. See also Joyce Appleby, "Ideology and the History of Political Thought," *Intellectual History Group Newsletter*, No. 2 (1980), 10–18.

19. Clifford Geertz, *Local Knowledge: Further Essays in Interpretative Anthropology* (New York: Basic Books, 1982), 84.

20. Ross, "Liberal Tradition Revisited," 117. See also Dorothy Ross, "Historical Consciousness in Nineteenth Century America," *American Historical Review*, 89 (1984), 911.

queline Reinier has linked child-rearing advice to the hope of sustaining subsequent virtuous generations.[21] Treating republicanism as a *cultural* as well as political phenomenon opens the way to evaluating the extent to which the experience of republicanism varied by gender. Montesquieu had, as in so much else, led the way. Explicitly, in *The Spirit of the Laws* and implicitly, in *The Persian Letters*, he had argued forcefully that it made a substantial difference to women whether or not they lived under a republican form of government. Despotic societies normally reduce women to a state of servitude: "In a government which requires, above all things, that a particular regard be paid to its tranquillity . . . it is absolutely necessary to shut up the women." Monarchies were apt to deflect elite women into vapid conspicuous consumption in the service of courtiers; women are better served by republics, where he assumed they are "free by the laws and [only] constrained by manners." In republics, Montesquieu suggested, women might have at least a modest degree of ability to forge their own political identities.[22]

Lester Cohen's recent subtle reading of Mercy Otis Warren provides a good example of how one woman reshaped the concept of republicanism to fit her own distinctive needs. Cohen argues that when Warren became disillusioned with Federalists, she drew on traditional political analysis and blamed Federalist failures on corruption. In an effort to forge her own personal identity as a republican and in an attempt to integrate public and private roles for herself, she subsequently developed, in Cohen's words, an analysis which identified "the role of mother with republican principles." Warren's answer to the question of how virtue can be preserved is that women would sustain civic virtue by subordinating their own self-fulfillment to the needs of the republic. They would raise their sons to be active citizens committed to the good of the republic; they would monitor their relations with their husbands and other men so as to reinforce and reward displays of civic virtue. The irony, as Cohen sees it, is that Warren was prepared to sacrifice her autonomy to republicanism at the moment when her male counterparts, though also committed Anti-Federalists, were drifting away from civic republicanism and were slowly being co-opted into

21. John E. Kasson, *Civilizing the Machine* (New York: Penguin Books, 1977); Jacqueline Reinier, "Rearing the Republican Child: Attitudes and Practices in Post-Revolutionary Philadelphia," *WMQ*, 3rd ser., 39 (1982).

22. Charles Louis de Secondat, Baron de Montesquieu, *The Spirit of the Laws*, trans. Thomas Nugent (New York: Hafner Publishing Co., 1949), I, 101–04.

positions of self-aggrandizement and of national power where they tested their principles and compromised on issues, participating in the complex development of postwar republicanism. Excluded from this experience, female republicanism became, Cohen concludes, an exercise in nostalgia.[23]

Although the language usually used gender-neutral terms, republicanism did indeed have different variants for men and for women. It could hardly be otherwise in a culture which had not begun seriously to question the inherited assumption that men and women have distinctive relationships and responsibilities to the state. Indeed the political incompatibility of men and women was embedded in the language of early modern political discourse. Virtue was understood to be a male attribute, not only because of its obvious derivation from the Latin root *vir* but also because it was steadily contrasted with its opposite, *Fortuna*—understood to be a feminine attribute. *Fortuna* was feminine not only because of its etymology, but also because it was personified as an eccentric, changeable, female quality, symbolized by her wheel, emblem of insecurity and chance. "This opposition," writes Pocock, "was frequently expressed in the image of a sexual relation: a masculine active intelligence was seeking to dominate a feminine passive unpredictability which would submissively reward him for his strength or vindictively betray him for his weakness." In a new, insightful study of Machiavelli's thought, Hanna Fenichel Pitkin takes her theme from a famous passage in *The Prince*, in which the distrust of women is explicit: "it is better to be impetuous than cautious, because Fortune is a woman and it is necessary to keep her under, to cuff and maul her."[24]

A political language fully composed of civil republican terms could not effectively describe an active role for women in the republic. Indeed, it was absolutely frozen at a standstill by the element in Florentine republicanism, derived directly from Roman republicanism, which assumed that the *sine qua non* of citizenship is the ability to bear arms in defense of the republic. Since Americans found the notion of the woman in arms outrageous, the

23. Lester Cohen, "Explaining the Revolution: Ideology and Ethics in Mercy Otis Warren's Historical Theory," *WMQ*, 37 (1980), 200–18, and idem, "Mercy Otis Warren: The Politics of Language and the Aesthetics of Self," *AQ*, 35 (1983), 481–98.

24. Pocock, *Machiavellian Moment*, 37, Hanna Fenichel Pitkin, *Fortune Is A Woman: Gender and Politics in the Thought of Niccolo Machiavelli* (Berkeley: Univ. of California Press, 1984), 152. The passage continues: "She more often lets herself be overcome by men using such methods than by those who proceed coldly; therefore always, like a woman, she is the friend of young men, because they are less cautious, more spirited, and with more boldness master her." See also chs. 5, 6, 11, 12.

Woman Question was enthralled in a circular argument: man is a political being; his virtue and reason can flourish only in political associations (the test of his commitment being his willingness and ability to risk his life for the republic); women are not part of political associations nor do they guarantee the security of the republic by their valor; therefore their virtue and reason do not flourish and they can not be considered political beings. Early modern political discourse virtually ensured that a republicanism which derived from it would be most comfortable in a political culture in which the common sense of the matter was that women could only be counted on to muck things up.

Understanding that the concept which I have elsewhere named "the republican mother" emerged from the older variant of republicanism helps us locate it with precision on the political spectrum. It is Janus-faced. Because it was framed in the language of civic humanism, it could lend itself, as Cohen shows in Warren's case, to a politics of nostalgia. (As Montesquieu suspected, even that hesitant politicization represented a major departure from the ancient tradition that women were not political creatures. Dedicated to raising virtuous citizens for the republic, a mother's traditional private duty took on a new element of public obligation.) In a society in which deference was fast eroding, republican mothers played a conservative, stabilizing role, deflecting the radical potential of the revolutionary experience. In effect, republican mothers were an important mechanism by which the memory of the standards of civic humanism was preserved long after it had faded elsewhere. Nostalgia was one face of republican motherhood. But consciousness of their civic obligation also meant that old boundaries on women's lives were stretched, making room for the questioning of hierarchies within the family and outside it, in the public world. In this way, republican motherhood could also sustain a major step in the direction of a liberal individualism which recognized the political potential of women.[25]

While we extend widely the scope of republicanism as a theme which helps us understand a complex culture, we must also be sensitive to issues which

25. Linda K. Kerber, "The Republican Mother: Women and the Enlightenment—An American Perspective," AQ, 28 (1976), 187–205 [and reprinted in the present volume]; idem, Women of the Republic: Intellect and Ideology in Revolutionary America (Chapel Hill: Univ. of North Carolina Press, 1980), ch. 9. Mary Beth Norton's characterization

republicanism *cannot* explain and did not solve. In his new book, *The Lost Soul of American Politics*, John Diggins argues that issues like labor, sectionalism, and equality do not lend themselves to formulation in terms of classical thought. Theories of mixed government which stressed reciprocal relations among the three orders of monarchy, aristocracy, and the people did not offer much advice to those who wanted to reduce the gaps between the orders. There were in fact "two languages of politics . . . that had 'liberty' as the key word in their vocabulary throughout the time span of the Machiavellian moment, c. 1500–c. 1800," explained J. H. Hexter. The Florentine language stressed participation as the foundation of civic virtue: its key words were participation, virtue and corruption. The other language was defensive, a "freedom *against* intrusion," whose key words were limited government, due process, and fundamental law.[26] As Isaac Kramnick has recently argued, we should take care lest we fall into assuming that the "republican tradition emphasizing citizenship and public participation" is sufficient to understand eighteenth-century politics without "the liberal individualist heritage preoccupied with private rights" and largely associated with Locke.[27]

This distinction has some elements of the arbitrary. In some hands Locke would not be contrasted so sharply with Bolingbroke. Henry F. May,

---

of my position in "The Evolution of White Women's Experience in Early America," *American Historical Review*, 89 (1984), 615, should be used with caution. I have not "contended that the postwar changes decreased . . . women's autonomy" except in certain specific cases, like the erosion of dower protection in Massachusetts. Rather I have argued that revolutionary claims by women for autonomy, initiative and independence were one side of an inherently paradoxical ideology of republican motherhood that legitimized political sophistication and activity while at the same time deflected political energy into domestic life.

26. J. H. Hexter, *On Historians*, 293–94, 301. "Citizen liberty available only to the members of the Consiglio Maggiore or to the electorate of the unreformed House of Commons leaves an awful lot of people out. The other idea of liberty is more ecumenical in its embrace. It does not profess, however, to give much to those it embraces. Mainly, it offers them some fairly clear constraints on the extent to which they can be rightfully booted about by current controllers of the machinery of political coercion." (302).

27. Kramnick, "Republican Revisionism Revisited," 629. See also John P. Diggins, *The Lost Soul of American Politics: Virtue, Self-Interest, and the Foundations of Liberalism* (New York: Basic Books, 1984), 12.

for example, links them together as exemplars of what he called "The Moderate Enlightenment."[28] But it does remind us that the American situation was not static, and that we should not be content when we have traced out the persistence of civic republicanism or Country habits of thought. Country politics provided a rhetoric, and even a general sort of political guidance, but it could not provide all political solutions; indeed it should not be expected to provide a context for thinking creatively about new issues that could not be said to mimic old ones. Targeted as it was at specifics of Walpolean politics, Country ideology had no need to raise basic questions about the relationship between the individual and authority, or between church and state.

Traditional republicanism, for example, had assumed that deference was the glue of society. Aristocrats were defined primarily by their property, but also by their manners and by the recognition that humble folks freely vouchsafed to them.[29] In this sense deference is not a passive, but an "active virtue"; it is for the masses what leadership is for the elite. Although the deference of the many to the elite was clearly evident in colonial society, it was a self-conscious sort of deference which eroded erratically but nonetheless rapidly in the Revolution. The shrill calls by the High Federalists to have it back after the war suggest it had disappeared. Republicanism of the older variety did not offer guidance about what to do with a society without deference, and, according to Pocock, "soon after the end of the War of Independence, the Revolution faced a crisis of confidence born of the realization that the naturally differentiated people, presupposed by every republican theorist from Aristotle to Machiavelli, had simply failed to appear."[30] The post-Revolutionary generation had to construct a republic without the mortar of deference; it would have to co-opt those whose deference could not be taken for granted. It is not by accident that the story of Andrew Jackson's inaugural, with the famous muddying of White House carpets and furniture, has become a staple of American political mythology. The story represents the co-optation of the nondeferential; it is the triumphant counterpart to the tale of the destruction of Governor Thomas Hutchinson's home by the revolutionary mob sixty-three years before. In

28. Henry F. May, *The Enlightenment in America* (New York: Oxford Univ. Press, 1979).

29. Pocock, *Machiavellian Moment*, 395, 485. See also J. G. A. Pocock, "The Classical Theory of Deference," *American Historical Review*, 81 (1976), 516–23.

30. Pocock, *Machiavellian Moment*, 516; 98, restating Giovanni Cavalcanti.

the task of understanding how Americans moved from the one to the other, inherited civic republicanism would be only of marginal and rhetorical help.

Republicanism of the civic humanist tradition circumvented the problem of slavery by confining itself to the relations between men who were already free. It did not offer clear solutions to the problem of representation and balance in an expanding territory. Indeed, as Gordon Wood has deftly shown, Florentine concepts of republicanism, tightly linked as they were to the idea that the "orders" of society were the one, the few, and the many, had to be jettisoned before Americans could begin to think in an original way about the relationship of state and society. Nor did civic republicanism appeal to those who felt the need for, as Robert Calhoun phrases it, "absorption into the sublime." It left the task of making political language congruent with religious language to the new evangelicals, who, in turn, led a religious revival that was complementary to the political revolution but not at all the same thing. As Rhys Isaac has argued, "the language and terms of classical republicanism that underlay the literate gentry's conception of the struggle could not readily arouse a populace whose limited experience of higher culture was of the Bible rather than the classics. More effective than the imagery of Roman republicanism was the Anglo-Virginian sense of identity as a Protestant people."[31]

Nor, finally, did traditional republican theory help either Jeffersonians or Federalists think creatively about the place of women in republican society. As we have seen, Mercy Otis Warren found the effect of traditional theory was to separate her from her male contemporaries. Lockean and radical Enlightenment ideas were needed for the development of new ideas about the role of women in political society, as the French showed in the Jacobin stages of their revolution. To deal with the woman question would require a political language derived not from the Moderate but from the Skeptical or Revolutionary Enlightenment (to use Henry May's categories). It would mean recourse back through time to Locke or forward in time to the liberal individualism of John Stuart Mill. It would require recognition

31. Wood, *Creation of the Republic*, 589. Robert Calhoun in letter to author, 1983; Rhys Isaac, *The Transformation of Virginia, 1740–1790* (Chapel Hill: Univ. of North Carolina Press, 1982), 246. Gordon Wood writes, "The new millenialism of many post-Revolutionary Americans represented both a rationalizing of revelation and a Christianizing of the Enlightenment belief in secular progress." Wood, "Evangelical America and Early Mormonism," *New York History*, 61 (1980), 359–86.

of the female restiveness and social problematic that Gary Nash points to when he recognizes that widows' poverty had become a significant social problem in northeastern cities on the eve of the Revolution.[32]

Happily, American political discourse was not fully dependent on civic humanist categories. Republican motherhood was a conceptualization which grafted the language of liberal individualism onto the inherited discourse of civic humanism. Because republican motherhood assumed that women's lives were shaped primarily by family obligations, it offered a politics congruent with the world as most women experienced it. Buttressed by Enlightenment commentary on natural rights, republican motherhood could be used effectively, as it was by Judith Sargent Murray and many others, to claim for women the independence and self-sufficiency that *Common Sense* had made a commonplace for adult men. Anyone who wants to start with the proposition that all are "by nature free, equal, and independent of one another," whether they be British radical artisans in the London Corresponding Society or Elizabeth Cady Stanton before the New York State Legislature in 1854, will need Locke, not Machiavelli.[33]

Our understanding of republicanism is now being greatly enriched by a major exploration of the interaction of the political revolution and economic development, particularly the Industrial Revolution. The juxtaposi-

---

32. On the important connection between citizenship and military obligation, see Pocock, *Machiavellian Moment*, 88–90, 390. In classical as well as early modern republican thought, Pocock points out, arms were understood to be the "*ultimo ratio* whereby the citizen exposes his life in defense of the state and at the same time ensures that the decision to expose it cannot be taken without him; it is the possession of arms which makes a man a full citizen, capable of, and required to display, the multiple versatility and self-development which is the crown (and the prerequisite) of citizenship." (90). I deal with this issue at greater length in " 'May All Our Citizens Be Soldiers and All Our Soldiers Citizens': The Ambiguities of Female Citizenship in the New Nation," in Robert Beisner and Joan Challinor, eds., *Arms at Rest: Peacemaking and Peacekeeping in American History* (Westport, Conn.: Greenwood Press, 1987). See also Lois G. Schwoerer, *"No Standing Armies": The Antiarmy Ideology in Seventeenth Century England* (Baltimore: Johns Hopkins Univ. Press, 1974). On widows' poverty, see Gary B. Nash, *The Urban Crucible: Social Change, Political Consciousness and the Origins of the American Revolution* (Cambridge: Harvard Univ. Press, 1979), 126–27, 182–89.

33. Kramnick, "Republican Revisionism Revisited," 648–49; Elizabeth Cady Stanton, "Address to the Legislature of New York, 1854," in Ellen DuBois, ed., *Elizabeth Cady Stanton/Susan B. Anthony—Correspondence, Writings, Speeches* (New York: Schocken Books), 45, 51.

tion of the two in time has long been noted, but especially in America it has been hard to see how they interacted.[34]

Now, haltingly, the narratives of political and economic development are being brought together by historians who recognize that actual political and economic development is necessarily synergistic. Isaac Kramnick describes the main elements in the sequence as it developed in England:

> America and the crisis over taxation introduced new noncountry issues into politics. The taxation controversy raised to the center of debate the issue of representation, which in its trail brought to the fore basic concerns about the origins of government and authority in general . . . It transcended the paradigms of country ideology to more class-based categories.

At the same time, the Industrial Revolution politicized an emerging middle class, "owners of small and moveable property" who resented their exclusion from the political process at the same time that their financial support of the state was demanded. "In Locke far more than in Bolingbroke and his ilk, the unenfranchised middle class and especially the Protestant dissenters found intellectual authority and legitimacy for their radical demands." Kramnick concludes, "The transformation . . . involved a changed emphasis on the nature of public behavior. The moral and virtuous man was no longer defined by his civic activity but by his economic activity. . . ." Adam Smith provided a different language for explaining how a stable and free social order could be maintained: not by disinterested and unspecialized citizenship, but by "economic productivity and hard work." It was understood that selfish private behavior in the marketplace could ultimately redound to the public good. "The world view of liberal individ-

---

34. Gerald Stourzh, *Alexander Hamilton and the Idea of Republican Government* (Stanford: Stanford Univ. Press, 1970). For Hamilton's correspondence, which suggested how closely early industrial manufacturing was tied to women's work at home, see Harold C. Syrett, et al., eds., *The Papers of Alexander Hamilton* (New York: Columbia Univ. Press, 1965), Volume 9, especially Nathanial Gorham to AH, 13 October 1790 (371); James Davenport to John Chester, 16 Sept. 1791 (340) and Peter Colt to John Chester, 21 July 1791 (320–23). The Report itself appears in Volume 10. For a summary of the process of home manufacture and its gradual transformation into factory work, see J. Bruce Sinclair, "The Merrimack Valley Textile Museum," *Publications of the Colonial Society of Massachusetts*, 18 (1966), 406–16. For a recent social history of the early stages of industrialization, see Gary Kulik, "The Beginnings of the Industrial Revolution in America: Pawtucket, Rhode Island, 1672–1829," Diss., Brown Univ., 1980.

ualism was fast pushing aside the older paradigms during the last three decades of the century. . . ."[35]

What Kramnick has done for England, Joyce Appleby has done, in more detail, for the United States in a series of essays which have appeared in scholarly journals in the course of the last ten years and, most recently, in *Capitalism and a New Social Order: The Republican Vision of the 1790's*. Appleby acknowledges that there were two vocabularies of republican discourse; like Kramnick, she views the liberal concept of liberty as fundamentally *incompatible* with the classical tradition. Drawing on her own extensive examinations of the debate on trade and the economy in seventeenth-century England, Appleby draws our attention to the fresh view of human psychology that accompanied the development of free market economics. The concept of liberty expressed by writers from Locke to Adam Smith was incompatible with the classical tradition because it treated *all* people—not just the gentry—as rational beings capable of making sensible decisions, first in the marketplace and, by extension, in political life as well.[36] The Jeffersonians, Appleby argues, continued this vein of argument. Far from being agrarian traditionalists or an American "country party," she maintains, the Jeffersonians embraced the international market enthusiastically. They welcomed the heightened European demand for American wheat and other agricultural products; they aggressively sought to enlarge America's share of the market by improvements in the quality of its produce.[37] For cosmopolitan, upwardly mobile people, whether they lived in cities or depended on urban markets to sell their produce, it was no longer natural to continue to function "within the old assumptions about a politically active elite and a deferential, compliant electorate. . . . The right of participation could not be extended to the many without changing the style and the substance of republican government." Thus the Jeffersonians transformed the traditional republicanism which they had inherited, developing its

35. Kramnick, "Republican Revisionism Revisited," 635, 637, 662–64.

36. See Joyce Appleby, "Ideology and Theory: The Tension Between Political and Economic Liberalism in Seventeenth-Century England," *American Historical Review*, 81 (1976), 499–515; idem, "Locke, Liberalism, and the Natural Law of Money," *Past and Present*, (1976), 43–69; idem, *Capitalism and a New Social Order: The Republican Vision of the 1790's* (New York: Oxford Univ. Press, 1984), 21. This work retains the agreeably conversational tone that characterized it when originally delivered as the Anson G. Phelps Lectures at New York University.

37. Appleby, "Commercial Farming and the Agrarian Myth in the Early Republic," *Journal of American History*, 68 (1982), 845.

Lockean ingredients, adding to it "the liberal position on private property and economic freedom," and "banishing the political distinction between the few and the many."[38]

Appleby asks a rhetorical question which forces historians to make a choice. "If the Revolution was fought in a frenzy over corruption, out of fear of tyranny, and with hopes for redemption through civic virtue, where and when are scholars to find the sources for the aggressive individualism, the optimistic materialism, and the pragmatic interest-group politics that became so salient so early in the life of the new nation?" In his expansive book *The Republic Reborn*, Steven Watts finds those sources in the writing and experience of a group of strategically placed articulate republicans who, he believes, "took the lead in moving liberal capitalist values from their emergent position in colonial America to one of cultural dominance in early national America." Watts' work is distinctive in its sensitivity to the ways in which personal experience articulated with political trends and in his extensive effort to include consideration of psychological tensions and literary imagery as they shaped political analysis. In the hands of Appleby, Kramnick, Watts, and others including Jeffrey Barnouw and John Diggins, the old civic humanist politics fades, and is replaced by a dynamic set of behaviors more congruent with the demands of bourgeois society and a capitalist marketplace.[39]

It may remain, however, possible that sharp choices between distinct alternatives do not have to be made. Edwin Burrows works out in detail the elements in the English Opposition tradition—especially the fear of a national debt—to which aspiring entrepreneurs like Albert Gallatin could resonate. In a very practical way, Gallatin was convinced that Hamiltonian finance would usher in economic privilege, encourage speculation, and

38. Appleby, *Capitalism*, 48–49, 73, 99, 101. In Appleby's formulation, the Federalists display a politics of nostalgia and unambivalent elitism. She provides little room for the distinctions between high and moderate Federalism made, for example, by David Hackett Fisher and most students of party politics in the early republic, except insofar as the two branches of the party echo Court-Country polarization. See David Hackett Fisher, *The Revolution of American Conservatism: The Federalist Party in the Era of Jeffersonian Democracy* (New York: Harper and Row, 1965). See note 46 below.

39. Appleby, "The Social Origins of American Revolutionary Ideology," *Journal of American History*, 64 (1978), 937; Steven Watts, *The Republic Reborn: War and the Making of Liberal America, 1790–1820* (Baltimore: Johns Hopkins Univ. Press, 1987). See also Jeffrey Barnouw, "The Pursuit of Happiness in Jefferson and Its Background in Bacon and Hobbes," *Interpretation: A Journal of Political Philosophy*, 11 (1983), 225.

underwrite patronage. He and his colleagues were all too sure that these had been the same policies which had once forced the British to the taxation which in turn had engendered the American Revolution. They thought Hamilton was set on course to replay the same drama. In many respects Gallatin—always in debt, always drowning in some land speculation or mercantile venture, a man, in Burrows's phrase, "on the make"—fits Appleby's characterization of American republicans as people who made their careers by taking advantage of new economic opportunities. Gallatin would have agreed with Appleby that Hamilton represented a reincarnation of Court politics. But Burrows's Gallatin would see no contradiction between embracing entrepreneurship on the one hand and acting to ensure that traditional sources of corruption could not operate. In employing Country principles for contemporary ends, he would have denied that he was operating from a politics of nostalgia.[40]

Thus an alternate interpretation is available, offered by historians who believe that the major concepts of the older republicanism retained their vitality longer than Appleby or Kramnick would concede and doubt that socio-psychological change occurred as sharply as the former group suspect. In *The Elusive Republic*, Drew McCoy describes a "hybrid republican vision," characteristic of American thinking as early as the 1770s, in which the "moral and social imperatives of classical republicanism" were adapted "to modern commercial society." Realistic republicans like Franklin sought to integrate "commerce and its consequences" into republican patterns of analysis: indeed, McCoy suggests that Poor Richard's maxims should be read as an effort to blend the "virtue" of traditional republicanism with the self-aggrandizement of assertive commercialism. By the time the decision for war to protect free trade was made in 1812, older definitions of virtue had given way to emphasis on individual industriousness; free trade meant that the state relied on the market to provide the social stability previously thought guaranteed only by self-restrained choices made by virtuous citizens. Although McCoy conceded that that decision might be regarded as a new departure, he emphasizes the ambivalence with which it was made: "Most Jeffersonians continued . . . to interpret the interdependent realm of

40. The phrase is Kramnick's; in full it is "the politics of nostalgia untainted by bourgeois liberal or individualist ideals," in "Republican Revisionism Revisited," 634. See Edwin Burrows, "Albert Gallatin and the Political Economy of Republicanism, 1761–1800," Diss., Columbia Univ., 1974.

polity, economy and society in the light of the same fears and concerns that had informed Franklin's outlook on the eve of the Revolution."[41]

In *Chants Democratic*, his subtle discussion of the political and economic transformation of the later years of the early republic, Sean Wilentz is less impressed by national prosperity than he is by "the subordination of wage labor to capital." The international industrial revolution and capitalist development altered the "locus and texture" of human relations "across the shifting barriers of trade, region, race, sex or ethnicity." In this transformed political economy, in which the middle-class entrepreneurs focused on by Kramnick and Appleby found the language of liberal individualism a close fit to the reality of their own experience, the independent artisans and craft workers who are the subjects of Wilentz's attention found themselves losing their options and pushed, in an inexorable cycle of downward mobility, into the sweated trades and the status of dependent wage earners. For them, the language of the individual freely contracting in a free market became less and less descriptive of a reality they welcomed; as they came ever nearer to the status of working class, the old dream of a commonwealth of cooperation and civic virtue became more attractive. Wilentz finds them apt to use the older language of traditional republicanism.[42]

Impressed by the persistence of the rhetoric, Wilentz insists—he has Gordon Wood in mind—that it is "premature to claim that classical politics died in 1787," or, for that matter, in 1812. There remained a resilient republican language which had absorbed, or fused with, major liberal ingredients and which continued to be central to American political discourse. Americans used this modern variant with no sense that they had created an oxymoron. "Early nineteenth century politicians and party spokesmen thought primarily not in straightforward liberal terms but in classical republican terms leavened by egalitarian notions of natural political rights— of a polity of independent virtuous citizens, working to build and maintain a commonwealth of political equality," writes Wilentz. He reads the Jack-

---

41. Drew McCoy, *The Elusive Republic: Political Economy in Jeffersonian America* (Chapel Hill: Univ. of North Carolina Press, 1980), 236–39. In E. James Ferguson, "Political Economy, Public Liberty, and the Formation of the Constitution," *WMQ*, 40 (1983), 389–412, the argument is made that currency finance strategies are in the Country political tradition.

42. Sean Wilentz, *Chants Democratic: New York City and the Rise of the American Working Class, 1788–1850* (New York: Oxford Univ. Press, 1984), 18–19, and ch. 3.

sonian party system as energized by "a specific conception of republican politics, one that *combined* republican rhetoric with a post-Madisonian liberalism." Daniel Walker Howe firmly makes the point that the pervasive vocabulary of Whig-Democratic debate—virtue, balance, luxury, degeneration, restoration—reveals the continued influence of long-familiar patterns of classical and Renaissance political thought. That Whigs and Democrats were both using this language helps explain why their debate was so bitter; "if they had not had such terms in common, they might not have understood each others' terms so well." Howe finds that "the staple of Whig political culture [in the 1840s] remained the Anglo-American 'country-party' tradition"; their intellectual ancestor was James Madison and his moderate Republican colleagues. The doubled concept of republican motherhood was a similar alloy.[43]

Whomever we choose as our guide, we arrive at the same place: the liberal individualism of the antebellum years and the capitalist free market economy. The distinctions made between the substitution of Court for Country, replacement of both by liberalism, or fusion of classical republicanism with liberalism, are not merely semantic. Appleby finds in the shift to liberalism a major social-psychological change which made democratic politics possible. "Instrumental, utilitarian, individualistic, egalitarian, abstract, and rational, the liberal concept of liberty was everything that the classical republican concept was not." Arguing for the persistence of classical republican thinking in post-Revolutionary America, Murrin suggests that because Americans have thought that their nation continued to be ruled by descendants of the anti-Court party (that is, by authentic dissidents and revolutionaries), incipient dissent may well have been inhibited and the sense of alienation kept to a minimum. "In America, except for the generation of older Federalists after 1800 and Southerners after 1850, alienation has been directed at the society rather than the polity, until our own Vietnam-Watergate era."[44] Wilentz and Howe give credit to an amalgam of classical and liberal ideology for deflecting class tensions in an industrializing society. Political elites were enabled to divert working-class hostility

43. Sean Wilentz, "On Class and Politics in Jacksonian America," *Reviews in American History*, 10 (1982), 54, 56. Italics mine. Daniel Walker Howe, *The Political Culture of the American Whigs* (Chicago: Univ. of Chicago Press, 1979), 78, 87, 90–91.

44. Appleby, *Capitalism and the Social Order*, 23; idem, "Social Origins," 955–58; Murrin, "Great Inversion," 428–30.

away from themselves and toward speculators, monopolists, and other people whom classical rhetoric had long since defined as enemies to the republic. One ingredient to the answer to the old question about why American political parties did not divide neatly along class lines may therefore be the continuing vitality of classical republicanism in American political discourse. Moreover, the old organic vision of community never fully disappeared, and was available for social critics to draw on as an authentic alternative throughout the nineteenth and into the twentieth centuries when an expanding economy had not made good on its promise to end major class distinctions, and capitalism and free trade no longer seemed quite as promising as they had appeared in the halcyon days of the early republic.

We may now be persuaded that Jeffersonians saw in their Federalist opponents the reincarnation of their British opponents of the prewar days. But even if this is not simply a matter of perspective, even if the Republicans were right in seeing the Federalists as a revival or continuation of the Court interest, I think we should also recognize that the Federalists had their own mythology. Federalists *also* believed themselves to be heirs of an authentic republican revolution, inheritors of the traditional understanding that republics were frail and required protection. Federalists would understand their role to be that they build a wall of protection around the republic. Their emphasis on the vulnerability of republics to both foreign and domestic enemies was also an authentic part of their inheritance from Florentine civic humanism. In seeking to understand the tensions of the post-Revolutionary years, we must concede that there was authenticity of belief on both sides of the partisan split.[45]

Federalists were captives of the belief that the good citizen was a political amateur, not a political technician. Observing their opponents professionalizing politics, Federalists concluded that it was the opposition which demeaned the integrity of citizenship. When Federalists said that Republicans aimed at subversion and were desperate men, they meant to certify that Republicans had become Court politicians, who would use all available means, with much energy and few scruples, and who were comfortable with the prospect of an open-ended, unpredictable future. This is a goal Federalists associated with Court and with connivance. They imag-

45. I have made this point in a different context in *Federalists in Dissent: Imagery and Ideology in Jeffersonian America* (Ithaca: Cornell Univ. Press, 1970).

ined, especially after the transfer of power in 1800, that the Republicans were heirs of Court politics.[46]

With both Federalists and Republicans racing as fast as they could to connect with and control the market economy of the Industrial Revolution, Jefferson's phrase of his First Inaugural, "We are all Federalists, we are all Republicans," takes on new vibrancy and new irony. The two parties shared a heritage of antique republicanism transformed by the political rivalries of Stuart and Hanoverian England. They shared a political language which had attached complex penumbra of meaning to certain words— among them *virtue, corruption,* and *liberty*. Useful though that language had been in helping them articulate their political resistance, it had never been sufficient; it had always been accompanied by an alternate liberal language that embraced competition and ambition as means to economic prosperity and political balance. During the years of the early republic, both parties groped toward economic modernization and a liberal politics. In the process, the very meaning of the code words shifted even as they continued in use. *Virtue* referred increasingly to individual choice, with perhaps religious overtones; *balance*, which had once referred to the relationship between "the one, the few, and the many," or King, Lords, and Commons, came to refer to the balancing of powers within the government as organized by the Federal Constitution. The sounds of civil republicanism persisted longer than the fact of it.

It may be that in a long perspective, historians of this generation will be seen to have devised yet another variant of consensus history, stressing the assumptions which Americans shared rather than the distinctions which divided them. Yet in their defense it should be recognized that historians who identified a republican consensus moved almost immediately to make distinctions within it, and to show that it in turn contained the possibility of contradictions. The language of early American politics reflected the absorption of Enlightenment ideas as well as Oppositionist ones, and was reshaped by real people, who had to make real judgments, as they moved toward the liberal, individualist, capitalist compromise which we have come to know.

46. In "What is Still American in the Political Philosophy of Thomas Jefferson?" Appleby argues that the Court-Country dichotomy was played out within the Federalist party: "the archetypal Country leader, Adams, found his prefigured enemy in the classical Court political, Hamilton." *WMQ*, 39 (1982), 307. This view contrasts sharply with the interpretations of Murrin and of Banning.

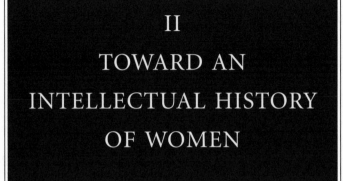

II

TOWARD AN

INTELLECTUAL HISTORY

OF WOMEN

SEPARATE SPHERES,
FEMALE WORLDS,
WOMAN'S PLACE
THE RHETORIC OF
WOMEN'S HISTORY

In no country has such constant care been taken as in America to trace two clearly
distinct lines of action for the two sexes and to make them keep pace one with the other,
but in two pathways that are always different.
ALEXIS DE TOCQUEVILLE, 1835

The Sphere of Woman and Man as moral beings [is] the same.
ANGELINA GRIMKÉ, 1838

Too much has already been said and written about woman's sphere.
LUCY STONE, 1855

A century and a half after the publication of Alexis de Tocqueville's account
of his visit to the United States, a mode of behavior that he may have been
the first systematic social critic to identify has undergone extraordinary
waves of analysis and attack. In four brief chapters in the third book of the
second volume of *Democracy in America*, published in 1840, Tocqueville
addressed the situation of women. His observations display Tocqueville's
habitual charm, his fearlessness in making broad generalizations, his mas-

I am deeply grateful for the good counsel provided on earlier versions of this essay by
Dorothy Ross, Tom Haskell, Barbara Sicherman, Alice Kessler-Harris, Mary Ryan,
Bruce Gronbeck, Drew Faust, Cindy Aron, Joan Jacobs Brumberg, Evelyn Brooks,
Allan Megill, Gerda Lerner, Susan Armeny, and the members of the Transformation
Project of the Philadelphia Center for Early American Studies, all of whom tried
valiantly to keep me from error and surely did not fully succeed.

159

tery of language. When *Democracy in America* was rediscovered and widely reprinted in the years after World War II, his chapters were among the few—perhaps the only—classic texts read by students of American history that seriously examined the situation of women in American society. When historians—whether inspired by Simone de Beauvoir or Eleanor Flexner or Betty Friedan—began again to study women's history, they could point to Tocqueville for evidence that at least one classic, Great Author had conceded the significance of their subject.

Tocqueville restricted his observations on women to a section entitled "Influence of Democracy on Manners Properly So Called." He alluded to the separation of male and female spheres in the course of his contrasting and impressionistic portraits of young middle-class American women. The breakdown of aristocratic government, he argued, had important implications for family life in that patriarchal authority was impaired, leaving young women with a high degree of independence, which encouraged a high degree of self-confidence. Yet when one of those same young women married, Tocqueville reported, "the inexorable opinion of the public carefully circumscribes [her] within the narrow circle of domestic interests and duties and forbids her to step beyond it." In this sentence he provided the physical image (the circle) and the interpretation (that it was a limiting boundary on choices) that would continue to characterize the metaphor. He ended by contrasting American women with European feminists who, he thought, wished to erase the boundaries between the spheres of women and of men, thus "degrading" both. Tocqueville concluded with what he thought was a compliment: "As for myself, I do not hesitate to avow that although the women of the United States are confined within the narrow circle of domestic life, and their situation is in some respects one of extreme dependence, I have nowhere seen women occupying a loftier position; and if I were asked, to what the singular prosperity and growing strength of the [American] people ought mainly to be attributed, I should reply: To the superiority of their women."[1]

1. Alexis de Tocqueville, *Democracy in America* (2 vols., New York, 1945), II, bk. 3, ch. 9–12, esp. 201, 211, 214. Just as Edward Pessen has taught us to distrust Tocqueville's observations on social mobility, it is now long past time to dispose of Tocqueville's observations on the condition of American women. Edward Pessen, "The Egalitarian Myth and the American Social Reality: Wealth, Mobility, and Equality in the 'Era of the Common Man,'" *American Historical Review*, 76 (Oct. 1971), 989–1034. George Wilson

When, more than a hundred years later, another generation began to search for explanations of women's lives, no concept seemed more promising than Tocqueville's. He had urged that the "circle of domestic life" be searched for the distinguishing characteristics of American women, and once we looked, the separation of spheres seemed everywhere underfoot, from crocheted pillows reading Woman's Place Is in the Home to justifications for the exclusion of women from higher education, to arguments against birth control and abortion. Women were said to live in a distinct "world," engaged in nurturant activities, focused on children, husbands, and family dependents.

The metaphor of the "sphere" was the figure of speech, the trope, on which historians came to rely when they described women's part in American culture. Exploring the traditions of historical discourse, historians found that notions of women's sphere permeated the language; they in turn used the metaphor in their own descriptions. Thus the relationship between the name—sphere—and the perception of what it named was reciprocal; widespread usage in the nineteenth century directed the choices made by twentieth-century historians about what to study and how to tell the stories that they reconstructed. The trope had an effect on readers as well, predisposing them to find arguments that made use of familiar language persuasive. "Common sense," writes Clifford Geertz, "is not what the mind cleared of cant spontaneously apprehends; it is what the mind filled with presuppositions . . . concludes." One of our culture's presuppositions

---

Pierson's careful list of Tocqueville's encounters with Americans includes few women and none as primary informants. George Wilson Pierson, *Tocqueville and Beaumont in America* (New York, 1938), 782–86. Tocqueville's women are stereotypes. Tocqueville claims, for example, "American women never manage the outward concerns of the family or conduct a business or take a part in political life, nor are they, on the other hand, ever compelled to perform the rough labor of the fields or to make any of those laborious efforts which demand the exertion of physical strength." Tocqueville, *Democracy in America*, II, 212. In *Democracy* we meet no adult single women, no widows. We learn nothing of women's relations with each other or of the revolutions in child nurture, women's education, and women's organizational life occurring at the very time of Tocqueville's visit. Although his companion Beaumont wrote a whole novel about the situation of a white woman who loves a black man, Tocqueville made no comment about women who sought to cross the barrier between the races. Gustave Auguste de Beaumont de la Bonninière, *Marie; or, Slavery in the United States: A Novel of Jacksonian America*, trans. Barbara Chapman (Stanford, 1958).

has been that men and women live in separate spheres. The power of presupposition may have been at work in the formulations of Erik H. Erikson, which gave the trope of separate spheres a psychological foundation. In 1964, reporting on play patterns of children, Erikson observed that little girls used blocks to construct bounded, interior spaces, while little boys used blocks to construct exterior scenes. He concluded that the differences between "Inner and Outer Space" "correspond to the male and female principles in body construction," to psychological identity, and to social behavior. For their part, historians were not immune to tropic pressures; the metaphor of separate spheres helped historians select what to study and how to report what they found.[2]

Writing in the mid-1960s, three historians substantially reinforced the centrality of the metaphor of separate spheres. Barbara Welter, Aileen S. Kraditor, and Gerda Lerner, all influenced to some degree by Betty Friedan and all writing in the climate created by the popular success of *The Feminine Mystique*, argued that American women's history had to be understood not only by way of events but through a prism of ideology as well. Between the historians and the reality of women's lives impinged a pervasive descriptive language that imposed a "complex of virtues . . . by which a woman judged herself and was judged by . . . society."[3]

Welter's 1966 essay was a frank attempt to do for the nineteenth century what Friedan had done for the twentieth. Retrieving sources resembling Friedan's—women's fiction and popular prescriptive literature—and reading them freshly, Welter identified a nineteenth-century stereotype, which she called the "Cult of True Womanhood" and for which she said a synonym might be "mystique." Among the cardinal virtues Welter found associated with women was domesticity (the others were piety, purity, and submissiveness); home was referred to as women's "proper sphere." She quoted a woman's revealing defense of that choice of sphere:

2. Clifford Geertz, *Local Knowledge: Further Essays in Interpretive Anthropology* (New York, 1983), 84. Erik H. Erikson, "Inner and Outer Space: Reflections on Womanhood," in *The Woman in America*, ed. Robert Jay Lifton (Boston, 1965), 1–26. These papers, originally read at a 1963 conference, include Alice S. Rossi, "Equality between the Sexes: An Immodest Proposal," *ibid.*, 98–143, and offer important evidence of the state of academic thinking about sex roles in the early 1960s.

3. Barbara Welter, "The Cult of True Womanhood: 1820–1860," *American Quarterly*, 18 (Summer 1966), 151–74, esp. 152; Betty Friedan, *The Feminine Mystique* (New York, 1963).

St. Paul knew what was best for women when he advised them to be domestic. There is composure at home; there is something sedative in the duties which home involves. It affords security not only from the world, but from delusions and errors of every kind.

And Welter concluded that American women of the nineteenth century, saddled with a stereotype so encouraging and yet so constraining, experiencing "guilt and confusion in the midst of opportunity," had been as much bemused by ideology as Friedan's (and Welter's) troubled contemporaries.[4] Unlike Tocqueville's, Welter's judgment of the separate sphere was a negative one. Separation denigrated women, kept them subordinate. The choice of the word "cult" was pejorative. Welter's essay—thoughtful, subtle, witty—was much cited and often reprinted; the phrase "cult of true womanhood" became an essential part of the vocabulary of women's history.

Less than two years later, Kraditor published *Up from the Pedestal*, still a striking anthology of documents. Considering what Kraditor called "the primitive state of historiography" in 1968, her introduction was pathbreaking. In it she identified what she called "the question of 'spheres'" as central to an understanding of American feminism. She contrasted "autonomy" with "women's proper sphere": "Strictly speaking," she wrote, "men have never had a 'proper *sphere*,' since their sphere has been the world and all its activities." She proposed that the separation of spheres was somehow linked to the Industrial Revolution, which "broadened the distinctions between men's and women's occupations and certainly provoked new thinking about the significance and permanence of their respective 'spheres.'" And she noted the persistent description of home as refuge in antifeminist literature, a refuge that had somehow become vulnerable long before Christopher Lasch coined the phrase "haven in a heartless world."[5]

Three years later, Lerner used the social history of women as a base for hypotheses about general political and economic questions in an important essay, "The Lady and the Mill Girl." Introducing class into the analysis and extending the link to the Industrial Revolution, Lerner argued that "American industrialization, which occurred in an underdeveloped economy with a shortage of labor, depended on the labor of women and chil-

4. Welter, "Cult of True Womanhood," 162, 174.

5. Aileen S. Kraditor, ed., *Up from the Pedestal: Selected Writings in the History of American Feminism* (Chicago, 1968), 9, 14, 10; Christopher Lasch, *Haven in a Heartless World: The Family Besieged* (New York, 1977).

dren" and that one "result of industrialization was in increasing differences in life styles between women of different classes. . . . As class distinctions sharpened, social attitudes toward women became polarized." Welter's "cult of true womanhood" was interpreted by Lerner as a *vehicle* by which middle-class women elevated their own status. "It is no accident," Lerner wrote in 1969, "that the slogan 'woman's place is in the home' took on a certain aggressiveness and shrillness precisely at the time when increasing numbers of poorer women *left* their homes to become factory workers."[6]

The careful reader of Kraditor and Lerner could hardly fail to notice that their description of women's sphere as separate from, and subordinate to, that of men was congruent with Marxist argument. For Lerner and Kraditor, the metaphor of sphere related not only to Tocqueville, but to Friedrich Engels's conceptualization of a dichotomy between public and private modes of life. Tracing the development of gender relations, Engels had argued that the "world-historical defeat of the female sex" had been accompanied by a shift in control of space: "The man took command in the home also." Engels gave classic expression to the concept of a public/private split, a split in which the most important psychic locus was the home, understood to be a woman's place, but ultimately controlled by man. "With . . . the single monogamous family . . . household management lost its public character. . . . It became a *private service.*"[7]

Rhetorically, Engels identified a psychological and legal shift (from matrilocality to patrilocality) and gave it a physical context: the nuclear fam-

6. Gerda Lerner, "The Lady and the Mill Girl: Changes in the Status of Women in the Age of Jackson," *Midcontinent American Studies Journal*, 10 (Spring 1969), 5–15, esp. 10–12. Lerner also observed that Friedan's "feminine mystique" is the continuation of the old myth of woman's proper sphere. With no reference to Lerner, Neil McKendrick made much the same argument for England: the literature of separate spheres was an effort of middle-class women to maintain the difference between themselves and working-class women. McKendrick also noted men's resentment of the new purchasing power of working women; the language of separate spheres expressed their view of the new earnings "as a threat to male authority, a temptation to female luxury and indulgence, and an incitement of female independence." Neil McKendrick, "Home Demand and Economic Growth: A New View of the Role of Women and Children in the Industrial Revolution," in *Historical Perspectives: Studies in English Thought and Society in Honour of J. H. Plumb*, ed. Neil McKendrick (London, 1974), 152–210, esp. 164–67.

7. Friedrich Engels, *The Origin of the Family, Private Property and the State*, ed. Eleanor Burke Leacock (New York, 1972), 120, 137.

ily's home. (Perhaps because this cultural shift had been accomplished long before his own time and had already come to seem the common sense of the matter, Engels did not feel the need to make explicit or defend the equivalencies he identified.) His strategy was to link private-home-woman and then to speak in synecdoche; any part of the triad could stand for any other part. He did so despite his explicit statement that the home was also a locus of men's behavior; indeed for Engels and for Karl Marx, the home is the locus of struggle between the sexes.

Awareness of the socially constructed division between public and private, often expressed through the image of sphere, gave energy to much Marxist-feminist writing in the late sixties and early seventies. "The contemporary family," wrote Juliet Mitchell, "can be seen as a triptych of sexual, reproductive and socializatory functions (the woman's world) embraced by production (the man's world)—precisely a structure which in the final instance is determined by the economy. The exclusion of women from production . . . is the root cause of the contemporary *social* definition of women as *natural* beings." At the end of her powerfully argued *Woman's Estate*, Mitchell reiterated that the central problem for women was their relegation to the home during their child-bearing years, "the period of adult psychic and political formation." Bourgeois and working-class women alike were deprived of the opportunity to learn from any but the most limited experience. "The spider's web is dense as well as intricate . . . come into my parlour and be a true woman," Mitchell concludes. "In the home the social function and the psychic identity of women as a group is found."[8]

The great power of the Marxist interpretation was that it not only described a separation of spheres, but also offered an explanation of the way in which that separation served the interests of the dominant classes. Separate spheres were due neither to cultural accident nor to biological determinism. They were social constructions, camouflaging social and economic service, a service whose benefits were unequally shared.

The idea of separate spheres, as enunciated by Welter, Kraditor, Lerner, and Mitchell, took on a life of its own. Women's historians of the mid-1960s had

8. Juliet Mitchell, *Woman's Estate* (New York, 1971), 148, 182. See also Karen Sacks, "Engels Revisited: Women, the Organization of Production, and Private Property," in *Woman, Culture, and Society*, ed. Michelle Zimbalist Rosaldo and Louise Lamphere (Stanford, 1974), 207–22; and Elizabeth Fox-Genovese, "Placing Women's History in History," *New Left Review* (May–June 1982), 5–29.

inherited a subject that had been, with only few conspicuous exceptions, descriptive and anecdotal. Books like Alice Morse Earle's *Home Life in Colonial Days* loomed large.[9] When earlier historians of women had turned to politics, a Whiggish progressivism had infused much of their work, suggesting that the central theme in women's history was an inexorable march toward the suffrage. The concepts of separate spheres and of a public/private dichotomy offered ways of addressing women's history that employed social and cultural, as well as political, material. Historians who did not think of themselves as Marxists were nevertheless deeply indebted to Marxist analysis. Social theory enabled women's historians to introduce categories, hypotheticals, and analytical devices by which they could escape the confines of accounts of "great ladies" or of "the progress of women." Still—whether handled by Erikson, who grounded the separation of spheres in what he took to be permanent psychological verities; Welter, who grounded it in culture; or socialist feminists (including Lerner and Kraditor), who grounded it in property relations—in the early 1970s separation was generally associated with subordination, deteriorating status, and the victimization of women by men.[10]

In 1975 Carroll Smith-Rosenberg offered a striking reinterpretation of the possibilities of separation in her pathbreaking essay "The Female World of Love and Ritual." Several years later she recalled: "I began with a question. How can we understand the nature of the emotionally intense and erotic friendships between eighteenth- and nineteenth-century married women and society's benign approval of such relationships?" Smith-Rosenberg maintained that separation could make possible psychologically sustaining and strengthening relationships among women. Victorians did not make rigid distinctions, as we do, between heterosexuality and homosexuality. A culture of separate spheres was not simply an ancestral culture differing from our own primarily in the extent of industrialization; it was, Smith-Rosenberg argued, a *dramatically* different culture in which boundaries were differently marked, anxieties differently expressed. Nineteenth-century women had available sources of psychological support that had eroded in our own day. Smith-Rosenberg's work implied that there had existed a distinctive women's culture, in which women assisted each other

9. Alice Morse Earle, *Home Life in Colonial Days* (New York, 1898).
10. See Barbara Sicherman et al., *Recent United States Scholarship on the History of Women* (Washington, 1980).

in childbirth, nurtured each other's children, and shared emotional and often erotic ties stronger than those with their husbands.[11]

Other work of the 1970s filled in details of the distinctive women's culture that Smith-Rosenberg had identified. In "Female Support Networks and Political Activism," Blanche Wiesen Cook focused on four women who had significant political careers in the late nineteenth and early twentieth centuries. Cook dealt with the probability of homosexual relationships among some of her subjects, arguing that politically activist women were sustained by complex and powerful friendships with other women. She maintained that such friendships were part of the history historians sought to trace and that, instead of ignoring them as irrelevant, historians should address them frankly, understanding that the "sisterhood" of which so many women spoke included female friendships that ran the gamut from acquaintance to long-sustained sexual relationships. Kathryn Kish Sklar's biography of Catharine Beecher analyzed the woman who did most to define the ingredients of the traditional women's sphere: domesticity, nurture, and education. Beecher took the position that women's sphere did not encompass politics, notably in exchanges with Angelina Grimké. Significantly, Beecher addressed extensively the elements of the physical location of the women's sphere, not only in abstractions like "the classroom" or "the home" but also in explicit and original physical plans for *The American Woman's Home*.[12]

In *The Bonds of Womanhood*, Nancy F. Cott explored the way in which "the doctrine of woman's sphere" actually was practiced in early nineteenth-century New England. Cott found in middle-class women's diaries and letters a distinctive "orientation toward gender" that derived from shared patterns of work. She found in those writings an understanding of domes-

11. Carroll Smith-Rosenberg, "The Female World of Love and Ritual: Relations between Women in Nineteenth-Century America," *Signs*, 1 (Autumn 1975), 1–29. Her later observations appeared in Carroll Smith-Rosenberg, "Politics and Culture in Women's History: A Symposium," *Feminist Studies*, 6 (Spring 1980), 55–64, esp. 60. See also her collected essays, Carroll Smith-Rosenberg, *Disorderly Conduct: Visions of Gender in Victorian America* (New York, 1985).

12. Blanche Wiesen Cook, "Female Support Networks and Political Activism: Lillian Wald, Chrystal Eastman, Emma Goldman," *Chrysalis* (no. 3, 1977), 43–61; Kathryn Kish Sklar, *Catharine Beecher: A Study in American Domesticity* (New Haven, 1973). In Catharine E. Beecher, *A Treatise on Domestic Economy* (Boston, 1842), 26–36, Beecher quoted Tocqueville at length and with admiration.

ticity that placed it in direct opposition to ongoing "social and economic transformation" and that emphasized the complexity of the role of motherhood. Organized church groups became one of the few institutional contexts in which women could "connect purposefully" to the community, and such groups, in turn, set a "pattern of reliance on female friendships for emotional expression and security."

Cott ended by proposing that the feminist political movement of the nineteenth century had grown out of the separation of spheres and taken its distinctive shape and interests *from* that separation. For Cott the "ideology of woman's sphere formed a necessary stage in . . . softening the hierarchical relationship of marriage." Although the idea of women's sphere was not necessarily protofeminist, domesticity and feminism were linked by "women's perception of 'womanhood' " as an all-sufficient definition and of sisterhood as implicit in it. That *consciousness*, Cott argued, was a necessary precondition for feminism, even though in opening up certain avenues to women because of their sex it barricaded all others.[13]

Like others before her, Cott sought an economic base for the social transformation she discerned. E. P. Thompson had argued that the crucial psychological change of the early stages of the Industrial Revolution was a shift from the task orientation of traditional artisan work patterns to the time discipline associated with modernity. Cott added the thought that married women's work became less like men's work in the early nineteenth century, as men's work was subjected to modern time discipline while women's work remained task oriented. Work patterns reinforced women's sense that their lives were defined differently from men's. Domesticity could even embody "a protest against that advance of exploitation and pecuniary values . . . by upholding a 'separate sphere' of comfort and compensation. . . . The literature of domesticity . . . enlisted women in their domestic roles to absorb, palliate, and even to redeem the strain of social and economic transformation."[14]

13. Nancy F. Cott, *The Bonds of Womanhood: "Woman's Sphere" in New England, 1780–1835* (New Haven, 1977), 200, 125, 70, 173, 197, 200, 205.

14. E. P. Thompson, "Time, Work-Discipline, and Industrial Capitalism," *Past and Present* (Dec. 1967), 56–97; Cott, *Bonds of Womanhood*, 58, 68–70. In 1964, David M. Potter had observed, "The profound differences between the patterns of men's work and women's work are seldom understood by most men, and perhaps even by most women." He noted that middle-class women's lives remained task-oriented deep into the twentieth century. David M. Potter, "American Women and the American Charac-

Perhaps the historian to use the concept of separate spheres most energetically was Carl N. Degler, whose book *At Odds: Women and the Family in America from the Revolution to the Present* was published in 1980. For Degler, the definition of separate spheres was an important nineteenth-century development that accompanied and made possible the replacement of patriarchal family relationships by companionate ones. Drawing on the work of Daniel Scott Smith, he suggested that women's political autonomy in the public world had been preceded by a form of sexual autonomy, or at least assertiveness, in the private world, and he pointed to the declining birth rate in the nineteenth century as evidence that women were able to exercise a growing degree of control in their sexual relations. Domesticity offered advantages as well as disadvantages to women, smoothing the way to popular acceptance of extrafamilial activities by women. "Separate spheres" deflected conflict; the very language anticipated negotiation. The metaphor of separate spheres helped Degler establish order among issues as disparate as abortion, suffrage, literacy, and friendship. Reference to the omnipresent ideology became a useful guide, enabling the historian to anticipate which changes Americans could be expected to support (for example, the entry of women into the teaching profession) and which they would resist (for example, suffrage, because it could not be accommodated to the concept of separate spheres). *At Odds*, a wide-ranging, fluent, and thoughtful survey of women's history and family history may well represent the high-water mark of reliance on separate spheres as an organizing device.[15]

The first stage of the development of the metaphor—in the late 1960s and early 1970s—was marked by an effort to identify separate spheres as a theme central to women's historical experience, locating the ideology in the context of antebellum American society. The second stage—in the later 1970s—encompassed an effort to refine the definition and identify complexities, introducing the liberating possibilities of a "women's culture." By

---

ter," in *History and American Society: Essays of David M. Potter*, ed. Don E. Fehrenbacher (New York, 1973), 277–303, esp. 287.

15. Carl N. Degler, *At Odds: Women and the Family in America from the Revolution to the Present* (New York, 1980), 9, 298. See also *ibid.*, 26–29, 50–54, 189, 283–98, 302–8, 317, 429. Daniel Scott Smith, "Family Limitation, Sexual Control, and Domestic Feminism in Victorian America," in *Clio's Consciousness Raised*, ed. Mary S. Hartman and Lois W. Banner (New York, 1974), 119–36.

1980 historians had devised a prism through which to view the diaries, letters, and organization records that had been freshly discovered and whose analytical potential was freshly appreciated.

But the language of separate spheres was vulnerable to sloppy use. Above all, it was loosely metaphorical. Those who spoke of "cult" did not, after all, mean a voluntary organization based on commitment to explicit ideological or theological tenets; by "sphere" they did not mean a three-dimensional surface, all points of which are equidistant from a fixed point. When they used the metaphor of separate spheres, historians referred, often interchangeably, to an ideology *imposed on* women, a culture *created by* women, a set of boundaries *expected to be observed* by women. Moreover, the metaphor helped historians avoid thinking about race; virtually all discussion of the subject until very recently has focused on the experience of white women, mostly of the middle class.[16]

In response to this problem, *Feminist Studies* published an exchange in which five historians—Lerner, Smith-Rosenberg, Temma Kaplan, Mari Jo Buhle, and Ellen DuBois—discussed the problems of usage inherent in the terms "women's sphere" and "women's culture." The *Feminist Studies* symposium of 1980 conveniently marks the opening of a third stage, in which historians have sought to embed women's experience in the main course of human development and to unpack the metaphor of "separate spheres." In this stage, historians have undertaken a conscious criticism of their own rhetorical constructions. The comments of the symposium contributors showed that the word "cult" had virtually dropped out of professional historians' usage, although its challenge—that we allocate how much was prescribed for women and how much created by women—remained. DuBois warned that pride in the possibilities of a distinct women's culture might blind historians to the facts of women's oppression. Her respondents tended to caution against conflating the terms "women's sphere," which they took to express a limiting ideology, and "women's culture," a term which embraced creativity in the domestic arts, distinctive forms of labor,

16. Note, however, Elizabeth Fox-Genovese, *Within the Plantation Household: Black and White Women of the Old South* (Chapel Hill, 1988), which addresses with subtlety the intersection of the spheres of slaveholding and enslaved women; and see Deborah Gray White, *Ar'n't I a Woman? Female Slaves in the Plantation South* (New York, 1985); and Jacqueline Jones, *Labor of Love, Labor of Sorrow: Black Women, Work, and the Family from Slavery to the Present* (New York, 1985).

and particular patterns of social relationships.[17] The need to break out of the restrictive dualism of an oppressive term (women's sphere) and a liberating term (women's culture) has propelled what I think is a third stage in the development of the metaphor of separate spheres. Taking an interactive view of social processes, historians now seek to show how women's allegedly "separate sphere" was affected by what men did, and how activities defined by women in their own sphere influenced and even set constraints and limitations on what men might choose to do—how, in short, that sphere was socially constructed both *for* and *by* women.

The first major characteristic of the third stage of understanding is the application of the concept to the entire chronology of human experience, rather than to the discussion of antebellum society where, perhaps by accident, perhaps thanks to Tocqueville, historians first encountered it. A great deal of recent work has made it clear that the separation of spheres was not limited to a single generation or a single civilization.

Surveys of the history of political thought have shown that the habit of contrasting the "worlds" of men and of women, the allocation of the public sector to men and the private sector (still under men's control) to women is older than western civilization. In *The Creation of Patriarchy*, Lerner locates the crucial moment in a prehistoric shift from hunting and gathering societies to agricultural ones and an accompanying intertribal "exchange of women" in the Neolithic period. "Women themselves became a resource, acquired by men much as the land was acquired by men. . . . *It was only after men had learned how to enslave the women of groups who could be defined as strangers, that they learned how to enslave men of those groups and, later, subordinates from within their own societies.*"[18]

The distinction between the private and the public was deeply embedded in classical Greek thought. As Hannah Arendt lucidly explained, the

17. Ellen DuBois, Mari Jo Buhle, Temma Kaplan, Gerda Lerner, and Carroll Smith-Rosenberg, "Politics and Culture in Women's History: A Symposium," *Feminist Studies*, 6 (Spring 1980), 26–64.

18. Gerda Lerner, *The Creation of Patriarchy* (New York, 1986), 212–13. Italics added. "For nearly four thousand years women have shaped their lives and acted under the umbrella of patriarchy," Lerner continues. "The dominated exchange submission for protection, unpaid labor for maintenance. . . . It was a rational choice for women, under conditions of public powerlessness and economic dependency, to choose strong protectors for themselves and their children." *Ibid.*, 217–18. See also *ibid.*, 27–28.

Greeks distinguished between the private realm, defined by the "limita-tion[s] imposed upon us by the needs of biological life," which preclude choice, and the public realm of action and choice. Women, "who with their bodies guarantee the physical survival of the species," were understood to live wholly on the private sector; in Greece they were confined to the large family household and did not mingle, promiscuously, with people on the streets. They were understood to lack the civic virtue that enabled men to function as independent moral beings. Men were advantaged; they lived in *both* the private and the public mode; men realized themselves most fully in the activities of the *polis*. For Aristotle, "the *sophrosyne* (strength of character) of a man and of a woman, or the courage and justice of a man and of a woman are not . . . the same; the courage of a man is shown in commanding, of a woman in obeying." In the ancient formulation, the separate world of women was located securely in a larger patriarchal social context. Classical assumptions about the appropriate relationship between men and women have been attacked only sporadically until recent times. Except for social writers, Western political theorists have treated women in what Susan Moller Okin has called a "functionalist" mode, which assumes that women cannot be dissociated from their function in the family.[19]

When Europeans ventured to the New World, they brought with them the long-standing Western assumptions about women's separate world. Colonial American culture made firm distinctions about what was appro-priate for each sex to do and took for granted the subordination of women. Whether viewed skeptically or sympathetically, English colonists in North America appear to have done little questioning of inherited role defini-tions. From northern New England to the Carolinas there stretched a society in which a woman was defined by her family life and acted in response to relatives' and neighbors' claims on her. The Christian faith of the immigrants ratified both distinctive roles and a subordinate status for women. "Of all the Orders which are unequals," wrote the Congregational

19. Hannah Arendt, *The Human Condition* (New York, 1958), 22–78, esp. 24, 72. Aristotle, *Politics*, trans. Benjamin Jowett (New York, 1943), 77 (1260a). I am grateful to Judith F. Hallett for this reference. Susan Moller Okin, *Women in Western Political Thought* (Princeton, 1979), 9–11, 233. Jean Bethke Elshtain, *Public Man, Private Woman: Women in Social and Political Thought* (Princeton, 1981), builds on a similar dichotomy, although Elshtain ends by decrying contemporary feminists for permitting the intru-sion of politics into the private sector. See also Ruth H. Bloch, "Untangling the Roots of Modern Sex Roles: A Survey of Four Centuries of Change," *Signs*, 4 (Winter 1978), 237–52.

minister Samuel Willard, ". . . [husband and wife] do come nearest to an Equality, and in several respects they stand upon even ground. . . . Nevertheless, God hath also made an imparity between them, in the Order prescribed in His Word, and for that reason there is a Subordination, and they are ranked among unequals." Recent studies of witchcraft have suggested that women at risk for accusation included those who pressed at the boundaries of expected women's behavior, intentionally or unintentionally. One of the major factors in the colonists' perception of Indians as uncivilized was the Indians' tendency to define gender relations differently than did Europeans. Europeans were particularly dismayed when Indian women played roles that were not subordinate or when Indian societies did not display a separation of spheres as Europeans understood them. (For example, Europeans found matrilocality indecipherable.)[20]

As the American Revolution began to impinge on white middle-class women, what Mary Beth Norton has called the "circle of domestic con-

20. Samuel Willard, *A Complete Body of Divinity in Two Hundred and Fifty Expository Lectures* (Boston, 1726), 609–12, quoted in Laurel Thatcher Ulrich, "Vertuous Women Found: New England Ministerial Literature, 1688–1735," *American Quarterly*, 28 (Spring 1976), 20–40, esp. 30. For skeptical views, see Lyle Koehler, *A Search for Power: The "Weaker Sex" in Seventeenth-Century New England* (Urbana, 1980). Laurel Thatcher Ulrich describes a social order in which men's and women's life roles were sharply distinct, overlapping, however, in the role of "deputy husband," which enabled women to act in the public sector if authorized by husbands and fathers. See Laurel Thatcher Ulrich, *Good Wives: Image and Reality in the Lives of Women in Northern New England, 1650–1750* (New York, 1982). Even Ulrich, however, represents a drastic revision of the generalizations about early American life made in the 1950s. See Daniel J. Boorstin, *The Americans: The Colonial Experience* (New York, 1958), 186–87. For the boundaries of witchcraft, see John Putnam Demos, *Entertaining Satan: Witchcraft and the Culture of Early New England* (New York, 1982), 281–83 (the maps of relationships between alleged witches and their accusers); and Carol F. Karlsen, *The Devil in the Shape of a Woman: Witchcraft in Colonial New England* (New York, 1987). On European attitudes toward sex roles in Indian societies, see James Axtell, *The Invasion Within: The Contest of Cultures in Colonial North America* (New York, 1985). For an example of Europeans who observed intensely, but rarely understood, Indian culture, see Paul Le Jeune, *Relation of What Occurred in New France in the Year 1633* in *The Jesuit Relations and Allied Documents*, ed. Reuben Gold Thwaites (73 vols., Cleveland, 1896–1901), V–VI. William Penn was a major exception to this rule. See, for example, "Letter to the Free Society of Traders," Aug. 16, 1683, in *William Penn and the Founding of Pennsylvania, 1680–1684: A Documentary History*, ed. Jean R. Soderlund (Philadelphia, 1983), 308–19.

cerns" bounded their lives: the choice of husband (an especially important decision in a virtually divorceless society), the nurture of children, the management or service of the household. The Revolution shook old assumptions about women's place and suggested new possibilities; guerrilla war made few concessions to alleged frailty, and many women, whether Loyalist or Patriot, were involuntarily given an accelerated course in politics and independence. By the end of the war, the domestic roles of women could no longer be taken for granted; such roles now required defensive ideological articulation. Thus emerged the antebellum prescriptive literature we have come to know.[21]

As I have argued elsewhere, the ideology of republican womanhood was an effort to bring the older version of the separation of spheres into rough conformity with the new politics that valued autonomy and individualism. Issues of sexual asymmetry dominated public discourse to an unprecedented extent as people tried to define a place for women in postrevolutionary society. Even as Americans enlarged the scope, resonance, and power of republicanism they simultaneously discounted and weakened the force of patriarchy. They recoded the values of women's sphere, validating women's moral influence on their husbands and lovers, ascribing world-historical importance to women's maternal role, and claiming for women a nature less sexual and more self-controlled than the nature of men. The ideology of republican womanhood recognized that women's choices and women's work did serve large social and political purposes, and that recognition was enough to draw the traditional women's "sphere" somewhat closer to men's "world." But to use the language of domesticity was also to make a conservative political choice among alternative options, rejecting the frankly feminist option, articulated by Mary Wollstonecraft in England and Etta Palm in France, that claimed for women direct connection with republican political life. Indeed, I believe that the American Revolution was kept from spinning on an outwardly expansive and radical track in part by the general refusal to

21. Mary Beth Norton, *Liberty's Daughters: The Revolutionary Experience of American Women, 1750–1800* (Boston, 1980), 298. Norton found reference to women's sphere in the late colonial period. Samuel Quincy wrote to Robert Treat Paine in 1756, fearing that women want "to obtain the other's Sphere of Action, & become Men," but hoped "they will again return to the wonted Paths of true Politeness, & shine most in the proper Sphere of domestick Life." *Ibid.*, 8. See also Linda K. Kerber, "Daughters of Columbia: Educating Women for the Republic, 1787–1805," in *The Hofstadter Aegis: A Memorial*, ed. Stanley Elkins and Eric McKitrick (New York, 1974), 36–59 [reprinted in the present volume].

entertain proposals for redefining the relationship between women and the Republic. By contrast, major changes in women's political life were associated with the radical stages of the French Revolution, and erasure of those changes was associated with the retreat from radicalism.[22]

The second major characteristic of the current stage of understanding is that we are giving more attention to questions about the social relations of the sexes and treating the language of separate spheres itself as a rhetorical construction that responded to changing social and economic reality. Tocqueville's visit occurred at the end of more than a half century during which one variant of the separation of spheres and the patriarchal culture in which it was embedded had been undermined by commercial, political, and industrial revolutions. Adam Smith had given voice to the great commercial transformation, the founders at Philadelphia had articulated the political one, and new technology embodied the industrial one. In each realm the world maintained itself by the spinning gyroscope of successive decision and choice. Political rules, like economic ones, had been written anew. In a world from which familiar boundaries had been erased, new relationships had to be defined, new turf had to be measured, and in Thomas L. Haskell's phrase, new "spheres of competition" had to be freshly aligned. In a system of laissez-faire, which relied on the dynamic force of self-interest in commerce and in politics, the "sphere of competition" was everywhere. In a Tocquevillean world of equality, where all the old barriers had been removed, little was left that was not vulnerable. Marvin Meyers discerned many years ago that Tocqueville's American Man was characteristically anxious, as well he might be in a world in which so little seemed reliably fixed.[23]

---

22. Linda K. Kerber, *Women of the Republic: Intellect and Ideology in Revolutionary America* (Chapel Hill, 1980), 185–231. See also Linda K. Kerber, "The Republican Mother: Women and the Enlightenment—An American Perspective," *American Quarterly*, 28 (Summer 1976), 187–205 [which is reproduced in the present volume]. For France, see Darline Gay Levy, Harriet Branson Applewhite, and Mary Durham Johnson, *Women in Revolutionary Paris, 1789–1795: Selected Documents Translated with Notes and Commentary* (Urbana, 1979). On sexuality, see Nancy F. Cott, "Passionlessness: An Interpretation of Victorian Sexual Ideology, 1790–1850," *Signs*, 4 (Winter 1978), 219–36. For the implications of republican ideology for the relations between women and men, see Jan Lewis, "The Republican Wife: Virtue and Seduction in the Early Republic," *William and Mary Quarterly*, 44 (Oct. 1987), 689–721.

23. Marvin Meyers, *The Jacksonian Persuasion: Politics and Belief* (Stanford, 1957), 45. Thomas L. Haskell used the phrase in a letter to me in May 1984.

The capitalist revolution also had deeply unsettling implications for women. As patriarchy eroded, social reality involved unattached individuals, freely negotiating with each other in an expansive market. The patriarchal variant of separate spheres was not congruent with capitalist social relations; capitalism required that men's and women's economic relations be renegotiated. A capitalist system tended to undermine an older scheme of property relations that, by keeping a woman's property under the control of the men to whom she was entrusted, could also keep it out of the marketplace, for example, when dower property was shielded from seizure for debt.

Capitalism had the potential to enhance the position of women by loosening patriarchal control of property and removing factors that shielded property from the pressures of the marketplace. The revised understanding of the relationship between women and the marketplace was embodied in the married women's property acts, devised state by state in the middle decades of the nineteenth century. Such statutes gave married women the right to hold and manipulate their own earnings and property. The statutes created a vast new group of property-holding, but unenfranchised, citizens; married women's property acts unintentionally but inexorably created an internally contradictory situation that was ultimately resolved by granting the vote—and with it, service on juries and the opportunity to hold public office. The franchise acknowledged women's connection to the political community as the law of property had acknowledged their entry into the marketplace. As the patriarchal corporate economy broke down, the traditional version of the separate sphere was destabilized. One plausible way to read nineteenth-century defenses of separate spheres, not least among them Tocqueville's, is to single out the theme of breakdown; the noise we hear about separate spheres may be the shattering of an old order and the realignment of its fragments.[24]

But the old order, like the parson's one-horse shay, took a long time

24. On fathers in commercial settings willing real estate to daughters, see Toby L. Ditz, *Property and Kinship: Inheritance in Early Connecticut, 1750–1820* (Princeton, 1986). For the anomalies of the impact of capitalism on the status of women, see Elizabeth Fox-Genovese and Eugene D. Genovese, *Fruits of Merchant Capital: Slavery and Bourgeois Property in the Rise and Expansion of Capitalism* (New York, 1983), esp. 299–336. For a succinct review of these developments, see Norma Basch, "Equity vs. Equality: Emerging Concepts of Women's Political Status in the Age of Jackson," *Journal of the Early Republic*, 3 (Fall 1983), 297–318, esp. 305.

breaking down. Patched up and reconstructed, it continued to rattle along for a long time. The first wave of married women's property acts did not seem to usher in a new era; they protected only property given or willed to women, expressing fathers' distrust of irresponsible sons-in-law. In protecting gift property from seizure for debts contracted by husbands, married women's property acts were debtor relief acts that directly benefited men. The new property acts expressed a relationship between men—as well as a revised relationship among men, women, and the marketplace. Only at the stage of revision—1855 in Michigan, 1860 in New York, later elsewhere—did the new statutes specifically protect married women's earnings and their right to manage their own property. Not until 1911 did Michigan law permit a married woman to define the full use of her own earnings; until then her husband had the right to decide whether or not a woman could work for wages.[25]

Thus the older property relations between husbands and wives persisted long after limited elements of those relations had been modified by statute. Studying nineteenth-century Michigan women's correspondence, Marilyn Ferris Motz has argued for the continuing instrumental usefulness of the separate female sphere as "a system of human relations" that provided a "cushion" against a legal system whose rules privileged the authority of husbands and fathers over married women's property relations during a lengthy transitional period. Because the early versions of married women's property acts protected only inherited and gift property, they created a paradox in which a woman exercised much more control over property she inherited from her parents than over property she had helped build—on a farm or in a family business—in the course of her marriage. In such a legal context, Motz argues, there was good economic reason for women to work energetically to establish and maintain networks of female kin. "Women attempted to balance their lack of authority within the nuclear family with the collective moral, social, and financial pressure of their kin networks," Motz observes, ". . . from whom [they] could inherit and to whom [they] could turn for alternative support." In an era when alimony was rare, women who wished to divorce their husbands leaned on female kin for support. A woman who faced early death in childbirth counted on her

25. Basch, "Equity vs. Equality." See also Norma Basch, *In the Eyes of the Law: Women, Marriage, and Property in Nineteenth-Century New York* (Ithaca, 1982); and Suzanne O. Lebsock, "Radical Reconstruction and the Property Rights of Southern Women," *Journal of Southern History*, 43 (May 1977), 195–216.

sisters to protect her children from mistreatment by possible future step-mothers. Young widows turned to their female kin to sustain them and their children; elderly widows counted on their daughters and daughters-in-law to nurse them in reciprocity for earlier care. Motz draws an analogy between the social dynamics that sustained the separate sphere of middle-class nineteenth-century Michigan women and the patterns of service and reciprocity traced by Carol B. Stack among twentieth-century working-class women. She argues forcefully that the "women's culture" and "wom-en's values" of the separate sphere rested on long-term economic and psychological self-interest.[26]

In Motz's Michigan, as in Cott's New England, the work patterns of men deviated ever farther from those of women, perhaps reinforcing the need to maintain the boundaries of the separate women's sphere. But as Tamara K. Hareven observed in 1976, members of families might be drawn into capitalist ways at different rates. When women worked in factories and taught in schools, their work was modernized and forced into the new time-bound, clock-measured matrix to which E. P. Thompson has given classical formulation. For the first time in history, substantial numbers of women could earn substantial amounts of cash. In a careful reading of the letters of Lowell mill women, Thomas Dublin criticizes the older assump-tion that mill women remained embedded in the traditional family econ-omy. "Work in the mills," he writes, "functioned for women rather like migration did for young men. . . . the mills offered individual self-support." Perhaps the clearest expression of that position comes in a letter written by a father on a farm to a foster daughter in the mills: "You now feel & enjoy independence trusting to your own ability to procure whatever you want, leaning on no one no one depending on you."[27]

26. Marilyn Ferris Motz, *True Sisterhood: Michigan Women and Their Kin, 1820–1920* (Albany, 1983), 29, 33–35, 121–25, 155–56, 168; Carol B. Stack, *All Our Kin: Strategies for Survival in a Black Community* (New York, 1974).

27. Tamara K. Hareven, "Modernization and Family History: Perspectives on Social Change," *Signs*, 2 (Autumn 1976), 190–206; McKendrick, "Home Demand and Eco-nomic Growth," 164–67; Thomas Dublin, ed., *From Farm to Factory: Women's Letters, 1830–1860* (New York, 1981), 22–23, 166. Class, race, ethnicity, location, and time all affected the psychological impact of work outside the home. Leslie Woodcock Tentler found that factory women in early twentieth-century Boston, New York, Philadelphia, and Chicago not only continued to think of themselves as embedded in the family economy, but also found in the workplace other young women who reinforced this traditional understanding. Leslie Woodcock Tentler, *Wage-Earning Women: Industrial*

How are we to find our way through the confusions of local idiosyncrasy, sometimes providing dependence, sometimes independence? Two important books, published in the early 1980s, both community studies built on demographic and quantitative research in documents revealing economic relationships, offer complex but carefully nuanced analyses. Together they testify to the dramatic force of capitalist pressures on women's sphere.

In antebellum Petersburg, Virginia, the language of domesticity and the deferential separation of spheres escaped explicit public challenge. But Suzanne Lebsock can unambivalently conclude from her intensive analysis of public records that "women in Petersburg experienced increasing autonomy, autonomy in the sense of freedom from utter dependence on particular men. Relatively speaking, fewer women were married, more women found work for wages, and more married women acquired separate estates." The changes occurred largely without the assistance of a politically oriented discourse. Separate estates—a legal device that deflected coverture and assured married women control over property—provided a shelter against family bankruptcy and an apolitical response to repeated economic panics. "It stands to reason," Lebsock writes, "that an ideology that tried to fix the boundaries of women's sphere should have become pervasive and urgent just as women began to exercise a few choices. . . . As women acquired new degrees of power and autonomy in the private sphere, they were confronted with new forms of subordination in the public sphere."[28]

The character of the women's sphere of the mid-nineteenth century as distinctive social construction is elaborately developed and richly argued in Mary P. Ryan's important study of Oneida County, New York, *Cradle of the Middle Class*. Stressing the connections between public and private realms, Ryan begins by describing the patriarchal assumptions of the traditional early modern domestic economy. In her reading, many aspects of patriarchy broke down in the early nineteenth century, under blows from an increasingly commercial economy that made unentailed estates and liquid inheritance advantageous to heirs. Instead of the language of separate spheres, Ryan speaks of the changing interests of families as a whole. Ryan

---

Work and Family Life in the United States, 1900–1930 (New York, 1979). See also Jacquelyn Dowd Hall et al., *Like a Family: The Making of a Southern Cotton Mill World* (Chapel Hill, 1987).

28. Suzanne Lebsock, *The Free Women of Petersburg: Status and Culture in a Southern Town, 1784–1860* (New York, 1984), xv, 234.

interprets the retreat to the private conjugal family as a way of mobilizing private resources for upward social mobility. Over a half century, from 1810 to 1855, the number of children per family dropped sharply, from 5.8 to 3.6, permitting more attention to each child. At the same time, the language of domesticity, which emphasized the role of mothers in raising children, was congruent with increased psychological investment in child nurture and education and, most important, with keeping *sons* out of the work force in order to extend their education and improve their chances for upward mobility. One major surprise is Ryan's finding that as boys were kept out of the work force, middle-class women and daughters were increasingly apt to work for pay—for example, by keeping boarders, or serving as domestics. Women's energy was used "to maintain or advance the status of men in their families."[29]

In Ryan's account, women's "separate sphere" was deeply paradoxical. The concept clearly served the interests of men with whom women lived. Yet, women also claimed it for their own, defining their own interests as inextricably linked to the upward mobility of their families, repressing claims for their own autonomy. When women went to work for pay, they entered a severely segregated work force (the white-collar jobs of clerks were still reserved for their sons and brothers). The diaries of their friendships show them circulating in a world of women. The logic of their situation drove a very few to political feminism, but for most, the "female world of love and ritual" and the ideology of domesticity that purported to explain it remained powerful and persuasive.

Black families were not immune to the ideology of separate spheres, and recent work by James Oliver Horton and Lois E. Horton, Dorothy Sterling, Jacqueline Jones, and Deborah Gray White has been particularly shrewd in tracing their ambivalent responses to it.[30] The American ideology was to some limited extent congruent with African traditions of matrilocality, of women's clear responsibilities for child support and child raising, and of a

29. Mary P. Ryan, *Cradle of the Middle Class: The Family in Oneida County, New York, 1790–1865* (Cambridge, Eng., 1981), esp. 56, 185.

30. James Oliver Horton and Lois E. Horton, *Black Bostonians: Family Life and Community Struggle in the Antebellum North* (New York, 1979); Dorothy Sterling, ed., *We Are Your Sisters: Black Women in the Nineteenth Century* (New York, 1984); Jones, *Labor of Love, Labor of Sorrow*; White, *Ar'n't I A Woman?* I am indebted to the interpretations of Evelyn Brooks, "The Problem of Race in Women's History," in *Coming to Terms: Feminism/Theory/Politics*, ed. Elizabeth Weed (New York, 1989).

A HAPPY FAMILY.

Authorities promoted the ideology of domesticity and separate spheres to southern
blacks, even when most still lived in slave cabins. Reproduced from Clinton B. Fisk,
Plain Counsel for the Freedmen (1866). Courtesy Library of Congress.

sex-linked division for child support and child raising, and of a sex-linked
division of labor. Enslaved men lacked the economic power that white men
exercised over their families; the nuances of relationships between slave
men and women are debated by historians. It is clear that directly after the
Civil War, prescriptive literature addressed to recently freed slaves, people
living in hovels with dirt floors, counseled delicacy among women and a

clear division of their work from men's work, implicitly promising that adoption of the ideology would ensure elevation to the middle class.[31]

The ideology of separate spheres could be both instrumental and prescriptive; its double character has made it difficult for historians to work with. In the first mode, it was an ideology women found useful and emotionally sustaining, a familiar link between the older patriarchal culture and the new bourgeois experience. This aspect could be particularly welcome as a hedge against secularization; religious women of virtually all persuasions sustained a pattern of separateness both in their religious activism and in their own religiosity.[32] It could also, as Gerda Lerner discerned, protect the interests of one class of women in a time of change. But in its prescriptive mode, the ideology of separate spheres required constant attention if it were to be maintained.

In *Beyond Separate Spheres*, Rosalind Rosenberg has located the beginnings of modern studies of sex differences in the Progressive Era. Two generations of brilliant social scientists, among them Helen Thompson, Jessie Taft, W. I. Thomas, Franz Boas, and Elsie Clews Parsons, established the foundation for a "fundamental shift that took place in the way women viewed themselves and their place in society." By the early twentieth century at least some psychologists, sociologists, and anthropologists were coming to understand that many sex differences were the result of socialization, not biology. Finally it became possible to imagine a culture that was not divided into separate spheres. Our own ideas about sex differences still rely heavily on their work.[33]

Yet the real world took its time catching up with what academics believed they knew. Quite as much energy, male and female, has gone to maintain boundaries as to break them down. One result of the traditional assumption that what women have done is trivial is that historians have severely underestimated the extent of the energy—psychological, political,

31. Sterling, *We Are Your Sisters*, 319–20.

32. Tamara K. Hareven's point that the rate of modernization may be different for men and women even within the same family applied to secularization as well. Nineteenth-century American Protestant women sustained a pattern of separateness in their religious activism and in their own religiosity. See Barbara Welter, *Dimity Convictions: The American Woman in the Nineteenth Century* (Athens, 1976), 83–102; and Joan Jacobs Brumberg, "Zenanas and Girlless Villages: The Ethnology of American Evangelical Women, 1870–1910," *Journal of American History*, 69 (Sept. 1982), 347–71.

33. Rosalind Rosenberg, *Beyond Separate Spheres: Intellectual Roots of Modern Feminism* (New Haven, 1982), xiv.

and legal—thus expended. Writing of rural communities in the nineteenth-century Midwest, John Mack Faragher describes the dynamics of the process: "the regulation of the sexual division of labor was achieved through the perpetuation of a hierarchical and male-dominant family structure, linked to a public world from which women were excluded. . . . Men were free to pursue the work of the public world precisely because the inequitable division of labor at home made them the beneficiaries of women's and children's labor."[34]

Examples of the energy put into maintaining boundaries abound. Thus Mary Kelley's *Private Woman, Public Stage* is in part an extended accounting of the price paid in pain and anguish by the first generation of professional women writers who sought to break their traditional intellectual isolation, and the "deprivation and devastation of spirit," the "subversion of intellect," to which the tradition of separate spheres had consigned them. Degler and Kraditor have emphasized the energy that antisuffragists dedicated to maintaining the boundaries of the separate spheres as they knew them. Cindy Sondik Aron's important study of the continuing negotiation of manners and reciprocal obligations in the mid-nineteenth-century civil service, the first large-scale labor force that was genuinely mixed in gender, shows that the ideology of separate spheres—like all ideology—is not frozen in time but is in a constant state of refinement until it fits reality so badly that a paradigm shift in conceptualization is unavoidable. Margaret W. Rossiter's *Women Scientists in America* provides, among many other things, a case study in the strategies of boundary maintenance and renegotiation. As women scientists successfully met the traditional markers of professional accomplishment, the standards themselves were redefined so as to enclose a sector of the population that was male.[35]

34. John Mack Faragher, "History from the Inside-Out: Writing the History of Women in Rural America," *American Quarterly*, 33 (Winter 1981), 537–57, esp. 550. Faragher proceeded to write a history that demonstrated the gendered nature of community formation and the uneven allocation of work and power. See John Mack Faragher, *Sugar Creek: Life on the Illinois Prairie* (New Haven, 1986).

35. Mary Kelley, *Private Woman, Public Stage: Literary Domesticity in Nineteenth-Century America* (New York, 1984), 187, 100; Cindy Sondik Aron, *Ladies and Gentlemen of the Civil Service: Middle-Class Workers in Victorian America* (New York, 1987); Margaret W. Rossiter, *Women Scientists in America: Struggles and Strategies to 1940* (Baltimore, 1982). Carl Degler pointed to the paradox that woman suffrage met severe resistance while other barriers to suffrage—property and race requirements for men—were being removed. He suggested that the resistance was in part due to the psychologi-

Feminist historians of the Progressive Era have been particularly sensitive to the force of opposition that women met when they sought public influence. The years 1870–1920 may be the high-water mark of women's public influence: through voluntary organizations, lobbying, trade unions, professional education, and professional activity. But women also met unprecedented hostility and resistance that seems disproportionate, even in the no-holds-barred political arena: When she opposed United States intervention in World War I, Jane Addams was attacked as " 'a silly, vain, impertinent old maid' who had better leave the fighting to the men." Barbara Sicherman asks, "Why did the Anti-Saloon League replace the WCTU as the leading temperance organization? Why were women's organizations especially subject to red-baiting in the 1920s?" We might add other examples from the 1920s and later: the extraordinary bitterness of the American Medical Association's campaign against the modest recommendations of the Sheppard-Towner Act; the bitterly vindictive, personal attacks on Eleanor Roosevelt throughout her life; the marginalization and isolation of political women like Oveta Culp Hobby in the 1950s; the rich resources of advertising used in the 1920s to redefine the housewife and again in the 1950s to sustain that definition. The evidence that the woman's sphere is a social construction lies in part in the hard and constant work required to build and repair its boundaries.[36]

In the last decade historians of working women have made it abundantly clear that the phrase "separate spheres" is a metaphor for complex power relations in social and economic contexts. Capitalist social relations from the late eighteenth century until now have balanced precariously on the fictions that women "help" rather than work, that their true "place" is in the home, that when they venture "out" of the home they are best suited to doing work that replicates housework. Such work is "unskilled," interruptible, nurturing, and appropriately rewarded primarily by love and secondarily by a segregated marketplace that consistently values women's work

---

cal investment that many women, as well as men, had in the status quo. Degler, *At Odds*, 340–61.

36. Barbara Sicherman, "Separate Spheres as Historical Paradigm: Limiting Metaphor or Useful Construct?" comment delivered at the annual meeting of the Organization of American Historians, Los Angeles, April 1984 (in Barbara Sicherman's possession); Cynthia Harrison, *On Account of Sex: The Politics of Women's Issues, 1945–1968* (Berkeley, 1988). Elaine Tyler May, *Homeward Bound: American Families in the Cold War Era* (New York, 1988).

less than men's. The point is not only that the marketplace is segregated by gender; it is also that the segregation has been constantly under negotiation and constantly reaffirmed. That these broad patterns are worldwide and cross-cultural was made clear in a special issue of *Signs* in 1977.[37]

The particulars of the American experience have been the target of sustained investigation by social historians who have developed a powerful feminist critique of Marxism for its conflation of the situation and interests of working-class men and working-class women. In *Out to Work*, published in 1982, Alice Kessler-Harris offered an important history of women's labor force participation. For Kessler-Harris, the dynamics of the marketplace and the ideology of separate spheres were interdependent, together defining a gender-segregated workplace, while forcing working-class women to live with the depressing ironies inherent in their situation as physically exhausted workers who were regarded as not really at work. Mary H. Blewett's studies of the work culture of shoemakers in preindustrial New England reveal that women were assigned the single task of binding the uppers of the shoes, a task housewives did in their kitchens, isolated from the shop, in a setting that denied them access to other aspects of the craft or to the collective experience of working with colleagues. Thus the industrial work culture of the nineteenth century inherited, writes Blewett, "gender categories [that] made it difficult for male artisans to regard women as fellow workers, include them in the ideology and politics based on their work culture, or see in the experience of working women what awaited all workers under industrialization."[38]

In the late nineteenth century, groups as disparate as the carpet weavers organized by the Knights of Labor, studied by Susan Levine; women socialists, studied by Mari Jo Buhle; and the Women's Trade Union League, studied by Nancy Schrom Dye and Robin Jacoby were torn in various ways by simultaneous commitments to "equal rights" in the public sector, to a

37. "Women and National Development: The Complexities of Change," *Signs*, 3 (Autumn 1977), 1–338.

38. Alice Kessler-Harris, *Out to Work: A History of Wage-Earning Women in the United States* (New York, 1982). The argument is developed forcefully in Alice Kessler-Harris, "The Just Price, the Free Market and the Value of Women," paper delivered at the Seventh Berkshire Conference on the History of Women, Wellesley, Mass., June 1987 (in Alice Kessler-Harris's possession). Mary H. Blewett, "The Sexual Division of Labor and the Artisan Tradition in Early Industrial Capitalism: The Case of New England Shoemaking, 1780–1860," in *"To Toil the Livelong Day": America's Women At Work, 1780–1980*, ed. Carol Groneman and Mary Beth Norton (Ithaca, 1987), 35–46, esp. 36.

New technologies were almost immediately segregated by gender. Switchboards, Cortland Exchange, c. 1890. Courtesy Library Company of Philadelphia.

future in which women would "return" to their "natural" sphere of the home and to an ugly reality in which working women labored in the public sector by day and returned to domestic chores by night. The result was to make the segregation of women in unskilled jobs a permanent feature of the American industrial scene. The boundaries of gender segregation were maintained by enormous efforts undertaken by elite owners of factories, middle-class managers, and unionized male workers. Judith McGaw has recently pressed the ironies further, arguing that the "unskilled" character of women's industrial work was itself a fiction that ensured a steady supply of cheap labor. The fiction devalued women's work because it was un-mechanized, obscuring the extent to which unmechanized work could require a degree of skill too high for machines to replicate, and the fact that unmechanized work fulfilled functions essential to factory production.[39]

39. Susan Levine, *Labor's True Woman: Carpet Weavers, Industrialization, and Labor Reform in the Gilded Age* (Philadelphia, 1984), 10, 148; Mari Jo Buhle, *Women and American Socialism, 1870–1920* (Urbana, 1981); Nancy Schrom Dye, *As Equals and As Sisters: Feminism, the Labor Movement, and the Women's Trade Union League of New York* (Columbia, 1980); Robin Miller Jacoby, "The Women's Trade Union League and

The dynamics have persisted. Sheila Tobias established male trade unionists' insistence on the exclusion of Rosie the Riveter from post–World War II factories, denying women who had joined the skilled work force during the war not only the jobs promised to returning veterans but their own earned seniority and thrusting a generation of working women into a pink-collar ghetto. Ruth Milkman has shown in convincing detail how even during World War II, unions and management cooperated to ensure that the work Rosie did was defined and redefined as women's work even if it involved skills and physical capacities previously understood to be male. Myra H. Strober has been demonstrating how in our own time, the new computer technology was quickly and emphatically assigned a gendered identity.[40]

Historians of working women have thus had especially good reason to understand that the language of separate spheres has been a language enabling contemporaries to explain to themselves the social situation—with all its ironies and contradictions—in which they understood themselves to be living. "Separate spheres" was a trope that hid its instrumentality even from those who employed it; in that sense it was deeply ambiguous. In the ambiguity, perhaps, lay its appeal.[41]

American Feminism," *Feminist Studies*, 3 (Fall 1975), 126–40; Judith A. McGaw, *Most Wonderful Machine: Mechanization and Social Change in Berkshire Paper Making, 1801–1885* (Princeton, 1987), 335–74. Judith A. McGaw, "No Passive Victims, No Separate Spheres: A Feminist Perspective on Technology's History," in *In Context: History and the History of Technology—Essays in Honor of Mel Kranzberg*, ed. Stephen Cutliffe and Robert W. Post (Bethlehem, Pa., 1988), argues that a transformation of housework *preceded* the Industrial Revolution and made many of its characteristics possible.

40. Sheila Tobias and Ruth Milkman, *Gender at Work: The Dynamics of Job Segregation by Sex during World War II* (Urbana, 1987); Myra Strober and Carolyn L. Arnold, "Integrated Circuits/Segregated Labor: Women in Computer-Related Occupations and High-Tech Industries," in *Computer Chips and Paper Clips: Technology and Women's Employment*, ed. Heidi Hartmann, Robert E. Kraut, and Louise Tilly (Washington, 1986), 136–82. For important studies of the "tipping" of an occupation from male to female, see Myra H. Strober, "Toward a General Theory of Occupational Sex Segregation: The Case of Public School Teaching," in *Sex Segregation in the Workplace: Trends, Explanations, Remedies*, ed. Barbara F. Reskin (Washington, 1984), 144–56; and Myra H. Strober and David Tyack, "Why Do Women Teach and Men Manage? A Report on Research on Schools," *Signs*, 5 (1980), 494–503.

41. "When we seek to make sense of such problematical topics as human nature, culture, society, and history, we never say precisely what we wish to say or mean precisely what we say," warns Hayden White. "Our discourse always tends to slip away

A third major characteristic of recent work, one whose potential is at last being vigorously tapped, is the use of "sphere" in a literal sense. Historians are paying considerable attention to the physical spaces to which women were assigned, those in which they lived, and those they chose for themselves. Stressing the interplay between the metaphorical and the literal, historians in the 1980s may be on their way toward a resolution of the paradoxes of women's politics/women's culture with which the symposiasts of *Feminist Studies* wrestled. Historians are finding it worthwhile to treat "sphere" not only as metaphor but also as descriptor, to use it to refer to domain in the most obvious and explicit sense.

In adopting that approach historians have learned much from anthropologists, who have long understood the need to scrutinize separate men's and women's spaces. Men's places were often clearly defined; menstruating women were often excluded from them. Men's space normally included the central community meeting place and the fields; that is, as Lucienne Roubin writes, the village government "tends to juxtapose and to fuse male space with public space." Women's space, by definition, is what is left: sleeping enclosures, gardens. In the mid-1970s historians found *Woman, Culture, and Society*, an anthology edited by anthropologists Michelle Zimbalist Rosaldo and Louise Lamphere, deeply resonant for its analyses of the significance of women's behavior in domestic settings.[42]

As we have seen, historians who examined sex roles were likely to link physical separation with social subordination. That was particularly true for historians of early America: as Lyle Koehler observed, "Puritan society

---

from our data towards the structures of consciousness with which we are trying to grasp them . . . the data always resist the coherency of the image which we are trying to fashion of them." Hayden White, *Tropics of Discourse: Essays in Cultural Criticism* (Baltimore, 1978), 1.

42. Lucienne Roubin, "Male Space and Female Space within the Provençal Community," in *Rural Society in France: Selections from the* Annales: Economies, Sociétés, Civilisations, ed. Robert Forster and Orest Ranum, trans. Elborg Forster and Patricia M. Ranum (Baltimore, 1977), 152–80, esp. 155. See also Michelle Zimbalist Rosaldo, "Women, Culture, and Society: A Theoretical Overview," in *Women, Culture, and Society*, ed. Rosaldo and Lamphere, 17–42; Sherry B. Ortner, "Is Female to Male As Nature Is to Culture?" *ibid.*, 67–87; and Louise Lamphere, "Strategies, Cooperation, and Conflict in Domestic Groups," *ibid.*, 97–112. Also important is Rayna R. Reiter, ed., *Toward an Anthropology of Women* (New York, 1975), especially Reiter's own essay, Rayna R. Reiter, "Men and Women in the South of France: Public and Private Domains," *ibid.*, 252–82 (her description of the "sexual geography" of a village).

was organized in a way that explicitly affirmed the belief in sex segregation as a reminder of men's and women's different destinies." In a 1978 essay, Mary Maples Dunn reversed the argument. In a brilliant examination of the way control of physical space could affect public behavior, Dunn argued that the spiritual equality that Quaker theology offered women was confirmed and authenticated by the device of separate women's meetings. Women's meetings enabled women to control their own agenda, to allocate their own funds, and to exercise disciplinary control over their members, especially by validating marriages. Those roles were reinforced by Quaker women's control over their physical space, in meetinghouses with sliding partitions in the center that provided "women and men with separate spaces for the conduct of their separate business." Women of no other denomination claimed such control over their space and their record keeping, and Dunn suggests that the elements of physical control were central to women's more autonomous spiritual role in the Quaker community.[43]

In 1979, Estelle Freedman published an important essay, "Separatism as Strategy: Female Institution Building and American Feminism, 1870–1930." In it she sought to overcome the simplifications of the traditional male-public/female-private hierarchy by a construction that bridged the two categories: the "public female sphere." By that she referred to the " 'female institution building' which emerged from the middle-class women's culture of the nineteenth century." She had in mind women's clubs (like Sorosis, which was initiated when the New York Press Club excluded women journalists in 1868); women's colleges; women's settlement houses, most notably Hull House; women's political organizations; women's trade unions; even the women's buildings at the International Centennial Exposition in 1876 and the World's Columbian Exposition in 1892. In each case, the refusal to merge their groups into male-dominated institutions gave women not only crucial practical and political experience but also a

43. Koehler, *Search for Power*, 41; Mary Maples Dunn, "Saints and Sisters: Congregational and Quaker Women in the Early Colonial Period," in *Women in American Religion*, ed. Janet Wilson James (Philadelphia, 1980), 27–46, esp. 45; originally published in *American Quarterly*, 30 (Winter 1978), 582–601, esp. 600. About the most clearly bounded women's religious social space—the convent—we know little. In the colonial period there was a convent in Montreal, but we have no studies of its internal dynamics, though we know that some American women captives chose to stay there rather than be repatriated. See Axtell, *Invasion Within*, 302–27. On the general problem, see Elizabeth Kolmer, "Catholic Women Religious and Women's History: A Survey of the Literature," in *Women in American Religion*, ed. James, 127–39.

place where they could rest the levers with which they hoped to effect social change. The space that Freedman ended by recommending to women was in part metaphorical: women needed their own networks, and they needed to nurture their own culture. Embedded in her essay, however, was also the observation that feminists had been most successful when they had commanded actual physical space of their own, which they could define and control.[44]

If we imagine Freedman as staking out an empty shelf in the bookcase of women's history in 1979, we could now say that the shelf is crowded with books and articles that illustrate her point. New studies of the history of domesticity have understood domesticity to be an ideology whose objective correlative is the physical space of the household. The "material feminist" reformers of Dolores Hayden's *The Grand Domestic Revolution*, who flourished between 1870 and 1930, sought to reappropriate that space and to redesign it to socialize domestic work. Central kitchens, cooked food delivery, professionalized home cleaning, and other efforts to reconstruct women's work within the domestic sphere severely challenged the traditional social order. Such inventions were squelched. Powerful interest groups countered them with home mortgage policies that privileged male-headed households, highway construction that encouraged diffuse suburban development, and urban design that stressed single-family homes lacking central services. Hayden's book was followed by detailed histories by Susan Strasser and Ruth Schwartz Cowan, which tracked the development of housework and household technology. Cowan argued that the definition of the home as women's sphere was accompanied by a change in household technology with the result that men—excused from chopping wood for fire, pounding meal, and other household tasks—found the home a place of leisure, a "haven in a heartless world" while it retained its character as a place of labor for women. The work of Faye E. Dudden on household service shows that women's domestic space was pervaded by class considerations; the home was a theater, in which the mistress of the house claimed her space and assigned to the servant the space she might occupy.[45]

44. Estelle Freedman, "Separatism as Strategy: Female Institution Building and American Feminism, 1870–1930," *Feminist Studies*, 5 (Fall 1979), 512–29, esp. 513.

45. Dolores Hayden, *The Grand Domestic Revolution: A History of Feminist Designs for American Homes, Neighborhoods and Cities* (Cambridge, Mass., 1981); Susan Strasser, *Never Done: A History of American Housework* (New York, 1982); Ruth Schwartz

Jane Addams in Hull House dining room with staff and guests, c. 1930.
Men are invited to women's space. Facing camera: Ida Lovett (smoking a cigarette),
Robert Morss Lovett, Alice Hamilton (face hidden), Addams; back to camera: Edith
de Nancrede, Rachelle Yarros. I am grateful to Mary Lynn McCree Bryan for the
identifications. Courtesy Swarthmore College Peace Collection.

The philosophy and ideology of other institutions are increasingly understood to be embedded in their arrangement of physical space. Helen Lefkowitz Horowitz has traced the complex relationships between the visions that women's college founders had for their institutions and the architecture that they commissioned. In her work, even intellectual history is understood to be deeply affected by its physical context. And a rich

Cowan, *More Work for Mother: The Ironies of Household Technology from the Open Hearth to the Microwave* (New York, 1983); Faye E. Dudden, *Serving Women: Household Service in Nineteenth-Century America* (Middletown, 1983).

outpouring of work on the women of the Hull House community has made it increasingly clear that having control of the physical institution of Hull House—which at its height included thirteen large structures spaced over two square blocks—provided an institutional base permitting women reformers, in Kathryn Kish Sklar's words, to "enter realms of reality dominated by men, where, for better or for worse, they competed with men for control over the distribution of social resources." Hull House was many things, not least among them a physical space in which the divorced Florence Kelley could find housing, community, and child care while she went to law school. Hull House's communal dining room was an innovative solution to the practical problems of self-maintenance for single professional women, a vigorous testimony to the advice of the material feminists whose work was chronicled by Hayden.[46]

Hull House was also a physical space in which women whose closest relationships were with other women could live comfortably in a world that increasingly scorned their relationships and their values. In this aspect of its services, the walls of Hull House were of enormous significance in marking an enclosure within which women could define the terms of their most private relationships and defend themselves against social criticism. In her memoir of her early days at Hull House, Kelley emphasized the significance of crossing the threshold into Hull House—a threshold no less metaphorical because it was also literal. Jane Addams was reticent about the psychological service Hull House performed for its residents; in *Twenty Years at Hull House* she reprinted, with apology, her classic essay on "The Subjective Necessity for Social Settlements" and then turned almost exclusively to an account of what the residents did for their neighbors. Only occasionally—"the fine old house responded kindly to repairs"—did her sense of the house as having a life of its own slip through her careful prose.[47]

The residents of Hull House understood that a city was not a single, unified entity. It was not merely that a city was *perceived* differently by

46. Helen Lefkowitz Horowitz, *Alma Mater: Design and Experience in the Women's Colleges from Their Nineteenth-Century Beginning to the 1930s* (New York, 1984); Kathryn Kish Sklar, "Hull House in the 1890s: A Community of Women Reformers," *Signs*, 10 (Summer 1985), 658–77, esp. 659.

47. Florence Kelley, "I Go to Work," *Survey*, June 1, 1927, pp. 271–74, 301; Jane Addams, *Twenty Years at Hull House, with Autobiographical Notes* (New York, 1910), 93.

Halsted Street view of Hull House, c. 1915.
Although its name suggested the cozy family home that was its original core, at its height Hull House included thirteen buildings and filled two city blocks. Courtesy Jane Addams Memorial Collection, Special Collections, University Library, University of Illinois at Chicago.

each observer; the single city was many cities, selectively constructed. They would have understood Christine Stansell's coinage "City of Women," a phrase evoking her vision of public space as inhabited on different terms by men and by women, "a city of women with its own economic relations and cultural forms, a female city concealed within the larger metropolis." The first major publication project of Hull House, after all, was *Hull-House Maps and Papers*, an innovative study in social geography that plotted the neighborhood around Hull House to make it plain that the Chicago appearing on the usual maps was not the Chicago Hull House residents knew. In remapping their neighborhood, they located the philosophical construction that was Hull House squarely in physical space. Moreover, the residents understood that the experience of the city varied with gender,

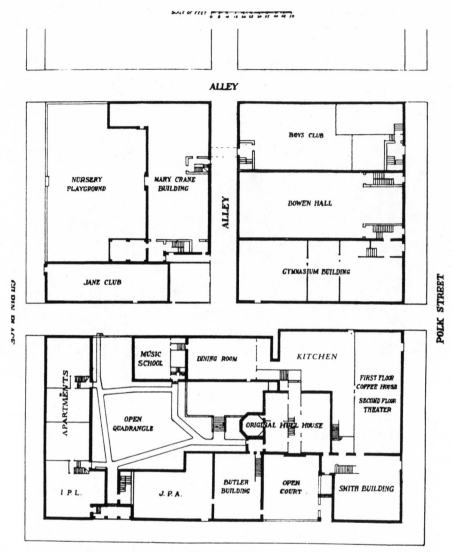

SCALE OF FEET

ALLEY

ALLEY

NURSERY
PLAYGROUND

MARY CRANE
BUILDING

JANE CLUB

BOYS CLUB

BOWEN HALL

GYMNASIUM BUILDING

MUSIC
SCHOOL

DINING ROOM

KITCHEN

FIRST FLOOR
COFFEE HOUSE

SECOND FLOOR
THEATER

APARTMENTS

OPEN
QUADRANGLE

ORIGINAL HULL HOUSE

I P.L.

J. P. A.

BUTLER
BUILDING

OPEN
COURT

SMITH BUILDING

HALSTED STREET

POLK STREET

Plan of the Hull House buildings, c. 1963.
Courtesy Jane Addams Memorial Collection, Special Collections,
University Library, University of Illinois at Chicago.

that working girls were particularly vulnerable in its public spaces. One
of the earliest Hull House projects was a small but significant effort to
claim city space for single women by establishing a cooperative residence
for working girls. By establishing the Jane Club, Hull House residents
announced their recognition that the physical spaces of the city were in-

hospitable to single women and suggested a practical model for redrawing that space.[48]

In *City of Women*, Stansell has given voice to a sweeping reformulation of social relations in urban places; the story she tells is of antebellum New York, but its point of view and its understanding of how geography can serve social analysis are of formidably broad applicability. The city of women has its own political economy, its own patterns of sociability, its own uses of the streets. It varies by class: the world of working-class women has not been the same as the world of middle-class women but neither has it been the same as the world of working-class men.

In Stansell's work, in Joanne Meyerowitz's study of the construction of space for working women in Progressive Era Chicago, and in work by Mary Ryan on the nineteenth-century urban creation of formal public spheres, one assigned to women, the other to men, whose boundaries shifted and overlapped, our understanding of the "separate sphere" is becoming both simpler and more complex.[49] It is simpler because the separate women's sphere can be understood to denote the physical space in which women lived, but more complex because even that apparently simple physical space was complexly structured by an ideology of gender, as well as by class and race. Courtrooms in which women appear singly as plaintiffs, defendants, or witnesses are male spaces; streets on which women are afraid to walk are male spaces; universities that women enter only at male invitation are male spaces. When Susan B. Anthony led a delegation of woman's rights activists to disrupt the public ceremonies celebrating the centennial of the Declaration of Independence in Philadelphia, they challenged both male control of public space and an anthropocentric interpretation of American rights and values. When the delegation of women marched to the other side of Carpenters' Hall, there to hear Anthony declaim her own centennial address, which called for the impeachment of all officers of government because they had been false to the values of the declaration (notably, "no taxation without representation"), they both asserted their

48. Christine Stansell, *City of Women: Sex and Class in New York, 1789–1860* (New York, 1986), xi; Residents of Hull-House, *Hull-House Maps and Papers* (New York, 1895). For the Jane Club, see Mary Kenny's reminiscence in Allen F. Davis and Mary Lynn McCree, eds., *Eighty Years at Hull-House* (Chicago, 1969), 34–35.

49. Joanne J. Meyerowitz, *Women Adrift: Independent Wage Earners in Chicago, 1880–1930* (Chicago, 1988); Mary P. Ryan, *Women in Public: Between Banners and Ballots, 1825–1880* (Baltimore, 1990).

own claim to public space and implicitly rejected a politics based on the separation of spheres.[50]

Tocqueville had discerned "two clearly distinct lines of action" for the two sexes. Actually he was reporting the discourse of separate spheres, which in his day was increasing in shrillness, perhaps to cover the renegotiation of gender relations then underway. But the task of the historiographer is to comment on historians more than to evaluate actual phenomena, and from the historiographer's perspective "separate spheres" was at least in part a strategy that enabled historians to move the history of women out of the realm of the trivial and anecdotal into the realm of analytic social history. Making it possible to proceed past Mary R. Beard's generalization that women have been a force in history, the concept of separate spheres proposed a dynamic by which that force was manifest.[51]

But if our predecessors were constrained by dualisms—home versus market, public versus private, household versus state—we need no longer be so constrained. In an important essay written late in her tragically abbreviated life, Michelle Zimbalist Rosaldo, who had made her reputation exploring the contrasts between the public and the private, nature and culture, argued forcefully that it was time to move on to more complex analyses. "The most serious deficiency of a model based upon two opposed spheres," she wrote, "appears . . . in its alliance with the dualisms of the past, dichotomies which teach that women must be understood not in terms of relationship—with other women and with men—but of difference and apartness." Approaches that attempt to locate "women's 'problem' in a domain apart . . . fail to help us understand how men and women both participate in and help to reproduce the institutional forms that may oppress, liberate, join or divide them."[52] To continue to use the language of

50. Elizabeth Cady Stanton, Susan B. Anthony, and Matilda Joslyn Gage, eds., *History of Woman Suffrage* (6 vols., Rochester, 1881–1922), III, 3–56.

51. Tocqueville, *Democracy in America*, II, 212; Mary R. Beard, *Woman as Force in History: A Study of Traditions and Realities* (New York, 1946).

52. M. Z. Rosaldo, "The Use and Abuse of Anthropology: Reflections on Feminism and Cross-cultural Understanding," *Signs*, 5 (Spring 1980), 389–417, esp. 409, 417. See also the important essay, Joan Kelly, "The Doubled Vision of Feminist Theory: A Postscript to the 'Woman and Power' Conference," *Feminist Studies*, 5 (Spring 1979), 216–27. "Woman's place is not a separate sphere or domain of existence but a position within social existence generally." *Ibid.*, 221. Jeanne Boydston is a historian who understands this point. See Jeanne Boydston, "To Earn Her Daily Bread: Housework and

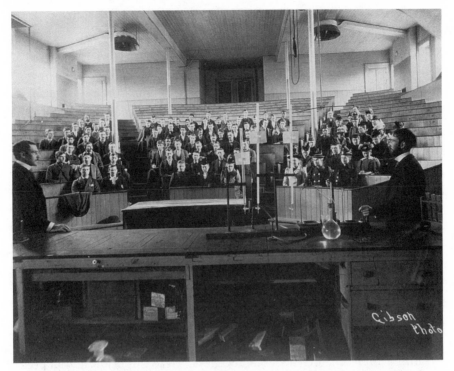

Men and women sit separately in a physics lecture room at the University of
Michigan, c. 1890. Courtesy University of Michigan Medical School Collection,
Michigan Historical Collections, Bentley Historical Library, University of Michigan.

separate spheres is to deny the reciprocity between gender and society, and
to impose a static model on dynamic relationships.

As we discuss the concept of separate spheres, we are tiptoeing on the
boundary between politics and ideology, between sociology and rhetoric.
We have entered the realm of hermeneutics; our task—insofar as it involves
the analysis and demystification of a series of binary opposites—is essentially one of deconstruction. What are we to make of this polarity between
the household and the world, an opposition as fundamental as the opposition between the raw and the cooked, the day and the night, the sun and the
moon? We do not yet fully understand why feminists of every generation—
the 1830s, the 1880s, the 1960s—have needed to define their enemy in this

---

Antebellum Working-Class Subsistence," *Radical History Review* (no. 35, 1986), 7–25;
and Jeanne Boydston, "Home and Work: The Industrialization of Housework in the
Northeastern United States from the Colonial Period to the Civil War" (Ph.D. diss.,
Yale University, 1984).

distinctively geographical way. Why speak of worlds, of spheres, or of realms at all? What is it in our culture that has made feminists think of themselves, in Mary Wollstonecraft's words, "as immurted in their households, groping in the dark?"[53]

The metaphor remains resonant because it retains some superficial vitality. For all our vaunted modernity, for all that men's "spheres" and women's "spheres" now overlap, vast areas of our experience and our consciousness do not overlap. The boundaries may be fuzzier, but our private spaces and our public spaces are still in many important senses gendered. The reconstruction of gender relations, and of the spaces that men and women may claim, is one of the most compelling contemporary social tasks. It is related to major social questions: the feminization of poverty, equal access to education and the professions, relations of power and abuses of power in the public sector and in the family. On a wider stage, the reconstruction of gender relations is related to major issues of power, for we live in a world in which authority has traditionally validated itself by its distance from the feminine and from what is understood to be effeminate.[54]

Little is left of Tocqueville except what he left to implication: that political systems and systems of gender relations are reciprocal social constructions. The purpose of constant analysis of language is to assure that we give power no place to hide.[55] But the remnants of "separate spheres" that still persist are symptoms, not cause, of a particular and historically located

53. Mary Wollstonecraft, *A Vindication of the Rights of Woman*, ed. Miriam Brody Kramnick (Harmondsworth, Eng., 1975), 87.

54. On gender in Nazi ideology, see Renate Bridenthal, Atina Grossman, and Marion A. Kaplan, *When Biology Became Destiny: Women in Weimar and Nazi Germany* (New York, 1984). On gendered language and birth images in contemporary strategic analysis, see Carol Cohn, "Sex and Death in the Rational World of Defense Intellectuals," *Signs*, 12 (Summer 1987), 687–718.

55. The reciprocal relationship of political and gender systems is developed far more explicitly throughout Charles Louis de Secondat, Baron de Montesquieu, *Persian Letters*, trans. C. J. Betts (Harmondsworth, Eng., 1973), esp. 270–81; and Baron de Montesquieu, *The Spirit of the Laws*, trans. Thomas Nugent (New York, 1949), 94–108. For a brilliant analysis, see Joan W. Scott, "Gender: A Useful Category of Historical Analysis," *American Historical Review*, 91 (Dec. 1986), 1053–75. And see Michael J. Shapiro, "The Political Responsibilities of the Scholar," in *The Rhetoric of the Human Science: Language and Argument in Scholarship and Public Affairs*, ed. John Nelson, Allan Megill, and Donald N. McCloskey (Madison, 1988), 380.

gender system. One day we will understand the idea of separate spheres as primarily a trope, employed by people in the past to characterize power relations for which they had no other words and that they could not acknowledge because they could not name, and by historians in our own times as they groped for a device that might dispel the confusion of anecdote and impose narrative and analytical order on the anarchy of inherited evidence, the better to comprehend the world in which we live.

CAN A WOMAN
BE AN INDIVIDUAL?
THE DISCOURSE OF
SELF-RELIANCE

Speaking in the midst of a major crisis of public confidence during the early years of the Massachusetts Bay Colony, Governor John Winthrop observed:

> [Civil or federal] liberty is maintained and exercised in a way of subjection to authority; it is of the same kind of liberty wherewith Christ hath made us free. The woman's own choice makes such a man her husband; yet being so chosen, he is her lord, and she is to be subject to him, yet in a way of liberty, not of bondage; and a true wife accounts her subjection her honor and freedom . . . Even so, brethren, it will be between you and your magistrates.[1]

Winthrop was struggling with the paradox that would occupy Rousseau a century later in *The Social Contract*; he needed a poetic image by which liberty on one hand and submission to authority on the other hand might comfortably be resolved. It seemed so obvious to Winthrop that wives embodied the paradox of authenticity and submission (as it later would to Rousseau—it was perhaps the only thing the two men had in common) that he felt no need to elaborate. Long after they had ceased to share Winthrop's assumptions about the proper relationship of church and state,

An earlier version of this essay was published under the title, "Women and Individualism in American History," in *The Massachusetts Review* (Winter 1989), 589–609.

1. John Winthrop's Journal, "History of New England," 1630–1649, ed. James Kendall Hosmer (New York: Scribner's, 1908), 2:239.

Americans considered his notions about the relationship of men and women to be the common sense of the matter.

Winthrop's formulation of liberty contrasts with one embedded in Elizabeth Cady Stanton's greatest speech, written when she was seventy-seven. The title of the speech is "The Solitude of Self."

> The point I wish plainly to bring before you on this occasion is the individuality of each human soul—our Protestant idea, the right of individual conscience and judgment—our republican idea, individual citizenship. In discussing the rights of woman, we are to consider, first, what belongs to her as an individual, in a world of her own, the arbiter of her own destiny, an imaginary Robinson Crusoe with her woman Friday on a solitary island. . . . The isolation of every human soul and the necessity of self dependence must give each individual the right to choose his own surroundings. The strongest reason for giving woman all the opportunities . . . for the full development of her faculties, her forces of mind and body . . . is the solitude and personal responsibility of her own individual life . . . as an individual she must rely on her self.[2]

Many years before, in the Seneca Falls Declaration of Sentiments of 1848, Stanton had attempted to cast the republican rhetoric of the American Revolution into terms congruent with women's experience. Now at the end of her life she was similarly recasting the individualist rhetoric of public discourse into terms congruent with women's experience. Both of her efforts may be understood as conservative efforts to link women to main themes in American political culture. Both were perceived by contemporaries as radical.

The concept of individualism has been linked to gender in ways that have generally eluded analysis. From John Winthrop through Tocqueville, and from Emerson to the team of sociologists headed by Robert Bellah, who recently published *Habits of the Heart*, most formulations of individualism in America have made the implicit assumption that the "individual" was male. Even when a vaguely generic language was adopted to make it seem that women were included, a careful reading reveals that virtually all commentators—except explicitly feminist ones like Stanton—contemplated the self-actualization of men. As R. W. B. Lewis named the individ-

2. The speech was given February 20, 1892. Elizabeth Cady Stanton, "The Solitude of Self," in *The History of Woman Suffrage*, ed. Susan B. Anthony and Ida Husted Harper (Rochester, N.Y., 1902), 4:189–90.

ual seeking autonomy in the American landscape, we habitually discuss "the American Adam." The basic formula for American fiction has been the hero, "homeless, timeless, and alone," thrust into adventure. The "authentic" American narrative has been taken to be "the individual going forth toward experience, the inventor of his own character and creator of his personal history, the self-moving individual who is made to confront the world." The classic American setting is the untamed forest (Cooper), the wild ocean (Melville), the broad Mississippi (Twain).[3]

Some twenty years ago, in "American Women and the National Character," David Potter laid down a classic challenge—that historians test every familiar generalization about the American past and ask whether it applied equally well, and with similar nuance, to women. I shall argue here that what we have identified as the classic statements of American individualism are best understood as guides to masculine identity; if we seek to understand a female quest for self-actualization, we must turn to an alternate, competitive literature that is no less "American."

William Hesseltine once remarked that writing intellectual history is like pinning jelly against a wall, and individualism is as slippery a concept as any. One is tempted to go off chasing something that one can put in a computer. However, as we are reminded at least every two years and certainly every four, during congressional and presidential elections, the rhetoric of individualism is deeply embedded in the language by which Americans explain themselves to each other; it is embedded in our national discourse. And if, indeed, this discourse is gender specific, it is time that we looked at it again.[4]

3. Myra Jehlen, *American Incarnation: The Individual, the Nation, and the Continent* (Cambridge: Harvard Univ. Press, 1986). Jehlen links the themes; as she puts it, "Incarnation—the idea that the methods of liberal individualism inheres in the American continent . . . ." The writers she discusses are a triad—Emerson, Hawthorne, Melville; the similarities between Emerson and Thoreau "are characteristic of American thought" (11). Jehlen sees the identification of the individual with the wide expanse of land as "the great American tautology" (235). Annette Kolodny has written thoughtfully about the implications of this way of thinking about the American landscape. See Annette Kolodny, *The Lay of the Land: Metaphor as Experience and History in American Life and Letters* (Chapel Hill: Univ. of North Carolina Press, 1975) and *The Land Before Her: Fantasy and Experience of the American Frontiers, 1630–1860* (Chapel Hill: Univ. of North Carolina Press, 1984).

4. As John William Ward wrote some years ago when he wrestled with the same subject, the concept of individualism has had "massive emotional associations. . . . American culture has a deep affective stake in the historical connotations of the con-

Let us begin with Winthrop. Ostensibly he was describing the relationship of the individual to society. But he also had a practical agenda: to quell restiveness among the freemen of Massachusetts Bay. His speech has made its way into standard documentary compilations as an attempt to connect political and religious issues and as an expression of ideas that seemed to be the common sense of the matter to articulate Puritans. Winthrop's contractualism rested on the unexamined assumption that the submissive woman was in fact free. This paradox was so much a part of the lives of his male audience that Winthrop expected that they, in turn, would find it logical to place themselves in a similarly ambivalent and paradoxical relationship to the state: "A true wife accounts her subjection her honor and freedom." On this base the political edifice that would reconcile choice and necessity rested. What the relationship might be of women to the state went unremarked.

At least Winthrop had a certain degree of consistency. He demanded of men of the middling ranks of society no more than the same degree of submissiveness that they were already demanding—and presumably receiving—from their wives. But although Winthrop's speech had a degree of rhetorical brilliance—it was, Perry Miller observed, the culminating expression of the Puritan ideal in New England—it did not have the effect Winthrop sought. It could call for but not create a constituency of submissive men who would defer to their social betters. Men understood the role Winthrop asked for as effeminate—the word also had pejorative connotations then—and refused to play it.

In fact, the first generation of Puritan settlers had brought with them sharply conflicting notions of the proper place of women in the community. On the one hand, they believed that each Christian woman was responsible for placing herself in the path of salvation and the knowledge of grace, just as each man was. This involved enough education to read the Bible for herself and to take substantial responsibility for the religious education of her children. This strain of Puritan influence would support relatively high levels of female literacy in New England as compared, for example, to the South, a disparity which persisted into the nineteenth century.[5]

---

cept of individualism and will not lightly surrender it on the grounds of being responsible to some intellectual demand for historical accuracy and logical consistency." "The Ideal of Individualism and the Reality of Organization," in *Red, White, and Blue: Men, Books and Ideas in American Culture* (New York: Oxford Univ. Press, 1969), 260.

5. Gerald Moran and Maris Vinovskis, "The Puritan Family and Religion: A Critical

On the other hand, the example of Eve implied that women were particularly likely to sin; after all, Eve had taken the initiative. Her sins—of pride and of disobedience—were understood to be characteristic women's sins. Women could easily be construed to be weak, vulnerable, in need of guidance for their own good. Although women, like men, sought to realize themselves through Christ, still the *self* they were to realize was to be characteristically submissive. "Godly men," Carol Karlsen has observed, "needed helpmeets, not hindrances; companions, not competitors; alter egos, not autonomous mates. They needed wives who were faithful and loyal; who assisted them in their piety, in their vocations . . . who revered them. . . ."[6]

Both themes would persist throughout the colonial period, but one would be strengthened at the expense of the other. Within less than two decades after settlement, Anne Hutchinson and other heretics were squelched and, as Mary Maples Dunn has shown, even believing women were silenced. Puritan women were automatically transferred from one church to another when their husbands moved, and older women ceased to have a voice in the disciplining of church members.[7] When the male church had been insecure and marginal, it treated women as valued allies. When it became more secure politically, it left women to their husbands and fathers. As we read Puritan sermon literature, for example, we do not find in it the assumption that the women to whom the minister is speaking are engaged in an intense search for their own individual religious voices or their own idiosyncratic conversion experience. The Christian virtues of patience and faith were invariably linked with the general female virtues of submissiveness and docility. Even tracts stressing the reciprocal duties of husband and wife, like William Secker's widely read *A Wedding Ring Fit for the Finger*, grounded this reciprocity on initial female submission. Man and wife were, Secker writes, "like the sun and the moon: when the greater

Reappraisal," *William and Mary Quarterly* 3d ser., 39 (1982): 42–49. See also William J. Gilmore, "Elementary Literacy on the Eve of the Industrial Revolution: Trends in Rural New England, 1760–1830," *Proceedings of the American Antiquarian Society* vol. 92, pt. 1 (1982): 87–171; and David D. Hall, *Worlds of Wonder, Days of Judgment: Popular Religious Belief in Early New England* (New York: Knopf, 1989), 32–34.

6. Carol Karlsen, *The Devil in the Shape of a Woman: Witchcraft in Colonial New England* (New York: W. W. Norton, 1987), 165.

7. Mary Maples Dunn, "Saints and Sisters: Congregational and Quaker Women in the Early Colonial Period," in *Women in American Religion*, ed. Janet Wilson James (Philadelphia: Univ. of Pennsylvania Press, 1980), 30–35.

light goes down, the lesser light gets up. . . . The wife may be a sovereign in her husband's absence, but she must be a subject in her husband's presence." A man is encouraged to choose a woman who will be "subject to [his] dominion."[8] Jonathan Edwards's account of Sarah Pierrepont's conversion experience is the unusual case.[9]

The great texts of the Enlightenment—notably those of Rousseau (especially the *Confessions* and his fiction) and of Montesquieu (especially *The Persian Letters*)—addressed directly and with great subtlety the problem of how to invent a state that has the power to preserve order yet in which it is also possible for individuals to preserve their own integrity and authenticity.[10] To be authentic, Montesquieu concluded, freedom in the public world had to be echoed by freedom within the private family; the individual is not free in the state unless also free at home. This was a formulation largely overlooked in America, where republicans used the more abstract formulations of *The Spirit of the Laws* in their argumentation. When, for

---

8. William Secker, *A Wedding Ring, Fit for the Finger; or the Salve of Divinity on the Sore of Humanity, With Directions to Those Men that Want Wives, How to Choose Them, and to Those Women that Have Husbands, How to Use Them*, 10th ed. (Portland, Maine: John McKown, 1806), 12, 14, 15, 22. Although Secker had died in 1681, his popular sermon was still being reprinted. On the extent to which gendered assumptions are embedded in the very conceptualization of rhetoric itself, and on the "mutually reflective relation between particular tropes and the orders they exemplify," see Patricia Parker, *Literary Fat Ladies: Rhetoric, Gender, Property* (London: Methuen, 1987), ch. 6, "Motivated Rhetorics: Gender, Order, Rule."

9. Clarence Faust and Thomas H. Johnson, eds., *Jonathan Edwards: Representative Selections* (New York: Hill and Wang, 1962), 56. Lacking as we do a large body of Puritan women's introspective literature, it is impossible to say how widely shared was the experience of "civil wars within," which Sacvan Bercovitch has so persuasively identified as the center of the Puritan man's religiosity. *The Puritan Origins of the American Self* (New Haven: Yale Univ. Press, 1975). In *Worlds of Wonder, Days of Judgment: Popular Religious Belief in Early New England* (New York: Knopf, 1989), David D. Hall offers a fresh and important interpretation of the mental world of Puritans that stresses the shared beliefs of women and men. But see Ivy Schweitzer, *The Work of Self-Representation: Lyric Poetry in Colonial New England* (Chapel Hill: Univ. of North Carolina Press, 1991), for a brilliant interpretation of Puritan thought which examines "the discursive deployment of the metaphor of woman," and argues "that the sexes experienced the Puritan regimentation of selfhood differently: while women were subordinated, men were coerced."

10. See Marshall Berman, *The Politics of Authenticity: Radical Individualism and the Emergence of Modern Society* (New York: Atheneum, 1970).

example, Abigail Adams argued in her famous letter of May 1776, "Put it out of the power of husbands to abuse us with impunity; remember all men would be tyrants if they could," John Adams coolly misread it as simply a plea for the vote.

It is possible to interpret the movement of resistance to England as energized in part by the urgency of a generation of middle-class men seeking careers by which to define themselves, who, finding their way blocked by England and English patronage appointees, turned in resentment to clear the way for self-fulfillment.[11] Even when one hastens to grant that this is only one among many reasons for resentment of England, the urgent demand for what the French, in their own Revolution, were soon to call "a career open to talents" was obvious.

The war and ensuing social change did indeed open up new choices for men—in the law, in politics, in trade, and in commerce. The language of the Declaration of Independence gave voice to an enlightened understanding that the nation existed for every man and not the reverse. But the Revolution offered women little except the chance to live vulnerable lives in a household from which men had gone to fight for one side or the other, to live in fear or in wonder, or to traipse after the troops, hanging on as one of the "women of the army" in a Brechtian world of cooks and laundresses.[12]

When women were actually "invited to war" as the title of one anonymous pamphlet put it, the war was not the war of the Revolution at all, but the great religious revival that began to build with the growth of Methodism in the 1780s and swelled into the Second Great Awakening of the first decades of the nineteenth century.[13] The women who followed Mother

11. For a subtle handling of this psychological pattern, see Peter Shaw, *American Patriots and the Rituals of Revolution* (Cambridge: Harvard Univ. Press, 1981).

12. See Holly A. Mayer, "Belonging to the Army: Camp Followers and the Military Community During the American Revolution," Ph.D. diss., College of William and Mary, 1990. I have discussed this phenomenon in *Women of the Republic: Intellect and Ideology in Revolutionary America* (Chapel Hill: Univ. of North Carolina Press, 1980), ch. 2, and " 'History Can Do It No Justice': Women and the Reinterpretation of the American Revolution," in *Women in the Age of the American Revolution*, ed. Ronald Hoffman and Peter J. Albert (Charlottesville: Univ. Press of Virginia, 1989), 3–42.

13. *Women Invited to War. Or a Friendly Address to the Honourable Women of the United States. By a Daughter of America* (Boston, 1787). In her essay on Mary Moody Emerson, cited below, Phyllis Cole discusses Emerson's concern "with eternity [rather] than time . . . this unworldly consciousness in itself one expression of time and place, of a woman's opportunities and exclusions in the years of the early Republic" (5).

Ann Lee or Jemima Wilkinson, or the Methodists and Baptists, found a mode of personal choice and individual authenticity that was inconceivable for women in secular language. Methodism had a particular appeal to women in the congruence of its rhetoric of method and system with the practical needs of housekeepers, and also in the honored figure of John Wesley's mother, Susannah. Susannah Wesley is a distinctive figure in that she was well read, admired for her judgment, and not afraid to speak in public. Indeed, during her husband's lengthy absences, she held worship services in her home, attended at their height by two hundred people, and successfully fended off complaints that they were an "illegal conventicle."[14]

It might be said that in the evangelical churches of the early Republic we find a revitalized tension between the individual and the community, which had leached out as the older churches became the province of women whose religious roles and social roles were comfortably congruent. The Second Great Awakening—whatever the denomination it affected— was characterized by what once would have been called the Arminian heresy: the assumption that one could affect the terms of one's own salvation. For women, heightened religiosity and a new community of believers could provide paths for self-fulfillment and an expression of personal independence possible in virtually no other sector of society.

Heightened religiosity could lead to mysticism, as it did in the case of Ralph Waldo Emerson's much-misunderstood aunt, Mary Moody Emerson. Though it risked leading one into eccentricity, mysticism also enabled one to carve out a private space that could command respect. If Mary Moody Emerson is remembered at all, it is as a rigid moralist and a religious eccentric who made a shroud for herself and wore it around the house in order, she said, to get accustomed to it. But in her voluminous diaries and letters we find an improvisation on Virginia Woolf's famous question about Shakespeare's sister. Ralph Waldo Emerson's aunt had great intelligence, a taste for writing, and absolutely no institutional context in which to exercise either. There was no Harvard College for her. As an adult woman without her own household to manage, she was vulnerable to the reproaches of her family, who expected her to define her life in terms of service to them. Ralph Waldo Emerson's widowed mother, Ruth, makes a

14. See Stephen A. Marini, *Radical Sects of Revolutionary New England* (Cambridge: Harvard Univ. Press, 1982); and Deborah Valenze, *Prophetic Sons and Daughters: Female Preaching and Popular Religion in Industrial England* (Princeton: Princeton Univ. Press, 1985).

unilateral decision to take in boarders, and then announces that of course her sister-in-law, Mary Moody Emerson, will come to assist with the work, and complains when she does not appear on the scene as soon as called. "I cannot find time in your absence to do even the necessary sewing of the family with my other cares and have not 4 or 5 shirts for the children which they need, waiting to be made."[15]

Caught in the inexorable cycle of the natural and domestic world, Mary Moody Emerson made the best of it by turning to contemplation and private piety: "Piety can supply to the feeble what the strong possess by nature." Her musings often approached the hypnotic: "The hill on which we rambled [October 1795] is become barren the sun has since cut short his journey, and the skies begin to frown. But, tho the face of nature is constantly changing and now threatens a dismal appearance; the subjects on which we dwell are ever the same, always interesting and sublime." But private, contemplative piety had no exterior consequence; if anything, it reinforced the old separation between the affective worlds of women and men.[16] In 1817, Mary Moody Emerson wrote, "Alass, with low timid females

15. Ruth Haskins Emerson to Mary Moody Emerson, July 20, 1813, Emerson Family Papers, Houghton Library, Harvard University. Cited by permission of the Ralph Waldo Emerson Memorial Association and the Houghton Library. See also Phyllis Cole, "The Advantage of Loneliness: Mary Moody Emerson's Almanacks, 1802–1855," in *Emerson: Retrospect and Prospect*, ed. Joel Porte (Cambridge: Harvard Univ. Press, 1983), 1–32.

16. Mary Moody Emerson Journals, Emerson Family Papers, Houghton Library, Harvard University. Cole begins "The Advantage of Loneliness" by quoting Mary Moody Emerson's journal, 1804: "Were the genius of the Xian religion painted, her form would be full of majesty, her mien solemn, her aspect benign . . ." Cole adds her own gloss: "A single female form, unaccompanied by parents or husband or children, friends or congregation—raises its eyes directly to Heaven, without the intercession of priest or even redeeming Christ. In fact she hopes herself to intercede for others. . . . She seems a New England Rachel or Virgin Mary, but also a Jeremiah: an explicitly female figure, she nonetheless goes beyond the conventional piety of New England women in her separation from the domestic sphere and her unfeminine prophetic power. Such an idealization of the solitary self was radical for both its gender and its time: indeed a significant anticipation of the self-reliance that Mary's nephew Ralph Waldo Emerson would articulate as the primarily masculine romantic vision of the next generation." Cole discusses Emerson's "holy individualism" (6n., 9).

Mary Moody Emerson understood herself to be a "daughter of the revolution"; her father had been chaplain to the Concord minutemen, and he died en route home from Ticonderoga in 1777. She was raised as the ward of an impoverished aunt. Phyllis Cole

or vulgar domestics how apt is this [moral grandeur] to lose its power when the nerves are weak. . . . But give me that oh God—it is holy independence—it is honor & immortality—dearer than friends wealth & influence. . . . I bless thee for giving me to see the advantage of loneliness."[17]

The journals of twenty-four-year old Eleanor Read, also a New Englander, reveal the ways in which religious conversion could provide psychological and intellectual options and the way that women might use the new evangelicalism for self-actualizing purposes.[18] She attended revival meetings in the fall of 1802, becoming increasingly interested; finally, she discovered that she was free of her jealousy of others who had found salvation. She gave way to "transports of joy" and saw everyone with "new eyes," in the traditional language of the evangelical conversion experience. In this spirit, she ventured to her baptism, no longer hesitating lest it imply reproach of her parents for the way they raised her, pleased that among the thirty with whom she was baptized were "young and old, illiterate and learned, rich and poor, and . . . a young mulatto man who had previously excited my indignation by mixing with others at conferences and other meetings." Now, shocking even herself, she looked on him as her "brother in Christ."[19]

---

writes: "William anticipated the Revolution as millennial glory: his daughter inherited the Revolution as social chaos, deprivation, orphanhood." On the fiftieth anniversary of the American Revolution, she writes, "Hail happy day—tho the revolution gave me to slavery of poverty & ignorance & long orphanship,—yet it gave my fellow men liberty" (7).

17. Quoted in Cole, "The Advantage of Loneliness," 10. See also Evelyn Barish, "Emerson and the Angel of Midnight: The Legacy of Mary Moody Emerson," in *Mothering the Mind: Twelve Studies of Writers and their Silent Partners*, eds. Ruth Perry and Martine Watson Brownley (New York: Holmes and Meier, 1984), 218–35.

18. Eleanor Read wrote in the long evangelical tradition of biography and autobiography that recounted an individual's struggle against sin. As David Hall has recently observed, this dramatization of the lives of ordinary men and women served some of the same functions that novels did in the imaginative lives of their readers. "Ordinary people thus learned that, whatever their worldly circumstances, they were actors in the greatest drama of them all. In this light we grasp why Bunyan wrote his masterpiece and why dozens of lay men and women in New England spoke and wrote so fluently about spiritual experience. Steady sellers—and remember, these were books presented to their readers as the truth—succeeded in the book trade because of their essential plot of sinners vitalized to overcome the Devil and gain saving grace." Hall, *Worlds of Wonder*, 57.

19. Samuel Worcester, *The Christian Mourning with Hope: A Sermon . . . on the*

After her conversion, Eleanor Read ceased to dwell on her human limitations; instead, she pressed at the boundaries of the possible. She stopped describing herself as anxious and indecisive. Her relationship with her mother now changed; instead of writing deferential letters, she wrote in a style verging on the impudent: "I have given myself away to God in a most solemn covenant. The child, whom you have so tenderly nursed, has sworn an eternal allegiance against you, unless you will serve my Lord and my God." She brought her religion into her classroom, overcoming her fear "that praying in my school would be deemed ridiculous enthusiasm." She decided that the injunction to women not to speak in church did not mean they could not pray in school. It was not usual (except among Quakers) for women to lead public prayer among their students, but Eleanor Read overcame her scruples and her fear of looking odd. (It clearly never occurred to her that she should keep her religious beliefs out of the classroom.)[20]

She traveled far from home, founding other schools in other communities, ultimately reaching Salem, Massachusetts, where she met the man she would marry. She argued with ministers—including her future husband—who thought women ought to confine their reading to religious tracts or who expected submissiveness in women.

> Let the man of real piety carefully examine the origin of that detested sentiment which leads him to consider learning and mental improvement as undesirable in a female. Upon a thorough investigation of this important subject, will not the honest Christian blush before his God for the unchristian and cruel degradation of the female mind? If the discerning and virtuous part of men would teach us to expect their esteem, only when our accuracy of thought and amiableness of conduct give us the appearance of rational beings, what a surprising reformation might be expected in the female world.[21]

We have reason to regret Eleanor Read Emerson's early death. Her journals provide evidence of the style with which at least one young woman

---

Occasion of the Death of Mrs. Eleanor [Read] Emerson . . . To Which Are Annexed Writings of Mrs. Emerson (Boston: Lincoln & Edmonds, 1809), 31–37, 55.

20. Ibid., 58–59, 39.

21. Ibid., 72. See also Joanna Bowen Gillespie, " 'The Clear Leadings of Providence': Pious Memoirs and the Problems of Self-Realization for Women in the Early Nineteenth Century," *Journal of the Early Republic* 5 (1985): 197–222.

bent religious revivalism in the direction of independence and her own search for authenticity. Eleanor Read's story can stand as an emblem for the thousands of white and black women who would follow her, discovering that the rhetoric of religion provided justification for behavior that a secular society would otherwise not countenance.

A third route to authenticity for women was articulated during and soon after the American Revolution by Judith Sargent Murray and others, male and female, who thought that the new Republic required a new woman as well as a new man. This set of ideas, the ideology of republican motherhood, called upon the women of the Republic to be forthright and practical, impervious to fashion and frivolity. They were to be prepared for a world that might literally turn upside down; a world in which violent changes, of the sort which the revolutionary generation had experienced, would be the rule rather than the exception. The rhetoric of republican virtue and independence provided the language for an insistence that women avoid subservience and docility, and, above all, be self-respecting. Women were called upon to assume an obligation to themselves and to the political society in which they lived, to educate themselves for economic competence and intellectual growth. For the first time in the history of the West, members of Murray's generation acknowledged and even welcomed female ambition—but only if ambition were developed in a context that also involved a companionable relationship with husbands and a pedagogical relationship with children. In the intensity of her insistence that a woman be trained to respect herself, to take pride in her own competence and to be prepared to support herself, Murray went far toward articulating a new model of female authenticity. But the model republican woman was still justified less on her own terms than by her service to her family and her children. The promise of service camouflaged and indeed undermined the independence and individualism that was also part of the concept. The promise of continued submission and deference made the republican woman politically palatable.[22]

These forms of individualism are by way of prehistory. The word "individualism" was not used until the 1820s, and then in France. It appears first in English in Alexis de Tocqueville's *Democracy in America*, published in

22. See Linda K. Kerber, "Separate Spheres, Female Worlds, Woman's Place: The Rhetoric of Women's History," *Journal of American History* 75 (June 1988): 9–39 [reprinted in the present volume].

1832. Tocqueville used *individualisme* to describe a celebration of the claims of the individual that he took to be distinctive to American society and that he thought had its own dangers.[23]

> Individualism is a mature and calm feeling, which disposes each member of the community to sever himself from the mass of his fellows and to draw apart with his family and his friends; so that after he has thus formed a little circle of his own, he willingly leaves society at large to itself.
>
> As social conditions become more equal, the number of persons increases who, although they are neither rich enough nor powerful enough to exercise any great influence over their fellows, have nevertheless acquired or retained sufficient education and fortune to satisfy their own wants. They owe nothing to any man, they expect nothing from any man; they acquire the habit of always considering themselves as standing alone, and they are apt to imagine that their whole destiny is in their own hands.
>
> Thus not only does democracy make every man forget his ancestors, but it hides his descendants, and separates his contemporaries from him; it throws him back for ever upon himself alone, and threatens in the end to confine him entirely within the solitude of his own heart.[24]

As he so often did, Tocqueville provided a name for what many agreed was a distinctive quality of postrevolutionary American society. The American was Crèvecoeur's "new man," who tilled his own soil, grew his own food, built his own home. The democratic hero was paradoxically not the person embedded in the *demos* but the autonomous individual, the man who imagined that his whole destiny was "in his own hands." Throughout Jacksonian political culture—in political thought, in economic theory, in literature, in the popular notions of the self-made man, ran the trope of the

23. See James T. Schleifer, *The Making of Tocqueville's Democracy in America* (Chapel Hill: Univ. of North Carolina Press, 1980), 245–59. Steven Lukes emphasizes that the French continue to stress "the opposition . . . between *individualisme* (implying anarchy and social atomization) and *individualité* (implying personal liberty and self-development). In French thought *individualisme* has almost always pointed to the sources of social dissolution. . . ." "Types of Individualism," in *Dictionary of the History of Ideas*, ed. Philip Wiener (New York: Charles Scribner's Sons, 1973), 2:594.

24. Alexis de Tocqueville, *Democracy in America* (1832; reprint, New York: Knopf, 1945), vol. 2, bk. 2, chap. 2.

individual posed *against* society. The concept, John William Ward observed, played the role of a "secular jeremiad, an exhortation to begin over again, sloughing off the complexities of society by returning to a natural state of grace."[25]

To Tocqueville's credit, he made it clear from the beginning (though many of his readers did not notice) that defining oneself as pure individual required a material base. The persons who may indulge in the notion "that their whole destiny is in their own hands" are those who have "sufficient education and fortune to satisfy their own wants." No economic independence, no individualism. Individualism in this sense is the psychological counterpart of liberalism and laissez-faire in the economic world; it is no accident that they appear in usage contemporaneously.[26]

What Tocqueville did not notice was that in a legal system molded by coverture, married women could not readily possess the material base that made individualism possible.[27] Mary Ryan's careful study of the changing political culture in Utica, New York, makes it clear that young men could take advantage of the opportunities of the new commercial world only if they were given the total resources of their families to draw on; in the end, mothers took in boarders and daughters aborted their educations in order that sons be kept in school longer and given a stake in society. "Self-made"

25. Ward, "The Ideal of Individualism," 237–38. But the meaning of individualism shifts; one must watch each author carefully for what they intend. In "Individualism Reconsidered," in *Individualism Reconsidered and Other Essays* (1951; reprint, Glencoe, N.Y.: Free Press, 1954), David Riesman opens by setting himself apart from "ruthless individualism" and, like David Potter, understands individualism to involve the freedom to develop one's private self and "escape from any particular group." Riesman wrote as social psychologist; concerned with the development of a "character-type," he set individualism off against the traditional town, with its "web of gossip and surveillance . . ." (35).

26. The link of individualism to the capitalist transformation has long been discussed; see C. B. MacPherson, *The Political Theory of Possessive Individualism* (Oxford: Clarendon Press, 1962); J. G. A. Pocock, *Virtue, Commerce and History* (Cambridge: Cambridge Univ. Press, 1985); and, most recently, Stephen Watts, *The Republic Reborn: War and the Making of Liberal America 1790–1820* (Baltimore: Johns Hopkins Univ. Press, 1987).

27. I have discussed the erosion of older systems of property relations by capitalism in "Separate Spheres, Female Worlds, Woman's Place: The Rhetoric of Women's History," *Journal of American History* 75 (June 1988): 21–23 [included in the present volume].

men were launched into the world by other people's sacrifices—some voluntary, most involuntary—and they knew it, although their language carefully screened that reality from their consciousness.[28]

Kenneth Lynn has recently pointed to a nice irony in the life of Ralph Waldo Emerson, the man who, more than perhaps any other American, articulated the ideal of the independent individual. Emerson's period of betrothal to the frail Ellen Tucker was marred by his frequent raising of what she called "the ugly subject"—her will. By the time he married her, he was securely embedded in her will, despite the reservations of her uncle and guardian. After Ellen Tucker Emerson's death a few years later, when he used the money to support himself and his relatives, Ralph Waldo Emerson remarked that she continued to benefit him even in death. Emerson refrained from forcing his own dismissal from the Second Church of Boston until after her uncle's lawsuit contesting the will had been settled in Emerson's favor. When Emerson gave the "American Scholar" address, calling on his listeners to spurn materialism and dedicate themselves to the life of the mind, he did not mention that he could rely on a steady income from his brief marriage.[29]

David Leverenz has recently explored the explicitly male language that Emerson employed. "Give me initiative, spermatic, prophesying man-making words," he wrote in his journal in 1841.[30] Emerson begins his essay "Intellect" with a verse that analogizes intellect to the "sower" who "scatters broad his seed."[31]

The individual mythologized by antebellum writers was male; he *had* to be a Natty Bumppo, a Huck Finn, or an American Scholar with $1,200 a

---

28. Mary P. Ryan, *Cradle of the Middle Class: The Family in Oneida County, New York 1790–1865* (New York: Cambridge Univ. Press, 1981). See also Richard Hofstadter, *The American Political Tradition and the Men Who Made It* (New York: Knopf, 1948) and John William Ward, *Andrew Jackson: Symbol for an Age* (New York: Oxford Univ. Press, 1955).

29. Kenneth S. Lynn, *The Air-Line to Seattle: Studies in Literary and Historical Writing About America* (Chicago: Univ. of Chicago Press, 1983), chap. 3, 27–32. See also Richard A. Grusin, " 'Put God in Your Debt': Emerson's Economy of Expenditure," *PMLA* 103 (1988): 35–44.

30. David Leverenz, "The Politics of Emerson's Man-Making Words," *PMLA* 101 (1986): 39. Leverenz is quoting a journal entry November–December 1841, in Joel Porte, ed., *Emerson in his Journals* (Cambridge: Harvard Univ. Press, 1982), 271.

31. "Essays: First Series," in *The Collected Works of Ralph Waldo Emerson* (Cambridge: Harvard Univ. Press, 1979), 191.

year. The myth of the lone individual is a trope, a rhetorical device. In real life no one is self-made; few are truly alone. Even those mythical lonely beings confronting the wilderness had companions to prepare their food and warn them of disaster. Trailing behind their real counterparts were wives, mothers, children, slaves, and servants to sustain the practical aspects of life. The myth of the wilderness either denied the reality of women (as in *Moby Dick*), trivialized them (as in Huck Finn), or, as Carroll Smith-Rosenberg has shown in a brilliant essay on Davy Crockett, indulged frankly in misogyny.

[In the stories, Crockett is obsessed with a sexuality that is] oral, exhibitionistic, violent, and nonproductive. . . . What emerges from the Crockett myth as natural, timeless and inescapable is . . . young male violence . . . directed toward women [and] . . . toward the inhabitants of the wilderness—toward Indians, Mexicans, and escaped slaves. . . . [misogyny] and racism are central to the myth.[32]

The language of individualism as it developed in antebellum America was not a woman's language. How could it be? It was a trope whose major theme was the denial of dependence; it was a response to social changes that were making men increasingly aware of their dependence and vulnerability in a culture that had, only the generation before, reified the idea of personal independence in the private world and political independence in the public sector. Before the nineteenth century, landed wealth was a high proportion of the total wealth, even for the middling sort; no one could pretend that inherited land was their own creation. But when manufacturing and human capital, expressed in paper money, accounted for more and more wealth, it was possible to indulge in the fiction of the self-made man.[33]

Dependence remained the condition of most women's lives, whether they were black or white, rich or poor—although the pain of that dependence varied enormously with social status. Embedded in a legal system that endowed her husband with control of her property at marriage, em-

32. Carroll Smith-Rosenberg, *Disorderly Conduct: Visions of Gender in Victorian America* (New York: Knopf, 1985), 105, 108.

33. See Carole Shammas, Marylynn Salmon, and Michel Dahlin, *Inheritance in America* (New Brunswick: Rutgers Univ. Press, 1987), which, by emphasizing how extensive inheritance as a source of wealth (about 80 percent) is and has been, undermines even further the language of the self-made.

bedded in an economy that offered white boys multiple career options, white girls only a handful, all of them marginal, and black women, even if free, virtually none, women first faced the intellectual and psychological task of *naming* their dependent condition. (The task of *rejecting* their dependent condition would not be faced until much later.)

In the early Republic, the woman who would, in Margaret Fuller's words, "beat my own self true to the heart of the world," had found that the most accessible path to female authenticity lay in heightened religiosity. In her own generation, Margaret Fuller attempted to move somewhat further in the direction of a secular definition of authenticity and independence for women, to connect women to Emersonian individualism, and to make the language of individualism congruent with the realities of women's lives. Her essays, which were printed in 1844 under the title *Woman in the Nineteenth Century*, had appeared first in *The Dial* under the impenetrable title "The Great Lawsuit: Man vs. Men, Woman vs. Women," by which she meant to contrast the ideal with the real. The essays combined the taste for the practical characteristic of Judith Sargent Murray with a mysticism close to that of Mary Moody Emerson—a mysticism that makes the essays occasionally impenetrable and accounts for their being honored but not widely read.

Fuller began by echoing Murray, offering as a model a fictional "Miranda" who was Fuller herself, only barely disguised; a girl raised by a father who respected even a girl child for possessing an "immortal intellect," who called upon her for "clear judgment, for courage, for honor and fidelity" and gave her, as all her portion, "a dignified sense of self-dependence," even though "self-dependence, which was honored in men, is deprecated as a fault in most women."[34] Like Murray, Fuller argued that a sure sense of self-worth would protect women against being seized by the current opinion that would try to sweep her "into the belief that she must marry, if it be only to find a protector."[35] Like Murray, she urged a richer education for women, a more serious cultivation of women's intellect; where she departed from Murray was that she was willing that women's education be *selfish*.

Too much is said of women being better educated, that they may become better companions and mothers for MEN. . . . a being of infinite

34. Margaret Fuller, *Woman in the Nineteenth Century* (New York: W. W. Norton, 1971), 38–40.

35. Ibid., 71.

scope must not be treated with an exclusive view to any one relation. Give the soul free course, let the organization both of body and mind, be fully developed, and the being will be fit for any and every relation to which it may be called.[36]

Whether they knew Fuller's work or not, other women would articulate in the mid-century years the claim she made; slowly it became conceivable to claim self-fulfillment, independence, and individualism simply because a woman was entitled to it. "Our right to individuality is what I would most assert," wrote the journalist Elizabeth Oakes Smith in 1851. "Men seem resolved to have but one type in our sex. . . . The laws of stubborn utilitarianism must govern us, while they may be as fantastic as they please."[37]

The question is, did the "individuality" of which they spoke mean the same thing to women as it did when men used the term? When a woman imagined herself as escaping the laws of utilitarianism, did she imagine herself escaping to the same "fantastic" place, the same unmapped wilderness to which men fled? To ask the question is to answer it. The myths of the self-reliant man and the self-reliant woman were not synchronized. Young men received fictional images such as Tom Sawyer and Huck Finn—lively boys who run off on splendid adventures and prove themselves able to outwit the challenges of the adult world. It is an adult world in which, as Nina Baym long ago made clear, "the encroaching, constricting, destroying society is represented with particular urgency in the figure of one or more women"; women are not only the "other," they are the enemy.[38] The fictive female counterparts of Huck and Tom would be the March sisters of *Little Women*, who, as Susan Gubar and Sandra Gilbert suggested some years ago, sent a mixed message. The usual assumption of literary critics has been that *Little Women* is about women's free choices and about the achievement of autonomy. Jo, wrote Elizabeth Janeway, is "the one young woman in

36. Ibid., 95.

37. Quoted in Susan Phinney Conrad, *Perish the Thought: Intellectual Women in Romantic America 1830–1860* (New York: Oxford Univ. Press, 1976), 123.

38. Nina Baym, "Melodramas of Beset Manhood: How Theories of American Fiction Exclude Women Authors," *American Quarterly* 33 (1981): 132–33. "Both . . . the entrammelling society and the promising landscape . . . are depicted in unmistakably feminine terms, and this gives a sexual character to the protagonist's story which does, indeed, limit its applicability to women. And this sexual definition has melodramatic, misogynist implication . . . the encroaching, constricting, destroying society is represented with particular urgency in the figure of one or more women."

nineteenth-century fiction who maintains her individual independence, who gives up no part of her autonomy as payment for being born a woman, and who gets away with it."

Janeway seriously misreads the novel. Alcott is explicit. Independence and autonomy do come at a price; they are not, in fact, fully achieved. *Little Women* is shot through with ever-repeated images of restraint, resignation, endurance. Only Meg has a personality congruent with the demands of her community, and only to her is contentment possible because she does not need to push at the margins of what is permitted in order to devise her own life. Beth makes a death so beautiful that Gubar and Gilbert call it virtually a suicide; Amy whines, manipulates, and gets her way at others' expense, and Jo must settle for an ambivalent happiness accomplished by denying her own instincts. No wonder the figure of Jo March has been a mystery that generations of girls have spent over a century trying to decipher. The most recent testimony comes from Cynthia Ozick, remembering her childhood: "I read *Little Women* a thousand times. Ten thousand. I am Jo in her 'vortex'; not Jo exactly, but some Jo of the future. I am under an enchantment; who I am must be deferred, waited for and waited for."[39]

Everyone remembers that Jo grows up to be a writer, but not everyone remembers that she also, with her husband, establishes a school. Sooner or later the search for female autonomy reverted to a dream of education. No sooner articulated, the rhetoric of female individualism quickly added the promise that it would not challenge men; that instead of lone individuals on unmapped frontiers, women would seek authenticity in schools and in communities of women.

Perhaps this was because for a long time the privately founded school, which might begin in one's own home or cheaply rented rooms, was the most accessible route for women to professional space and steady income. Perhaps it was because education was one of the few modes of work that offered gentility and protected at the same time against accusations of masculinity. Perhaps it was because to deflect restive women into educational institutions meant that they did not immediately threaten the hegemony of the male middle class, but were instead redefined as a group serving the male middle class. Perhaps it was because no dream dies harder than the one

39. Elizabeth Janeway in *New York Times Book Review*, September 29, 1968; Sandra M. Gilbert and Susan Gubar, *The Madwoman in the Attic: The Woman Writer and the Nineteenth-Century Imagination* (New Haven: Yale Univ. Press, 1979), 483; Cynthia Ozick in *New York Times Book Review*, January 31, 1982.

that promises that we will save the world if we can only square things for the next generation. And perhaps it was because, just as a cigar is sometimes just a cigar, women's education was clearly the next thing on most folks' agenda.

As early as 1776, Adam Smith had noted without criticizing the narrow practicality of women's education; "They are taught what their parents or guardians judge is necessary or useful for them to learn; and they are taught nothing else. Every part of their education tends . . . either to improve the natural attraction of their person, or to form their mind to reserve, to modesty, to chastity, and to economy; to render them both likely to become the mistresses of a family, and to behave properly when they have become such." There is, he concluded, "nothing useless, absurd, or fantastical" in the education of women.[40] But for women like Elizabeth Smith, or Margaret Fuller, "the fantastical" was just the point.

And therefore throughout the nineteenth century, from Emma Willard opening an academy in her home in Middlebury, Vermont, at its beginning, to Annie Nathan Meyer raising money on Park Avenue for Barnard College at its end, independence for women was frequently defined in terms of schools. "Don't ever dare to take your college as a matter of course," wrote one women's college alumna in 1939, "because like freedom and democracy, many people you'll never know anything about have broken their hearts to get it for you."[41]

Women had to find room to develop their intellects without eliciting male hostility and contempt. It was assumed that the course of study for women required special justification; a standard question was: what studies are appropriate for the female mind? Adam Smith had said that what women needed was a continuation of what had been learned in the home and could be used directly and practically in adult life: "no absurdities." In the nineteenth century, the list of appropriate studies lengthened; it became respectable for women to contemplate a widening range of activities. But few would say with Margaret Fuller, "Let them be sea-captains if they will," and fewer would maintain that women might properly indulge in any form of study.[42]

40. Adam Smith, *An Inquiry into the Nature and Causes of the Wealth of Nations*, ed. Edwin Canaan (New York: Modern Library, Random House, 1937), bk. 5, 734.

41. Alice Duer Miller, quoted in Virginia Crocheron Gildersleeve, *Many a Good Crusade* (New York: Macmillan, 1954), 227–80.

42. Both colleges and political organizations could provide space that empowered women to make these claims. See, for example, Antoinette Brown's address at the

To take the old language of individualism at face value could be dangerous. In the first third of the twentieth century, Rose Wilder Lane decided to assume that it was possible for a girl to link herself to the myth of the lone individual that she understood to be part of the American vision. Preparing herself by writing biographies of two exemplars of the self-made man, Jack London (whose *Call of the Wild* delineated a pure frontier for a new generation) and Herbert Hoover, Lane launched herself into the life of a free-lance journalist, arriving in Europe immediately after the war was over, reporting from devastated Eastern Europe, traveling with only one female companion to Albania, nearly as isolated from the West as it was until 1989. Expecting to "make it" on her own, beholden to no one, she broke most friendships not long after they were made, proud of hanging on in a world of magazines that was feast or famine, briefly becoming one of the best paid popular feature writers for the *Saturday Evening Post*, but also suffering long stretches without pay.

During these stretches, she returned to her family home in the Ozarks, where her father and her mother, Laura Ingalls Wilder, hung on, leaning on her for support. In the years of the depression, Lane and her mother became increasingly embittered with a society in whose promises of success to the individual they had believed. Lane announced that she would no longer write so that she would not have to pay taxes to a New Deal government, but she did write fiction romanticizing the hardships of the homesteader on the late-nineteenth-century frontier, and she rewrote the rough drafts of her mother's memoirs, "passing them through my typewriter" and turning them into the *Little House* books in which the isolated family is pitted against the elements and makes it—or doesn't—with no help from the community. The self-reliance celebrated in the *Little House* books turns

---

Oberlin Ladies Department graduation, "Original Investigation Necessary to the Right Development of Mind," *Oberlin Evangelist*, September 29, 1847. Cited in Carol Lasser and Marlene Deahl Merrill, eds., *Friends and Sisters: Letters between Lucy Stone and Antoinette Brown Blackwell, 1846–93* (Urbana: Univ. of Illinois Press, 1987), 11. Planning a women's rights meeting in Worcester, Massachusetts, Lucy Stone wrote to Antoinette Brown: "The Anti-Slavery women I think are more intelligent than most women, at any rate they have *thought* more, and they talk good sense. Still many of them, are not accustomed to take comprehensive views, as men are. How long it will be before Women will even *begin*, to be what they ought to be. Still a great change is working, and the right *will come uppermost*. I dont now, ever wish that I was a man." Stone to Brown, June 9, 1850, ibid., 73.

sour at their end, when Laura and Almanzo must face a reality unmediated by their parents. By the end of her life, untrammeled individualism had become for Lane a shrill anticommunism.[43]

In the years of the cold war, years which saw on American campuses the creation of programs in American Civilization (a shrill insistence that America *had* a civilization), the old image of the individual poised against society was moved into the core programs in liberal education. The theme of Columbia University's famous and widely imitated curriculum in contemporary civilization used the conflict between individual and society as its central theme: the American Civilization programs claimed Matthiessen's canonical American literature resting heavily on Emerson, Melville, and Twain. Offered to an undergraduate population that was half female, these selections made the easy assumption that the great work of the world had been done by men, and that the true American image was the lone male adventurer, pitting himself against the unknown, and that what he could expect from women was opposition, not camaraderie. We are beginning now to understand this canon as a cliché that served a wide range of only dimly acknowledged political purposes and political needs.[44]

This was not simply the antebellum trope revisited; rather, I think, it was a continuation of an ideology that had made World War II endurable by posing individual freedoms against Fascist states that offered no breathing space outside of group solidarity. The concept of individualism, as a mark of the limits of society's claims, which promised options outside the tyranny of the group, resonates through David Riesman's *The Lonely Crowd*. Riesman reinterpreted the old ideology of the self-made into the "inner-directed" individual; his extraordinarily popular book offered a sympathetic reading of the anxieties of modernism. But even Riesman wrote from inside the paradigm, still assuming that it is men who make the choices that define the individual and only occasionally considering whether his gener-

43. Linda K. Kerber, "Laura Ingalls Wilder," in *Notable American Women: The Modern Period*, ed. Barbara Sicherman and Carol Hurd Green (Cambridge: Harvard Univ. Press, 1980), 732–34. Rose Wilder Lane's papers are at the Herbert Hoover Presidential Library, West Branch, Iowa. For her influence on Laura Ingalls Wilder's work, see especially Box 12.

44. See, for example, Richard Pells, *The Liberal Mind in a Conservative Age* (New York: Harper and Row, 1985), 117–18. I have discussed this issue in "Diversity and the Transformation of American Studies," *American Quarterly* 41 (1989): 415–31.

alizations held up when applied to women.[45] The image of the male adventurer pitting himself, like Natty Bumppo, against the unknown was not a very practical image for young men whose career options lay in insurance or advertising; it was almost valueless for the young woman who knew that whatever she tried to do professionally she would need to be a support to a young man. Thus Adlai Stevenson, speaking at a Smith College commencement in 1956:

> You may be hitched to one of these creatures we call "Western man" and I think part of your job is to keep him Western, to keep him truly purposeful, to keep him whole. In short—while I have had very little experience as a wife or mother—I think one of the biggest jobs for many of you will be to frustrate the crushing and corrupting effects of specialization, to integrate means and ends. . . . This assignment for you, as wives and mothers, has great advantages. In the first place, it is home work—you can do it in the living room with a baby in your lap . . .

"The language of individualism," wrote Robert Bellah and his colleagues recently in *Habits of the Heart*, "is the primary American language of self-understanding." That language is inadequate, Bellah argues, because it "limits the way people think." It permits a deracinated selfishness that makes the self-interest of the observer into the measure of value and shields people from confronting great social and moral issues.[46]

But that language is also inadequate, also limits the ways in which people

45. When Riesman was invited to address women directly, however, as he did in a graduation address at a women's college, he would urge the students to make their own claims to an education that would "put pressure on life," open up new worlds of learning, encourage new ambitions, and make room for the problematic. See "Continuities and Discontinuities in Women's Education," Paper presented at commencement, Bennington College, 1956.

46. Robert Bellah et al., *Habits of the Heart: Individualism and Commitment in American Life* (Berkeley: Univ. of California Press, 1985). Although quotations from women are scattered throughout the book, only one of the main subjects of the interviews was a woman, and the descriptions of work that are central to the argument invariably refer to the significance of paid professional work to men. Thus Bellah can come to the easy conclusion that "a less frantic concern for advancement and a reduction of working hours for both men and women would make it easier for women to be full participants in the workplace without abandoning family life—and men would be freed to take on an equal role at home and in child care." His conclusion makes the assumption that there is a consensus that the methods of work *ought* to be made less brutally competitive or that men in large numbers will agree to do what women do.

think, because it has not been acknowledged that the language of individualism has been a male-centered discourse, that its imagery has traditionally served the self-interest of men, whatever their class. In the context of a bourgeois social order, an order of sexual politics that assumed continued deference from women toward their men and continued interruption of women's most private, imaginative lives so that domestic tasks could be done, the paradoxes of republican motherhood and the contradictions inherent in achieving female authenticity could not be resolved—not by the antebellum generation, not by the Progressive generation, not by any of the subsequent generations of the twentieth century, not even our own.

Years ago Antonio Gramsci put his mind to the problem of how ruling groups maintain consent to their power and argued that they do not do it by force alone. Rather, they use a language that limits the way other groups can *think* about their place in society. If the language is not available it becomes difficult to locate the source of unease. Unable to conceptualize a challenge to hegemonic language, women seem to have played the role of a "historical bloc" in Gramsci's sense—a group not completely distracted by the prevailing cultural hegemony and permanently in the process of groping for a language to describe its own perception of reality. I would say that in the long sweep of women's history there have been times—ours is one of them—when women have been particularly aggressive and imaginative in seizing their culture's tools of expression. And I would also say in the long sweep of American cultural history, the language of individualism helped them very little.

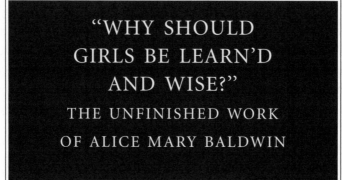

"WHY SHOULD GIRLS BE LEARN'D AND WISE?"

THE UNFINISHED WORK OF ALICE MARY BALDWIN

Col. [Thomas Wentworth] Higginson said that one of the great histories yet to be written is that of the intellectual life of women.
ANNA GARLIN SPENCER, *Women's Share in Social Culture,* 1925

Alice Mary Baldwin was a formidable American educator. A historian who received her Ph.D. from the University of Chicago in 1926, she is best known as the author of a long-standard monograph on New England ministers in the era of the American Revolution.[1] Baldwin spent most of her career as dean of the Woman's College of what is now Duke University. Overworked and underpaid, she had trouble fitting research projects into her day and published little after her doctoral dissertation.

This essay is a revised and expanded version of " 'Why Should Girls Be Learn'd and Wise?' Two Centuries of Higher Education for Women as Seen through the Unfinished Work of Alice Mary Baldwin," originally published in John Mack Faragher and Florence Howe, eds., *Women and Higher Education in American History* (New York: W. W. Norton, 1988). I am greatly indebted to Kenneth Cmiel, Mary Ann Dzuback, Leon Fink, and Barbara Sicherman for thoughtful and helpful comments, to Leslie Taylor for smart research assistance, and to the National Humanities Center for collegial surroundings.

1. Alice Mary Baldwin, *The New England Clergy and the American Revolution* (Durham, N.C.: Duke University Press, 1928). Alice Mary Baldwin was born in 1879. The most complete account of her life is found in Dianne Puthoff Brandstadter, "Developing the Coordinate College for Women at Duke University: The Career of Alice Mary Baldwin, 1924–47" (Ph.D. diss., Duke University, 1977).

Baldwin's life and work exemplify some of the key issues and major patterns in the history of the intellectual life of American women. In the course of her career she was forced to reflect on the position of intellectual women and on women's formal education; at the end of her life this restrained, discreet woman set on paper her own bitter criticism of the way Duke University had treated its women's college and its dean. She ordered this account sealed for twenty years; it has only recently been opened. In the fraction of her time that she could devote to research in early American history, Baldwin found herself increasingly drawn to the study of women's experience. Through her notes and drafts of essays, we can watch a fine mind struggling to write women's history without the matrix of support on which we can now rely. In 1938 she could not command attention for her narrative of two colonial sisters who hungered for intellectual challenge except by offering them as "quaint." By the time she died, in 1961, she was no longer treating women's experience apologetically. Left unfinished among her papers were notes and drafts for an essay tentatively called "The Reading of Women in the Colonies before 1750." In this essay she set herself to defend colonial women from the charge that they "ordinarily read very little" and that "intellectual accomplishments were not expected of the weaker sex."[2]

I do not know whether Baldwin suspected that her own career and the research on which she embarked were parts of the same large story, that she was in effect a character in a late chapter of a narrative featuring her heroine, the eighteenth-century Bostonian Jane Colman Terrell, in its first chapter. For all its complexity, the intellectual history of women in America has been at base a single story: a continuing quest by determined women to claim access to books, instruction, and opportunity to interpret, always resisting the assumption—as much a part of our legacy from the Greeks and Romans as is the architecture of the Parthenon—that women's minds are naturally limited to the trivial. Individual women had to struggle to clear a space for their own intellectual activity and to defend themselves against the charge that intellectual effort was inappropriate, even dan-

2. All references to Baldwin's work are based on the Alice Mary Baldwin papers in the Duke University Archives and are quoted by permission of the Duke University Archives. See especially the typescript "Two Sisters of Old Boston," circa 1938; her miscellaneous notes on cards and on sheets of paper, filed as "The Reading of Women," circa 1961; and her typescript memoir, "The Women's College as I Remember It," 1959, opened in 1980.

Alice Mary Baldwin before her retirement in 1947 as dean of the Woman's College of Duke University. Courtesy Duke University Archives.

gerous, when attempted by a woman. What they knew was, in Michel Foucault's terms, treated as "subjugated knowledges"—knowledges "disqualified as inadequate to their task or insufficiently elaborated"—knowledges instantly devalued once claimed by a woman.[3] African Americans were systematically excluded from Western systems of literature, learning, and publication; as Henry Louis Gates recently pointed out, fifty-six years elapsed between the publication of Phillis Wheatley's *Poems on Various Subjects, Religious and Moral* in 1773 and the next book of poetry published by an African American, George Moses Horton, in 1829. The first book of

3. Michel Foucault, "Two Lectures," in *Power/Knowledge: Selected Interviews and Other Writings, 1972–1977*, trans. Colin Gordon, Leo Marshall, John Mepham, and Kate Soper; ed. Colin Gordon (New York: Pantheon Books, 1980), 82. For an example, see discussion of the gendered dimensions of social science knowledge in the early twentieth century in Barbara Laslett, "Gender In/And Social Science History," *Social Science History* 16 (Summer 1992): 177–95.

essays published by an African American was Ann Plato's in 1841.[4] Before a black woman could claim Virginia Woolf's "room of her own," she had first to claim her own body, her own mind, and her own house—physical as well as metaphoric—in which to place that room.

As David Hollinger has shrewdly observed, intellectual history in America has traditionally been written in a manner that "treats . . . ideas, for the most part, as a structure, and attributes the structure to a community of interacting minds." The paradigm for intellectual history has long been Perry Miller's *New England Mind*, published in 1953. What was novel and exciting about *The New England Mind*, Hollinger observes, was that the life of the mind was "depicted as a *life*," conveyed through "a succession of disputes, of discussions, of arguments" rather than as "a set of discrete units of thought," like the idea of progress or the Great Chain of Being.[5] Indeed, Hollinger observes, intellectual history as it has been written in America "focuses on arguments made by people whose chief business it was to argue. . . ."[6] What for a long time went virtually unnoticed was that although Miller was describing the arguments carried on by New England's ministers and political leaders, he offered and his readers accepted this as an account of an entire *generation*: "the premises," Miller said, "of all Puritan discourse."[7]

Hollinger's connection of intellectual history to the discourse of intellectuals suggests questions about the extent to which communities of intellectuals—"people whose chief business it was to argue"—have fashioned themselves in large part by class and by gender. If the site of intellectual life in colonial New England is understood to be the arguments of ministers and women were excluded from the ministry—even, as Anne Hutchinson tragically discovered, from informal claims to theological authority—then women were neither part of a profession nor part of an intellectual community. If women are not "people whose chief business it was to argue," then we are unlikely to find the intellectual history of women in the usual places. The theater for women's intellectual life has rarely been institu-

4. Henry Louis Gates, Foreword to *The Schomburg Library of Nineteenth-Century Black Women Writers* (New York: Oxford University Press, 1988), x–xi.

5. David Hollinger, "Historians and the Discourse of Intellectuals," in *New Directions in American Intellectual History*, ed. John Higham and Paul K. Conkin (Baltimore: Johns Hopkins University Press, 1979), 47.

6. Ibid., 49.

7. Ibid., 47.

tional. Its locus was necessarily wherever women gathered to argue: in antislavery societies, where they wrestled with ideas about the limits of individualism, or in social meetings, where they struggled with concepts of the authentic relationship between labor and capital, or around kitchen tables, where, after a day of labor, they gathered informally to discern the essential elements of the social and economic system in which they felt trapped. The task of constructing themselves into something called "an intellectual" was different for women than it was for men because as a group women were understood to be differently situated in relation to argument, reason, and particularly abstraction. The culture of argument involved also a culture of oratory, a culture as old as Demosthenes. The "learned" professions—the ministry, law, and the professoriate—involved not only reason and argument but also forceful public speaking, barred to women by law and custom. With few exceptions, women would not begin to insert themselves into public space as orators until the antislavery and women's rights movements of the second third of the nineteenth century; indeed, the presence of women in public argument has only recently begun to be normalized.

To write women into intellectual history as American historians have traditionally understood it, we would have to wait for the creation of institutions in which women can carry on argument. That is, the history of women's intellect, unlike the history of women thinking, would have to wait for the building of institutions in which women argued and in which they exercised authority.[8] Those institutions were built only gradually, at first informally, and always with many variations. A wide range of sites in which argument took place was developed—the lyceum lectures women attended and discussed, the literary societies in boardinghouses in Lowell and other mill towns, women's literary and debating societies at coeducational colleges. Women's study and book discussion groups, which flourished from the 1880s through the twentieth century, have only recently been understood to be a site of intellectual development and argument.[9]

8. Mary Kelley is now exploring the connections between women's improved learning and their intrusion into the public sector. See especially " 'Vindicating the Equality of Female Intellect': Women and Authority in the Early Republic," *Prospects* 17 (1993): 1–27.

9. Mary Ann Dzuback, personal communication. On sites of argument, see Theodora Penny Martin, *The Sound of Our Own Voices: Women's Study Clubs 1860–1910* (Boston: Beacon, 1987). Adrienne Rich, "Toward a Woman-Centered University," in *On*

Until quite recently, whether women were included in historians' narratives of intellectual history depended heavily on whether they had intense personal relationships with men's intellectual communities, from Margaret Fuller among the transcendentalists to Mary McCarthy among the *Partisan Review* circle.[10]

We may discern four distinct periods or stages in the framing of women's formal intellectual claims. To evaluate each, we need to know something about the levels of literacy—both elementary and sophisticated—among women as compared with men; their opportunities to participate in formal and informal intellectual practices—access to books and newspapers, correspondence, schooling—and the extent to which they were able to establish formal and informal communities of colleagues who examined ideas critically. Despite their usual claim to be free of social inequities—to be an "ivory tower"—these communities have reflected patterns of racial, ethnic, and gender segregation at work in the societies of which they have been a part. It is still the very rare intellectual community in which the men and women participate in equal numbers on equal terms.

In the first era, the colonial period, female literacy grew slowly and erratically, and there were no formal institutions of higher education for females. Literacy was tightly tied to race and class and was connected to residence in an urban commercial environment. By the end of the period, basic literacy was widespread among white women in the Northeast; some authors have argued that it was close to universal in that region by the time of the Revolution.[11] Women who aspired to an education more complex than the three Rs, however, had to find their own mentors in a culture that was highly skeptical of their efforts.

The years between the Revolution and 1833, the opening of Oberlin College to women, might be labeled the Era of the Great Debate over the Capacities of Women's Minds. These years were marked by continuing

---

Lies, Secrets and Silence: Selected Prose 1966–1978 (New York: W. W. Norton, 1979), 125–55, is a bitter and insightful indictment.

10. Even the book in which Hollinger's essay appeared—itself marking an important historiographic moment for intellectual history—and in which many authors paid obeisance to Merle Curti's pioneering work on the social context of American thought, failed to identify gender as part of that social context. Yet Curti's own work and career has been marked by a receptivity to women scholars and to women's history.

11. See, for example, William Gilmore, "Elementary Literacy on the Eve of the Industrial Revolution: Trends in Rural New England 1760–1830," *Proceedings of the American Antiquarian Society* 92, part 1 (1982): 87–178.

improvement in female literacy, a political revolution that articulated the need for the education of succeeding generations of moral citizens, and the assertion by some articulate women of their need for institutional support. Inherited assumptions about women's incapacity for higher education were questioned; schools for girls with serious aspirations, whether for learning or for upward social mobility, were established. The founding of Oberlin marked the end of one era and the beginning of another. Although Oberlin offered somewhat different tracks to white men, to white and black women, and to black men, it created the first coeducational and interracial student body and made an important statement about the range of people in whom genius might be found.[12]

The years between Oberlin's founding and roughly the turn of the century may be thought of as a third era, characterized by women's increasing access to institutions of higher education. State colleges and universities were opened to women; some followed the model of the University of Iowa, founded in 1847, which was coeducational and admitted women from the moment of its founding. In the Reconstruction years, institutes and colleges for black students were established, and virtually all were coeducational. Among the most exciting were Wilberforce University in Ohio, founded in 1856; Atlanta University, founded in 1865; Fisk University, founded in 1866; and Howard University, founded in 1867. Indeed, despite the fame of the women's colleges established in the last quarter of the century—Wellesley and Smith in 1875, Spelman in 1881, Bryn Mawr and Randolph-Macon in 1884, and Barnard in 1889—coeducational institutions would always account for the largest number of women students. (In the South, however, women were most likely to attend women's colleges.) In 1775 not a single institution of higher education included women among its students; a century later over a hundred allowed white women to enter, and a handful—Oberlin, Antioch, Fisk, Atlanta—admitted black women. Not many by today's standards, certainly, but an extraordinary contrast with a century before.

12. Lori D. Ginzberg, "'The Joint Education of the Sexes': Oberlin's Original Vision," in *Educating Men and Women Together: Coeducation in a Changing World*, ed. Carol Lasser (Urbana: University of Illinois Press, 1987), 67–80. See also Barbara Miller Solomon, "The Oberlin Model and Its Impact on Other Colleges," in *Educating Men and Women Together*, ed. Lasser, 83. African Americans entered Oberlin in the early 1860s.

A fourth period in women's higher education may be said to extend from the first decade of the twentieth century, when strong backlash against women's intellectual claims frequently excluded them from the newly developing research universities, to the 1970s, when Title 9 of the Higher Education Act of 1972 prohibited sex discrimination in most schools that receive federal financial assistance, and one after another elite colleges and universities admitted women to their student bodies.[13] The first two decades of the twentieth century were characterized by, in Barbara Miller Solomon's words, an "explosion in female enrollments"; between 1900 and 1920 women moved from constituting one-third of all students enrolled in institutions of higher education to nearly one-half.[14] Their more visible presence, coupled with their academic success, "precipitated yet another round in the cycle of criticism."[15] The opening years of the twentieth century were notable for the complaint that women were "taking over" the universities; it sometimes seemed that the higher their achievement, the more opposition was expressed to their equal access to educational institutions. When women students earned more awards than men did, writes Solomon, Stanford University ignored "the university statute requiring 'equal advantages in the University to both sexes' "; between 1904 and 1933 it maintained an admissions ratio of three males to each female, and admissions on a roughly equal basis was not established until the 1970s. The University of Chicago went to the length of establishing a separate junior college to push women out of the undergraduate college when, in 1902, it realized women accounted for a majority of those achieving Phi Beta Kappa status. The segregated system was short-lived. An effort to segregate women into a separate teachers' college at the University of Wisconsin in 1907 was only narrowly defeated, as was a similar effort at the University of South Carolina in 1913. Women were admitted only to upper-division courses at the University of North Carolina in 1898, and they would not be admitted on an equal basis with men until a court order in 1972; no women

13. Exceptions from Title 9 were made for single-sex and religious institutions. See statistics on number of colleges open to men and women 1870–1981 in Solomon, "The Oberlin Model," 44.

14. Ibid., 63.

15. Barbara Miller Solomon, *In the Company of Educated Women: A History of Women and Higher Education in America* (New Haven, Conn.: Yale University Press, 1985), 58.

at all were admitted to the University of Virginia in Charlottesville until the threat of a court order in 1970.[16]

Even when efforts to resegregate academic institutions failed, they left behind a general sense that women had entered into space controlled by men and stayed only so long as men found it convenient. When wartime conscription, particularly during World War II, drew men out of the pool of prospective students, colleges vigorously welcomed women, but when men flooded back after the war, hostility to women's presence was again expressed. Women's enrollment in institutions of higher learning declined after 1920, reaching a twentieth-century low of 30 percent in 1950, when space was given to veterans and popular magazines ran articles questioning whether women should take up spaces that would otherwise go to men.[17] Moreover, coeducation in universities extended only to the student body; faculties, administrators, boards of trustees were overwhelmingly male. During the twentieth century, it could be said that women's relationship with academic intellectual communities has intensified but generally been uneasy.

Through all these years there hummed, like the steady continuo of the harpsichord, the constant complaint versified by John Trumbull at the end of the eighteenth century:

> Why should girls be learn'd and wise?
> Books only serve to spoil their eyes.
> The studious eye but faintly twinkles
> And reading paves the way to wrinkles.[18]

16. Ibid., 58–61, is the best brief summary of these developments. Lynn D. Gordon's shrewd chapters on women at the University of California and the University of Chicago are indispensable. See Lynn D. Gordon, *Gender and Higher Education in the Progressive Era* (New Haven, Conn.: Yale University Press, 1990), chap. 2, 3. For the southern institutions, see Amy Thompson McCandless, "Maintaining the Spirit and Tone of Robust Manliness: The Battle against Coeducation at Southern Colleges and Universities, 1890–1940," *NWSA Journal* 2 (Spring 1990): 199–216. For the University of Virginia, see *Kirstein v. Rector and Visitors of the University of Virginia*, 309 F. Supp. 184 (1970), in which a three judge panel approved a consent order.

17. On the exclusion of women from postwar enrollments, see Alma Lutz, "Women Need Education, Too," *Christian Science Monitor*, July 20, 1946. On the persistence of this perspective, see Philip Ward Burton, "Keep Women Out of College!" *This Week*, February 9, 1958.

18. John Trumbull, "The Progress of Dulness," in *Satiric Poems: The Progress of Dulness and M'Fingal*, ed. Edwin T. Bowden (Austin: University of Texas Press, 1962), 88.

In the late 1930s Alice Mary Baldwin wrote a narrative she called "Two Sisters of Old Boston." It serves well as an introduction to our first era, when most women had only the most marginal literacy and those who acquired more than the rudiments did so through informal instruction in their own families.[19] Although Baldwin did not explicitly mark the Colman sisters as emblems of the fate of the colonial woman who hungered for learning, that implication is embedded in her account.[20]

Jane and Abigail were the daughters of Benjamin Colman, a graduate of Harvard in 1692 and the minister of the Brattle Street Church in Boston. Jane, the older, was born in 1702. The girls read the poems of Elizabeth Singer Rowe, Alexander Pope, Richard Blackmore, and Edmund Waller. Jane probably was familiar with some of the Latin poets as well, since later she wrote a poem in imitation of Horace. Jane's poems testified to her hunger for learning:

> Come now, fair Muse, and fill my empty mind,
> With rich ideas, great and unconfin'd . . .
> O let me burn with *Sappho*'s noble Fire,
> But not like her for faithless man expire.

Benjamin Colman respected Jane's quest for "great and unconfin'd" ideas; in 1725 he admitted that "with the Advantages of my liberal Education at School & College, I have no reason to think but that your genius in writing would have excelled mine." At the same time, however, he warned her that writing poetry was indulgent; she should spend her time in reading and in devotion.

But Jane Colman was unlucky in her husband. Ebenezer Terrell was a minister at Medford; Baldwin assessed him as a smart but humorless man who monopolized control of the books and ideas circulating in their household.[21] "The story," wrote Baldwin, "told in the old letters and in the phrasing of the day, makes very clear the demands upon her young body and the conflicts of her mind and spirit." By the time Jane was twenty years

19. See Joel Perlmann and Dennis Shirley, "When Did New England Women Acquire Literacy?" *William and Mary Quarterly*, 3d ser., 48 (January 1991): 50–67; and response by Mary Beth Norton, *William and Mary Quarterly*, 3d ser., 48 (October 1991): 639–45.

20. This summary of the story draws on Baldwin's draft and on her 1961 notes.

21. Tom Leonard at the School of Journalism, University of California–Berkeley, is exploring the control of printed matter in the household and also examining painting and prints for depictions of the use of reading to reinforce hierarchy.

old she had come to be fearful for her salvation and to regret her reading of fiction. When she died at the age of twenty-seven, her father's colleague, the Reverend John Adams, thought he was doing her honor by praising her as

> Free from ambition . . .
> Nor was she vain, nor stain'd with those Neglects,
> In which too learned Females lose their Sex—

The story of the younger sister, Abigail, is even more tormented. "Nabby," as she was called, was twelve when Jane gave up romances to please her husband. Abigail nevertheless "gave herself to reading from her Childhood," reported her father, "and soon to writing. She wanted not a Taste for what was excellent in Books, more especially of a Poetical Turn or Relish. . . . Thus run her too soon and too far into the reading of Novels, &c., for which God in his righteous Providence afterwards punished her by suffering her to leave her Father's House, to the grief of her Friends and the Surprise of the Town."

Colman assumed a clear connection between Nabby's reading and her elopement with the young rake Alfred Dennie, who took her to New Hampshire, where, to the family's horror, they were married by "a Priest of the Church of England." There were desperate fights over Nabby's inheritance and Dennie's expenditure of her money; Dennie was accused of giving his wife "a foul disease." Nabby claimed that she loved Dennie "with a Love stronger than Death"; she did indeed die shortly thereafter, but not before observing that "I ought to be the subject of a Tragedy as noble as that of Cato's."

Stories like Abigail's would be told and retold for at least another century as a way of warning young girls to avoid misalliance. The genre would reach its apogee in the 1790s in Susannah Rowson's *Charlotte: A Tale of Truth* (1791) and Hannah Webster Foster's *Coquette* (1797). Each is a political cautionary tale in which the price of sexual adventure is death. Each is also a bitter criticism of a world in which upwardly mobile men use women for their own purposes. In a commercial society in which all rests on promises and credit, marriage promises themselves could not be trusted.[22] Young women read fiction literally to save their own lives.

22. See Linda K. Kerber, *Women of the Republic: Intellect and Ideology in Revolutionary America* (Chapel Hill: University of North Carolina Press, 1980), chap. 8, esp. 240–52. See also Cathy N. Davidson, "The Life and Times of *Charlotte Temple*: The Biography of a Book," in *Reading in America: Literature and Social History*, ed. Cathy N. Davidson (Baltimore: Johns Hopkins University Press, 1989), 157–79; and Carroll

Baldwin understood both sisters as emblems of caution against reading. Abigail's reading was thought to have drawn her into irresponsible behavior. Jane managed to maintain her intellectual interests without discrediting her character, but it seemed, as the Reverend John Adams put it, a near thing. In 1961 Baldwin decided to find out how typical the Colman girls had been. She suspected that the worry about novel reading had been overstated and not only for poor Nabby: "In the wills and inventories which I have been able to find [in New York] there is no mention of any novel or romance." In fact, there were few novels or romances in the colonies before 1750. "Usually authors have been contented to say that for the most part women were interested in household affairs, in embroidery, painting, perhaps a smattering of French. . . ." Baldwin was skeptical; she also suspected that these authors were repeating each other. She embarked on a search of wills, printed library lists, and diaries. She found women reading *The Spectator*, William Shakespeare, Robert Burton's *Anatomy of Melancholy*, Joseph Addison, Richard Price, William Congreve, Alexander Pope, and John Dryden. She even found a woman who supervised the studies of her descendants after death: in 1780 one Mrs. Latham saw "the specter of an elderly woman," an ancestor who had willed her books to her descendants and who now appeared "to reprove her for reading a novel on the Sabbath Day."[23] Baldwin died before she could finish this essay, but she had clearly established that the range of women's reading was far wider than her contemporaries had thought.

In *The Wealth of Nations*, published in 1776, Adam Smith sensitively noted that there were few institutions in England dedicated to the education of women. He suggested that this was because women were not thought to need an education that would draw them into a world of commerce, politics, and the unpredictable. Boys, in contrast, required an education that gave them the skills needed to respond to the public world. Smith wrote, "There is nothing useless or absurd or fantastical in the common course of women's education. They can be taught what their

---

Smith-Rosenberg, "Engendering Virtue," in *Literature and the Body: Essays on Populations and Persons*, ed. Elaine Scarry, Selected Papers from the English Institute, 1986, new series, no. 12 (Baltimore: Johns Hopkins University Press, 1988), 160–84.

23. The book at issue was Giovanni Paolo Marana's *Letters Writ by a Turkish Spy . . .* (London: G. Strahan, 1734), which may have been the model for Montesquieu's *Persian Letters* and which included a passage supporting extended education for women.

parents or guardians judge necessary or useful for them to learn. They are taught nothing else."[24] Since parents, in effect, can predict what a woman is going to need to know, she can be trained at home to face that life. It was not anticipated that women would encounter the uncertain and the unexpected, "the absurd or the fantastical." A reasonably sophisticated level of literacy is the crucial means of access to the community of argument, but in the first era the girl who, like Jane Colman, hungered for more literacy and argument than she "needed" was incomprehensible to her contemporaries.

Beneath a veneer of stability, major changes were under way throughout the eighteenth century and would come with breathtaking speed at the end. A second era in women's intellectual history may be discerned in the years of the early Republic—roughly including the Revolution and the first decades of the nineteenth century—when competence in skills increased markedly, especially for white middle-class women, and claims were made with some frequency that women's intellect was at least comparable to men's. A virtual revolution in literacy was under way, encouraged by the transition of the economy to a print culture and reinforced by a technology that made printed materials more widely available and injected them into new areas of life, and by an ideological campaign that linked reading to rationality, upward mobility, and control of one's own life. Although literacy did not increase at the same rate for each class or each sex within each class, what might be called a "literacy gap" between free white men and women gradually closed during the first half-century of the Republic's history. This gap had been a double one; reading and writing were differently gendered. As Jennifer Monaghan has shown, in the colonial era reading was understood to be appropriate for girls as well as boys and was normally taught to children by women, whether their mothers or other adult women in "dame schools." But "writing was considered a craft . . . a male job-related skill, a tool for ministers and shipping clerks alike."[25] Studying towns in the upper Connecticut River Valley for the years of the early Republic, William Gilmore reports nearly universal literacy for men of all classes by the 1780s and 80 percent female literacy for the richest

24. Adam Smith, *An Inquiry into the Nature and Causes of the Wealth of Nations*, ed. Edwin Canaan (New York: Modern Library, 1937), bk. 5, chap. 1, pt. iii, pt. 2, 734.

25. E. Jennifer Monaghan, "Literacy Instruction and Gender in Colonial New England," in *Reading in America*, ed. Davidson, 60–61.

eight-tenths of the population.[26] Skills once regarded as those of the power-ful—reading and writing—were distributed among American women to an unprecedented extent. White women in New England seem to have been the most literate women in the Western world.

These figures cannot be generalized for the entire United States. They are specific to region: the South lagged far behind; as late as 1850 one out of five white women in the South was illiterate.[27] They are specific to race: literacy was denied to slaves by law; free blacks lacked both opportunity and institutional support for extended study. Yet the literacy of free blacks was much higher than, until recently, it has been assumed, and urban African Americans quickly narrowed the gap between the races after the Civil War. In 1910, when 36 percent of all rural African Americans were illiterate, less than 6 percent of urban African Americans in western cities were, a slightly lower level of illiteracy than prevailed among white foreign born in the same cities.[28]

For people on the margins of society, achieving literacy could mean the opening of wonderful, even magical new horizons. But not necessarily. Nowhere is the ambivalence of the marginal person toward reading—and toward the life of the intellect in general—expressed with more precision than by Harriet A. Jacobs in her thinly disguised autobiography, *Incidents in the Life of a Slave Girl*.[29] In that account, literacy is no predictor of moral integrity. When Jacobs's grandmother stands on the auction block, placed there by her privileged and literate masters, she is saved by "a feeble . . . maiden lady, seventy years old, the sister of my grandmother's deceased mistress. . . . [She] could neither read nor write; and when the bill of sale

26. William Gilmore, *Reading Becomes a Necessity of Life: Material and Cultural Life in Rural New England, 1780–1835* (Knoxville: University of Tennessee Press, 1989). See also Linda Auwers, "Reading the Marks of the Past: Exploring Female Literacy in Colonial Windsor, Connecticut," *Historical Methods* 13 (Fall 1980): 204–14; and Richard D. Brown, *Knowledge Is Power: The Diffusion of Information in Early America, 1700–1865* (New York: Oxford University Press, 1989).

27. Maris Vinovskis and Richard Bernard, "Beyond Catharine Beecher: Female Education in the Antebellum Period," *Signs* 3 (Summer 1978): 856–69.

28. Bureau of the Census, Department of Commerce, *Negro Population, 1790–1915* (Washington, D.C.: Government Printing Office, 1918), 417.

29. Harriet A. Jacobs, *Incidents in the Life of a Slave Girl, Written by Herself*, ed. L. Maria Child (1861); ed. Jean Fagan Yellin (1987) (Cambridge, Mass.: Harvard University Press, 1987 [1861]).

was made out, she signed it with a cross. But what consequence was that, when she had a big heart overflowing with human kindness? She gave the old servant her freedom."[30]

The generations of women who lived through the American Revolution and the first years of the early Republic were aware—to varying degrees—that they were living through a strategic moment in the history of the female intellect. The republican ideology of the revolutionary years made literacy a moral obligation; the diffusion of knowledge was the responsibility of a republican society. There was understood to be a reciprocal relationship between an informed people and a virtuous people—an ideology given its classic expression in Thomas Jefferson's remark to the effect that he would choose a free press over other republican institutions. Believing as they did that republics rested on the virtue of their citizens, revolutionary leaders needed to believe that Americans of subsequent generations would continue to display the moral character that a republic required. The role of a guarantor of civic virtue, however, could not be assigned to a particular branch of government. Instead, it was hoped that other agencies—churches, schools, families—would fulfill that function. Within families, the crucial role was thought to be the mother's, a role combining political and educational obligation that I have called the "Republican Mother."[31]

Republican ideology thus combined with Protestant encouragement of Bible reading and the increasingly print-oriented commercial trading networks to sustain not only basic literacy but an enlarged range of knowledge, for girls as well as boys, women as well as men. Formal facilities for teaching girls multiplied; it is estimated that "nearly four hundred exclusively female academies were founded between 1790 and 1830."[32] In New York City, as Carl Kaestle has shown, "common pay schools" charged modest fees, enrolled approximately one girl for every two boys, and were

30. Ibid., 12.

31. See Kerber, *Women of the Republic*, chap. 7, 9; Linda K. Kerber, "The Republican Mother: Women and the Enlightenment—An American Perspective," *American Quarterly* 28 (Spring 1976): 187–205; and Linda K. Kerber, "The Republican Ideology of the Revolutionary Generation," *American Quarterly* 37 (Fall 1985): 474–95 [both essays reprinted in the present volume].

32. Kelley, " 'Vindicating the Equality of Female Intellect,' " citing Lynne Templeton Brickley, " 'Female Academies Are Every Where Establishing': The Beginnings of Secondary Education for Women in the United States, 1790–1830" (Qualifying paper, Harvard Graduate School of Education, 1982).

accessible to students from a wide range of social classes.[33] In Philadelphia Sarah Mapps Douglass opened a school for African American children in 1820; by 1853 she was in charge of the girls' primary department of the Philadelphia Institute for Colored Youth. Quaker women formed societies to support the education of girls and black children and hired younger women to teach.[34] Moravians established pairs of schools for boys and girls. New England schools began to hold summer sessions for girls and younger children. As public moneys were allocated to pay female teachers' salaries, the functions of the summer schools were gradually integrated into the year-round public grammar school.

Many interesting things might be said about the girls' schools of the early Republic: their size; their social composition; the extent to which they opened careers to talented teachers and administrators like Sarah Pierce, Emma Willard, and Sarah Mapps Douglass; the impact they had on the women of the next generation. These schools provided the requisite groundwork for a subsequent demand for even more advanced, or "higher," education. Before there could be colleges, there would have to be elementary schools, academies, and seminaries.[35] For the young women who taught and managed schools in the early Republic, Joan Jensen argues, teaching "provided an essential transition—for some women at least—from a functional to a liberating literacy through which they could interact with the social and intellectual life of the new nation in ways that only males had done earlier. . . . The teaching daughters were an essential link between Republican motherhood and feminist sisterhood."[36]

These new opportunities—to move "from a functional to a liberating literacy"—were regarded with great ambivalence. They could be welcomed with excitement, but they were also met with profound distrust. Indeed, they became the subject of a bitter debate—in student essays, in graduation orations, in newspaper columns—on the merits of female education. The

33. In 1796 thirteen-year-old Washington Irving, whose father was assessed for £1500 in real estate and £350 in personal property, had as a classmate Catharine Steddiford, daughter of an auctioneer who had no real estate at all and only £250 in personal property. In New York, charity schools also enrolled girls as well as boys. Carl F. Kaestle, *The Evolution of an Urban School System: New York City, 1750–1850* (Cambridge, Mass.: Harvard University Press, 1973), 44–49.

34. Joan Jensen, *Loosening the Bonds: Mid-Atlantic Farm Women 1750–1850* (New Haven, Conn.: Yale University Press, 1986), 170–71, 181–82.

35. Ibid., 172; see also Kaestle, *The Evolution of an Urban School System*, 38–40.

36. Jensen, *Loosening the Bonds*, 182–83.

hostility with which educated women were greeted is akin to the skepticism with which upper classes have traditionally regarded the spread of literacy among the poor or the fear whites displayed of freed black people's drive for learning before and after the Civil War. Approval of the new competence was balanced by a fear that new knowledge might make its holders more troublesome. As literate women moved into a male world of print and the professions, they found themselves criticized for transforming the roles that were initially theirs by virtue of their sex. They encountered a variant of the anti-intellectualism that Richard Hofstadter identified as a distinctive feature of American life in times of stress.[37] This consisted of the assertion that women did not need learning, for they could not be wise. This idea can be found in Plato; it retained its vigor down through the centuries. The complaint that the learned woman crossed the boundaries of her sex, a complaint lodged against Jane Colman Terrell, received fresh energy during the anxious years of the early Republic. Indeed, that it was made shows us, as in mirror image, that women were reaching for access to higher education and gaining enemies in the process. "Women of masculine minds," thundered the Boston minister John Sylvester John Gardiner, "have generally masculine manners, and a robustness of person ill calculated to inspire the tender passion."[38]

Still, virtually no one explicitly defended marginal literacy for women. Education for girls began to be welcomed as a path to an upwardly mobile marriage, and, increasingly, there were those who took Mary Wollstonecraft's arguments to reflect the common sense of the matter: that is, limits on female intelligence were more a matter of educational opportunity than the result of nature.[39]

37. Richard Hofstadter, *Anti-Intellectualism in American Life* (New York: Alfred A. Knopf, 1963).

38. *Massachusetts Mercury and New-England Palladium* (Boston), September 18, 1801. See also verses headed "To a Lady, Who Expressed a Desire of Seeing a University Established for Women," *American Museum* 3 (February 1788): n.p. On the long tradition in Western thought in which "women out of their place—in tropes subject to decorum and to warnings against 'excesse' or abuse—are part of a potentially dangerous invasion of linguistic into social responsibility," see Patricia Parker, *Literary Fat Ladies: Rhetoric, Gender, Property* (London: Methuen, 1987), esp. chap. 6 (quote on 111).

39. See, for example, the graduation debate between Mr. Little and Mr. Bannister in 1797, Dartmouth College Archives. For a classic statement of progressive male students' attitudes at the time, see James Iredell, Jr. (son of the Supreme Court Justice), "On the Female Sex," February 18, 1805, Iredell Papers, University of North Carolina, Chapel

Finally, and perhaps most significantly, women welcomed learning as a route to power and as an expression of ambition. One is struck by some women's hunger for learning and for access not only to skills but also to wisdom and by their expression of resentment for being excluded from the world of books. The distinguished playwright and novelist Susannah Rowson wrote in 1794, "There is no reason why we should stop short in the career of knowledge, though it has been asserted by the other sex that the distaff, the needle, together with domestic concerns alone should occupy the time of women. . . . The human MIND, whether possessed by man or woman, is capable of the highest refinement and most brilliant acquirements."[40]

In an era in which Jefferson was shocked to find Hamilton acknowledging his hunger for fame frankly and openly, it was the more startling to find Judith Sargent Murray writing that young women's minds ought to be taught to aspire. Murray did not arrive at that conclusion easily or without pain; indeed her major work, three volumes of essays published as *The Gleaner* in 1798, originally had been offered with a male authorial voice.[41] Not until the final installment, "The Gleaner Unmasked," did Murray identify herself as the Constantia who had "filled some pages" in the *Boston Magazine* and the *Massachusetts Magazine*. She had passed "in the masculine character" because, she said, she was "ambitious of being considered *independent as a writer*"; she had kept her secret even from her own husband.[42] In so misogynist a culture, "observing . . . the contempt, with which female productions are regarded," she even now feared that "it will be affirmed, that the *effeminacy* and *tinsel glitter* of my style could not fail of betraying me at every sentence which I uttered."[43] The political voice was so deeply understood to be specific to men that a woman who wished to enter into the dialogue needed, as it were, to dress in men's clothes. The secret, however, was soon out, and an increasingly wide audience knew Murray's columns as those of a woman. In these columns she argued that ambition

---

Hill, N.C. I am grateful to Don Higginbotham for this reference. I have commented on the exclusion of women from classical studies in *Women of the Republic*, 190–93.

40. Susannah Rowson, *Mentoria: Or the Young Ladies Friend* (Philadelphia: n.p., 1794), preface.

41. Judith Sargent Murray, *The Gleaner*, vol. 1 (Boston: I. Thomas and E. T. Andrews, 1798), 13.

42. Ibid., vol. 3, 314–15.

43. Ibid., 313.

was a noble principle and urged that girls be taught "to reverence them-selves. . . . that is, their intellectual eminence," insisting that self-respect and intellectual power went together. She warned against attempts by parents to eliminate pride; properly understood, pride (or "self-complacency") seemed to her a useful defense against false flattery and manipulation by others, especially men.[44]

"There are some ambitious spirits," observed Emma Willard comfort-ably in 1819, "who cannot be confined in the household and who need a theatre in which to act. . . ." Instead of being distressed at the possibility of ambition in women, she proposed they use their energies to establish and direct female academies.[45] A female poet, writing an attack on Alexander Pope, claimed:

> In either sex the appetite's the same
> For love of power is still the love of fame. . . .
> In education all the difference lies;
> Women, if taught, would be as learnd and wise
> As haughty man, improved by arts and rules. . . .[46]

A recurrent theme in these prescriptions for women's education was, as Murray had said, that a woman ought to be taught "to reverence herself." The study of history had an important role in this and was often com-mended as an antidote to novels. Women harbored some doubts, however. Miss Morland, in Jane Austen's *Northanger Abbey*, explains why she prefers popular novels to history: "I read it [history] a little as a duty, but it tells me nothing that does not either vex or weary me. The quarrels of popes and kings, with wars or pestilences, in every page; the men all so good for nothing, and hardly any women at all."[47]

Feminist writers and teachers responded to such skepticism by compil-ing lists of accomplished women and anthologies of historical episodes. Women's history as a subject of study in the United States may be said to

44. Judith Sargent Murray, "Desultory Thoughts upon the Utility of Encouraging a Degree of Self-Complacency, Especially in Female Bosoms," *Gentlemen and Ladies Town and Country Magazine*, October 1784, 251–52.

45. Emma Willard, *An Address to the Public . . . Proposing a Plan for Improving Female Education* (Middlebury: n.p., 1819), 34.

46. "On Pope's Characters of Women," by a Lady, *American Museum* 11 (June 1792): Appendix 1.

47. Jane Austen, *Northanger Abbey and Persuasion*, ed. John Davie (London: Oxford University Press, 1971), 97.

have begun with the late eighteenth-century search for a usable past, one that would link girls to heroic women of the past and attempt, however hesitantly, to provide women a place in the civic culture. Compilers of "ladies repositories," ladies' magazines, and textbooks for girls' schools ransacked their libraries, tumbling historical examples about. They were often heedless of chronology: Charlotte Corday might be paired with Lady Jane Grey, Margaret of Anjou with Catherine of Russia. Not until Oberlin's opening years were coherent histories of American women available for the female audience. Samuel L. Knapp's *Female Biography* appeared in 1834, Lydia Maria Child's *History of the Condition of Women in Various Ages and Conditions* in 1835, Elizabeth Ellet's great compilation of the activities of women during the American Revolution in 1848, and Sarah Josepha Hale's *Woman's Record* in 1853. The generation of antebellum activist women could read histories that challenged the canon and made claims for women's presence and the significance of women's actions. Ellet's *Domestic History of the American Revolution*, published in 1850, was perhaps the very first history of any war to give men's and women's activities equal space, offering accounts of civilian women's steady patriotic resistance and occasional heroism interchangeably with accounts of male battles.

Hesitantly, carefully, it became possible for a young woman, growing to maturity in the early nineteenth century, to contemplate advanced education as an attractive option. The curriculum of the girls' seminaries was, of course, not often rigorous; even the "Ladies' Course" at Oberlin would now appear to be that of a secondary school rather than a college. But the path of Mary Ann Shadd, daughter of a leading free African American abolitionist and educated in a West Chester Quaker school, who spent her career as a teacher, lecturer, antislavery and emigration advocate and, at the age of sixty, earned a law degree from Howard University, epitomizes not only an individual woman's own educational quest for also women's use of institutional options that Jane Colman Terrell could not have imagined.[48]

In the third era, from 1833 to the early twentieth century, formal supports for intellectual communities of women were created by the establishment

48. Shadd's career is summarized in Jensen, *Loosening the Bonds*, 181–82, and in *Notable American Women, 1607–1950: A Biographical Dictionary*, vol. 1, ed. Edward T. James, Janet Wilson James, and Paul S. Boyer (Cambridge, Mass.: Belknap Press, 1971), 300–301, under "Mary Ann Shadd Cary." Another example of use of the new options is the career of Lucy Stone, which took her from her town school, to rather marginal

of institutions. The number of schools grew steadily—seminaries at a faster pace than colleges. The temptation for the modern observer to tell an institutional story here is very great. It is easy enough to chart intellectual opportunity in terms of the growth in the number of classrooms, teachers, and growing access to professions. The dramatic expansion of public "common" schools, initiated in the 1840s and nurtured by regional leaders like Horace Mann, created a substantial community of solidly instructed girls, a small proportion of whom continued on to high school, seminaries, and even college. Their numbers steadily increased throughout the nineteenth century; in many communities girls tended to stay in schools longer than boys did. Selwyn Troen has charted this growth between 1840 and 1880 for St. Louis, where more than half of the children between ages seven and twelve attended schools and where a free high school was available to whites. St. Louis did not, however, establish a public high school for black students until 1875.[49] That high school was one of only four such schools open to black students in all of the South; as late as 1915 twenty-three of the forty-two southern cities with populations over twenty thousand lacked even a single public high school for African Americans. There was no public high school for African Americans in Atlanta until 1924.[50] On the other hand, many of the high schools that were open to African Americans in the years 1850–1916 offered challenging college preparatory curricula, including Latin, Greek, and advanced mathematics; all were coeducational.[51]

But there was an extra-academic, extra-institutional aspect of American

----

female seminaries, to Mount Holyoke Female Seminary, and finally to Oberlin, where she became the first Massachusetts woman to take a college degree.

49. Selwyn K. Troen, *The Public and the Schools: Shaping the St. Louis System, 1838–1920* (Columbia: University of Missouri Press, 1975), 119–24. Troen persuasively links the disparity in length of school attendance to the wider range of remunerative and skilled work available to boys when they left school. Eighteen percent of the boys of sixteen who were not in St. Louis schools had white-collar jobs, but fewer than 2 percent of the girls did; on the other hand, 26 percent of the boys were unskilled workers, but nearly 40 percent of the girls were in unskilled occupations ranging from domestic service to prostitution.

50. Among these cities were Atlanta, New Orleans, Charleston, and Montgomery. See James D. Anderson, *The Education of Blacks in the South, 1860–1935* (Chapel Hill: University of North Carolina Press, 1988), 186–237, esp. tables 6.3 and 6.4.

51. Ibid., 199. By the early 1920s, however, most of these schools had been transformed into "industrial" schools offering only limited vocational training.

intellectual life, as there still is; it was very strong in the nineteenth century, and it had particular relevance for women. In a world in which only a few thousand women were in college or university in any given year, most "higher" education was necessarily self-education.[52] Women shaped their intellectual lives out of their own reading, diary keeping, and letter writing. Their study was squeezed in between the domestic tasks that their families—even the most supportive—required of them. "Dear Friend," wrote Sarah Bradford to Mary Moody Emerson in 1814, "You will have me write— what? The interesting detail of mending, sweeping, teaching? What amusement can you reasonably require at the hand of a being secluded in a back chamber, with a basket of stockings on one side, and an old musty heathen on the other?" Yet her letters testify to a wide and dense range of reading: Josephus, Virgil, Friedrich Klopstock, David Hume. "Oh, how I envy the scholar, the philosopher, whose business, whose profession, is science!" Bradford observed. Like Mary Moody Emerson's, her studies were undisciplined; years later Sarah Bradford was to recall accurately of her friend, "She has read, all her life, in the most miscellaneous way. . . ." One may be permitted to wonder whether Mary Moody Emerson would have rambled on in her writing had there been a public audience for it, as there was for the writing of her nephew?[53]

Justifications for study fell into three categories, only two of them considered respectable: religious self-appraisal of the sort especially sanctioned by Calvinist tradition, service to the family by preparing oneself to teach one's children, and self-indulgence. "I am sometimes almost tempted to wish I knew nothing about Latin, and had not a taste for studies that subject me to so many inconveniences; for the time I now employ in study I should then spend in reading books which would enable me to join in the

52. The usually cited figure is 11,000 in 1870, but that includes seminaries; 3,000 is closer to the mark for colleges. See Solomon, *In the Company of Educated Women*, 63, 44; and Helen Lefkowitz Horowitz, *Alma Mater: Design and Experience in the Women's Colleges from Their Nineteenth Century Beginnings to the 1930s* (New York: Alfred A. Knopf, 1984).

53. Sarah Bradford to Mary Moody Emerson, November 9, 1814, and Sarah Bradford Ripley to Mr. Simmons, October 7, 1844, in *Worthy Women of Our First Century*, ed. Sarah Butler Wister and Agnes Irwin (Philadelphia: Lippincott, 1877), 130, 175. See also Phyllis Cole, " 'The Advantage of Loneliness': Mary Moody Emerson's Almanacks, 1802–1855," in *Emerson: Retrospect and Prospect*, ed. Joel Porte (Cambridge, Mass.: Harvard University Press, 1983), 1–32.

conversation and partake of the pleasures of fashionable ladies, but now I am as careful to conceal my books and as much afraid of being detected with them as if I were committing some great crime," Sarah Bradford confessed.[54] In the private writing of mid-century women, we can sense this need for a justification for learning that was self-fulfilling as well as self-indulgent, a rationale for learning that enabled one to shape one's own self or affect one's own community. This wish and this need may well have been embedded in the choice that thousands of women made by reading Mme. de Staël's *Corrine*. One of the most popular novels of the early nineteenth century, *Corrine* offered, as almost no other novel did until George Eliot began to publish, a woman who sought to please herself and who made demands on the society of men.[55]

The experiences of Lydia Maria Child and Margaret Fuller suggest some of the pains of trying to structure an intellectual career without institutional support. Child's formal education extended no further than dame school, though her brother Convers Francis, to whom she was very close, graduated from Harvard and studied at the Harvard Divinity School. Yet she read widely and seriously. At fifteen she was complaining to her brother about "Milton's treatment of our sex" in *Paradise Lost*; at eighteen she was teaching school in Maine and searching for a religious identity, which she found in the Unitarian church; and at twenty-two she was writing her first novel. *Hobomok: A Tale of Early Times* (1824) was political fiction that entered into public argument about the status of Indians, interracial marriage, and Puritan history.[56] The success of *Hobomok* prompted the Boston Athenaeum to offer Child an honorary membership that provided free access to its library; it was an unusual compliment, signaling that as an intellectual woman she could literally enter male space. When, a few years later, she offended conservatives with her trailblazing antislavery pamphlet,

54. Sarah Bradford to Mary Moody Emerson, circa 1810, in *Worthy Women of Our First Century*, ed. Wister and Irwin, 126–27.

55. As Gail Parker has observed, "Madame de Stael had suggested that it was possible for a woman to be Byronic—at least if she were willing to die young." Gail Parker, *The Oven Birds: American Women on Womanhood* (New York: Doubleday, 1972), 13.

56. The novel has recently been reprinted with a thoughtful introduction. See Lydia Maria Child, *Hobomok and other Writings on Indians*, ed. Carolyn L. Karcher (New Brunswick, N.J.: Rutgers University Press, 1986). See also Linda K. Kerber, "The Abolitionist Perception of the Indian," *Journal of American History* 62 (June 1975): 271–95, esp. 271–73.

An Appeal in Favor of That Class of Americans Called Africans (1833), her library privileges were abruptly withdrawn.[57] Thereafter she would proceed—as did most of her male and all of her female contemporaries—without institutional support for her studies. She found intellectual and political sustenance in the overlapping communities of transcendentalists and abolitionists and in friendship and dialogue with women who became informal colleagues—Margaret Fuller among them.[58]

Everyone who knew Margaret Fuller seems to have agreed that she had a fine mind; she spent much of her life restlessly searching for a context in which to exercise it effectively and consequentially. Unlike Child, she was deeply skeptical of voluntary associations; unlike Catharine Beecher, she found teaching girls' schools deeply frustrating.[59] Her "Conversations," an effort to guide the learning of other women, were constructed in criticism of women's educational options. She opened the first session in 1839 with the following declaration:

> Women are now taught, at school, all that men are; they run over, superficially, even *more* studies, without being really taught anything. When they come to the business of life, they find themselves inferior, and all their studies have not given them that practical good sense, and mother wisdom, and wit, which grew up with our grandmothers at the spinning-wheel. But, with this difference; men are called on, from a very early period . . . to put to use what they have learned. But women learn without any attempt to reproduce. Their only reproduction is for purpose of display.[60]

57. Lydia Maria Child to Samuel J. May, n.d., 1867, in *Letters of Lydia Maria Child with a Biographical Introduction by John G. Whittier and an Appendix by Wendell Phillips* (New York: Negro Universities Press, 1969 [1883]), 195, and comment on the affair by Wendell Phillips, 264.

58. See Milton Meltzer and Patricia C. Holland, eds., *Lydia Maria Child: Selected Letters, 1817–1880* (Amherst: University of Massachusetts Press, 1982), chap. 1, 2.

59. See her letters on teaching in Providence in 1837 in Robert N. Hudspeth, ed., *The Letters of Margaret Fuller*, vol. 1 (Ithaca, N.Y.: Cornell University Press, 1983), 288ff.

60. In *Memoirs of Margaret Fuller Ossoli*, vol. 1 (Boston: Phillips, Sampson, 1852), 329. See Charles Capper, "Margaret Fuller as Cultural Reformer: The Conversations in Boston," *American Quarterly* 39 (Winter 1987): 509–28, and his splendid biography, *Margaret Fuller—An American Romantic Life: The Private Years* (New York: Oxford University Press, 1992). Fuller intended, she wrote to Sophia Ripley in a letter exten-

Fuller's relationship with the transcendentalist writers, exhibited through shared work on *The Dial* and in the volume of memoirs that her American male friends compiled after her untimely death, has seemed to suggest she was their colleague. But this collegiality is problematic; Caroline Healey Dall reported on one set of "Conversations" offered to both men and women, where Emerson was present. "Emerson pursued his own train of thought. He seemed to forget that we had come together to pursue Margaret's."[61]

In 1885 Annie Nathan, an eighteen-year-old New York girl, began to read the *Memoirs of Margaret Fuller* and not long thereafter organized a reading group called the Seven Wise Women. "The idea came to me last year while reading of M. Fuller's social gatherings. . . . The idea is to study these women carefully—& write an essay upon each: Hannah More, Mary Wollstonecraft, E. B. Browning, Mary Somerville, M. Fuller, Harriet Martineau, Caroline Herschel, Geo. Eliot."[62]

By 1885, however, there was a substantial institutional context for the aspirations of girls like Annie Nathan. She knew of authentic colleges for women: Vassar was already twenty years old, Smith and Wellesley had opened ten years before, Spelman had been in operation for four years and Bryn Mawr for a year. The 1870s were something of a "take-off" decade for coeducational, especially public, institutions in the North and women's colleges in the South; often the increased need for women's higher education was ascribed to a superfluity of young women, whose male peers had been killed in the Civil War and who therefore needed to be self-supporting.[63] In

---

sively quoted by Capper, "to systematize thought . . . [and to] give a precision in which our sex are so deficient" and to enlarge the range of subjects about which women thought so that they might "make the best use of our means of building up the life of thought upon the life of action" (513).

61. Caroline Healey Dall, *Margaret and Her Friends: Or Ten Conversations with Margaret Fuller upon the Mythology of the Greeks and Its Expression in Art* (Boston: Roberts Bros., 1897), 46.

62. Journal of Annie Nathan Meyer, October 18, 1885, box 12, folder 5, Annie Nathan Meyer Papers, American Jewish Archives, Cincinnati, Ohio. For shrewd observations on the meaning of reading to women of Meyer's generation, see Barbara Sicherman, "Sense and Sensibility: A Case Study of Women's Reading in Late-Victorian America," in *Reading in America*, ed. Davidson, 201–25.

63. Patricia Palmieri, "From Republican Motherhood to Race Suicide: Arguments on the Higher Education of Women in the United States 1820–1920," in *Educating Men and Women Together*, ed. Lasser, 49–64, esp. 53.

1885 the Mississippi State College for Women, the first female public institution in the South, opened its doors.[64] In 1896 Washington Duke gave
$100,000 to Trinity College in Durham, North Carolina, with the provision
that the college admit women, "placing them in the future on an equal
footing with men, enabling them to enjoy all the rights, privileges and
advantages of the college. . . ."[65] At the University of Wisconsin and the
University of Missouri women reasserted their claim to a liberal education
in the same classes with men, instead of segregated in a normal school; at
the University of Michigan a fundraising campaign to provide the $100,000
necessary to establish the female department promised by the university's
charter finally succeeded. In Nathan's own city of New York the options
were more constricted, but Columbia College had just established an "An-
nex" through which women could be examined by Columbia professors,
although they could not take courses. Annie Nathan entered this marginal
academic setting. Within a few years she had committed herself to a major
fundraising campaign to endow a women's college. Before five years were
up, Barnard College was in existence, and Annie Nathan was writing, "Felt
happy and proud to see evidence of my work. I can always look to Barnard
College even if I am only 23 & feel if I die tomorrow, I have not lived in vain.
I do hope that next year this time we have an endowment of $250,000."[66]

The intensity of young Annie Nathan's feelings about her college experience seems characteristic of her generation. College women in the late
nineteenth century knew they had made an unusual commitment. "We
worked in those years," Jane Addams recalled of her time at Rockford in the
1870s, "as if we really believed the portentous statement from Aristotle . . .
with which we illuminated the wall occupied by our Chess club[:]. . . .
There is the same difference between the learned and the unlearned as
between the living and the dead."[67] Yet they still had to defend their access
to learning. "The world of thought," Anna Julia Cooper ruefully observed

64. Solomon, *In the Company of Educated Women*, chap. 4.

65. Brandstadter, "Developing the Coordinate College for Women," 31.

66. Journal of Annie Nathan Meyer, October 6, 1890, Annie Nathan Meyer Papers.
See also Lynn D. Gordon, "Annie Nathan Meyer and Barnard College: Mission and
Identity in Women's Higher Education 1889–1950," *History of Education Quarterly* 26
(Winter 1986): 503–22.

67. In *Twenty Years at Hull House*, quoted in *The American Woman: Who Was She?*
ed. Anne Firor Scott (Englewood Cliffs, N.J.: Prentice-Hall, 1971), 65–66. See also
Palmieri, "From Republican Motherhood to Race Suicide," 56, on the ambiguous
experience of the first generation of college women.

in 1892, "moved in its orbit like the revolutions of the moon; with one face (the man's face) always out, so that the spectator could not distinguish whether it was disc or sphere." Cooper counted herself among the mere thirty African American women to whom B.A. degrees had ever been awarded; gently she challenged African American men to raise funds to increase that number: "While our men seem thoroughly abreast of the times on almost every other subject, when they strike the woman question, they drop back into . . . the idea that women may stand on pedestals or live in doll houses, (if they happen to have them) but they must not furrow their brows with thought to attempt to help men tug at the great questions of the world." Cooper called for scholarships earmarked for "ambitious" girls "with pluck and brain . . . to offset and balance the aid that can always be found for boys who will take theology."[68]

African American women who founded schools, as Mary McLeod Bethune did in 1904, often began them as elementary schools because of the absence of good facilities for black children. By 1922 Bethune's school, which had begun with an enrollment of five girls aged eight to twelve whose parents paid fifty cents weekly tuition, had merged with Florida's first college for black men to become Bethune-Cookman College. "When I walk through the campus," Bethune wrote in 1941, "with its stately palms and well-kept lawns, and think back to the dump-heap foundation, I rub my eyes and pinch myself."[69] Mary Church, the daughter of one of the very few wealthy black businessmen in the country, was sent to study languages at Oberlin and in Europe; her father wished her education to be an ornamental one. Her commitment to teaching other black students—first at Wilberforce, then at the high school for Negro students in Washington—required gumption. "As some girls run away from home to marry the man of their choice," Mary Church Terrell wrote in her memoirs, "so I left home and ran the risk of permanently alienating my father from myself to engage in the work which his money had prepared me to do."[70]

68. Anna Julia Cooper, "The Higher Education of Women," in *A Voice from the South* (New York: Oxford University Press, 1988 [1892]), 56, 75, 78–79. I am indebted to Elizabeth Alexander of the University of Chicago for sharing her unpublished work on Cooper.

69. Mary McLeod Bethune, "Faith that Moved a Dump Heap," *Who: The Magazine about People* 1 (1941): 54.

70. Mary Church Terrell, *A Colored Woman in a White World* (Washington, D.C.: Ransdell, 1940), 63.

Many, like Cooper, Terrell, and Addams, felt a strong sense of obligation that their learning be used for some larger social good, but it also began to be possible to be part of a "group of women who have gone on acquiring knowledge for themselves," as one Vassar alumna put it in 1895. By the 1920s the struggles of these women had begun to fade from consciousness. "Don't ever dare to take your college as a matter of course," Alice Duer Miller admonished the students at Barnard, "because, like freedom and democracy, many people you'll never know anything about have broken their hearts to get it for you."[71]

The opening of research universities to women brings us back to Alice Mary Baldwin. Baldwin graduated from Cornell University in 1900. She had chosen to transfer there after a year at coeducational Bates College because Cornell, also coeducational, offered more career options, but co-education at Cornell was contested; although classes were open to women, many male students thought women did not belong in college activities. Baldwin joined a women's student organization that fought vigorously to protect the right of women students to participate in elections, publications, and committees.[72] She stayed on at Cornell for two years after her graduation to earn a master's degree, with a thesis on enlightened despotism in Sweden. A traveling fellowship offered by the Association of Collegiate Alumnae gave her the chance to study briefly at the Sorbonne and the University of Berlin and to travel in Europe. She enrolled in the history department at Columbia in 1903.[73] Financial difficulty following the death of her father seems to have forced her to drop graduate school, briefly take a job teaching languages in a New Jersey high school, and then spend an unhappy two years as dean of women and instructor in history at Fargo College in North Dakota. In 1906 she returned to the East to teach history at the Baldwin School, one of the best preparatory schools in the country, founded explicitly as a "feeder school" for Bryn Mawr. She remained there for fifteen years. In 1921, when it appeared that she was likely to be named headmistress, she took a leave of absence and enrolled at age forty-two in the history department of the University of Chicago.[74]

71. Quoted in Marian Churchill White, *A History of Barnard College* (New York: Columbia University Press, 1954), 139.

72. Brandstadter, "Developing the Coordinate College for Women," 12.

73. Ibid., 10–13.

74. Ibid., 13–15.

The University of Chicago was, along with Columbia University in New York, one of the few research universities that made women graduate students reasonably welcome.[75] Baldwin's advisers at Chicago knew how to take advantage of the skills of such a mature and experienced student. She was awarded a graduate research assistantship and studied with the distinguished historian Andrew McLaughlin. Her dissertation on the New England clergy in the era of the American Revolution was a search for her own roots, although she would have said it was less a search than an appreciation. In the introduction to the published version, she situated herself in a male line of intellectual descent: "The following study has not been for me one of merely academic interest. My grandfather . . . my father . . . and my uncle . . . were all congregational clergymen; and it was through them that I first learned to appreciate, in some measure, the ministers of New England."[76]

In her second year Marion Talbot, the innovative dean of women, appointed Baldwin head of a women's residence hall. It was a role Baldwin viewed with ambivalence. Her career goal was a faculty appointment in a college history department, preferably in a research institution; Talbot might be offering Baldwin opportunities to train herself to be a dean elsewhere, but it was not an opportunity Baldwin welcomed. She had already spent enough of her career arranging the lives of the young.

When she came close to achieving her Ph.D., however, the jobs open to her involved administration. The one everyone *but* Baldwin thought she ought to accept was the position of dean of women at Trinity College, a small coeducational institution in Durham, North Carolina. As she hesitated, McLaughlin undertook the duty of telling his student the facts of academic life. "The . . . question relates to the future at Chicago, the most distant future," he observed in response to her letter. "I am afraid there is not any future. . . . You and I agreed in our conversation that whether it be just or not, the fact is that in the University there is not much opportunity for women. I would not wish to have such a sentiment proclaimed aloud from the housetops; and I am not sure that I should lay it down as a policy.

75. See Rosalind Rosenberg, *Beyond Separate Spheres: Intellectual Roots of Modern Feminism* (New Haven, Conn.: Yale University Press, 1982), esp. chap. 2; Gordon, *Gender and Higher Education in the Progressive Era*, esp. chap. 3; and Ellen Fitzpatrick, *Endless Crusade: Women Social Scientists and Progressive Reform* (New York: Oxford University Press, 1990).

76. Quoted in Brandstadter, "Developing the Coordinate College for Women," 16.

You know the conditions as they actually exist, and as I have said, I under-stand that you look upon those conditions very much as I do. . . ."[77] Forty-four years old, with substantial administrative experience and a Ph.D., Baldwin was in demand for a job that, remembering her unhappy years in North Dakota, she emphatically did not want. Trinity College in North Carolina recruited her vigorously as dean of women; she accepted because she had no other options, but only after she followed McLaughlin's advice to insist on an appointment to the faculty as well as the deanship. It was well that she did.[78]

The very next year a $40 million bequest from James B. Duke trans-formed Trinity into a university with law, medical, and graduate schools. The male undergraduate college was formed of the men who had formerly attended Trinity; a Woman's College—it bore the generic name until its demise in 1972—was formed of their female counterparts. The creation of the Woman's College in 1927 reflected a widespread reaction against coed-ucation and a break with Washington Duke's instruction of less than thirty years before that the women of Trinity be placed "on an equal footing with men."[79]

In the new configuration, Baldwin was dean of the Woman's College; her job would be to fight for "equal footing" of the single-sex colleges within the coeducational university. "My chief aims," she wrote, "were to have full opportunities for the women to share in all academic life."[80] She was warmly welcomed by the older male historians, and she was the first woman to teach an upper-level course in history to a mixed class of men and women.[81] She encountered more resistance from administrators, who had trouble dealing with her "as a fellow administrator, not simply as a woman to be treated with Southern courtesy."[82] Just as she had insisted on a

77. Andrew McLaughlin to Alice Mary Baldwin, July 6, 1923, quoted in ibid., 22–23.

78. On her recruitment, see her memoir, "The Woman's College as I Remember It," 1–5 (hereafter AMB Memoir).

79. Brandstadter, "Developing the Coordinate College for Women," 31.

80. AMB Memoir, 16. Her fellow administrators were all men, "none of [whom]," she wrote later, "had worked with a woman who had any real authority or faculty standing. . . ." Ibid., 4.

81. Ibid., 35. She was touched when, at the first faculty meeting that she "rather hesitatingly" attended in 1924, two elderly members made a point of rising and "wel-comed me, sat me between them . . .[and] old Dr. Pegram said, 'Miss Baldwin, I have longed to see this day.'" Ibid., 14.

82. Ibid., 15.

faculty appointment for herself, she now insisted that the women students in the college be understood to be students in the university, receiving their degrees from the university.[83] As dean of the Woman's College, she claimed "the same authority" that the dean of Trinity had. Moreover, she set herself absolutely against the addition of home economics courses to the women's curriculum.[84]

Yet as even the architecture of the newly configured campus made clear, the new Duke University was really two separate institutions. The firm of Frederick Law Olmsted, the nineteenth century's greatest landscape architect, designed the male university with collegiate gothic buildings claiming an implicit link to medieval learning; the phallic towers of the central chapel aggressively pointed skyward. The Woman's College, two miles away, was placed on a space less than one-quarter the size of the university campus, in neoclassic buildings whose lines emphasized peacefulness and repose; its major buildings no more than three stories high, capped not by towers but by rounded womblike domes.[85] Only with difficulty did Baldwin dissuade President William Preston Few from adding "a big, decorative iron fence around the quadrangle to be locked at night for the safety of the girls."[86] Alice Mary Baldwin intended to forge a women's intellectual community at Duke—and she did succeed in hiring a number of women faculty (Katherine Gilbert in philosophy, Hertha Spooner in botany, Julia Dale in mathematics)—but she had to do it in an institutional setting that denied women the opportunity to argue with men.[87] President Few assumed that

83. This required her to resist the university president, who entertained the idea that it ought to be "possible for a woman to receive a degree for work done entirely on our campus." Ibid., 16–18.

84. Brandstadter, "Developing the Coordinate College for Women," 58ff, 88. She was not fully successful. "In 1936–38 questions arose concerning the desirability of differentiating in any way between the courses offered men and women: for example,. in physical education, home economics, etc. I remember talking with Prof. Hatley about making the experiments in the physics classes for women somewhat different, tho not in any way less difficult, than those in the men's classes, and with Dr. Robert Smith about work in Economics dealing especially with questions likely to arise in a woman's life. For a time a course in what might be called household economics was offered, but it did not become especially popular." AMB Memoir, 59.

85. See Annabel Wharton, "Gender, Architecture, and Institutional Self-Presentation: The Case of Duke University," *South Atlantic Quarterly* 90 (Winter 1991): 175–217.

86. AMB Memoir, 21.

87. See Anne Firor Scott, "Duke Women: Visible and Invisible," in *Proceedings, the*

women's persuasive options were confined to the narrow range between the simple request and the tearful appeal to emotions. Among his first questions to Baldwin was whether she "could take criticism and disappointment without weeping."[88] Years later Baldwin assured a colleague "that she had never cried at any of their meetings."[89] Baldwin was caught in the trap of a status that required forthright argument but an institution that required decorum—her original fears were not off the mark.

Required by her vulnerable position to exercise the greatest discretion, Baldwin offered her criticisms of the state of women's education only in passing, interweaving them between the lines of carefully guarded accounts of her own college. Occasionally, it is possible to see what she really thought. In 1932 Baldwin called for "real coordination rather than subordination" when a women's college was part of a university. "There should be women on the board of trustees." The budget should not be wholly in the hands of men. There should be "a reasonable number of women of fine personality and ripe scholarship" on the faculty.[90] By 1949 she had concluded that "in the larger coeducational institutions . . . the interests of the women students, always in the minority, tend to be submerged in those of the men. . . . Perhaps the most serious loss is in the part played by the women themselves; in their sense of unity, of belonging to a college which is peculiarly their own and for which they are in large part responsible. . . ." Her posthumous memoir provides the evidence that she knew herself to be undervalued and underpaid throughout her life at Duke, and she was outraged not only for herself but also for the women of the college whom she served.[91]

Changing Patterns of Our Lives: Women's Education and Women's Studies, A Sesquicentennial Symposium, Duke University, March 3–5, 1989, 7–15, Duke University Archives.

88. Soon after this question was posed by Few, "Mr. Flowers and Dr. Wannamaker came also, asking identical questions, including my ability to refrain from tears," AMB Memoir, 4–5.

89. Brandstadter, "Developing the Coordinate College for Women," 60.

90. "Proceedings," Association of Colleges and Secondary Schools of the Southern States, 1932, box 17, Alice Mary Baldwin Papers. On petty problems that could nevertheless be demoralizing, see AMB Memoir, passim (e.g., the failure of Trinity College administrators to inform her of changes in their class schedule, 50–51).

91. "History of Woman's College on Its Twenty-fifth Anniversary," box 17, Alice Mary Baldwin Papers. On being underpaid, see AMB Memoir, 38, 78–80. The configuration of Baldwin's career is not idiosyncratic. Mary Ann Dzuback of Washington University, St. Louis, who has intensively studied the careers of women social scientists,

Alice Mary Baldwin's world was far removed from that of her predecessors, Jane Colman Terrell, Judith Sargent Murray, Emma Willard, and Margaret Fuller, or even that of Anna Julia Cooper and Mary Church Terrell in her own time. One theme linked them, however. They all lived in a culture deeply skeptical of learned women. It is true that as time went on, levels of literacy improved, opportunities for its active use—especially in correspondence and in print—increased, informal and institutional sites for argument expanded, and women found more allies in their quest for intellectual freedom and opportunity. Skepticism was voiced with more delicacy; no minister thundered from the pulpit that the learned woman was necessarily masculine. But such women were still regarded as oddities. As learned women, they were still viewed with suspicion. Baldwin's memoirs show that, though she spent her entire life as an intellectual and a scholar, she knew she was not welcomed to fellowship with her male colleagues, and it hurt.[92]

For two hundred years it was assumed that learning in men and learning in women could not be quite the same. Women had to find room for their educations and for critical thinking without eliciting male hostility and contempt. It was assumed that the learning for women required special justification; the standard question was, "What studies are appropriate for the female mind?" Adam Smith said that women needed a continuation of what had been learned in the home and could be used directly and prac-

---

has identified a long list of scholars of Baldwin's generation who found that the only academic situations open to them were primarily administrative ones. Among these women might be included Lucy Flower, Violet Jayne, and Ruby Mason, deans of women at the University of Illinois; Sarah Gibson Blanding, dean of women at the University of Kentucky (1923–41), dean of Cornell's College of Home Economics (1941–46), and president of Vassar; and Eleanor Harris Rowland, dean of women at Reed College. Personal communication, April 30, 1991. See also Paula A. Treichler, "Alma Mater's Sorority: Women and the University of Illinois, 1890–1925," in *For Alma Mater: Theory and Practice in Feminist Scholarship*, ed. Paula A. Treichler, Cheris Kramarae, and Beth Stafford (Urbana: University of Illinois Press, 1985), 5–61, esp. 23ff.

92. The general pattern of Baldwin's career, as well as the human pain that was inescapably part of such a career, was not limited to the discipline of history. See especially the exemplary account of the career of the distinguished American philosopher Suzanne Langer offered by Bruce Kuklick, *The Rise of American Philosophy: Cambridge, Massachusetts, 1860–1930* (New Haven, Conn.: Yale University Press, 1977); and the ironic Marjorie Nicolson, "Scholars and Ladies," *Yale Review* 19 (September 1929): 775–95.

tically in adult life; he called for "no absurdities." In the nineteenth century the list of appropriate studies lengthened; it became respectable for women to contemplate a widening range of activities. But few would say with Margaret Fuller, "Let them be sea-captains if they will," and fewer still would maintain that women might properly indulge in any form of study. As recently as 1956 it was fresh and unusual for the Harvard sociologist David Riesman to propose for women an education that would be *discontinuous* with what had come before, that would "put pressure on life," open up new worlds of learning, encourage new ambitions, make room for the problematic and, in Adam Smith's word, the "fantastical."[93] Even in the twentieth century, communities of male scholars based in research universities maintained distanced and ambivalent relationships with the most distinguished women intellectuals—Charlotte Perkins Gilman, Mary Ritter Beard, Margaret Mead, Hannah Arendt—who, in a mixture of choice and necessity, built their careers outside of the academy.[94] The renewed women's movement of the early 1970s had an often unappreciated intellectual and institutional component in what Adrienne Rich has called the "women's university-without-walls," which burst into life in the early 1970s and continues to thrive "in the shape of women reading and writing with a new purposefulness, [in] . . . feminist bookstores, presses, bibliographic services . . . libraries, art galleries . . . all with a truly educational mission. . . ."[95] When the Ivy League colleges opened their doors to women in the 1970s, they responded to the claims that women were making, answering the question of what studies are appropriate for the female mind by taking

93. David Riesman, "Continuities and Discontinuities in Women's Education" (Bennington College commencement address, 1956). See also David Riesman, *Constraint and Variety in American Education* (Lincoln: University of Nebraska Press, 1956), 139–43. Riesman's position was contested; two years later, in a commencement address at Smith, Adlai Stevenson would counsel the women graduates to use their learning to soothe the cares of "western man." Smith College Archives, Sophia Smith Library, Smith College, Northampton, Mass.

94. Mead had an adjunct appointment at Columbia; her base was the Museum of Natural History. Mary Beard scorned the academy. See Nancy F. Cott, *Mary Beard: A Woman Making History* (New Haven, Conn.: Yale University Press, 1991), 39–40. Hannah Arendt held occasional visiting and part-time academic appointments throughout her American career, but she identified herself as one "*nicht vom Fach*, not from the profession." Elizabeth Young-Bruehl, *Hannah Arendt: For the Love of the World* (New Haven, Conn.: Yale University Press, 1982), 410.

95. Rich, "Toward a Woman-Centered University," 126.

Riesman's, Judith Sargent Murray's, and Margaret Fuller's positions: all studies are appropriate for the female mind; no one need any longer fear undermining her own character by what she chooses to study.

But if we have resolved in this generation the question of whether women's minds are fit for serious thought, we have not yet fully resolved the related issue of whether women's experience is as important a part of our cultural inheritance as the medieval cathedral and whether it is as important for men to study women's experience as it has been for women to study men's. The revolution that is feminist studies addresses that issue; the hyperbolic response that women's texts destabilize the canon of the great work of Western thought is evidence of the vigor and complexity of that revolution.

The educational challenge before us is to transform our institutions of higher education so they not only accept both men and women as students but also provide an understanding of the world in which the record of women's experience, needs, and accomplishments is regarded with as much respect and as much pride as the record of men is. The story of Jane Colman Terrell is of interest not because it was "quaint" but because she was silenced. Her story is as much a part of American educational history as the story of Harvard College is. Alice Mary Baldwin was seeking to find a way to tell us this when she died. I think she would be pleased to know that many voices have now been added to hers and that the issues she had to tiptoe around are now being contested and directly confronted.

III

FINDING GENDER
IN AMERICAN
CULTURE

THE PARADOX OF
WOMEN'S CITIZENSHIP IN
THE EARLY REPUBLIC
THE CASE OF *MARTIN VS.*
MASSACHUSETTS, 1805

No Cit[izen]ess to my name, I'll have, says Katey, . . . *[it] means,*
"A Woman of the town."
(Boston) *Columbian Centinel*, March 16, 1793.

In February 1801, James Martin submitted a writ of error to the Supreme Judicial Court of Massachusetts, the highest court of appeals in the state. He demanded the return of properties confiscated from his mother twenty years before, toward the close of the American Revolution. In responding to Martin's lawsuit, leading lawyers and judges of the early republic were forced to articulate publicly their understanding—normally left unexpressed—of the nature of women's relationship to the postrevolutionary civic order and particularly their understanding of the obligations married women citizens owed to the state. The outcome was ironic: recognizing the claims of Anna Gordon Martin and her heirs entailed a refusal to construe her as an autonomous citizen with her own civic responsibility.

The political community fashioned by the American war was a deeply gendered one in which all white adults and a few black adults were citizens

This essay was first presented as one of the Jefferson Memorial Lectures, University of California, Berkeley, 1989. I thank the Department of History and the Jefferson Memorial Lectures Committee for many courtesies on that occasion. It was drafted when I was National Endowment for the Humanities Fellow of the Philadelphia Center for Early American Studies (PCEAS) at the University of Pennsylvania in 1987 and at the Center for Advanced Study of the University of Iowa in 1989. I am deeply grateful to the

but white men's voices were privileged. For men, political institutions—the army, the militia, the state legislatures, the Continental Congress, organizations of artisans—facilitated collective experience. A notable male elite, whose patriarchal character has since been encoded in its identification as the "Founding Fathers," articulated political republicanism and embedded it in successive manifestos and institutions. They said they acted in the name of all Americans, even though they formally consulted propertyless white men only rarely and consulted neither black men nor any women, whatever their race or class.[1] Drawing on what they had learned from the great European theorists of the social contract (Hobbes, Locke, Montesquieu, Rousseau), they constituted themselves as citizens whose allegiance was contractual, the corollary of that point being that an allegiance freely chosen could also be annulled.[2] This aspect of radical ideology sustained yeomen and artisans in making claims on their social betters; it sustained free blacks in making claims on the republic; it sustained those in Congress who devised for the Northwest Territory a pathbreaking ordinance proclaiming that the United States would be an expansive empire without colonialism. Only belatedly, however, would it sustain women in making claims on the republic.

Citizenship involves claims of rights, notably suffrage but also the right to pursue happiness and to be free of constraints. It involves a wide range

---

College of Liberal Arts of the University of Iowa for generous support throughout this project and to the John Simon Guggenheim Foundation and the National Humanities Center for support in 1990–1991. This essay could not have been written without the shrewd instruction and guidance that I received from Wayne Bodle and other colleagues at the PCEAS, Hendrik Hartog, Bruce Mann, and Alan Taylor. I am grateful for the research assistance of Kathy Hermes of Duke Law School, Leslie Taylor of the University of Iowa, and Alexandra Gillen of the University of Chicago, and also for the advice of Sydney V. James, Martha Minow, H. Jefferson Powell, Kathryn T. Preyer, Aviam Soifer, and Laurel Thatcher Ulrich. I received indispensable archival help from Stanley Tozeski, Federal Records Center, Waltham, Mass.; Elizabeth Bouvier, Massachusetts State Archives; and Cynthia Harrison, Federal Judicial History Center, Washington, D.C.

1. Further comments on this point are in my essay " 'I Have Don . . . much to Carrey on the Warr': Women and the Shaping of Republican Ideology after the American Revolution," in Harriet B. Applewhite and Darline G. Levy, eds., *Women and Politics in the Age of the Democratic Revolution* (Ann Arbor, Mich., 1990), 227–57 [which is reprinted in the present volume].

2. James H. Kettner, *The Development of American Citizenship, 1608–1870* (Chapel Hill, N.C., 1978), 173 and following.

of civic obligations, among them patriotic loyalty, the payment of taxes, and service on juries and in the military. The political discourse of citizenship has been gendered since its origins, in ways that historians are only beginning to comprehend. "Excluded from honours and from offices, we cannot attach ourselves to the State of Government from having held a place of Eminence," Abigail Adams observed toward the end of the American Revolution. "Even in freest countrys our property is subject to the controul and disposal of our partners, to whom the Laws have given a sovereign Authority. Deprived of a voice in Legislation, obliged to submit to those Laws which are imposed upon us, is it not sufficient to make us indifferent to the publick Welfare?" Abigail Adams concluded that, given the situation, women's patriotism must be "the most disinterested of all virtues"; there was practically no way in which women's service to the state could be directly rewarded. Indeed, one of the few issues on which Patriot and Loyalist men generally agreed was their belief that the only service to the state of which women were capable was financial, and therefore there were few reciprocal obligations—notably, the obligation of single women to pay taxes—that women owed the state.[3]

Political republicanism in America rested heavily on a definition of citizenship, inherited from the civic republicanism of the Renaissance and of the eighteenth-century British Whig opposition, that favored men for qualities that distinguished them from women. "Luxury, effeminacy and corruption" was as much a revolutionary-era triad as "life, liberty and the pursuit of happiness."[4] Republican ideology was antipatriarchal in the sense that it voiced, as Tom Paine accurately sensed, the claim of adult men to be freed from the control of male governors who had defined themselves as rulers and political "fathers" in an antique monarchical system. The language of the revolution was permeated by claims to unsettle traditional patriarchal relationships. The rhetoric of the revolution positioned the colonists as sons who had outgrown patriarchal constraint and as adult

3. Abigail Adams to John Adams, June 17, 1782, in L. H. Butterfield, *et al.*, eds., *Adams Family Correspondence* (Cambridge, Mass., 1963–   ), 4:328. She went on: "Yet all History and every age exhibit Instances of patriotic virtue in the female Sex; which considering our situation equals the most Heroick." For thoughtful comment on obligation, see Joan R. Gundersen, "Independence, Citizenship and the American Revolution," *Signs*, 13 (1987): 59–77, esp. 61–62.

4. See, for example, George Washington to James Warren, October 7, 1785, *Writings of Washington, From the Original Manuscript Sources, 1745–1799*, John C. Fitzpatrick, ed. (Washington, D.C., 1931–44), 28: 290.

men unfairly enslaved by the British.[5] But republican ideology did not eliminate the political father immediately and completely; rather, it held a liberal ideology of individualism in ambivalent tension with the old ideology of patriarchy. Thus George Washington quickly became the "father of his country"; at the Governor's Palace in Williamsburg, Virginia, the life-size portrait of George III was quickly replaced by a life-size portrait of Washington in the same pose.[6] The men who remodeled the American polity after the war remodeled it in their own image. Their anxieties for the stability of their construction led them, as they emphasized its reasonableness, its solidity, its link to classical models, also to emphasize its manliness and its freedom from effeminacy. The construction of the autonomous, patriotic, male citizen required that the traditional identification of women with unreliability, unpredictability, and lust be emphasized. Women's weakness became a rhetorical foil for republican manliness.[7]

Yet women were citizens of the nation; they could be naturalized; they were subject to its laws; as single adult women, they were vulnerable to taxation. "The spirit of liberty," in John Adams's famous phrase, "spread where it was not intended." Women's national citizenship contained deep within it an implicit challenge to coverture, the legal system that governed relationships between men and women. Patriot men rarely spoke about this issue, but their actions speak for them. The generation of men who radically transgressed inherited understandings of the relationship between kings and men, fathers and sons, and who radically reconstructed many basic elements of law, nevertheless refused to destabilize the law governing relations between husbands and wives, mothers and children. Coverture—the system of law that transferred a woman's civic identity to

5. Edwin Burrows and Michael Wallace, "The American Revolution: The Ideology and Psychology of National Liberation," *Perspectives in American History*, 6 (1972): 167–306. See also Winthrop D. Jordan, "Familial Politics: Thomas Paine and the Killing of the King, 1776," *Journal of American History*, 60 (1973): 294–308.

6. Now on display in the Museum of Decorative Arts there. Michael Grossberg, *Governing the Hearth: Law and the Family in Nineteenth-Century America* (Chapel Hill, N.C., 1985), also stresses persistence of patriarchal thought.

7. Tracing changes in voting law in New Jersey, Gundersen argues that in the early republic, "dependency" was redefined as a "sex-specific trait, [transforming] dependent males into independent voters, while subsuming single women, who were in every practical sense independent, into a category of dependence"; Gundersen, "Independence, Citizenship," 66. See also Ruth Bloch, "The Gendered Meaning of Virtue in Revolutionary America," *Signs*, 13 (1987): 37–58.

her husband at marriage, giving him use and direction of her property throughout the marriage—was incompatible with revolutionary ideology and with the liberal commercial society developing in the early republic. Even as patriot men proudly attacked patriarchy, choosing John Locke over Sir Robert Filmer, *Two Treatises* over *Patriarcha*, they carefully sustained their own patriarchal law.[8] They even continued to refer to the body of law of coverture by its traditional name, "the law of baron et feme," that is, not the reciprocal "husband and wife" or "man and woman" but "lord and woman."[9]

A rare sign that revolutionary legislators glimpsed the incompatibility of coverture with republican ideology is the elimination of the crime of *petit treason* from the statute books of the early republic. The traditional reasoning had been that, at marriage, the husband became the wife's lord and stood to her as king did to subject; thus the killing of a husband by a wife was analogous to regicide and treason, and the penalties for *petit treason* were worse than those for murder. The killing of a wife by her husband, however, remained murder. The concept was not much enforced in early America, but neither was it eliminated from the statutes until the revolution.[10] With that exception, neither the government of the Articles of Confederation nor the federal government of the Constitution directly challenged the legal system of coverture.

As anthropologists have long understood, the laws and practices of domestic relations echo other aspects of a culture. The American Revolution was preeminently a crisis of authority; a democratizing society and a patriarchal family were discordant. "Do not put such unlimited power into the

8. Carol Pateman, *The Sexual Contract* (Stanford, Calif., 1988), 48–49 *et passim*.

9. See, for example, Tapping Reeve, *The Law of Baron and Feme, Parent and Child, Guardian and Ward, Master and Servant, and of the Powers of Courts of Chancery* (1816; 2d edn., Burlington, Vt., 1846). Nathan Dane, *General Abridgment and Digest of American Law* (Boston, 1823), headed the chapter on the relationship between husband and wife "Baron and Feme"; vol. 1, chap. 19, pp. 331–78. William Blackstone, *Blackstone's Commentaries: With Notes of Reference . . .*, St. George Tucker, ed. (Philadelphia, 1803), vol. 1, book 1, chap. 15 reads, "her husband is called her lord."

10. See, for example, "An Act for annulling the Distinction between the crimes of Murder and Petit treason," March 16, 1785, in Asahel Stearns, *et al.*, eds., *The General Laws of Massachusetts . . .* (Boston, 1823), 1: 188. *Petit Treason* also involved the killing of a master by a servant, and it endured in the slave South longer than in the North. See Kathryn Preyer, "Crime, the Criminal Law and Reform in Post-Revolutionary Virginia," *Law and History Review*, 1 (1983): 56–58.

hands of the Husbands," Abigail Adams wrote in 1776; "Remember all men would be tyrants if they could."[11] The challenge the revolution posed to patriarchal relationships was expressed dramatically in the excoriation of the father figure of George III in the pages of *Common Sense* and in the ritual pulling down and melting of his statues in the streets. But, as Michael Grossberg has recently emphasized, although the tradition that sustained the authority of the male governor in the home "by granting him control of its inhabitants as well as of family property and other resources" became increasingly anachronistic, it nevertheless persisted in a new order otherwise characterized by "a deep aversion to unaccountable authority and unchecked governmental activism, the equation of property rights with independence, a commitment to self government, a belief that individual virtue could prevent the abuse of power, and a tendency to posit human relations in contractual terms"—all themes that, on the face of it, should have been incompatible with patriarchy.[12] Adult men who were differently situated in terms of class—as artisans, farmers, merchants, planters—were similarly situated in regard to gender. Benefiting from the established practice of coverture, they felt no need to renegotiate it. Anxiety combined with self-interest to restrain male legislators from addressing the inherited system.

In stabilizing the revolution and eliminating inherited class distinctions among whites, founding-era legislators, it could be said, created a social system that, while certainly not classless, minimized differences between white men in comparison to what they had been before the war, and they adopted an ideology and a rhetoric that minimized differences between white men even more sharply than these differences were minimized in fact. But the founders kept in place a legal system that promoted legal differences between free women and men, especially between married women and men. They maintained difference while denying its significance.[13] As men increasingly freed themselves from the constraints of pa-

11. Abigail Adams to John Adams, March 31, 1776, Butterfield, *Adams Family Correspondence*, 1: 369–70.

12. Grossberg, *Governing the Hearth*, 5–6.

13. "At least until the middle years of the nineteenth century, being married meant subjecting oneself to a known and coercive public relationship," wrote Hendrik Hartog in an important essay on the conceptualization of marital relations in the early republic. Hartog, "Marital Exits and Marital Expectations in Nineteenth Century America," *Georgetown Law Journal*, 80 (1991): 95–129, quote 96; see also Hartog, "Mrs. Packard on Dependency," *Yale Journal of Law and Humanities*, 1 (1988): 79–103. Some

triarchy, they left in place a fully developed, complex system of law based on the principle that married women were "covered" by their husbands' legal identity. Even when modest modifications were made in this law (as, for example, on the matter of *petit treason*), legislators of the early republic showed no disposition to reconsider the system as a whole. As both Hendrik Hartog and Carole Shammas have recently observed, the system of law that developed around the *feme covert* was not attacked directly until the second quarter of the nineteenth century and not radically altered until the third quarter.[14] Indeed, major elements have persisted in American law until our own time.

James Otis was one of the few political activists of the revolutionary era who followed the implications of women's citizenship to their logical end. "If all were reduced to a state of nature," Otis asked in 1764, not long after his famous Writs of Assistance argument, "had not apple women and orange girls as good a right to give their respectable suffrages for a new King as the philosopher, courtier . . . and politician? Were these and ten millions of other such . . . consulted?"[15] Perhaps in retribution for raising the question at all, he soon went mad.

Were women—even Otis's apple women and orange girls—part of the new social compact? Or did they remain in a patriarchal social order in which their only freely chosen obligation was to their husbands? As I have argued elsewhere, women who lived through a revolutionary era could not

---

years ago, Gerda Lerner warned that women's status should be evaluated not only in abstract terms but in relationship to changes in men's status; see Lerner, "The Lady and the Mill Girl: Changes in the Status of Women in the Age of Jackson," *Midcontinent American Studies*, 10 (1969): 5–15.

14. "The keystone of family capitalism," according to Shammas, "was the male household head's ability to control both his and his wife's wealth . . . [W]hen women received the legal right during the nineteenth century to possess property that they had inherited, it greatly diminished the percentage of total wealth owned by men. Such legislation, however, did not appear until after corporate forms had evolved sufficiently so that the family was relieved of the chore of being the prime organization involved in the management of capital"; Carole Shammas, "Early American Women and Control over Capital," in Ronald Hoffman and Peter J. Albert, eds., *Women in the Age of the American Revolution* (Charlottesville, Va., 1989), 154. Shammas discusses this point at greater length in her unpublished essay, "Re-Assessing the Married Women's Property Acts" (1990), cited by permission of the author.

15. James Otis, *The Rights of the British Colonies Asserted and Proved* (Boston, 1764), reprinted in Bernard Bailyn, ed., *Pamphlets of the American Revolution 1750–1776* (Cambridge, Mass., 1965), 419–22.

help but explore the potential of the new politics for freeing them to develop their own relationships with the republic. Because the revolutionary generation emerged into the republic with its system of law governing relations between men and women largely intact, those who wished to reconsider the role of women in the republic had little space in which to negotiate. It would be two generations before Elizabeth Cady Stanton and her colleagues could clearly articulate the incompatibility of coverture and liberalism.[16] The old civic republicanism, developed in the Renaissance and transmitted through the British Whig opposition, made property owning and arms bearing central to the political community; in that tradition, women were the timeless representations of ambition, luxury, and lust; qualities understood to be effeminate were qualities to be feared.[17] In this unfriendly theoretical context, critics were able to develop their formal political claims to the compromise point that I have called the politics of "republican motherhood"; that is, they could claim political participation only so long as they implicitly promised to keep their politics in the service of the men of their family, using it to ensure republican authenticity on the part of their husbands and sons.[18]

Most historians, including myself, have assumed that this limited definition of female citizenship was all that the revolutionary discourse would permit, that no more fully inclusive definition could be conceived at the time. It is generally thought to be both unfair and ahistorical to expect of the revolutionary generation that it initiate radically new conceptualizations of female citizenship. For the most part, the records on this matter have been silent, and we have tended to take the silence of contemporaries literally, assuming that they were silent about that relationship because

16. Linda K. Kerber, *Women of the Republic: Intellect and Ideology in Revolutionary America* (Chapel Hill, N.C., 1980), chaps. 7 and 9. Carole Pateman, who has written the most shrewd analysis of this point, concludes that coverture meant it was impossible for a wife ever to be the "possessive individual" who is central to the new liberal state, "the proprietor of his person and his attributes," in C. B. Macpherson's terms, the person who, in Locke's words, "has a Property in his own Person. This no body has any right to but himself"; Pateman, *Sexual Contract*, 55–56.

17. On this point, see Hanna Fenichel Pitkin, *Fortune Is a Woman: Gender and Politics in the Thought of Niccolo Machiavelli* (Berkeley, Calif., 1984).

18. Linda K. Kerber, "The Republican Mother: Women and the Enlightenment—An American Perspective," *American Quarterly*, 28 (1976): 187–205, and "The Republican Ideology of the Revolutionary Generation," *American Quarterly*, 32 (1985): 474–95 [both included in the present volume].

they were not thinking about it. But silence itself is a social construction, related to an ability to verbalize and a control of access to the forums of public discussion. It is our task as historians to be alert to occasions on which silence is broken. I now would argue that it *was* possible for contemporaries to conceive of alternatives: they dismantled *petit treason*, and, as we have seen, James Otis opened the broader question. Moreover, it should now be possible for historians to reconsider what counts as citizenship. If we require that discussions of citizenship be limited to claims to voting and office holding by women, then the early republic offers us mostly silence. If we broaden the discussion and recognize that citizenship involves wide-ranging issues of claims of rights and of political behavior, as well as matters of allegiance, support, and analysis, then it is not difficult to find many occasions when women addressed political matters. If we adopt an even more inclusive definition, seeking to understand how citizenship is continually being reconstructed, particularly during a postrevolutionary era; if we seek to discern the gendered implications of superficially neutral rhetoric, tracing the ways in which political language was used to emphasize and sometimes redefine the meaning of masculinity; and, if we understand that an ideology that takes enormous pains to exclude women is, by that very fact, an ideology interactive with women, then we can see more clearly how the problem of women's relationship to the state in the postrevolutionary era infused republican ideology and reflected the gender dynamics of the generation that created it.[19]

For a moment at the beginning of the nineteenth century, in a Massachusetts courtroom, the discourse opened to suggest that it was not inconceivable that women might be citizens with their own responsibilities to the state. All the participants in this discussion were men; we have no record of a woman's voice in this conversation. Yet, in men's discussion of women, we can hear evidence of the gendered construction of citizenship

19. Some reflections on this point appear in Linda K. Kerber, "History Can Do It No Justice: Women and the Reinterpretation of the American Revolution," in Hoffman and Albert, *Women in the Age of the American Revolution*, 3–44 [reprinted in the present volume]. Wayne Bodle explores the implications of one woman's extensive effort to claim compensation from the Royal Commission on American Loyalists in "Jane Bartram's 'Application': Her Struggle for Survival, Stability, and Self-Determination in Revolutionary Pennsylvania," *Pennsylvania Magazine of History and Biography*, 115 (1991): 185–220. See also the important work of Mary P. Ryan, *Women in Public: Between Banners and Ballots 1825–1880* (Baltimore, Md., 1990); and Joan Landes, *Women and the Public Sphere in the Age of the French Revolution* (Ithaca, N.Y., 1988).

in the postrevolutionary republic. The case of *Martin vs. Commonwealth of Massachusetts* broke the silence and yielded a counter-revolutionary resolution. It suggests that there had been radical alternatives to the conservative outcome. It suggests how forcefully the courts in one major state were willing to act in order to maintain the gendered relationships on which they understood their community to rest.

James Martin's family had rejected a revolutionary connection. His father, William Martin, had been an officer in the Royal Regiment of Artillery, the one regiment in which commissions were not purchased and in which careers were, therefore, open to talent. William Martin was born in England; in 1742, he joined the artillery and was stationed in the colonies during the Seven Years' War. Sometime before 1752, he married Anna Gordon, the daughter of James Gordon, a wealthy Boston merchant and landholder who was briefly a warden of King's Chapel. Over the years, William Martin rose slowly in rank and was posted to a number of places; he and his wife spent some years in Halifax, Nova Scotia. When the revolution broke out, William and Anna Martin fled Boston with the British and traveled to Halifax, then to British-occupied New York City.[20] Ultimately, William Martin served on the staff of Brigadier-General James Pattison;

20. The Commonwealth of Massachusetts: Middlesex: Court of Common Pleas at Cambridge, December 24, 1782. These Common Pleas records of the revolutionary era have been lost, but sections were reprinted in *Martin v. Commonwealth of Massachusetts*, 1 *Mass. Reports*, 348 (1805). Other information making it possible to reconstruct William Martin's career appears in Court Files No. 148.112, *Martin v. Gordon*, Superior Court of Judicature Records, Suffolk County, Archives of the Commonwealth of Massachusetts, Columbia Point, Boston; *Martin v. Gordon*, Record Book, Superior Court of Judicature, Suffolk County 1773–74, pp. 20–21, June 14, 1773, Archives of the Commonwealth, Columbia Point; "Letters Communicated by Mr. Noble," in Massachusetts Historical Society, *Proceedings*, 2d ser., 13 (1900): 379–96; Massachusetts Archives, ms. vol. 154, p. 253, in Archives of the Commonwealth of Massachusetts, Columbia Point; *A List of the General and Field Officers, As They Rank in the Army* (London, 1763–84); "Memorial of Colonel William Martin of the Royal Regiment of Artillery, Massachusetts & N. Hampshire" (London, 1784), Great Britain, Public Record Office, Records of the American Loyalist Claims Commission, Film 263, Audit Office Transcripts Microfilm [hereafter, AO] 13/47/622–25; "Examination of Colonel William Martin of the Royal Artillery . . . February 5–7, 1789," AO 12/71/102–08. See also AO 13/6/370. Martin is described in E. Alfred Jones, *The Loyalists of Massachusetts: Their Memorials, Petitions, and Claims* (London, 1930), 211; and Peter Wilson Coldham, *American Loyalist Claims* (Washington, D.C., 1980), 335.

when Pattison returned to England on sick leave in 1780, Martin took his place as commander of artillery until the evacuation of New York in 1783, when he and his family left for England.[21]

What wealth William Martin had seems to have come largely from his marriage. His relationship to that wealth was precarious. After James Gordon's death in 1770, Anna Gordon Martin inherited one-third of his estate—a double share went to her brother. When the property was actually divided in 1773, she received at least 844 acres of land, improved and unimproved, in New Hampshire and central Massachusetts, at least one farm in Braintree, and a house on the Boston Harbor, with a wharf and stables for ten or twelve horses.[22]

As was usual in the eighteenth century, even though Anna Martin was a married woman under coverture, real estate that came to her by bequest was set off to her directly, thus keeping it in the Gordon line (assuming that William Martin, who had control of it during his lifetime, did not waste it). Anna Martin had a right of remainder in it, and it would descend to her heirs.[23] William Martin was "seized and possessed" of Anna Martin's prop-

21. Brigadier-General James Pattison to [William Martin], March 31, 1778, Pattison Letterbooks, Microfilm, Royal Artillery Institution Library, Woolwich, England, microfilm copy at the David Library of the American Revolution, Washington's Crossing, Pennsylvania. I am grateful to Wayne Bodle for identifying this letter, as well as other references to Martin in the papers of Guy Carleton, and among the Brigade Orders of the Royal Artillery, Royal Artillery Institution Library, microfilm at the David Library of the American Revolution. See also Public Record Office Microfilm AO 13/6/376. Martin conducted the formal inquiry into the causes of the great fire that destroyed much of New York in 1776; see the "Minutes of a Commission, (1783) to investigate the causes of the Fire in New York City," New-York Historical Society.

22. The house, which was destroyed by the British, sat on a plot of ground that stretched 2,000 feet from the street to low water. It was rented for £30 a year to Major General James Robertson when he was in Boston; AO 12/71/105. See also listing in Massachusetts Historical Society, *Proceedings*, 2d ser., 10 (1895): 180–81. The Braintree property is described in AO 14/47/637–38. The New Hampshire property is described in AO 13/47/622–38. The properties and their disposition can be traced in Suffolk County, Probate Docket vol. 72, pp. 281–84, 524; vol. 76, p. 22; vol. 102, pp. 302, 377, 415; vol. 106, p. 507, and file papers no. 14734, Office of Register of Probate, Suffolk County Courthouse, Boston.

23. *The Laws Respecting Women, as they regard their natural rights, or their connections and conduct; in which their interests and duties as daughters, wards, heiresses, spinsters, sisters, wives, widows, mothers, legatees, executrizes, &c, are mentioned and enumerated: also, the obligations of parent and child, and the condition of minors . . .*

erties only "during his natural life."[24] William Martin's "ownership" was limited to a life estate in the property; he held the property "in right of his wife." In other words, when he died, it would pass not to his heirs but to Anna Martin and her heirs. Because William and Anna Martin fled with the British, they lost all this property; Massachusetts and New Hampshire confiscated it in 1781. Massachusetts seized the property under the Massachusetts Confiscation Act of April 30, 1779, and it was this property for which James Martin sued in 1801.[25]

————

(London, 1777), 183; Dane, *General Abridgment and Digest of American Law*, 341–42; Reeve, *Law of Baron and Feme*, 162.

24. James Martin (Plaintiff in Error) *versus* The Commonwealth and William Bosson and Others, Ter-tenants, *Reports of Cases Argued & Determined in the Supreme Judicial Court* (September 1804–June 1805), 1: 348; hereafter, *Martin v. Commonwealth*. The manuscript file papers related to this case, including the writs submitted to the court and detailed descriptions of the property involved, are in the records of the Supreme Judicial Court, Suffolk County, March 1805, Archives of the Commonwealth of Massachusetts, Columbia Point, Boston.

25. "An Act to Prevent the Return to this State of Persons therein named . . . who have left this State . . . & joined the Enemies thereof," October 16, 1778, in *The Acts and Resolves, Public and Private, of the Province of Massachusetts Bay* . . . (Boston, 1886), vol. 5, chap. 24, pp. 912–18. William Martin was named in this statute. Massachusetts Archives (manuscript), vol. 154, p. 338; October 3, 1781, account of sale of estates of "Conspirators and Absentees," Archives of the Commonwealth of Massachusetts, State House, Boston. The only closely parallel situation I have been able to find is a suit apparently brought in the U.S. Circuit Court by Ward Nicholas Boylston to recover his family estate in Roxbury. It had been confiscated from his father, Benjamin Hallowell, who had been named as a "notorious conspirator" in the statute of April 13, 1779; Boylston (who had taken his mother's maiden name) claimed, as James Martin would do, that the property had actually been owned by his mother, and consequently the confiscation could operate "upon the life estate of Mr. Hallowell, in right of his wife, but did not convey the fee." The estate had been acquired by Isaac Rand, who sold it to a French immigrant, Dr. Lewis Leprilete, in 1791. Boylston's suit was successful in 1803; that success might have prompted James Martin's action. George Blake, who had served as Leprilete's lawyer, would make an opposite argument as Martin's lawyer. See "Confiscated Estates," *New England Genealogical and Historical Register*, 12 (1858), 71–72; Jones, *Loyalists of Massachusetts*, 281–84. I am deeply grateful to David Maas for this reference. *Ward Nicholas Boylston v. Lewis Leprilete*, U.S. Circuit Court, Mass. District, October 1801, copy in Court of Common Pleas, Suffolk County, files, January 1802, *Leprilete v. Rand*, Judicial Archives, Archives of the Commonwealth, Columbia Point, Boston. See also Supreme Judicial Court, Suffolk County, Record Book, 1803–1804, *Rand v. Leprilete*, Judicial Archives, Archives of the Commonwealth.

Confiscation was one among many ways in which patriots defined theirs as an authentically new social order. Virtually every state gave force to this commitment with a fairly standard trio of statutes, solidly in place by 1778, linking treason, oaths of allegiance, and the establishment of a system of confiscation. Together, the three were gestures of commitment to the revolution; the penalties could not be easily undone or forgiven. Treason—the act of aiding the enemy—and misprision of treason—the knowledge and concealment of an enemy plot—was to be punished with death, banishment, or enforced service on a naval vessel (from which escape was virtually impossible). Oaths, in the eighteenth-century religious system, were understood to be existentially binding. And the confiscation of property reached not only to self-interest but to the conditions for individual autonomy. The state of Massachusetts was unusual in the care it took to include women in each aspect of the triad.

Throughout the nation, treason and misprision of treason were understood to be crimes that either sex might commit. The statutes were written in terms of "persons." The penalty provisions sometimes eschewed the generic male pronoun in favor of the specific: North Carolina provided, for example, that those judged guilty of high treason "shall suffer Death without Benefit of Clergy, and his or her Estate shall be forfeited to the State."[26] The New Jersey statute was similar, but it added the provision that the condemned person might receive a pardon if he enlisted in the Continental Navy. Since women were not welcome in the navy, an alternative punishment was provided for them: a fine of up to three hundred pounds and imprisonment for up to one year.[27]

Massachusetts' 1777 treason statute made an even more explicit claim to women's allegiance. The statute applied to all "Members" of the state, who were defined as "all persons abiding within . . . and deriving protection from the laws." When the General Court defined the punishments for treason, it made sure that the implication of "all persons" was clear: "every

26. April 1777, in *First Laws of the State of North Carolina* (Raleigh, N.C., 1791), 1: 284. A New York statute against spying provided that "he or she" might be put to death after courtmartial. See *Laws of New York*, vol. 1, June 30, 1780, p. 282; and March 30, 1781, p. 370. See also discussion in Bradley Chapin, *The American Law of Treason: Revolutionary and Early National Origins* (Seattle, Wash., 1964), 37–45; and my discussion in *Women of the Republic*, 121–23.

27. "Act for Constituting a Council of Safety," September 1777, in *Acts of General Assembly of the State of New Jersey . . .* (Trenton, N.J., 1784), 87.

person who shall be attainted of treason within this State, whether male or female, shall be punished by being hanged by the neck until they are dead."[28] Although the statutes explicitly applied to women, and women were accused of misprision of treason, it was exceedingly rare for a woman to be accused of treason. No person was executed for treason in Massachusetts in the course of the revolution.[29]

The gendered dimension of oaths of allegiance was more murky. Although occasionally framed in terms of all residents, oaths seem almost always to have been selectively imposed on men. The strategy of requiring oaths assumed a community of Christians who truly believed their immortal souls to be at risk should they forswear themselves. When tension built between the colonies and the empire in the 1770s, tests of loyalty were instituted. Throughout the colonies, women were encouraged to support boycotts by changed patterns of consumption. But only in Massachusetts were women also explicitly included among the signatories of the evidence of commitment, the Solemn League and Covenant, drafted by the Assembly and circulated in the early summer of 1774. Contemporaries report "every adult of both sexes putting their names to it, saving a very few."[30]

Those who refused to swear loyalty when it was demanded of them faced physical and financial punishment. Even the most primitive government provides the basic service of overseeing the orderly transmission of property—by exchange, sale, or inheritance. This was a service the patriots were absolutely committed to maintain, for their understanding of a new political order rested solidly on the guarantee of the security of property. More-

28. "An Act Against Treason and Misprision of Treason," passed by the General Court, February 1, 1777, when sitting in exile from Boston at Watertown. *Acts and Resolves, Public and Private, of the Province of Massachusetts Bay* (1886), vol. 5, chap. 32, p. 615. The Massachusetts statute was closely modeled on the treason statute of the Continental Congress, June 24, 1776: "That all persons residing within any of the United Colonies, land deriving protection from the laws of the same, owe allegiance to the said laws, and are members of such colony"; *Journals of the Continental Congress*, 5: 475–761; quoted in Kettner, *Development of American Citizenship*, 179. For an insightful examination of the gradual transformation of the concept of the king's "subject" to the republic's "citizen," see Kettner, chap. 7.

29. Chapin, *American Law of Treason*, 46. There were no executions in Virginia, either. There were dozens of arrests for treason in New York, New Jersey, and Pennsylvania, however, and some executions. Chapin, 48–62.

30. Harold M. Hyman, *To Try Men's Souls: Loyalty Tests in American History* (Berkeley, Calif., 1960), 63–64.

over, patriots' understanding of individual independence and autonomy assumed that the active citizen had sufficient property to assure that he acknowledged no one as master. But patriots felt no obligation to oversee the orderly transfer of *loyalist* property down through a series of heirs. Including the explicit refusal to do so was one of the ways in which patriots defined the Rubicon they had crossed.[31]

To confiscate a loyalist's property required the property to be identified precisely. In English law, coverture ensured that the property a married man held was almost never fully his, free and clear; one-third of his real estate was encumbered to his wife for her use as dower property during her widowhood—that is, until she remarried or died. This dower property (the widow's thirds) was understood to be an equitable recompense for the woman who had given up control of her property at marriage, and British law treated her rights to it with great care. The dower property even of widows of men who had been hanged, drawn, and quartered for treason was carefully preserved. In confiscating loyalist property, most patriot legislatures left dower as a recognized claim on the estate. They did so partly because of long-established tradition, partly on the practical grounds that to assign dower would prevent the wives and children of absentees from becoming a burden on public charity (although their standard of living would obviously drop precipitously). This restraint was congruent with the

31. The fullest account of confiscation in revolutionary Massachusetts is found in David E. Maas, "The Return of the Massachusetts Loyalists" (Ph.D. dissertation, University of Wisconsin, 1972), esp. chap. 6. Maas stresses the complications and contradictions of Massachusetts policy: the fears of patriots when the British occupied Boston, the self-interest of private citizens who helped themselves to the property of absentees, the desire not to leave abandoned members of loyalist families dependent on patriot public charity—"leaving a wife in Massachusetts was the major method of protecting real estate"; p. 314. After the war, Thomas Astney, the British agent for loyalist claims, was surprised at how little the rebellious state government had profited from confiscation; p. 270. Maas concludes that, in Massachusetts, confiscation "failed as a method of financing the revolution"; p. 313. This failure made it practical for Tories to return and reclaim their land. Maas replaces the older, and much briefer, review of confiscation legislation in Massachusetts: Andrew McFarland Davis, "The Confiscation Laws of Massachusetts," *Publications of the Colonial Society of Massachusetts*, 8 (1903): 50–72. Although Harry Yoshpe does not deal directly with the extent to which confiscation served as "a method of financing the revolution," his conclusions for New York are roughly congruent with those reached by Maas; see Harry B. Yoshpe, *The Disposition of Loyalist Estates in the Southern District of the State of New York* (New York, 1939).

generally restrained approach American revolutionaries took toward the law of inheritance.[32]

Confiscation statutes varied widely in their treatment of dower right; most left the matter to implication. Connecticut and New York made no mention of dower right at all.[33] Rhode Island and South Carolina not only made no mention of dower but also claimed all property of loyalist absentees, whether held "in possession, reversion or remainder."[34] Others, among them New Jersey, New York, and Delaware, made no mention of dower right but may have included it by implication in the "just debts" to be liquidated before confiscated property was transferred or sold.[35] A few

32. See Stanley N. Katz, "Republicanism and the Law of the Inheritance in the American Revolutionary Era," *Michigan Law Review*, 76 (1977): 28. Carole Shammas, Marylynn Salmon, and Michel Dahlin, *Inheritance in America from Colonial Times to the Present* (New Brunswick, N.J., 1987), also stresses the limits of the changes made in inheritance law in the revolutionary era, see esp. 63–79.

33. "An Act directing certain confiscated Estates to be sold," *Acts and Laws of the State of Connecticut in America* (New London, Conn., 1794), 56–57. "An Act, for the forfeiture and sale of the estates of persons who have adhered to the enemies of this State . . . 22 October 1779," *Laws of the State of New York . . .* (Albany, N.Y., 1886), 1: 173–84. See also "An Act for the speedy sale of the confiscated and forfeited estates . . . 12 May 1784," *ibid.*, 736–59. But after the revolution, the New York legislature passed a number of private bills that restored dower claims. See, for example, "An Act for the relief of Clara Service and others," 3: 717 and following.

34. The quoted words are from "An Act for disposing of certain estates," February 26, 1782, in John Faucheraud Grimké, ed., *The Public Laws of the State of South Carolina . . .* (Philadelphia, 1790), 204 and following. The language of the Rhode Island statute covered "all and every the lands, tenements and hereditaments whatsoever, whether held in fee simple, fee tail, for term of life or years; and all estates in remainder or reversion, and all goods and chattels, rights and credits of every kind"; "An Act for the confiscating the estates of certain persons . . ." (October 1779), in John Russell Bartlett, ed., *Records of the State of Rhode Island and Providence Plantations in New England* (Providence, R.I., 1863), 8: 609–14. That the committees appointed to supervise the sales of these properties did not automatically reserve the dower right is suggested by the fact that Sarah Wanton had to petition for support for herself and son from the rents of a portion of her deceased husband's confiscated estate. March 1781, *Records of the State of Rhode Island*, 9: 350–51.

35. "An Act for taking Charge of and leasing the Real Estates, and for forfeiting the Personal estates of certain Fugitives and Offenders . . ." April 18, 1778, *Acts of the General Assembly of the State of New Jersey*, 43–52; "An Act for forfeiting to, and vesting in, the State of New Jersey, the Real Estates of certain Fugitives . . . ," December 11, 1778, *ibid.*, 67–68; "An Act to direct the Agents of forfeited Estates . . . to proceed to the Sale . . . ,"

states, New Hampshire and Pennsylvania, did not mention dower right directly but did provide for the support of the absentees' families out of confiscated estates.[36] In Georgia, a Board of Commissioners in each county, charged with confiscation and sale, could allocate half the estate—and if the estate was very small, all of it—to a wife or child left behind.[37] Only a few states, however, Virginia, North Carolina, and Massachusetts, specified that dower would be recognized if the woman had stayed in America.[38]

December 16, 1783, *ibid.*, 354–56; "An Act of free pardon and oblivion . . . ," June 26, 1778, *Laws of the State of Delaware* (New Castle, Del., 1797), 2: 636–43; "A Supplement to an act, intitled, An act of free pardon . . . ," June 5, 1779, *ibid.*, 658–65; "An Act, for the forfeiture and sale of the estates of persons who have adhered to the enemies of this State . . . ," October 22, 1779, *Laws of the State of New York* [1777–1784] (Albany, N.Y., 1886), 1: 173–84; "An Act for the speedy sale of the confiscated and forfeited estates . . . ," May 12, 1784, *ibid.*, 736–59.

36. In Pennsylvania, the justices of the Supreme Court could set aside parts of forfeited estates to support wives and children of absentees and traitors; dower may have been treated as an encumbrance on the estate. See "An act for the attainder of divers traitors . . . 6 March 1778," *Laws of the Commonwealth of Pennsylvania* (Philadelphia, 1803), 2: 165 and following, esp. 173–76. New Hampshire provided that committees of confiscation (in 1778) and probate judges (in 1779) could "make such allowance for the wives and children of such absentees out of their estates as they shall judge proper." No specific mention was made of dower or of the necessity to reside in the United States. "An Act in Addition to an Act intituled 'An Act to Confiscate the Estates of Sundry Persons' . . . 26 June 1779," in Henry Harrison Metcalf, ed., *Laws of New Hampshire . . .* (Bristol, N.H., 1916), 4: 216–18.

37. "An Act for attainting such persons as are therein mentioned of high treason, and for confiscating their estates . . . 1778," in Robert and George Watkins, ed., *A Digest of the Laws of the State of Georgia . . .* (Philadelphia, 1800), 208 and following, esp. sect. 22: 218. See also "An Act for inflicting penalties on, and confiscating the estates of such persons as are therein declared guilty of treason . . . ," 1782, *ibid.*, 242 and following, sect. 12.

38. In Virginia, widows or wives without children could claim dower, and the property of British subjects with children, whether the wife was alive or not, was exempt from confiscation if the heirs resided in the state. William Waller Hening, ed., *The Statutes at Large: Being a Collection of All the Laws of Virginia . . .* (Richmond, Va., 1823), 10: 71, chap. 14, May 1779. For a discussion of loyalist wives who remained, see Adele Hast, *Loyalism in Revolutionary Virginia: The Norfolk Area and the Eastern Shore* (Ann Arbor, Mich., 1982), 127–31. North Carolina also reserved dower claims for wives of absentees who remained "in or under the protection of the . . . United States." They were "allowed" as much of the confiscated estate as if the absentee had died intestate, that is, their dower right, which in North Carolina was one-third of the lands and a

The Massachusetts legislation was "ardent," wrote one of its historians, and did not leave dower claims to implication.[39] The statute that passed in 1779, after several drafts, provided "That where the wife, or widow, of any of the [loyalists] aforenamed and described, shall have remained within the jurisdiction of any of the said United States, and in parts under the actual authority thereof, she shall be [e]ntitled to the improvement and income of one third part of her husband's real and personal estate (after payment of debts) during her life, and continuance within the Said United States; and her dower therein shall be set off to her by the judges of probate of wills, in like manner as it might have been if her husband had died intestate and a liege subject of this state."[40] The explicit requirement that she remain in the

---

portion of the personal property. North Carolina added the provision that in small estates, wives of absentees could receive "so much of the personal property, including all the household goods . . . as will be sufficient for the reasonable support of the wives, widows and children," and if the lands were small and impoverished, the county court might set aside all of it for the support of wife and children." "An act to Carry into effect an Act . . . entitled An Act for Confiscating the Property . . . 1778," in Walter Clark, ed., *The State Records of North Carolina* . . . (Goldsboro, N.C., 1905), vol. 24, Laws 1777–1788, pp. 209–14. Note esp. sects. 6, 15. North Carolina went further than other states by specifying that confiscated properties could also be reserved for the support of aged parents of the absentee who were otherwise unable to maintain themselves. See "An Act to carry into effect . . . Act for confiscating the property of all such persons as are inimical [of November 1777]," Clark, vol. 24, p. 268, sect. 17; and "An Act directing the sale of Confiscated Property," Clark, pp. 424–29 (1782), chap. 6, sect. 21.

39. Richard D. Brown, "The Confiscation and Disposition of Loyalists' Estates in Suffolk County, Massachusetts," *William and Mary Quarterly*, 3d ser., 21 (1964): 537. Brown distinguishes between the legislation, which he characterizes "as the most ardent and vengeful . . . justifying the confiscations in blatant Whig terms," and the modest extent of its enforcement: "Except for a few conspirators, none of the loyalists was ruined by confiscations carried out for purely, or even principally, political reasons . . . The General Court's most active concern, both in sequestration and confiscation, was always the protection of creditors"; p. 550.

40. "An Act for Confiscating the Estates of Certain Persons Commonly Called Absentees," May 1, 1779, chap. 49, *Acts and Resolves, Public and Private, of the Province of Massachusetts Bay*, 5: 968–69. Details of the legislative history of this statute appear on 1053 and following. On the law of dower, see Marylynn Salmon, *Women and the Law of Property in Early America* (Chapel Hill, N.C., 1986), chap. 7. The efforts of one absentee's wife to have set off to her one-third of her husband's real estate, "for her dower therein during her life & continuance within the United States of America" may be

state implied that wives of absentees who fled with their husbands could not claim dower in confiscated property. An early draft was even stronger; its explicitly revolutionary preface attacked the king, it required that debts owed to Americans were the first lien on the estates and that proceeds from the sale of loyalist estates be used to relieve both inhabitants who had suffered in the war and the wives and children of dead American soldiers.[41] There is no parallel to this last clause in the confiscation legislation of any other state.

By spelling out what was probably the usual expectation throughout the United States, Massachusetts made that expectation into a self-limiting proposition: not that most cases would relate to wives who stayed on but that all cases should. Thus Massachusetts enacted a statute that contained within it a deeply radical and broader set of claims for a revolutionary relationship between the married woman and the state. Anna Martin's heir did not claim her dower property; he claimed property that she had held in her own right. But because she had fled the revolution, the state of Massachusetts did not think the property should be returned to her estate.

James Martin was forty-eight years old, and the twenty-year statute of limitations was about to run out when he brought his complaint to the Supreme Judicial Court.[42] His case was heard by a four-judge panel—Francis Dana, Theodore Sedgwick, Simeon Strong, and George Thatcher—all men who were Federalist by conviction and deeply conservative by temperament. The careers of the judges had involved decades of extensive interaction with each other and with the attorneys who now argued both sides of the *Martin* case.[43] The political affiliations of the opposing pairs of

---

traced in detail in the John Chandler Transcripts, Octavo Volume C and Folio Volume C, American Antiquarian Society, Worcester, Massachusetts. See also Andrew McFarland Davis, *The Confiscation of John Chandler's Estate* (Boston, 1903).

41. Manuscript draft, October 8, 1778, Acts 1778, chap. 48, Archives of the Commonwealth of Massachusetts, Columbia Point, Boston. This packet includes three other versions drafted between October 1778 and April 1779.

42. *Martin v. Commonwealth*, 348 and following.

43. On the longstanding tension between Dana, Sullivan, and Sedgwick, see Thomas Dwight to Theodore Sedgwick, March 20, and April 21, 1798, Theodore Sedgwick Papers, Vol. C, Massachusetts Historical Society; between Parsons, Dana, and Sullivan, see Theophilus Parsons II, *Memoir of Theophilus Parsons* (Boston, 1859), 79; for tension between Parsons and Sedgwick, see Richard E. Welch, Jr., "The Parsons-Sedgwick Feud

attorneys—there was a Democratic-Republican and a Federalist on each team—suggests how close, even overlapping, political positions could be in the early republic, especially among members of the political and economic elite.[44]

Martin's case was presented by George Blake, a well-established Boston lawyer who had been appointed to the "lucrative" office of federal district attorney by the Jeffersonians in 1801.[45] Blake situated himself on the conservative edge of the Republican Party; it was often difficult to tell him from a Federalist. Some years later, for example, Blake became a leading opponent of the effort to achieve full disestablishment of religion in Massachusetts; he allied himself with conservative Federalists on the issue and fought vigorously for nearly two decades. In the 1820s and 1830s, when moderate Jeffersonians had moved into the ranks of Jacksonian Democrats, Blake was a leader of the Whigs, along with conservative Jeffersonians and many former Federalists.[46]

Blake's colleague in Martin's claim was Theophilus Parsons, a prominent Federalist with whom John Quincy Adams had studied law. The following year, Parsons was elevated to the post of chief justice in the court in which he now appeared as attorney. Parsons had close Tory connections and was a

---

and the Reform of the Massachusetts Judiciary," *Essex Institute Historical Collections*, 92 (1956): 171–87. For Sullivan's role in shaping the postwar judiciary system in Massachusetts, "Bills Drawn by James Sullivan, 1782," in Robert Treat Paine Papers, Massachusetts Historical Society. On the culture of courts and lawyers in this period, see Gerard W. Gawalt, *The Promise of Power: The Emergence of the Legal Profession in Massachusetts 1760–1840* (Westport, Conn., 1979), chaps. 2–3; and Van Beck Hall, *Politics without Parties: Massachusetts 1780–1791* (Pittsburgh, 1972), 46–48.

44. Oscar Handlin and Mary Flug Handlin pointed this out some years ago, but they made a distinction between national and local issues that now seems arbitrary. See Handlin and Handlin, *Commonwealth: A Study of the Role of the Government in the American Economy, Massachusetts, 1774–1861* (1947; Cambridge, Mass., 1969), 57–58.

45. Thomas C. Amory, *Life of James Sullivan: With Selections from His Writings* (Boston, 1859), 2: 88. George Blake (1769–1841) graduated from Harvard in 1789 and read law with James Sullivan; he was admitted to the bar in 1792 and served as U.S. attorney 1801–1809. Alfred S. Konefsky and Andrew King, eds., *The Papers of Daniel Webster: Legal Papers*, Vol. 1: *The New Hampshire Practice* (Hanover, N.H., 1982), 137.

46. Blake's positions on disestablishment can be traced in William G. McLoughlin, *New England Dissent 1630–1883: The Baptists and the Separation of Church and State* (Cambridge, Mass., 1971), 2: 1074, 1158, 1173, 1177–78, 1218–19. His later legal career and his friendship with Daniel Webster can be followed in Charles M. Wiltse, ed., *The Papers of Daniel Webster: Correspondence* (Hanover, N.H., 1974, 1976), vols. 1 and 2.

leader of the most conservative wing of the Massachusetts Federalists, among whom Tory sympathies were common.[47]

The state's lawyers also came from both parties. Daniel Davis, the solicitor general for the Commonwealth of Massachusetts, had built his career on the Maine frontier. He was a moderate Federalist, whom Jefferson promptly removed as U.S. attorney for Maine in 1801; Massachusetts' Federalist governor, Caleb Strong, had equally promptly appointed Davis solicitor general. Davis held the office for the rest of his professional life. Although he wrote two minor treatises, he was known primarily as a solid trial lawyer; a memoirist conceded "he was not a student, nor a book lawyer, but was quick in his perceptions, and argued his cases well."[48] Davis's colleague was the state's attorney general, James Sullivan, who at the time of the trial was the Republican candidate for the governorship, challenging Caleb Strong's bid for reelection.[49]

47. For Parsons' politics, see Parsons, *Memoir of Theophilus Parsons*, 27 and following; and David Hackett Fischer, *The Revolution of American Conservatism* (New York, 1965), 254. Fischer stresses Parsons' elitism: about the Massachusetts constitutional convention of 1779–1780, Fischer writes, Parsons "worked at cross-purposes with John Adams . . . [and sought to extend the power of the 'natural aristocracy'] throughout the government, without check or balance." For Parsons' conservative views of marriage, see Grossberg, *Governing the Hearth*, 72–73. James Sullivan's biographer stresses the collegial relations the two men maintained on the circuit; see Amory, *Life of James Sullivan*, 2: 39–42. Daniel Webster was then a young man reading law in Boston; his admiring comments on Parsons and his critical comments on Sullivan appear in his note "Some Characters at the Boston Bar, 1804," in Konefsky and King, *Papers of Daniel Webster*, 1: 41–42.

48. William Willis, *A History of the Law, the Courts and the Lawyers of Maine from Its First Colonization to the Early Part of the Present Century* (Portland, Me., 1863), 114–15. Willis says that the office of solicitor general had been "created especially" for Davis, and when he retired from it, the office was eliminated. I am grateful to Alan Taylor for this reference.

49. See (Boston) *Columbian Centinel*, March 6, 13, April 20, 1805. Not until 1806 did a Boston newspaper mention the *Martin* case or Sullivan's connection with it. Then William Bosson, who had purchased the confiscated property and lost it in the lawsuit, charged that Sullivan, though acting on behalf of the state as attorney general, had also and inappropriately charged him (Bosson) a twenty-dollar fee for legal services. Sullivan defended himself in print; see *Boston Chronicle*, March 24 [?], 1806, reprinted in Amory, *Life of James Sullivan*, 2: 413–14. On the election rivalry, see Moses Sampson, *Who Shall be Governor, Strong or Sullivan? Or, the Sham-Patriot Unmasked* (Hudson, N.Y., 1806). For Sullivan's bitter reflections after the election, see Sullivan to Thomas

James Sullivan's historical reputation has been eclipsed by that of his more famous brother John, a revolutionary war general. But James Sullivan played an active and sometimes ambiguous role in Massachusetts politics throughout the early republic. If we are to understand the context in which he and Davis made their arguments against Martin's claim, it is important to understand his career, in all its complexity and occasional contradiction. Sullivan was a Jeffersonian who sometimes played the Federalists' game, sometimes resisted it; Ronald Formisano locates him as one of the "Republicans of the revolutionary center."[50]

Born in Berwick, Maine, in 1744, son of an Irish immigrant, Sullivan was sixty-one years old at the time of the *Martin* trial. Although he lacked, in John Adams's words, "an Accademical education," had begun "with neither learning, books, Estate, or any Thing, but his Head and Hands," suffered from epilepsy, and was badly lame as a result of a boyhood accident, Sullivan moved quickly from the frontier to the town of Durham to study law with his equally ambitious older brother John, and married Hetty Odiorne, daughter of a shipbuilder and royal commissioner.[51] When

---

Jefferson, June 20, 1806: "I am now before a Supreme Judicial Court, artful, malignant, and cruel, fully determined to ruin me if possible. The Governor [Caleb Strong] will give them all the countenance he can . . . If I would retire to private life, they would not think me worth their persuit [*sic*], but I can not endure the idea that these malignant men should review me as in a situation chased away by the federalists, and neglected by my own party." See also Sullivan to Jefferson, June 20, 1805, April 21, 1806, Sullivan Papers, Massachusetts Historical Society.

50. Ronald Formisano, *The Transformation of Political Culture: Massachusetts Parties, 1790–1840* (New York, 1983), 60 and following. Sullivan exchanged more letters with Jefferson than have been published; those published show Jefferson urging Sullivan to be of good cheer despite Federalist attacks. See Jefferson to Sullivan, February 9, 1797, in Paul Leicester Ford, ed., *The Writings of Thomas Jefferson* (New York, 1896), 7: 116–18; Jefferson to Sullivan, May 21, 1805, 8: 354–56, and Jefferson to Sullivan, June 19, 1807, 9: 75–78, congratulating him on his election as governor of Massachusetts.

51. John Adams to Abigail Adams, June 29, 1779, *Adams Family Correspondence*, 1: 113. Amory, *Life of James Sullivan*, 1: 28. The best biographical essay on Sullivan is Clifford K. Shipton's; see *Sibley's Harvard Graduates: Biographical Sketches of Those Who Attended Harvard College . . .* (Boston, 1970), 15: 299–322. From the pre-revolutionary war years and throughout their lives, Sullivan supported Sam Adams and John Hancock. This often meant that he was to be found in alliances that John Adams opposed; indeed, in 1788, Sullivan tried to gather support for Hancock instead of Adams as vice-president. For Sullivan's defense of Stamp Act rioters and Adams's defense of their target, see *Adams Family Correspondence*, 1: 132–33.

Gilbert Stuart, *James Sullivan*.
Courtesy Massachusetts Historical Society, Boston.

the Boston Port Bill closed the city's trade, Sullivan was elected to the General Court from Biddeford; thereafter, he remained in public service, on one revolutionary committee or another, in the General Court, the Provincial Congress, or as attorney general.[52] He was a member of the General Court while the statutes regulating the return of absentees and the con-

52. Biddeford, Maine, elected Sullivan to its Committee of Safety and sent him as its delegate to three pre-revolutionary congresses between 1774 and 1775. In 1776, he became its delegate to the new state legislature. In 1778, Sullivan moved to the central

fiscation of their property were debated and enacted.[53] During his time in the Provincial Congress, Sullivan endorsed strong, even punitive confiscation law.[54] After the war, Sullivan was often found on the side of those who were making it difficult for Tories to return.[55]

Sullivan's strong support for the revolution was buttressed by his admiration for his heroic brother, General John Sullivan, and by his grief for another brother, Daniel, who died on a British prison ship. Sullivan had made his career in the crucible of the revolution. He understood the society of the early republic to be a postrevolutionary one, committed to the promises the revolutionary generation had made. He was hesitant when the Federal Convention bypassed the amendment procedures of the Articles of Confederation, was skeptical of the Three-Fifths Compromise, and worried about the future of civil liberties under the new Federal Constitution in view of the absence of a bill of rights with a strong guarantee of trial by jury.[56] When the French Revolution broke out, Sullivan wrote at least one pamphlet supporting it and emphasizing its parallels with the American experience.[57] While he was arguing the *Martin* case, Boston's major

---

Massachusetts town of Groton and soon afterward was appointed to the Superior Court of Judicature, the predecessor of the Supreme Judicial Court. He continued to serve concurrently in the legislature; he later moved to Boston.

53. Samuel A. Green, *An Account of the Lawyers of Groton, Massachusetts, Including Natives Who Have Practised Elsewhere, and Those Also Who Have Studied Law in the Town* (Groton, Mass., 1892), 22 and following.

54. James Sullivan to James Warren, March 24, 1777, in Amory, *Life of James Sullivan*, 1: 96, see also 64.

55. Amory, *Life of James Sullivan*, 1: 146–48. Sullivan served on legislative committees that drafted stiff laws for returning Tories in 1784; these drafts were ultimately modified because they were not congruent with the promises of the Treaty of 1783. See Maas, "Return of the Massachusetts Loyalists," 450–51, 475; and James Sullivan to Richard Henry Lee, April 11, 1789, James Sullivan Papers, Massachusetts Historical Society, cited in Maas, 504. Sullivan was a lawyer for those who resisted payment of debts to Tories (despite the provisions of the peace treaty); Maas, 528, see also 447 n. 8, 475, and 508 n. 27.

56. Amory, *Life of James Sullivan*, 1: 221. See also [James Sullivan], *A Dissertation upon the Constitutional Freedom of the Press . . .* (Boston, 1801).

57. In this pamphlet, Sullivan powerfully defined the United States as a postrevolutionary society. If Americans were unrepentant—as he thought they should be—for tar and feathers, for the humiliation and jailing of traitors, for confiscated estates, then they had ought not castigate the French for similar vigor; indeed, they ought to acknowledge their similarities and their debt. Novion [James Sullivan], *The Altar of Baal*

Federalist newspaper castigated Sullivan as a "Jacobin" and alleged that, nine years before, Sullivan had been part of a "self-created society" whose politics echoed those of "the mother club, in Paris, under Robespierre and Marat."[58]

Nevertheless, in the politics of Maine, and in Massachusetts politics in general, Sullivan played a cautious role. He looked to metropolitan Boston for his alliances, not to the explosive backcountry. If he attacked some returning Tories, there were others whom he assisted.[59] He was unambivalently opposed to Daniel Shays and his rebellion. As attorney general, Sullivan aggressively prosecuted the state's interest against the proprietors of large speculative endeavors, but he had also, Alan Taylor reports, "been a lawyer for both the Plymouth Company and for Henry Knox," one of the largest land speculators in Maine.[60] Sullivan's fullest statement of his understanding of the marketplace is his 1792 pamphlet, *The Path to Riches*, in which he bitterly denounced Alexander Hamilton's Bank of the United States for favoring speculators in stocks and bonds and strongly urged making bank stock available to small investors.[61] Although he had grown

---

Thrown Down: Or, the French Nation Defended, Against the Pulpit Slander of David Osgood, A.M. Pastor of the Church in Medford (Boston, 1795). *An Impartial Review of the Causes and Principles of the French Revolution, by an American* (Boston, 1798) is also attributed to Sullivan; in this, too, he makes comparisons between the French and American experience; see esp. 33, 65, 84, 98.

58. *Columbian Centinel*, March 23, 1805. Sullivan denied that he had written the group's constitution but insisted there was nothing wrong with the Massachusetts Constitutional Society. (Boston) *Independent Chronicle*, March 11, 1805.

59. Amory, *Life of James Sullivan*, 1: 138 and following. Sullivan undertook the defense of the returning Tory Sylvester Gardiner in return for title to one of Gardiner's estates, an arrangement that was revealed only by David Maas in 1972 (Maas, "Return of the Massachusetts Loyalists," 526). Another Tory he assisted was William Vassall (Maas, 533). By 1787, he was in collegial correspondence with Richard King's son, the Federalist senator Rufus King.

60. In 1798, Judge Francis Dana nearly threw Sullivan out of the courtroom for his expressed sympathy for squatters. Thomas Dwight to Theodore Sedgwick, April 21, 1798, Sedgwick Papers, Massachusetts Historical Society. But he also took positions that the speculators endorsed. "The Federalist Great Proprietors," Alan Taylor writes, "should have known that they had little to fear from the new politicians, because so many of the leading Jeffersonians used to work for them"; Taylor, *Liberty Men and Great Proprietors: The Revolutionary Settlement on the Maine Frontier* (Chapel Hill, N.C., 1990), 216, see also 23–24.

61. [James Sullivan], *The Path to Riches: An Inquiry into the Origin and Use of Money;*

wealthy not only as a result of shrewd land purchases but also because of the elite connections of his father-in-law, Sullivan understood himself to be a self-made man, devoted to the free market, certain that in earning his wealth he had done nothing but what the free play of the market permitted. He was, in short, a moderate Jeffersonian and a classic liberal.

Sullivan was consistent in his liberalism, committed to making "all law compatible with a society of individuals exercising free choice."[62] He was on the bench when the first in the series of Quock Walker cases was decided in 1781; he believed that public opinion had made slavery untenable in Massachusetts and that the nation as a whole should adopt a long-range program of gradual emancipation coupled with equal education for children black or white.[63] Sullivan was skeptical of capital punishment[64] and an ardent advocate of religious liberty; he defended the Universalists—a high proportion of whom were women—both in court and in print at a time when they were very unpopular.[65]

And, most important, for our purposes, Sullivan was willing to follow consent theory where it led, certainly as far as the elimination of property requirements for voting and, long before the *Martin* case, up to the boundaries of gender. In the spring of 1776, Sullivan wrote to Elbridge Gerry:

Every member of society has a right to give his Consent to the Laws of the Community or he owes no Obedience to them. This proposition will never be denied by him who has the least acquaintance with true republican principles. And yet a very great number of the people of this Colony have at all times been bound by Laws to which they never were

***

and *Into the Principles of Stocks and Bonds, to which are Subjoined Some Thoughts Respecting a Bank for the Commonwealth* (Boston, 1792).

62. These words are from Alan Taylor, personal letter to Linda K. Kerber, May 27, 1991.

63. On Quock Walker, see Amory, *Life of James Sullivan*, 1: 115, 120; and John D. Cushing, "The Cushing Court and the Abolition of Slavery in Massachusetts: More Notes on the 'Quock Walker Case,'" *American Journal of Legal History*, 5 (1961): 121 n. 6, 137. Sullivan's most extended comments on slavery appear in letters to Jeremy Belknap, April 9, July 30, 1795, in Massachusetts Historical Society, *Collections*, 5th ser., 3 (1877): 402–03, 412–16.

64. See essay signed "Marcus" in *Independent Chronicle*, February 7, 1793, and essay signed "Plain Truth," *Independent Chronicle*, August 2, 1793.

65. *An appeal to the impartial public by the Society of Christian Independents Congregating in Gloucester* (Boston, 1795). See also James Sullivan to [?], June 25, 1785, Sullivan Papers, Massachusetts Historical Society.

in a Capacity to Consent not having estate worth 40/per annum &c . . . Why a man is supposed to consent to the acts of a Society of which in this respect he is absolutely an Excommunicate, none but a Lawyer well dabled in the feudal Sistem can tell.

Sullivan distrusted the rich as well as the poor—"Stupid Souls . . . are as often found on the throne as on the Dunghill"—and urged that voting for legislation that did not include new taxes should involve "every person out of wardship that is bound thereby."[66] Gerry sent Sullivan's long letter on to John Adams, who was representing Massachusetts at the Continental Congress in Philadelphia and daily facing the problem of how to turn the claims of the consent of the governed into practical devices for a new political order. Sullivan's letter came hard on the heels of Adams's own correspondence with his wife on this point: "In your new code of laws," Abigail Adams had written, "I pray you remember the Ladies." Together, Abigail Adams and James Sullivan forced John Adams to a consideration of the composition of "the public." In response to Sullivan, John Adams wrote the powerful, now well-known letter of May 26, 1776, in which he contemplated the question "Whence arises the Right of the Men to govern Women, without their Consent?" Sullivan had said that "every person out of wardship" should participate in legislation in some way, and Adams might well have responded that coverture placed married women in "wardship" to their husbands. But Adams construed Sullivan's letter to imply that women and children were governed without their consent, and he could see that the logic of liberalism, pressed as extensively as Sullivan was willing to press it, led inexorably to a challenge to coverture. "Depend upon it, sir," Adams warned, "it is dangerous to open So fruitfull a Source of Controversy and Altercation, as would be opened by attempting to alter the Qualifications of Voters. There will be no end of it. New Claims will arise. Women will demand a Vote."[67]

Sullivan continued to align himself with those who supported various challenges to women's subordination. Kathryn Kish Sklar finds him active

66. Sullivan to Elbridge Gerry, May 6, 1776, in *Papers of John Adams*, Robert J. Taylor, *et al.*, eds. (Cambridge, Mass., 1979), 4: 212–13. Sullivan had read his Paine: "Government is founded on the Authority of the people, and by them only is Supported and is as the writer of Common Sense observes, not founded so much in human Nature, as in the depravity of it." He suggested a two-tier voting system that took relative wealth into account.

67. Adams to Sullivan, May 26, 1776, in Taylor, *Papers of John Adams*, 4: 208–13.

in 1792, as state attorney general, persuading a jury "that girls had equal rights under the constitution and could not be expelled from school" when the selectmen of the town of Northampton refused to allocate funds for the schooling of girls.[68]

In short, Sullivan's role in the *Martin* case was congruent with the unusually consistent liberalism he displayed throughout his career. Believing that society was composed of equal individuals, he spun out the implications of that belief in a wide range of issues as they presented themselves—banking and the economy, religious freedom, an end to slavery, and even gender relations.

As they faced each other in court, each of the attorneys and judges had a high—and, in the cases of Dana, Sedgwick, Sullivan, and Parsons, formidable—political profile. Two men had actually served in the General Court (Dana on the Council, Sullivan in the House) when the confiscation legislation was passed in 1779. The strategy of the attorneys who spoke for Martin was to confine the case to narrow grounds. Had the Court of Common Pleas had appropriate jurisdiction? Had there been procedural due process? Was William Martin's title clear? The strategy of the two opposing lawyers, Davis and Sullivan, explicitly located the case in its revolutionary context, defended the choices of the revolutionary era legislature, and urged the court to sustain the radical implications of that legislation.

As the case was tried, the argumentation developed along two lines. One, whether the Martins had been granted due process of law, was relatively free from gendered considerations. I will not try to reconstruct it in this essay, but I will note that, while Martin's lawyers emphasized claims to due process, James Sullivan introduced a political dimension by claiming that a loose interpretation of statutes was permissible in time of war. The other line of reasoning challenged the relationship of a married woman to the state.

No one denied that if William Martin had possessed property, the state had a right to seize it. Martin had met virtually all the requirements of the confiscation statute: as an officer in the Royal Regiment of Artillery, he had levied war against the government and people of the United States; he had

68. Kathryn Kish Sklar, "Popular Sources of Change in the Schooling of Girls in Massachusetts, 1750–1820," unpublished paper, c. 1990, cited with permission of the author.

withdrawn from Massachusetts to a place "under the power of the fleets or armies of the . . . king," and he had not taken "an oath of allegiance to [the United] . . . states."[69] No one denied that Anna Martin possessed property. She, too, met the explicit conditions of the statute: she, too, had absented herself from the state of Massachusetts after April 19, 1775. Did the state have the right to seize her property as well? On what terms might it make such a claim?

The answer would be found, George Blake argued in his opening statements, in a close reading of the text. His voice reaches across the centuries to make explicit what had always been encoded in the concept of *feme covert*. The Confiscation Act addressed itself to "every *inhabitant* and *member* of the state." Women were inhabitants of the state; were they also members? Blake thought not. "Upon the strict principles of law, a *feme covert* is not a member; has no *political* relation to the *state* any more than an alien . . . the legislature intended to exclude femes-covert and infants from the operation of the act; otherwise the word inhabitant would have been used alone, and not coupled with the word member." As we have seen, confiscation had been linked legislatively with oaths of allegiance and with definitions of treason. Blake drew on these oaths and definitions for analogies by which to maintain his point: "A *feme-covert* was never holden to take an oath of allegiance." Like treason statutes, he went on, the confiscation "statute is highly penal" and therefore demanded very narrow interpretation. When Blake read the preamble, he construed it in gender-specific terms:

> "Whereas every government hath a right to command the *personal services* of all its *members*, whenever the *exigencies of the State* shall require it, especially in times of an impending or *actual invasion*, no *member* thereof can then withdraw *himself* from the jurisdiction of the government, and thereby deprive it of *his personal services*, without justly incurring the forfeiture of all *his* property, rights and liberties holden under and derived from that constitution of government, to the support of which *he* hath refused to afford *his aid and assistance*" . . . The object [of the preamble] was not to punish, but to retain the physical force of the state . . . How much physical force is retained by retaining married women? What are the *personal services* they are to render in opposing *by force* an actual invasion? What *aid* can they give to an enemy? So far are

69. "An Act for Confiscating the Estates of Certain Persons Commonly Called Absentees."

women from being of service in the defence of a country against the attacks of an enemy that it is frequently thought expedient to send them out of the way, lest they impede the operations of their own party.[70]

Blake proceeded to run through a long list of British precedents, easily found, for under the common law rule that "*as a woman is supposed to have acted under the coercion of the husband,*" she is regularly excused for acts, otherwise illegal, committed with him.

"And can it be supposed"—one imagines him thundering—"in the case before the Court, that the legislature contemplated the case of a wife withdrawing with her husband? It ought not to be, and surely was not, intended that she should be exposed to the loss of all her property for withdrawing from the government with her husband. If he commanded it, she was bound to obey him, by a law paramount to all other laws—the law of God."[71]

Blake's argument is important because it spelled out, in politically intense and loaded language, what his contemporaries took to be the political implications of the concept of the *feme covert*. As inhabitants of the state, women were merely residents. Only men were members of the commonwealth; indeed, the eighteenth-century euphemism for penis underscored the gendered implications of the contemporary concept of the "citizen": at some level, to be a "member" was necessarily masculine and generative. Implicit in this understanding was the antique definition of citizen, a definition as old as the Roman republic: the citizen was the man who is prepared to take up arms to defend the republic and so, in reciprocal relationship, has a right to claim a voice in the decision to resort to arms.[72] Thus Blake could speak in terms of "personal services" and the right of the state "to retain the physical force of the state." Once this was established, much else followed; at its extreme, the *feme covert* "has no *political* relation to the *state* any more than an alien." It would be hard to be more direct

70. *Martin v. Commonwealth*, 362–63, emphasis in original. The governor of North Carolina had received a plea to permit female absentees to claim dower right in confiscated property even if they left the state. Samuel Johnson wrote at the end of the war, "their return to the Country would have added very little to the Strength of our defense nor were they in any instance bound to find Substitutes." Johnson to Governor Adeneas Burke, April 1, 1783, in Clark, *State Records of North Carolina*, 16: 953–54.

71. *Martin v. Commonwealth*, 364.

72. J. G. A. Pocock summarizes this relationship in *The Machiavellian Moment* (Princeton, N.J., 1975), 90.

than this. Many years later, claiming a political voice for women, the abolitionist Angelina Grimké would ask plaintively, "Are we aliens because we are women?" Blake's answer, obviously, was yes.[73]

In a striking example of how contemporary discourse shapes the thoughts it is possible to think, no one in the courtroom was able to separate women from infants. Blake could not imagine that by "inhabitant and member" a state might have wished to identify adults who were competent to make judgments of their own, that infants might be inhabitants but not members, that married women might be both. Blake elided the issue by simple assertion: "The legislature *intended* to exclude *feme covert* and infants . . . otherwise the word inhabitant would have been used alone." Even in his own terms, this was not an accurate assertion, for, earlier in his argument, Blake had given the Treason Act of 1777 a close reading for other purposes, and he surely had cast his eyes on the opening words of that document, which began by saying that every *person* was an "inhabitant and member" of the commonwealth. If women could not be separated from infants, neither could women and infants be separated from men in the revolutionary definition of "inhabitant and member." But Blake was speaking a quarter-century after the revolutionary statute, and it was becoming possible to construe it in other ways.

In what was, so far as I can tell, an unprecedented argument, the attorney general and the solicitor general for the state of Massachusetts undertook to challenge what Blake offered as the common sense of the matter. They insisted that Anna Martin met the clear terms of the law: she had withdrawn from the state. Was she excused because she was *feme covert*? The statute said "any person." The provisions that confiscated dower provided that dower would not be confiscated for women who stayed, suggesting that married women had the "power of remaining or withdrawing, as they pleased." This element of choice, of course, had traditionally been absent from the repertory of the married woman. To introduce it was a challenge to traditional discourse. It was indeed possible to think what we have heretofore assumed to be unthinkable. James Sullivan attacked Blake's assertion that women were not included in clauses phrased with masculine pronouns; that is, attacked Blake's denial of the generic he: "almost all the provisions of the act are masculine." On this point, Sullivan was outraged:

73. Angelina Grimké, *Appeal to the Women of the Nominally Free States* (Boston, 1838), 19.

The same reasoning would go to prove that the *Constitution* of the Commonwealth does not extend to women—secures them no rights, no privileges—for it has no words in the feminine gender; it would prove that a great variety of crimes, made so by statute, could not be committed by women, because the statutes had used only the words *him* and *his* . . . Surely a *feme-covert* can be an inhabitant in every sense of the word. Who are members of the body-politic? are not all the *citizens*, members; infants, idiots, insane, or whatever may be their *relative* situations in society? Cannot a *feme-covert* levy war and conspire to levy war? She certainly can commit treason—and if so, there is no one act mentioned in the statute which she is not capable of performing.

Together, Davis and Sullivan articulated a case for the politicized married woman. Shaking loose of traditional assumptions about women's vulnerability, their incompetence, their distance from issues of concern to the commonwealth, Davis and Sullivan offered the court a woman who had been redefined as a competent citizen by revolutionary legislation and challenged to make her own political choices in the crucible of revolution.[74]

Sullivan's language was politicized; it was part of a discourse of revolution. He accused the other side of being unfaithful to the intent of revolutionary legislation: "If all the decisions which were had during war . . . are in time of peace, liable to be reversed, there would be instant cause of war, and there would be no end of war." For Sullivan and Davis, the revolution had claimed the loyalty of all *persons*, defining them as "inhabitants and members" of the state and broadening the obligations of citizenship to stretch past physical service and include the emotional and mental act of allegiance.[75] Women could share this sort of citizenship, and, they concluded, women could also share its obligations. They leaned on natural law more

---

74. *Martin v. Commonwealth*, 362, 375–76. Sullivan's position was, indeed, congruent with the traditional understanding that the husband who abjured the realm was civilly dead, leaving his wife as *feme sole* and thus vulnerable to the direct claims of the state. See, for example, *Laws Respecting Women*, 171; Dane, *General Abridgement and Digest of American Law*, 335; Reeve, *Law of Baron and Feme*, 98–105. I am grateful to Hendrik Hartog for this observation. In these cases, however, it was assumed that the husband (but not the wife) had left the realm, and that he had surrendered his claim to the body of his wife.

75. He might here have cited the Treason Act of 1777, which had specified "All *persons* . . . owe allegiance and are members of the State"; "An Act Against Treason and Misprision of Treason."

than common law; indeed, they abandoned the common law principle of "unity of person" accomplished by marriage and substituted a natural law understanding of the possibilities of reason to shape political behavior. To this effect, Davis cited Jean Jacques Burlamaqui on *The Principles of Natural Law*: "Reason being the first rule of man, it is also the first principle of morality, and the immediate cause of all primitive obligation." It may be that the woman Sullivan and Davis envisaged bore some debt to Mary Wollstonecraft's construction, which offered competence and capability as preconditions of citizenship. "How can a being be generous who has nothing of its own? or virtuous who is not free?" Wollstonecraft had asked. If Anna Martin were to be a member of the commonwealth, she would have to be defined as a being who had something of her own.[76]

The end of the story is quickly told. The politics of the courtroom pitted the republican candidate for governor against a panel of judges committed to his political defeat. The two days of argument took place before a bench composed of men in late middle age—Thatcher, the youngest, was fifty-one; Dana, the eldest, sixty-two—who had moved in and out of elective politics.[77] All four judges voted to support James Martin's claim to his mother's property, thus reversing the lower court's decision. Three addressed the issue of the nature of female citizenship in a republic; the most extensive of these was offered by Theodore Sedgwick.

Sedgwick had been a cautious supporter of the revolution and now was a conservative Federalist.[78] In his written opinion, he began with the revo-

76. J. J. Burlamaqui, *The Principles of Natural and Politic Law*, 5th edn. (Cambridge, 1807), 149; Mary Wollstonecraft, *Vindication of the Rights of Woman*, Miriam Brody, ed. (1792; London, 1985), chap. 9, p. 259.

77. Sedgwick, Thatcher, and Dana were formally identified with the Federalist Party; Simeon Strong had been briefly arrested as a loyalist during the revolution and subsequently confined himself to the private practice of law. He was appointed to the bench by Federalist governor Caleb Strong in 1801. See William T. Davis, *Bench and Bar of the Commonwealth of Massachusetts* (New York, 1974), 246; Gawalt, *Promise of Power*, 48, 69; Shipton, *Sibley's Harvard Graduates*, 93–95.

78. Sedgwick had held this position for a long time. As early as 1778, he had, in correspondence with his Loyalist friend Henry Van Schaack, described Tories as "Persons who have done no more than in meer opinion to dissent from the rest of the Country." Theodore Sedgwick to Henry Van Schaack, August 24, 1778, quoted in Maas, "Return of the Massachusetts Loyalists," 402 and 422 n. 38. As a member of the General Court in the early 1780s, Sedgwick had voted against harsh treatment for returning

lution, offering a curiously apolitical interpretation of what it had been, stressing its elite origins and respecting those who from "principles of duty and conscience" could not support it. Rereading the charges, Sedgwick emphasized that William and Anna Martin had been *jointly* charged with levying war, adhering to the king of Britain and withdrawing themselves. "[W]e are called upon . . . to say whether a *feme-covert*, for *any* of these acts, *performed with her husband*, is within the intention of the statute; and I think that she is not." The common law, Sedgwick argued, exempts a married woman from punishment for most crimes when performed with her husband because of the strength of his "authority" and "her duty of obedience." How can we have a situation, Sedgwick asked, in which women are not held responsible for independent judgment on straightforward ethical matters like theft and yet would be held to independent judgment on political matters in which even "men of great powers and equal integrity . . . [are] divided"?

> Can we believe that a wife for so respecting the understanding of her husband as to submit her own opinions to his, on a subject so all-important as this, should lose her own property, and forfeit the inheritance of her children? Was she to be considered as criminal because she permitted her husband to elect his own and her place of residence? Because she did not, in violation of her marriage vows, rebel against the will of her husband?[79]

In this way, Sedgwick came to articulate the issue of the relationship of women to rebellion and disorder. Did the state intend—was it possible to imagine the revolutionary coalition in Massachusetts as having intended—to call upon married women to rebel against their husbands? It had certainly called upon sons to rebel against their fathers. But, Sedgwick thought, the state could not possibly have tried to recruit women; there was nothing they could contribute to the rebellion.

> A *wife* who left the country in the company of her husband did not *withdraw* herself—but was, if I may so express it, withdrawn by him. She did not deprive the government of the benefit of her personal services—she had none to render—none were exacted of her . . . Can any one believe it

---

Tories. Maas reports that Sedgwick enthusiastically arranged for the return of Peter and Henry Van Schaack, even to the point of bribing the justices of the peace; 444 and following. See also Gawalt, *Promise of Power*, 48–49.

79. *Martin v. Commonwealth*, 392–93, 391.

was the intention of the legislature to demand of *femes-covert* their *aid and assistance* in the support of their constitution of government?

Sedgwick proceeded to reconstruct the preamble, which defined it as the duty of all the "*people* . . . to unite in defence of their common freedom, and *by arms* to oppose the fleets and armies of the said King; yet, nevertheless, divers of the *members* of this [state] . . . evilly disposed . . . did withdraw themselves." He asked:

> [C]an it be supposed to have been the intention of the legislature to exact the performance of this duty from *wives* in opposition to the will and command of their husbands? Can it be believed that a humane and just legislature ever intended that wives should be subjected to the horrid alternative of, either, on the one hand, separating from their husbands and disobeying them, or, on the other, of sacrificing their property? It is impossible for me to suppose that such was ever their intention.

In the end, all four judges chose common law over natural law, English precedent over republican potential, narrow interpretation over loose construction. They chose James Martin's private claim over the public claim of the Commonwealth of Massachusetts. The judges spoke in terms of deference, of obligation, of what women owed to their husbands, what men had a right to demand of their wives. Dana spoke of the "duty, which, by the laws of their country and the law of God, [women] . . . owed to their husbands"; Sedgwick spoke of the propriety of women's submission to her husband's opinions and judgments, even when they were evil; Strong observed that the married woman "is bound to obey his commands . . . except *perhaps* in treason and murder."[80]

The marriages these men describe are not companionate marriages. The women they describe are not "republican wives" in Jan Lewis's terms; they certainly do not have the freedom to be republican mothers.[81] Theirs is a language of constraint, of control and of force. Sir William Blackstone had defended coverture as protective; the woman, he said, was a "favorite" of the laws of England. But there is little in the language of the judges or of the plaintiff's attorneys that suggests favoritism and protection: all is force, violence, constraint. In odd juxtaposition, the Federalists spoke of the revolution—on the face of it, a locus of force and violence—in mild terms.

80. *Martin v. Commonwealth*, 390–92.

81. Jan Lewis, "The Republican Wife: Virtue and Seduction in the Early Republic," *William and Mary Quarterly*, 3d ser., 44 (1987): 689–721.

They referred to the revolution primarily in connection with giving extended time for loyalists to make up their minds about allegiance, in referring to the persistence of English common law despite the revolutionary fault line. To construct a married woman this way in the context of the *Martin* case was to deny the claims of the American citizens—the purchasers of the confiscated property, as well as the state of Massachusetts—and to privilege the claims of the alien and Tory; yet this conclusion was reached by all the judges. The paradox was that, in order to sustain the state's claim that Anna Martin had been a "member" of the Commonwealth, she and her heirs would have had to forfeit their property.[82]

Federalist judges ruled on behalf of the Tory claimant as they had often done in the past.[83] The significance of the *Martin* case lies not so much with the substance of the decision, which was congruent with long-term trends

82. The *Martin* case is unusual for the clarity with which the matter of women's status was discussed. There are some similarities between it and *Lessee of Pemberton v. Hicks*, 1799, in Horace Binney, *Reports of Cases Adjudged in the Supreme Court of Pennsylvania* (Philadelphia, 1809), 1: 1–24, in that the property of the wife of a loyalist was also at issue. But the facts of the case were significantly different. Joseph Galloway had not only been a loyalist but an attainted traitor, who had fled to England. He had held property "in right of his wife," Grace Galloway, who, like Anna Martin, had inherited land from her father, which Joseph held as tenant by courtesy. But Grace Galloway had met the requirement that she stay in the United States in order to maintain her claim on the property. As a traitor, Joseph Galloway was regarded as "civilly dead," thus all rights reverted to her, and for civil purposes she was treated as a widow. When she willed the property to her son-in-law, the Supreme Court of Pennsylvania upheld her claim. Yet, even in this lawsuit, one of the judges who voted with the majority made the point that he was "averse to visiting the sins of the father upon the children"; p. 12. The dissenting judge argued that the property had been properly confiscated when Galloway was attainted, since the purpose of deterring treason would not be served if the property remained in the family. "The only human consideration which can withhold [traitors] . . . from endangering the nation, is their attachment to their wives and children . . . Besides, property is created and preserved by government and laws; consequently every government may regulate it in such a manner as the society deems most conducive to the good of the nation"; p. 18. Judge Smith was, like Sullivan, willing to sustain the radical purposes of revolutionary legislation, but the status of Grace Galloway did not enter into the argument.

83. David Maas finds that, with a few brief exceptions in the immediate postwar period, Tory claimants won more cases than they lost; Maas, *Divided Hearts: Massachusetts Loyalists 1765–1790; A Biographical Directory* (Boston, 1980), xxiii. See also Maas, "Return of the Massachusetts Loyalists," 524–25 *et passim*.

in Massachusetts and elsewhere, but in the texture of the argument. The Federalist jurists rallied around a traditional, corporate vision of society in which the family was still a "little commonwealth" headed by a benevolent patriarch. Ironically, they may have been blinded from understanding how restrictive their decision was precisely because they understood themselves to be personally generous, even indulgent, toward the women of their own families. Sedgwick took enormous pride in having freed the family's slave, "Mumbet," who took the name Elizabeth Freeman, and in nurturing his own daughter's love of reading—Catharine Maria Sedgwick, fifteen years old in 1805, who grew up to be a leading novelist of her generation. Yet that personal generosity itself left patriarchal relations intact; the father who chose to be indulgent toward his dependents had the option of choosing otherwise.[84]

That conservative public politics should be thus linked with patriarchal private relations comes as no surprise, except insofar as these Federalist judges and lawyers are unusually explicit in their denial of the civic capacity of women. They were voicing an interpretation of marital relations that we now understand to be anachronistic in light of what would follow, but they did not have the benefit of hindsight. The state predictably assumed the defense in order to sustain its own claims to the confiscated property. What is intriguing is that James Sullivan and Daniel Davis should have offered the arguments they did in favor of the civic capacity of women. Sullivan and Davis moved far beyond the claim of mutuality in marriage to a vision of marriage in which the partners were independent moral actors, a vision of family life in which wives as well as husbands had to evaluate the revolution, take a position, and risk their property and prosperity on the choice they made. Sullivan and Davis argued that if patriarchy in politics is rejected, so too must be patriarchy in marriage. The Federalist judges wanted it both ways—to abandon patriarchy in politics but maintain it, in sentimental form, in their private lives. Many judges clung to this position for the rest of the nineteenth century; the longest-lived aspect of the pre-revolutionary past would be, Michael Grossberg argues, "judicial patriarchy."[85]

Sullivan's comments in the *Martin* case suggest the outer limits of arguing the Woman Question. The seizure of a married woman's property

84. See Catharine Maria Sedgwick, *Hope Leslie: Or, Early Times in the Massachusetts*, Mary Kelley, ed. (New Brunswick, N.J., 1987), ix–xxi. I owe this paragraph to conversations with Alan Taylor.

85. Grossberg, *Governing the Hearth*, 296.

because she had not remained in the republic and made her own political commitment was as far as one could go. In Sullivan's language, the insistence that married women had the power to make choices was associated with a vision of the revolution as violent. It was congruent with other positions Sullivan took throughout his career and with positions others articulated—briefly—in the radical spaces of the revolution. Sullivan was consistent in his liberalism, supporting a free market not only in the economy but in ideas, not flinching when that position suggested that women were necessarily part of the polity. No one joined Sullivan and Davis out on their limb, and they did not venture out there again.[86]

A quarter-century later, Supreme Court Justice Joseph Story brought the issue to one kind of closure in his thoughtful and lengthy opinion for the

86. The *Martin* decision was reaffirmed by Theophilus Parsons, in his role as chief justice of the Supreme Judicial Court, in *Esther Sewall v. Benjamin Lee*, 9 *Mass. Reports* (1812): 363–70. See also Lewis Bigelow, *A Digest of the Cases Argued and Determined in the Supreme Judicial Court of the Commonwealth of Massachusetts from Sept. 1804 to Nov. 1815* . . . (Cambridge, Mass., 1818), 238.

James Martin subsequently brought four different and successful ejectment actions against holders of property he claimed he inherited from his mother. These cases can be traced in the records of the U.S. Circuit Court, Massachusetts District, Docket Book, vol. 2, 1804–09, Record Book, vol. 2, 1806–11, and accompanying file papers for *James Martin v. John Bosson*; *Martin v. Benjamin Cargyll*; *Martin v. Winslow Parker*; *Martin v. Levi Thayer*; *Martin v. Paul Thayer*, Federal Records Center, Waltham. Blake served as Martin's attorney in all the suits; Sullivan, in his private capacity, was counsel for Bosson and Cargyll.

There are a few other revolutionary-era cases in which women figure prominently as plaintiffs or defendants, notably *Rutgers v. Waddington*, New York City Mayor's Court, 1784, and *Kempe's Lessee v. Kennedy*, 5 *Cranch* 173. But none became the occasion for the detailed expression of ideas about the relationship of women to the state or of a debate on what the civic order owed to married women. Elizabeth Rutgers, for example, was a widow—that is, not a *feme covert*—who sued Joshua Waddington, a British merchant, for "forcibly" occupying and using her brewery during the British occupation of New York City. He had done so by virtue of the authority of the occupying British army, and the argument in the court related to the extent to which the independent United States should, in 1784, recognize authority the British had exercised in 1778. Rutgers' status was never in question: "she was an inhabitant of this city," observed the court, "who by reason of the invasion of the enemy, left her place of abode, and . . . hath not since voluntarily put herself into the power of the enemy . . . [she is] a compleat Plaintiff." Richard B. Morris, ed., *Select Cases of the Mayor's Court of New York City, 1674–1784* (Washington, D.C., 1935), 302–05 and following.

majority in *Shanks vs. Dupont*, decided in 1830.[87] Story had known many of the principals in the *Martin* case. As a member of the General Court, he had served on a committee that examined the election returns in 1806; though a Republican, he had refused to vote along party lines and had awarded the disputed election to Caleb Strong rather than to Sullivan.[88] Story made brief reference to *Martin* in his opinion. Although the issue was inheritance rather than confiscation, the *Shanks* case turned on the question of the allegiance of Ann Scott Shanks. Like Anna Gordon Martin, Shanks was born in the colonies, a subject of the king; she married a British officer in 1781 (that is, before the war's end and while American claims to independence were therefore in some doubt) and returned with him to England. Was she to be treated as a British subject toward whose claims for property the United States was neutral, was she to be understood to be a *feme covert* with no capacity to make a political decision, or was she to be considered an American citizen who had renounced her allegiance? What choices did Shanks have the capacity to make as a *feme covert*? Coverture was still the rule in the United States, and Story did not try to undermine it explicitly. He acknowledged that the act of marriage was "the only free act of her life . . . for from thence she continued *sub potestate viri.*" But Story did widen the range of choices available to a *feme covert*.

Story argued that "marriage with an alien, whether a friend or an enemy, produces no dissolution of the native allegiance of the wife. It may change her civil rights, but it does not affect her political rights or privileges." Ann Scott had not lost her American citizenship simply by marrying Joseph Shanks. But, Story argued, she did dissolve her allegiance by going "voluntarily under British protection, and adhering to the British side, by her removal with her husband." Two nations, Britain and America, claimed her allegiance, "but they virtually allowed her the benefit of her choice." Story explicitly denied that "her situation as a *feme covert* disabled her from a change of allegiance." He pointed out that the United States had treated as citizens "British *femes covert*, residing here with their husbands at the time of our independence, and adhering to our side until the close of the war." The court concluded that Ann Shanks, whom the British government had never ceased to treat as a British subject, *was* a British subject and that her heirs could claim her property under the terms of the Treaty of 1783. Story

---

87. *Ann Shanks et al. v. Abraham Dupont et al.*, 3 *Peters* (1830): 242–68.

88. R. Kent Newmyer, *Supreme Court Justice Joseph Story: Statesman of the Old Republic* (Chapel Hill, N.C., 1985), 56–57, 401 n. 88.

made a distinction between the "incapacities . . . provided by the common law [that] apply to [married women's] . . . civil rights, and are for their protection and interest," and married women's "political rights [that] . . . stand upon the more general principles of the law of nations." These political rights, he argued, are not undermined by coverture, nor do they prevent married women from "acquiring or losing a national character." In this way, Story's decision in *Shanks vs. Dupont* opened the door for a broader conceptualization of the political capacity of married women. The woman with political capacity was a woman who could choose not only her husband but also her political allegiance. She would become an alien only by an intentional act, not "because we are women."[89]

Citizenship is basic to other claims individuals make on the state or the state makes on them. By pulling the concept of political rights out from under coverture, Story's decision helped markedly in the redefinitions that would have to occur before it was possible to establish the full political identity of American women, and it pointed the way toward the unambivalent claim of women's civic capacity that was voiced in the Seneca Falls Declaration of Sentiments in 1848. But, not long after that claim was articulated, it was attacked. A statute passed in 1855 provided that an alien woman who married an American citizen "shall be deemed and taken to be a citizen." It said nothing about the converse situation, American women who married aliens. American courts were often prepared to argue that a married woman's citizenship "naturally" followed that of her alien husband, especially if she moved abroad. Such women were said to have "suspended" their citizenship. What "suspended" citizenship meant was not clear, but in some cases women who married aliens were indeed treated as aliens. In practice, they might even be stateless. In 1907, this position was written into law; American women who married aliens lost their citizenship, even if they continued to reside in the United States. The Supreme Court upheld the statute in 1915, arguing in *Mackenzie vs. Hare* that by voluntary marriage to an alien, a native-born woman gave up her citizenship and adopted the nationality of her husband.[90]

89. *Shanks v. Dupont*, 246–48.

90. The best succinct analysis of changes in women's status as citizen is provided by Virginia Sapiro, "Women, Citizenship and Nationality: Immigration and Naturalization Policies in the United States," *Politics and Society*, 13 (1984): 1–26. My paragraph relies heavily on this incisive essay. See also Waldo Emerson Waltz, *The Nationality of Married Women: A Study of Domestic Policies and International Legislation* (Urbana, Ill.,

Not until national women's suffrage was won, and a vigorous national women's lobbying effort was undertaken, were these statutes revised. The process was long, complex, and has still not been fully analyzed. The Cable Act of 1922, which stated that "the right of a person to become a naturalized citizen shall not be denied to a person on account of sex or because she is a married woman," permitted American women who married foreigners to retain their citizenship but only if they married men from countries whose subjects were eligible for U.S. citizenship—that is, not from China or Japan. Even then, American-born women who married aliens were treated as naturalized citizens who would lose their citizenship should they reside abroad for two years. The Cable Act was extended by amendments well into the 1930s, but loopholes remained, and not all of it was made retroactive. As late as the 1950s, some American-born women were denied passports because they had married aliens before 1922.[91]

The extent to which the American Revolution was radical or conservative remains to be calibrated precisely. The story of *Martin vs. Massachusetts* suggests that the early national period was Thermidorean. Men who had supported the revolution nevertheless undertook in its aftermath to defuse the memories of revolutionary violence and upheaval, to constrain the renegotiation of gender roles, and to limit the political responsibilities of married (by which they actually meant adult) women. They found it impossible to imagine adult women as anything other than wives. They could not separate the sexual monopoly that a man exercised over his wife in marriage from the political monopoly he was understood to exercise over her property. At the height of the French Revolution, an anonymous contributor to a conservative Boston newspaper had offered the epigraph with which this article began, expressing conservative confusion on this point; the potential of female citizenship is dismissed with a linking of a woman of the *polis* to a woman of the streets.

But the story of *Martin vs. Massachusetts* also contains evidence that an

---

1937), esp. 25–28, 37; Luella Gettys, *The Law of Citizenship in the United States* (Chicago, 1934), esp. chap. 5, "The Effect of Marriage on Citizenship," 111–41; and the recent study by Candice Dawn Bredbenner, "Toward Independent Citizenship: Married Women's Nationality Rights in the United States: 1855–1937" (Ph.D. dissertation, University of Virginia, 1990).

91. Sapiro, "Women, Citizenship and Nationality," 11–15; personal communication from Lawrence Gelfand to Linda K. Kerber, September 24, 1991.

alternate scenario existed, also written by men. This alternative acknowledged the authenticity of the republican break with the past, pointed the way to a reconstruction of the relationship of women to real property, and explicitly claimed for women the responsibility of assuming the obligations of citizenship. The important point is not that this path proved too rocky for the revolutionary generation. The important point is that, for a brief moment, it was glimpsed.

WOMEN
AND MEN
BOREDOM, VIOLENCE
AND POLITICAL
POWER

My title comes from a lecture prepared by the distinguished American lawyer and civil rights activist Dorothy Kenyon, written in 1971, the last year of her long life. So far as I know, this speech has never been published or even quoted in print.[1] She knew she was passing a baton to a younger generation, and she wanted to say something meaningful about relations between the sexes—as they were, and as she hoped they would become. The themes she chose epitomize the central contested sites of gender relations in her own time, themes which—like much of her career, seemed idiosyncratic at the time—resonate in the present moment as central subjects of feminist discourse. Kenyon's words and her work link the problems of sex relations across the long twentieth century, offering a ground on which we can stand as we squint into the future.

Dorothy Kenyon was born in 1888 and graduated from college twenty years later. Late in her twenties she entered New York University Law School, one of the few major law schools that welcomed women, and was admitted to the New York Bar in 1917. Entering the profession as the United States entered World War I, one of her first jobs involved research for the 1919 peace conference. For the rest of her life social justice at home and internationally would absorb her energies. When the League of Nations established a Committee for the Study of the Legal Status of Women in 1937, Dorothy Kenyon was the American member of the group of seven

---

1. The manuscript can be found in Folder 241, Box 23, Dorothy Kenyon Papers, Sophia Smith Collection, Smith College, Northampton, MA.

Dorothy Kenyon, in 1970, speaking at a meeting of the Parent-Teachers Association of Public School 33 in New York City. Dorothy Kenyon Papers, Sophia Smith Collection, Smith College, Northampton, Massachusetts.

jurists who comprised it. The Committee struggled to do its work even after the outbreak of war.

It was reconstituted after the war as the United Nations Commission on the Status of Women; Kenyon served as the U.S. delegate from 1946 to 1950.[2] As she conducted her own private legal practice, she also maintained her concern for women's condition internationally. She kept up a vigorous career as an advocate for civil liberties and for a broad interpretation of the implications of the Fourteenth Amendment's "equal treatment" provisions as they concerned women. At the end of her life she initiated ACLU discussion of abortion rights for women. Ruth Bader Ginsburg, who was recently appointed to the United States Supreme Court, built upon Kenyon's work and is in some ways her direct intellectual successor. The clues Kenyon left

2. Dorothy Kenyon Papers, Smith College, esp. Boxes 51–52, 56–64.

in her unpublished papers encourage us to study continuities in relations between men and women across the twentieth century. They remind us that our generation is not the first to understand that relations between men and women are socially constructed.

In her 1971 speech, Kenyon referred to "boredom." She meant the emotional state men often displayed when the subject of *women* was raised, the assumption that "the woman question" is tediously devoid of interest or trivial and frivolous. Kenyon interpreted that boredom and frivolity as "a shield, a protection of some sort," a strategy which gave men permission to ignore intractable problems. By "violence" she meant to convey that unequal relations between the sexes are invisibly sustained by the fear of the violence men were capable of exhibiting if they did not have their way, just as hierarchical race relations are also sustained by a violent subtext.[3] And finally, Kenyon was convinced that change for the better in relations between men and women was a political matter. She wrote just before the Supreme Court, for the first time in its history, declared discrimination on the basis of sex an example of unequal protection of the laws, but lower court decisions were already pointing in that direction. Kenyon had worked throughout her life in expansive political movements which sought to develop equal, rather than unequal relations between men and women, not only in the United States but throughout the world. The implications of these themes—boredom, violence, political power—still resonate for us.

The League of Nations was founded at a moment not unlike our own: a time of enormous optimism about the prospects for a revitalized and peaceable international order in which the quality of life for all people, all over the globe, would improve and flourish. It was founded at a time of a strong feminist presence on the international scene; indeed the word "feminist" had only recently been coined in English. In the United States and in the United Kingdom, women had at last won the right to vote; in the Soviet Union, women were members of the Executive Committee of the Bolshevik Party and their role in the state and party was asserted to be central. An energetic international movement to make birth control information and technology available flourished. It was increasingly recognized that in all

3. She had in mind Gunnar Myrdal's work on race relations, as well as the "sadistic displays of brutality and cruelty" in television and movies which, she believed, instruct "all our male children, as the younger generations came along, [in] the niceties of killing and gun play generally."

cultures women were less likely to be literate than men, have less access to health care than men, be more vulnerable than men to sexual exploitation and to oppressive working conditions. It was increasingly recognized that relations between men and women, even men and women of the same families, were usually hierarchical, were rarely authentically reciprocal. These generalizations remain accurate descriptions of contemporary life.

Women's issues were implicit in the agendas for the League's work and for the committees that sustained that work in Geneva. It was generally assumed that women's problems would be included in more general headings: "Welfare," "Diseases," "Refugees," "Slavery," "Nutrition." As improvements were made in these areas it was thought that women, like men, would necessarily benefit. But even so, the League added other categories. Early in its existence, the League sponsored an International Conference on Traffic in Women and Children [Geneva, June 30–July 5, 1921] and, taking the advice of the conference, established in 1922 an Advisory Committee on the Traffic in Women and Children. In 1936 this committee was, along with the Child Welfare Committee, merged into the Advisory Committee on Social Questions. The League's Legal Section early marked the problems of the legal status of women under international law as difficult ones.

For example, in places where women derived citizenship from their husbands' status they were particularly vulnerable to statelessness. Toward the end of its life, the League established a Committee for the Study of the Legal Status of Women [September 30, 1937]. This Committee—on which Kenyon served—struggled to do its work even after the outbreak of war. The Committee provided, in turn, the basic foundation for the United Nations Commission on the Status of Women, which has continued into the present, emphasizing the codification of international law relating to women and expressing a concern for improving women's status in an international context. The "Scheme of Work" devised by the League Committee for the Study of the Legal Status of Women does not seem outdated.[4]

4. See, for example, the "Report on the Progress of the Enquiry, Adopted on January 10, 1939" and *Legal Status of Women: A Survey of Comparative Law* [Rome, 1942]. See also "Confidential: Not for Publication. Committee for the Study of the Legal Status of Women. Scheme of Work. April 12th, 1938," Folder 504, Box 51, Dorothy Kenyon Papers. A very helpful map of League concerns is Hans Aufricht, *Guide to League of Nations Publications: A Bibliographical Survey of the Work of the League, 1920–1947* (New York: Columbia University Press, 1951).

The United Nations continued this commitment by developing its World Conferences on Women, which have met every fifth year, and by establishing the United Nations Convention on the Elimination of All Forms of Discrimination Against Women [CEDAW] which was opened for signature and ratification in 1979.[5]

When I examine the agenda of the men and women who, like Kenyon, sought in the 1920s and thereafter to assess the relations between men and women and to change those relations in the direction of increased equity, equality and reciprocity, I find myself somewhat less impressed by progress and more impressed by the extent to which the agenda which we face is similar to the agenda that was outlined nearly a century ago. To inspect the work of the League of Nations on relations between men and women is to be humbled by the recognition that many of the most intractable problems we face are not new problems. The League reports, the early UN reports, and the reports of the UN International Conference on Human Rights in Vienna in the spring of 1992 are congruent documents.

When the League and the UN gather information on the status of women they are in fact measuring *relations* between men and women. The allocation of social resources that establishes status is an expression of power relations. For example: early in the twentieth century, the League undertook the first substantial systematic investigation of the international dimensions of the "traffic in women."[6] In our own time, the collapse of the Soviet Union and the Warsaw Pact has resulted in aggressive "trade" in vulnerable women for prostitution rings in arrangements all too reminiscent of enterprises which flourished in the first two decades of the twentieth century.[7] State power as embodied in border patrols and in civilian

5. The Convention was drafted in 1976. A revised draft was passed by consensus in the General Assembly at the end of 1979; by the Copenhagen Conference on Women in 1980, 52 states had signed. CEDAW is in force as of Sept. 1981; in 1993, 119 states had signed. The Committee on the Elimination of Discrimination Against Women is chosen pursuant to CEDAW; it called the Second World Conference on Human Rights, held in Vienna in June 1993. See Lars Adam Rehof, *Guide to the Travaux Preparatoires of the United Nations Convention on the Elimination of All Forms of Discrimination Against Women* (Dordrecht: Martinus Nijhoff Publishers, 1993).

6. *Report on the Traffic in Women and Children* [1927], discussed in H. Wilson Harris, *Human Merchandise: A Study of the International Traffic in Women* (London: Ernest Benn Ltd., 1928?), pp. ix–x; see also 259–70.

7. *Time*, June 21, 1993, pp. 45–51.

and military police, is complicit in this construction of females as potential objects of pleasure for men.[8]

The war in the former Yugoslavia has demonstrated the systematic use of sexual violence as a strategy of war, calling our attention not only to its use in the present but in the past. Rape is a protected form of torture; protected in the sense that the perpetrator "explains" that he is only expressing "natural" urges, and protected in that structures of shame in civilian society often inhibit victims from reporting their experiences, lest they be subsequently regarded as tainted.[9]

The League worried about infanticide. In our own time, we know about the widespread use of ultrasound technology in China to guide the abortions of female fetuses; it is estimated that more than 12 percent of all female births have been aborted. Misuse of amniocentesis for similar purposes is widespread in India.[10] These accounts of female infanticide or selective abortion tell us also of relationships in societies that choose boys over girls. We will not be surprised when demographers find, as the distinguished economist Amartya Sen has so effectively reported, systemic deprivation of food and basic health care to girls as compared to boys. Gendered disparities can be observed "in the division of labour within the household, in the extent of care or education received, in liberties that

8. Historian Bruce Cumings has written movingly of "the social construction of every Korean female as a potential object of pleasure for Americans" over the entire course of the American relationship with Korea from neo-colonial authority to ally between 1945 and the present, analogizing the "free" enterprise of prostitution under American occupation to the "comfort girl" system under the Japanese occupation. See Cumings, "Silent But Deadly: Sexual Subordination in the U.S.-Korean Relationship" in Saundra Pollock Sturdevant and Brenda Stoltzfus, eds., *Let the Good Times Roll: Prostitution and the U.S. Military in Asia* (New York: The New Press, 1992), pp. 168–69. On the policing of prostitution in the environs of the U.S. Naval Station in Subic Bay, see Aida F. Santos, "Gathering the Dust: The Bases Issue in the Philippines," in *Let the Good Times Roll*, pp. 32–44; also Cynthia Enloe, *Bananas, Beaches & Bases: Making Feminist Sense of International Politics* (Pandora Press, 1989; American Edition, University of California Press, 1990).

9. Amnesty International has recently undertaken a major project to identify gendered practices of violence in more than 40 countries.

10. Nicholas Kristof reports that the number of male births in China has skyrocketed from the normal ratio of 105 for every 100 female births to 118 males for every 100 females; there is real reason to suspect that girls whose births come as a surprise because the ultrasound tests were misleading are abandoned, killed, or sent for international adoption. *New York Times*, July 21, 1993.

different members are permitted to enjoy."[11] The United Nations estimates that in Asia and Africa, women work as much as 13 hours more per week than men do.[12] These are measures not only of the status of women, but of the relationship between men and women; the subtext, as Kenyon suspected, is the violent denial of social resources to females and the allocation of these resources to males.

The terms of the Convention on the Elimination of All Forms of Discrimination Against Women are encouraging. Among them is the principle that women should have citizenship in their own right and not as a derivation of their husbands' status, an issue which was contested in the United States in Kenyon's time and took more than 20 years of vigorous political work to change. When Kenyon served on the League's Committee on the Legal Status of Women, vulnerability to statelessness was a major problem for women; although it has been resolved in the United States, it remains a problem elsewhere and is highlighted in CEDAW. But the principles of CEDAW remain matters of dispute and there are no enforcement mechanisms. Many parties signed with reservations; some, like the United States, signed but did not ratify. Yugoslavia signed and ratified CEDAW more than a decade ago, but the effect on gender relations inside the region is not today discernible.[13]

United Nations reports describe three systems of relations between men

11. Amartya Sen, *Inequality Reexamined* (Cambridge, MA: Harvard University Press and the Russell Sage Foundation, 1992), pp. 122–24. See also Amartya Sen, "More Than 100 Million Women Are Missing," *New York Review of Books*, Dec. 20, 1990, pp. 61–66, and Marge Koblinsky, et al., *The Health of Women: A Global Perspective* (Boulder: Westview Press, 1993). UNICEF has described what are sometimes called "cultural discriminations"; in Malaysia, for example, the weekly duration of work for little girls aged 5–7 is 75% longer than that for boys of the same age, without counting the "invisible" work they do at home. In Jordan, baby boys between 4 and 8 months are four times more likely to be well nourished than baby girls. Sixty percent of children in the world who have no school education are girls. *Women of Europe*, No. 68, February/ May 1991, p. 35.

12. *The World's Women 1970–1990: Trends and Statistics* Series K, No. 8, Social Statistics and Indicators (New York: United Nations, 1991), p. 1.

13. This discrepancy between statements of principle and lived experience is not unusual. For example, the United Nations' most recent summary statement on the status of women observed that "the Bangladesh Constitution guarantees the equal rights of men and women and sanctions affirmative action programmes in favour of women but . . . the status of women in Bangladesh is among the lowest in the world." *The World's Women*, p. 7.

and women in the world today. In the "developed world" female literacy, education and access to health care is increasingly comparable to that of men. That is to say, in the societies of the developed world, girls and boys, women and men, can make roughly similar claims to the resources of their families and of society. They remain constrained by their class positions, it is true, and maintaining equal access in practice often requires political action and attention. But women and men have roughly equal access to education and health care at virtually all levels; we can observe women increasingly claiming competence in fields which had been previously monopolized by men, and we can note that men and women are increasingly likely to relate to each other as colleagues as well as kin and lovers.

But there are two other worlds—a "developing world" of Latin America and North Africa; and an "underdeveloped world" of sub-Saharan Africa and southern Asia, and, it should be said, sectors in the societies of the "developed" world—in which limited resources are clearly allocated differentially on the basis of gender as well as class. These are societies in which women work harder than men, die younger than men, are less literate than men, and have virtually no role in social decision-making. In these worlds, Amartya Sen's terrible statistics tell us—as the best social science almost always does—that the surface of what counts as "normal" hides unpleasant social secrets. In this context, what are we to say of relations between women and men? What words can we use that do not signal tension, resentment and exploitation—however implicit or unconscious—of one sex by the other? There remain many in whose interest it is to insist that women's issues are boring and tiresome; many who live in societies in which resources are violently torn from some and given to others. In all worlds, as Dorothy Kenyon discerned, relations between women and men are a matter of politics as well as a matter of emotion.

Future public policy is rarely the historian's metier. We dream of shaping the future by telling over more precise stories of the past. For historians like myself, two major theoretical shifts have taken place since Kenyon wrote that have changed the questions we ask of the past and the strategies we use for developing our answers. They make possible more precise analysis and perhaps offer grounds for optimism about progressive change. The first shift was articulated powerfully by Mary Beard shortly after World War II and again in the early 1960s by David Potter. By 1971 historians were taking up their challenge, which required that we question generalizations by asking whether they hold for women as well as they do for men. Virtually no generalization in the major historical narratives held up against that question. American historians, for example, who had long considered the frontier the major locus of social and economic opportunity, found that generalization is gender specific; the city, not the frontier was more likely to be a site of opportunity for women. The effects of social and intellectual change also turned out to be gender-specific; eras that seemed to improve the status of men—like the Renaissance—could be periods of decline and demoralization for women.

The insight was a simple one, but it required a re-examination of many conclusions about the past that had been regarded as well-established. It meant that the grand narratives we have inherited, built as they were on the assumption that men's experience is normative and women's experience is trivial, are partial narratives. It required that historians recognize women as historical actors, vulnerable as men are to forces beyond their control, striving as men do to shape the contours of their lives as best they can. The new approaches sustained a generation of exciting and productive scholarship across a wide spectrum of historical topics.

By the mid-1980s, the new lines of investigation were leading almost inexorably to the second major theoretical shift: to introduce into historical work the analysis of gender relations. The work of women's history expanded to include not only those experiences particular to women but the complex relations between men and women. Asking questions about how men and women construct meaning for their historical experience, historians now understand that gender itself is socially constructed. Gender is a culturally specific system of meaning that, as Alice Kessler-Harris has observed, "orders the behavior and expectations of work and family, influences the policies adopted by government and industry, and shapes perceptions of equity and justice."[14]

Dorothy Kenyon understood that women had interests to which male legislators generally did not respond. What she could not understand was why when she raised those issues, male eyes glazed over; in the speech from which I have been quoting, she said frankly "I sense [a] little hostility in the

14. Alice Kessler-Harris, "A New Agenda for American Labor History: A Gendered Analysis and the Question of Class," in J. Carroll Moody and Alice Kessler-Harris, eds., *Perspectives on American Labor History: The Problems of Synthesis* (DeKalb: Northern Illinois University Press, 1989), p. 226.

air . . . Nothing seems taken very seriously . . . One feels somehow or other put in 'one's place,' whatever that is."[15] We can now say that Kenyon felt that discomfort because she lived in a culture which constructed men as the ungendered norm. Only women were thought to have gender; in such a culture, it was almost impossible to situate a gendered self as a professional colleague. In America whites were not understood to have race; only blacks had race. Other cultures racialized other marginal groups, not necessarily on the basis of skin color—Jews, Gypsies, untouchables in India, the people who used to be known as Burakumin in Japan.[16] Every society is capable of creating an unracialized norm and a racialized other. The physical body of the asker is itself part of the discourse.

Like all academic and professional women of her time, Kenyon found that almost anything that she said or wrote was treated, at least in part, as what Foucault has called "subjugated knowledge"—knowledge marked by the knower's gendered social identity—as though no other knower also had gendered social identity. Since the community of historians had already concluded that the history of women was not serious, it became necessarily radical to claim women as the object of knowledge if one were oneself a woman. Understanding gender as a social construction helps us understand why women like Kenyon, who, in the post–World War I world, thought that the accomplishment of suffrage was a sign that they could enter politics, the academy and workplace as equals, were bound to be disappointed.

Understanding gender to be a social construction also helps us comprehend how it happened that the serious and extensive work on relations between men and women undertaken by League committees and United Nations commissions bore so little fruit; we may get some clues about how to interrupt this unfortunate pattern. For all their detail and force, the reports about women, especially when women were linked with children, were received as "subjugated knowledge,"—marginal, separate from the "real work" of the League, which involved negotiations over reparations, or over boundaries; separated from the "real work" of the UN. To resituate these reports as something more substantive, another theoretical move was required.

15. "Men and Women . . . ," p. 6. Dorothy Kenyon Papers.

16. For a thoughtful examination of the racializing of Gypsies, see Katie Trumpener, "The Time of the Gypsies: A 'People without History' in the Narratives of the West," *Critical Inquiry* XVIII (1992): 843–84.

That shift involved the recognition that generalizations need to be tested simultaneously by their resilience in the face of differences of race and class as well as gender. What had been separated as political history, diplomatic history, working-class history, women's history, and the histories of races marked by skin color or of racialized ethnicities we can now try to place in dynamic relationship to each other on battlefields of contested historical knowledges. Class resides in class formation; gender lies in the process of naming, displaying and giving meaning; race in the social construction of the other. The triad race, class and gender is *not* a mantra; and it should not be the monopoly of left-leaning historians or of social historians. It is not only a set of abstract concerns but modes through which relations of power are claimed and constructed. In most recent investigations, it has become increasingly clear that race, class and gender are not separate modes of analysis but are inextricably linked in complex relationships, each participating in the construction of the other in ways of which we have been only dimly aware, and all participating in the construction of political and economic power relations.

The "Scheme of Work" that guided the League Committee for the Study of the Legal Status of Women sensed this challenge. The Committee was warned that the category "women" was not monolithic; they were not only to "describe the position of women as such but also to deal with differentiations made between women themselves on the ground of marriage, age, education, number of children, etc." For the most part, however, the Committee was instructed to gather descriptive information, for example: "I.f. Position of women as regards personal freedom and safety, liberty of speech and of assembly. I.g. Fiscal laws affecting women as such. II.b.e. Rights of a married woman to carry on business or industry. II.b.a. Law of adoption as it affects women. III.e. Prostitution and traffic in women. III.f. The law of vagrancy as it affects women."

Framing the assignment in this way meant the League Committee would discuss the structure of law relating to women as though it stood alone, unrelated to the structure of law covering men with which it was always necessarily in dialogue. This structure was maintained even though as they worked in the late 1930s, fascist politics were not only effectively marking Jews as targets but constructing Jewish men as effeminate and Jewish women as masculine; that is, reconstructing gender and race simultaneously. Kenyon would later be impressed by the work of Gunnar Myrdal, whose devastating study of American race relations, blamed a "paternalistic order of society" and linked the problems of women and African Americans. In recent years, scholars whose work has been informed by post-structuralist analysis have urged us to understand language not only as systems of words and grammatical rules but as systems of thought through which meaning is constructed. As Jane Sherron De Hart has put it, through language "meanings are reproduced differentially, through contrasts and oppositions, and hierarchically, through the assignment of primacy to one term and subordination on the other. Pairings such as objective/subjective, public/private, equality/difference, and male/female are key examples."[17]

These pairs convey, superficially, that they name symmetrical relationships, but invariably they describe asymmetrical relationships, relationships in which the first part of the pair is privileged and the second is understood to be supplementary. The superficial equality between the two has the effect of masking the power relationship between them. For example, the public/private dichotomy has often been accompanied by a description of women as living in a "separate sphere" or "private sector" of their own. In this language, "public" and "private" seemed to be reciprocal social constructions.[18] But this discourse masks the way the power of the state intrudes upon and shapes intimate, "private" relationships—by laws governing marriage, by systems of taxation, by rules of divorce and child custody, by cultural climates in which literacy is differentially available—reifying difference and sustaining the dependence of women on men. When the League's "Scheme of Work" listed topics in law "as it affects women" it also inadvertently conveyed that it is possible to speak of one part of the pair without necessarily constructing meaning for the other part.

Scholars from a variety of disciplines have also come to understand "the contingent, constructed character of presumably neutral, universal concepts and principles."[19] Carole Pateman has argued that even the abstraction "the social contract," in which individuals are understood to legitimate civil government by voluntary and free "exchange [of] the insecurities of

17. In much of what follows, I am indebted to Jane Sherron De Hart, "Equality Challenged: Equal Rights and Sexual Difference," *Journal of Policy History* VII (1994): 40–72. See also Joan W. Scott, "Deconstructing Equality-Versus-Difference: or, the Uses of Poststructuralist Theory for Feminism," *Feminist Studies* XIV (1988): 32–38.

18. I have discussed this point at length in "Separate Spheres, Female Worlds, Woman's Place: The Rhetoric of Women's History," *Journal of American History* (1988): 9–39 [which is included in the present volume].

19. De Hart, "Equality Challenged," p. 57.

natural freedom for equal, civil freedom which is protected by the state," describes in fact not "all adult individuals" but only relationships among men. The liberal order in which every man claimed, in Locke's words, "a property in his own person" did not sustain women in claiming a property in *their* own persons. Pateman argues that lurking behind the social contract that sustains liberal society is a *sexual contract* which defines women as politically irrelevant and personally subordinate.[20] The rational individual on whom liberal political theory is based, one who can display autonomy and independence, is necessarily an adult male unmarked by class or race.[21]

Pateman's work helps explain why even in liberal, egalitarian political systems, even when they are of the same families and the same economic classes, men and women are differently situated in relation to the social order. Indeed, for those who are differently situated, it is possible for the application of equal rights to be punitive. Kenyon's contemporaries could not explain this fully, but they could sense it; the beginning of the "Scheme of Work" carries the warning that "In some cases . . . a law which *prima facie* affects both sexes equally is in reality of a nature to operate adversely to women." The "Scheme" went no further; but it was pointing to the phenomenon which the lawyer Martha Minow has recently characterized as "the difference dilemma."

By the difference dilemma Minow means that the very act of naming difference is to risk reifying it. "[S]ocial and legal constructions of difference have the effect of hiding from view the relationships among people, relationships marked by power and hierarchy," Minow writes. ". . . Difference, after all, is a comparative term. It implies a reference . . . A short person is different only in relation to a tall one. But the point of comparison is often unstated. Women are compared with the unstated norm of men, 'minority' races with whites . . ." It is more important, Minow sug-

20. Carole Pateman, *The Sexual Contract* (Stanford: Stanford University Press, 1988), pp. 4–9. I have discussed the impact of these disparities during the revolutionary era in the United States in "The Paradox of Women's Citizenship in the Early Republic: The Case of *Martin vs. Massachusetts*, 1805," *American Historical Review* (April 1992): 349–78 [reprinted in the present volume].

21. Minow, p. 147: "Rights analysis offers release from hierarchy and subordination to those who can match the picture of the abstract, autonomous individual presupposed by the theory of rights. For those who do not match that picture, application of rights analysis can be not only unresponsive but also punitive . . . In short, rights analysis preserves rather than alters the dilemma of difference: difference continues to represent deviance in the context of existing social arrangements. . . ."

gests, to be skeptical about what counts as difference, and to examine not the "traits inherent in the 'different person'" but rather "the relationships between people who have and people who lack the power to assign the label of difference."[22]

As we develop new and more expansive historical enterprises—global history, environmental history—we will need to resist the temptation to write a history driven by abstract "forces." We need to strive, instead, to link social transformation to political and economic change. We will not be able to adopt national histories as traditionally written, for they convey primarily what has traditionally counted as centers of authority—emperors and popes, patriarchs and legislatures—activities by which men claim, articulate and enact relations of power, without much attention to how the participants in these relations are named or chosen.[23] Traditional historical practice has generally failed to interrogate the ways in which the invisibility of women sustains the power of the men of their class and kin. Driven by a need to understand how difference is enacted even while it is denied, we can insist on asking—of any society—questions that haunt us now. Many are like the questions which the members of the League committees struggled to articulate nearly a century ago. Now, one hopes, we can frame the problems with more precision and address them more successfully.

We can, for example, resist treating as "natural" relationships which we know are socially constructed, named "natural" by state power which seeks to make itself invisible. We can recognize that gender is implicit in many questions which have been assumed not to involve gender at all. When we study routes to public authority, whether legitimate or illegitimate, we can ask not only who has travelled them successfully, but also examine who

22. Martha Minow, *Making All the Difference: Inclusion, Exclusion, and American Law* (Ithaca: Cornell University Press, 1990), pp. 22–23. We reify difference, for example, when health insurance systems cover all nonpregnant persons, a strategy which apparently treats men and women equally, but which leaves women without medical coverage for an expensive disability which is marked female. For the litigation of this issue, see *California Federal Savings v. Guerra* 107 S. Ct 683 (1987).

23. Two recent issues of the *American History Review* filled with fine review essays on the state of the field for histories of Eastern Europe and of the Middle East are instructive for the virtual absence of attention to the relationship of social relations and structures of political power. But now that new archives are opening up—at least in Eastern Europe—we will find that we need not be dependent on inherited histories as written.

found resistance when they embarked on the journey. We can investigate how gender, race and class have affected access to authority and to power. We can ask what happened to gender relations during the Nazi and Fascist achievement of power? or during the U.S. occupation of Japan? or in the course of revolutionary transformations anywhere, including the last four years in Europe after the fall of the Berlin Wall? We can ask how changes in gender relations in moments of violent social upheaval have participated in changing power relations, understanding that it is likely that these changes were not necessarily peripheral but may have been central to the new configurations of social power. We can ask under what conditions ethnic differences have been marked as racial? and under what conditions has it become imperative to effeminize racially marked men?

Asking questions like these may have significant policy implications. For example, studies of intellectual history undertaken in this spirit will take as their subject the knowers as well as what is known. Before we complain about the absence of female intellectuals, we need to ask who learns to read, and we will come up against the harsh statistics of female literacy. In the United States, the first census which showed women as likely to be literate as men was not taken until 1840, and there is evidence that this relationship did not persist after the great waves of immigration at the end of the century. In the world today, 40% of young women, and 75% of women over age 25 are illiterate in much of Africa and in southern and western Asia.[24]

Our account of the social history of intellectuals, or of the absorption of colonial intellectuals into metropolitan culture must recognize that the sites of argument—universities, journals, even coffee houses and taverns— have for much of the past been gendered as spaces accessible to men.[25]

The most heartbreaking problems are gendered: Who is fed in time of famine?[26] Who gets to be a refugee? Who gets left behind? Because single

24. *The World's Women*, pp. 46–47.

25. David Hollinger has thoughtfully observed that intellectual history "focuses on arguments made by people whose chief business was to argue." See David Hollinger, "Historians and the Discourse of Intellectuals," in John Higham and Paul K. Conkin, eds., *New Directions in American Intellectual History* (Baltimore: Johns Hopkins University Press, 1979), pp. 47–49.

26. Paul R. Greenough considers gender-selective survival strategies in *Prosperity and Misery in Modern Bengal: The Famine of 1943–1944* (New York: Oxford University Press, 1982).

men travel alone more easily and invisibly they have had somewhat more success fleeing oppressive regimes.[27]

Dorothy Kenyon concluded her 1971 speech by observing that relations between men and women involved political power. The reason that women had no influence in government for so long, she pointed out, was that in order to get the vote they had to persuade men to give it to them; only in France had the decision on votes for women been opened to a national plebiscite in which women voted. But suffrage alone, Kenyon warned, could not revolutionize political relationships; so long as "men controlled every policy making agency in government," women would have little voice in choosing candidates, setting agendas, managing legislative bodies, choosing what is to be debated and the order of debate.[28] Recent political experience in the United States, when the Anita Hill/Clarence Thomas hearings set off a firestorm of political activity which resulted in the election of more women to Congress than ever before in its history, sustains Kenyon's point, and suggests how heightened gender consciousness can be related to heightened political activism and efficacy.[29]

The work of women's historians in the three decades since Kenyon spoke has made it possible for us to address the issues she raised with more precision, but the categories she identified remain salient. As we face the 21st century, we would do well to heed Kenyon's warnings, guarding against the temptation to marginalize women as different and understanding that the language of marginalization is itself a clue that power relations are at work.

27. See essay by Sybil Milton in Atina Grossmann, et al., *When Biology Became Destiny* (New York: 1984).

28. Kenyon, "Men and Women—Boredom, Violence and Political Power," conclusion. Folder 241, Box 23, Dorothy Kenyon Papers.

29. See Sue Tolleson-Rinehart, *Gender Consciousness and Politics* (New York: Routledge, 1992).

INDEX

Abolitionists, 77–78, 228

Abortion, 12, 308

Adams, Abigail, 64; on women and politics, 15, 57, 263, 287; on men, 57, 129, 205–6, 265–66; on *Common Sense*, 107n

Adams, Hannah, 85n

Adams, John, 108; and women's political rights, 37, 57, 129, 206, 287; on property qualifications, 88; on "spirit of liberty," 95, 264; and *Common Sense*, 107n; and Murray's *Gleaner* essays, 116, 119; and Patience Wright, 127; on republicanism, 131; and James Sullivan, 282, 287

Adams, Rev. John, 234, 235

Adams, John Quincy, 280

Adams, Randolph G.: *Political Ideas of the American Revolution*, 132

Adams, Sam, 282n

Addams, Jane, 184, 191 (ill.), 249; "The Subjective Necessity for Social Settlements," 192; *Twenty Years at Hull House*, 192

Advice literature, 129

African Americans. *See* Blacks

Alcott, Louisa May: *Little Women*, 217–18

Almond, Gabriel, 59n

Almshouses, 89, 109

Ambition, 90, 121, 211, 241–42

American army: women in, 70, 71, 72–74; recruitment and training, 78

American Civil Liberties Union (ACLU), 12, 304

American Historical Association (AHA), 9; Rose Committee Report, 9, 10–12

American Indians, 173

American Magazine, 24, 33

American Medical Association, 184

American Philosophical Society, 29

American Quarterly, 14

American Revolution: and "republican motherhood," 16, 174; effects on gender roles and relations, 38, 68, 69, 95, 96, 98, 173–75, 301; women's participation in, 63, 64–69, 70–74, 79, 84, 102, 103, 128, 206; and social hierarchies, 69–70, 74–75, 98, 146; and women's political rights, 84, 87–88, 90–91, 96–99, 128, 174–75; and historical cycles, 93; and patriarchalism, 102, 262, 263–64, 265–66; and republican ideology, 111, 128–29, 140, 201, 263–64; churches and, 124; taxation and, 137, 152; and corruption, 151; laws for punishment of loyalists in, 273–75. *See also* Revolutionary War

American Studies Association, 4

Andrews, E. T., 117

Anthony, Susan B., 7, 195

Anti-Federalists, 133, 142–43

Antigone, 84–85, 87, 92

Anti-intellectualism, 240

Anti-Saloon League, 184

Appleby, Joyce, 150–51, 152, 153, 154; *Capitalism and a New Social Order*, 150

Applewhite, Harriet, 103

Apprenticeship, 89, 109–10n

Arendt, Hannah, 16, 171–72, 257

Aristocracy, 137, 146

Aristotle, 172, 249

Arminianism, 207

Aron, Cindy Sondik, 183

Articles of Confederation, 265

Astney, Thomas, 275n

Atlanta, Ga., 244

Atlanta University, 230

Austen, Jane: *Northanger Abbey*, 242

Authors, women, 24, 33, 112, 120, 183

Bache, Sarah Franklin, 57, 81, 82 (ill.), 91

Bailyn, Bernard, 52, 132

Baker, Keith Michael: *Condorcet*, 48n

Baldwin, Alice Mary, 18, 226 (ill.), 258; academic career, 224–25, 251–56; "The Reading of Women in the Colonies before 1750," 225; "Two Sisters of Old Boston," 233, 235

Baldwin School, 251

Bancroft, George, 84
Bangladesh, 309n
Bank of the United States, 285
Banning, Lance, 138
Barnard College, 2, 3, 4, 5; founding of, 219, 230, 249
Barnouw, Jeffrey, 151
Baym, Nina, 217
Beard, Mary R., 11, 257, 310; *Woman as Force in History*, 1, 196
Beauvoir, Simone de, 160
Becker, Carl: *The Declaration of Independence*, 132
Beecher, Catharine, 167, 247; *Treatise on Domestic Economy*, 40
Bellah, Robert N.: *Habits of the Heart*, 201, 222
Bercovitch, Sacvan, 205n
Berkshire Conference, 11
Berthoff, Rowland, 139
Bethune, Mary McLeod, 250
Bethune-Cookman College, 250
Bible, 43, 44, 203, 238
Birth rates, 169, 180, 308n
Blacks, 312, 313–14; denial of educational opportunity to, 8, 226, 237, 240; women, 180–81, 216, 227, 230, 250; and "separate spheres," 180–82; authors, 226–27; schools for, 230, 239, 244, 250
Blackstone, Sir William, 37, 295
Blake, George, 272n, 280, 289–91
Blanding, Sarah Gibson, 256n
Blewett, Mary H., 185
"Bluestockings," 32, 39, 40
Blumenthal, Walter Hart, 70
Boas, Franz, 182
Bolingbroke, Henry St. John, first Viscount, 138, 145–46, 149
Bosson, William, 281n
Boston, Mass., 24
Boston Athenaeum, 246
Boston Committee of Correspondence, 77
Boston Magazine, 120, 241
Boston Massacre, 80, 106–7
Boston Weekly Magazine, 24
Boycotts, 76–78, 81, 274

Boylston, Thomas, 81, 104
Boylston, Ward Nicholas, 272n
Bradford, Sarah, 245–46
British army, 70, 74
Brown, Antoinette, 219–20n
Brown, Charles Brockden, 23, 24, 28, 40; *Ormond*, 26–27; *Alcuin*, 36–37, 57
Brown, Richard D., 278n
Bruns, Gerald L., 140
Bryn Mawr College, 230, 248
Buhle, Mari Jo, 170, 185
Burgh, James, 52
Burgoyne, John, 70
Burke, Edmund, 16, 81, 140
Burlamaqui, Jean Jacques: *The Principles of Natural Law*, 293
Burrows, Edwin G., 53, 105, 107, 151, 152

Cable Act (1922), 301
Calhoun, Robert, 147
Capitalism, 150–51, 153, 154, 155; and women, 176, 179, 184–85
Carter, Elizabeth, 28
Cassandra, 84–85, 87, 92
Catherine II (empress of Russia), 243
Chicago, Ill., 193
Child, Lydia Maria, 246–47; *History of the Condition of Women*, 243; *Hobomok*, 246; *An Appeal in Favor of That Class of Americans Called Africans*, 246–47
Child rearing, 94, 141–42, 180
Children, 47; education and, 24, 28–30, 50, 239; gender roles and, 28, 180; women's influence on, 38–39, 44; in Revolutionary War, 73; apprenticeships, 89, 109–10n; family size, 180
China, 301, 308
Christianity, 123, 172, 204
Church, Mary, 250
Churches, 76, 87, 112, 121, 124–25
Cities, 192–95
Citizenship: Fourteenth Amendment and, 12; gendered definitions of, 19, 92, 128, 263, 269–70, 290, 301; civic obligations of, 19, 262–63; education and, 27; Condorcet on, 46; women excluded from,

46, 88, 90, 143–44, 290; Montesquieu on, 58–59; "republican motherhood" and, 58–59, 144, 268; "deferential citizen," 59–60; military service and, 87–88, 90, 91–92, 97, 143–44, 148n, 290; revolutionary redefinition of, 87–88, 91–93, 268–70, 292–93, 301; women's claims to, 91, 93, 97, 267–68, 292, 301–2; republican ideology and, 92, 128, 263, 269; Federalists and, 155; and married women, 264–65, 292–93, 299–301, 306, 309; *Martin v. Massachusetts* and, 270, 293, 301–2; international law and, 306, 309

Class differences, 154–55, 164, 266, 313

Clinton, Cornelia, 93

Cohen, Lester, 142, 143, 144

Cold War, 2, 4

Cole, Phyllis, 206n, 208–9n

Colleges and universities: American Civilization programs, 3–4, 221; women faculty, 8, 10; women's, 10, 191, 230, 248–49; admittance of women, 230, 231–32, 249, 251, 252, 255, 257–58; and black students, 230, 250

Colman, Abigail, 233, 234, 235

Colman, Benjamin, 233

Colman, Jane, 225, 233–34, 235, 236, 240, 243, 258

Columbia College, 39, 94, 249

Columbia University, 2, 6, 221, 252

Commercialism, 152

Common law, 290, 292–93, 294, 295, 300

Condorcet, Marie Antoine Nicolas Caritat, Marquis de, 105–6; on political role of women, 46–48, 52, 55, 56; *Esquisse d'un tableau historique de progrès de l'esprit humain*, 47–48

Congregational churches, 121

Conkin, Paul K., 140

Connecticut, 276

Conscientious objectors, 124

Constitutional Convention, 133, 136, 284

Continental Congress, 100, 127, 128, 274n

Convents, 189n

Cook, Blanche Wiesen: "Female Support Networks and Political Activism," 167

Cooper, Anna Julia, 249–50

Cooper, James Fenimore, 202

Cooper, Thomas, 28–29

Coordinating Committee on Women in the Historical Profession (CCWHP), 9–10, 11

Copley, John Singleton, 115

Coplon, Judith, 2

Corday, Charlotte, 243

Cornell University, 251

Corruption, 137, 138, 142, 151

Cosway, Maria, 42

Cott, Nancy F., 178; *The Bonds of Womanhood*, 167–68

Countryman, Edward, 112

Court and Country parties, 138–39, 146, 152, 154, 155–56

Coverture, 271, 295; "republican motherhood" and, 16–17, 268; revolutionary republicanism and, 129, 264–65, 266–67; separate estates and, 179; and women's individualism, 213; and women's citizenship, 264–65, 268, 287, 299, 300; and confiscation of property, 275

Cowan, Ruth Schwartz, 190

Crane, Elaine, 109n

Cray, Robert E., 109n

Crèvecoeur, J. Hector St. John, 212

Crockett, Davy, 215

Cumings, Bruce, 308n

Curti, Merle, 229

Dale, Julia, 254

Dall, Caroline Healey, 248

Dana, Francis, 279, 285n, 288, 293, 295

Danto, Arthur, 97

Darragh, Lydia, 65

Davidson, Cathy N., 18

Davis, Daniel, 281, 288, 292, 293, 297, 298

Declaration of Independence, 88, 97, 195, 206

Declaration of the Rights of Woman, 102

Deferential citizen, 59–60

Degler, Carl N., 183, 183–84n; *At Odds*, 169

De Hart, Jane Sherron, 314

Delaware, 276

Democracy, 60, 75, 133n, 212
Democratic Party, 154
Demosthenes, 228
Dennie, Alfred, 234
Dennie, Joseph, 24
De Pauw, Linda Grant, 71
Despotism, 142
Dial, 216, 248
Diggins, John P., 151; *The Lost Soul of American Politics*, 145
Discrimination, 12, 231, 305
Divorce, 177
Domesticity, 167–68, 169, 173–74, 180, 190; republican ideology and, 59; and revolutionary involvement, 76–77; Tocqueville on, 160–61; virtues of, 162–63. *See also* "Women's sphere"
Dorr War, 134
Douglas, William O., 64
Douglass, Sarah Mapps, 239
Dower property, 275–79
Dred Scott v. Sandford (1857), 134
Drinker, Elizabeth, 34–35, 85n
Dublin, Thomas, 178
DuBois, Ellen, 170
Dudden, Faye E., 190
Dueling, 90
Duke, James B., 253
Duke, Washington, 249, 253
Duke University, 224, 225, 254
Dunn, Mary Maples, 189, 204
Dwight, Timothy, 29–30, 35–36
Dye, Nancy Schrom, 185
Dzuback, Mary Ann, 255–56n

Earle, Alice Morse: *Home Life in Colonial Days*, 166
Economic dependence, 89, 91
Economic development, 148–50
Edenton, N.C., 77
Education, 310; blacks and, 8, 226, 230, 237, 239, 240, 244, 250; Benjamin Rush on, 24, 25, 29, 30–31, 32, 38, 40, 58; and marriage, 24–25, 26, 39, 240; and women's independence, 25–26, 27, 117, 118, 218, 219; Judith Sargent Murray on, 26, 28,

29, 30, 38, 118, 242, 257–58; republican ideology and, 27, 38–40, 238; deficiencies of women's, 28–29, 37–38, 218–19, 247; establishment of girls' schools, 29, 238, 239, 243–44; curriculum for women, 29–32, 243; opposition to women's, 32–34, 37, 239–40, 256; Rousseau on, 41, 49, 50; Adam Smith on, 50n, 219, 235–36, 256–57; and women's literacy rates, 112, 203, 229–30, 236, 239–40; religion and, 122, 203; Margaret Fuller on, 216–17, 247, 257–58; college, 230–32, 248–51, 257–58; gender discrimination in, 231–32; women's ambition and, 241–42; self-education, 245–46
Edwards, Jonathan, 205
Eliot, George, 246
Elkins, Stanley, 1
Ellet, Elizabeth F., 63–65, 68, 79, 84, 85, 97; *Women of the American Revolution*, 65, 66–67; *Domestic History of the American Revolution*, 65–67, 243
Elliott, Barnard, 66
Ellis, Joseph, 14–15
Elshtain, Jean Bethke, 85n
Emerson, Eleanor Read. *See* Read, Eleanor
Emerson, Ellen Tucker. *See* Tucker, Ellen
Emerson, Mary Moody, 122, 206n, 207–9, 216, 245
Emerson, Ralph Waldo, 201, 208n, 214, 221, 248; "Self-Reliance," 95; "Intellect," 214
Emerson, Ruth, 207–8
Employment, women's: discrimination in, 5, 89, 108, 187, 309; necessity to families, 108–9; Industrial Revolution and, 163–64, 168, 178; and "separate spheres," 164, 168, 178, 184, 185–87; segregation of, 180, 184–85, 186
Engels, Friedrich, 164–65
English Civil Wars, 107–8
Enlightenment, 156, 205; and women, 41–42, 52, 59, 147; "republican motherhood" and, 61, 148; and state of nature, 105–6; "Moderate," 145–46; French Revolution and, 147
Enloe, Cynthia, 69

Equality, sexual, 46–47, 172–73, 288
Erikson, Erik H., 162, 166

Families: women's roles in, 38, 45n, 172, 180; Whig political theory and, 53; American Revolution and, 69–70; working-class, 108–9; patriarchal, 160, 179, 265–66, 297; public/private dichotomy and, 164–65; commercial capitalism and, 179–80; middle-class, 180; black, 180–82
Faragher, John Mack, 183
Fascism, 221, 313
Fashion, 24–25, 28
Federalist, The, 55–56, 133–34
Federalists, 142, 154, 279–80, 296–97; quarrel with Jeffersonians, 14, 155–56; and political parties, 119; and republicanism, 133, 146, 155; elitism among, 146, 151n
Female Advocate, 56–57
Feminism, 43, 190, 305; academic, 3, 258; and women's history, 7, 12–13, 242; and "separate spheres," 18, 163, 168, 197–98; critique of Marxism, 185
Feminist Studies, 170, 188
Few, William Preston, 254–55
Fiction writing, 112, 129–30, 202, 217–18, 234
Filmer, Sir Robert: Patriarcha, 43–44, 265
Fisher, David Hackett, 151n
Fisk, Clinton B.: Plain Counsel for the Freedmen, 181
Fisk University, 230
Flexner, Eleanor, 160; Century of Struggle, 1
Florentine republicanism, 137, 141, 143, 145, 147, 155
Flower, Lucy, 256n
Formisano, Ronald, 282
Fortuna, 143
Foster, Hannah Webster: Coquette, 234
Foucault, Michel, 226, 312
Founding Fathers, 102, 262
France, women's suffrage in, 318
Francis, Convers, 246
Franklin, Benjamin, 125, 126–27, 152–53
Franklin, John Hope, 12

Freedman, Estelle: "Separatism as Strategy," 189–90
Freeman, Elizabeth, 297
Free market economics, 150, 154
French Revolution, 70, 79, 206, 284; and women's political rights, 98, 102, 103, 119, 147, 175; public rituals, 124
Friedan, Betty, 160; The Feminine Mystique, 162, 164n
Friendships between women, 166–67, 168
Frontiero v. Richardson (1973), 12
Fuller, Margaret, 229, 246; Woman in the Nineteenth Century, 216; on women's education, 216–17, 219, 247, 257–58; "Conversations," 247–48; Memoirs, 248

Gadsden, Christopher, 76
Gallatin, Albert, 151–52
Galloway, Grace, 296n
Galloway, Joseph, 296n
Gannett, Deborah, 23
Gardiner, John Sylvester John, 33, 240
Gardiner, Sylvester, 285n
Garvin, Eleanor, 109n
Gates, Henry Louis, 226
Gay, Peter, 41
Geertz, Clifford, 140–41, 161; "Ideology as a Cultural System," 140; "Common Sense as a Cultural System," 141
Gender, social construction of, 69, 312, 313
Gender relations, 303, 306; American Revolution and, 69–70, 95; French Revolution and, 98; war and social upheaval and, 104, 317; republican ideology and, 143; American Indians and, 173; "separate spheres" and, 196, 198–99; defined as submission of women, 200–201; UN reports on, 307–8, 309–10; women's history and, 311; political power and, 318
Genet, Edmond, 93
George III (king of England), 264, 266
Georgia, 277
Gerry, Elbridge, 286–87
Gilbert, Katherine, 254
Gilbert, Sandra M., 217, 218
Gilman, Charlotte Perkins, 257

Gilmore, William, 236–37
Ginsburg, Ruth Bader, 8, 12, 304
Godwin, William, 35
Gordon, Anna. *See* Martin, Anna Gordon
Gordon, James, 270, 271
Gordon, Thomas, 138
Gouges, Olympe de, 102
Graham, Patricia Albjerg, 9, 11
Gramsci, Antonio, 223
Gray, Hanna Holborn, 9
Great Awakening, Second, 86–87, 125, 206–7
Great Britain, 137, 206; in World War I, 79; Court and Country factions, 138–39
Greene, Catherine, 71
Greene, Nathanael, 72n, 124
Grey, Lady Jane, 243
Grimké, Angelina, 159, 167, 291
Grimm tales, 67–68
Gross, Robert, 18
Grossberg, Michael, 266, 297
Gubar, Susan, 217, 218
Guilds, women's, 103, 104
Gundersen, Joan R., 108, 264n
Gutridge, Molly, 124

Habermas, Jürgen, 110
Hacker, Barton, 73
Hale, Sarah Josepha: *Woman's Record*, 243
Hall, David, 209n
Hall, Sarah, 24
Hallowell, Benjamin, 272n
Hamilton, Alexander, 151–52, 241, 285
Hancock, John, 282n
Hareven, Tamara K., 178, 182n
Hartford Patriotic and Economic Association, 77
Hartog, Hendrik, 266n, 267
Haskell, Thomas L., 175
Hayden, Dolores, 192; *The Grand Domestic Revolution*, 190
Hays, Mary ("Molly Pitcher"), 70, 72, 74
Health care, 12, 308, 310
Health insurance, 316n
Hesseltine, William, 202
Hexter, J. H., 135, 145

Higginson, Thomas Wentworth, 224
Higher Education Act (1972), 231
Hill, Anita F., 318
Historians, 18, 310–11; women, 9–10, 11–12; and "separate spheres," 18, 161, 162, 165–66, 169–70, 187, 188, 196; and republicanism, 131–32, 135–36, 139–40
Historical cycles, 93, 141
Historiography, 18, 196
History, study of, 242
Hobbes, Thomas, 105–6
Hobby, Oveta Culp, 184
Hodgkins, Sarah, 68–69
Hofstadter, Richard, 1, 6, 14–15, 240
Hohendahl, Peter, 110
Hollinger, David, 5, 227, 317n
Homosexuality, 166, 167
Hoover, Herbert C., 220
Hopkinson, Emily, 24
Horowitz, Helen Lefkowitz, 18, 191
Horton, George Moses, 226
Horton, James Oliver, 180
Horton, Lois E., 180
Howard University, 230
Howe, Daniel Walker, 154
Howe, John R., 136
Hull House, 189, 191–95, 193 (ill.), 194 (ill.)
Hull-House Maps and Papers, 193
Humanism, 139, 141, 144, 147, 148, 151, 155
Humphries, Richard, 34n
Huntington, Faith Trumbull, 69
Hutchinson, Anne, 204, 227
Hutchinson, Thomas, 95, 146

Ideology, 140–41
Independence, women's: American Revolution and, 23, 108, 111; education and, 25–26, 27, 117, 118, 218, 219; economic and political, 26, 91; Tocqueville on, 160; religion and, 210–11; fiction and, 217–18
India, 308, 312
Individualism, 149–50, 151, 153, 154; republican ideology and, 128, 264; "republican motherhood" and, 144, 148, 174, 211; and women, 201, 211, 216, 217, 218, 220; association with maleness, 201–2, 214–15,

221–23; Tocqueville on, 211–12, 213; French words for, 212n; "self-made man," 212–14, 215, 220, 221

Industrial Revolution, 153, 156; and political revolution, 148–49; and "separate spheres," 163–64, 168

Infanticide, 308

Institution building, female, 189–90

Intellectual history, 17–18, 19, 112, 202, 225–29; republican ideology and, 43; literacy and, 229–30, 236, 317; schools and, 230, 243–44; self-education and, 244–46, 257

Interest-group politics, 151

International Centennial Exposition (1876), 189

International Conference on Human Rights (1992), 307

International Conference on Traffic in Women and Children (1921), 306

International law, 306

Irving, Washington, 239n

Isaac, Rhys, 147

Jackson, Andrew, 66, 131, 146

Jackson, P. W., 38–39

Jacobs, Harriet A.: *Incidents in the Life of a Slave Girl*, 237–38

Jacoby, Robin, 185

James, Janet Wilson, 8

Jane Club, 194–95

Janeway, Elizabeth, 217–18

Japan, 301, 312

Jayne, Violet, 256n

Jefferson, Thomas, 138–39, 156, 238, 241, 281, 282n

Jeffersonian Republicans, 14, 150–51, 152–53, 155–56

Jehlen, Myra, 202n

Jensen, Joan, 239

Jews, 5, 6, 313

Jones, Jacqueline, 180

Jordan, 309n

Kaestle, Carl F., 238–39

Kames, Henry Home, Lord, 41; *Sketches of the History of Man*, 51–52

Kaplan, Temma, 170

Karlsen, Carol, 204

Kasson, John E.: *Civilizing the Machine*, 141

Kelley, Florence, 192

Kelley, Joan, 17

Kelley, Mary, 18; *Private Woman, Public Stage*, 183

Kelley, Robert, 139

Kenyon, Dorothy, 304 (ill.), 313; on gender relations, 303, 304–5, 309, 310, 311–12, 318; on League of Nations committee on women, 303–4, 306, 309

Kessler-Harris, Alice, 311; *Out to Work*, 185

Kettner, James H., 91–92

Kin networks, 177–78

Knapp, Samuel L.: *Female Biography*, 243

Knights of Labor, 185

Knowles, Mrs., 28

Knox, Henry, 285

Knox, Samuel, 30n

Koehler, Lyle, 188–89

Korea, 308n

Kouwenhoven, John, 3, 4; *The Columbia Historical Portrait of New York*, 3

Kraditor, Aileen S., 162, 183; *Up from the Pedestal*, 163

Kramnick, Isaac, 145, 149, 150, 153

Kristof, Nicholas, 308n

Labor, sexual division of, 98, 180–82, 183, 190. *See also* "Separate spheres"

Lady's Magazine and Repository, 24, 25, 33–34, 112–13, 114

Lafayette, Marie-Joseph du Motier, Marquis de, 102

Lamphere, Louise: *Woman, Culture, and Society*, 188

Lane, Rose Wilder, 220, 221

Langston, Dicey, 64–65, 67

Lasch, Christopher, 163

League of Nations: Committee for the Study of the Legal Status of Women, 303–4, 306, 309, 313; founding of, 305; and women's issues, 306, 307, 312; "Scheme of Work," 306, 313, 314, 315; and infanticide, 308

Lebsock, Suzanne, 179

Lee, Mother Ann, 122, 124, 206–7

Leprilete, Lewis, 272n

Lerner, Gerda, 1, 8, 18, 170, 182; "The Lady and the Mill Girl," 163–64; *The Creation of Patriarchy*, 171

Lessee of Pemberton v. Hicks (1799), 296n

Leverenz, David, 214

Levine, Susan, 185

Levy, Darline G., 103

Lewis, Jan, 295

Lewis, R. W. B., 201–2

Liberty, 145, 150, 154, 200

Literacy: rates for men and women, 60n, 109–10, 236–37, 310, 317; women's education and, 112, 203, 229–30, 236, 239–40; Puritan influence and, 203; improvements in women's, 229–30, 236, 256; blacks and, 237, 240; republican ideology and, 238

Locke, John, 105–6, 136, 145, 147, 148, 149; *Two Treatises on Government*, 43–45, 51, 265

Lockridge, Kenneth, 60n

London, Jack: *Call of the Wild*, 220

Louis XVI (king of France), 112

Loyalists, 124, 275

Lukes, Steven, 212n

Luther v. Borden (1849), 134

Lynn, Kenneth S., 214

Maas, David E., 275n

Macaulay, Catharine, 28, 42, 52, 53

McCarthy, Mary, 229

McCoy, Drew: *The Elusive Republic*, 152–53

McDougall, Alexander, 80–81

McDougall, Hannah Bostwick, 80–81

McGaw, Judith A., 186

Machiavelli, Niccolò, 148; *Discourses*, 88; *The Prince*, 143

McIntosh, Millicent, 5

McKendrick, Neil, 164n

Mackenzie v. Hare (1915), 300

McKitrick, Eric, 1

McLaughlin, Andrew, 252–53

Madison, James, 133–34, 138–39, 154

Magazines, 24

Malaysia, 309n

Mann, Horace, 244

Margaret of Anjou, 243

Marriage: women's education and, 24–25, 26, 39, 240; Wollstonecraft on, 35, 36; Locke on, 44n; restriction of women's property rights, 108, 176, 215–16, 264–65, 271–72, 297–98; republican ideology and, 129, 264–65, 295; "separate spheres" and, 168; women's property reform laws, 176, 177; submission of women in, 204–5, 294, 295, 297; fiction and, 234; and women's citizenship, 264–65, 292–93, 299–301, 306, 309

Martin, Anna Gordon, 261, 270, 271–72, 279, 289, 291, 293, 294, 296

Martin, James, 261, 270, 272, 279, 293, 295, 298n

Martin, William, 270–72, 288–89, 294

Martin v. Commonwealth of Massachusetts (1805), 270, 279–80, 288–98, 301–2

Marx, Karl, 165

Marxist analysis, 164, 165, 166, 185

Mason, George, 138–39

Mason, Priscilla, 31–32, 36, 37

Mason, Ruby, 256n

Mason, Sally, 89

Massachusetts, 280; Supreme Judicial Court, 261, 279; Confiscation Act (1779), 272, 275n, 277, 278–79, 288–89; and women as citizens, 273, 274, 278–79; Treason Act (1777), 273–74, 291

Massachusetts Bay Colony, 200, 203

Massachusetts Magazine, 26, 116, 120, 241

Materialism, 151, 214

Mather, Cotton, 121

Matthiessen, Francis O., 221

May, Henry F., 145–46

Mead, Margaret, 14, 257

Mecom, Jane, 126

Melville, Herman, 202, 221

Men: women and moral development of, 38–39, 40, 58–59, 93, 94, 174; women's submission to, 44, 118–19, 171, 172–73, 200–201, 203, 204–5, 295; and citizenship rights, 46, 49, 87–88, 90, 92, 143–44, 261–62, 263, 290; Abigail Adams on, 57, 129, 205–6, 265–66; democracy and, 60, 61, 212; literacy rates, 60n, 109–10, 236–37, 310, 317; Revolutionary War soldiers, 70, 72, 73, 78–79, 90; women and sinfulness of, 86, 123; military service obligation, 87–88, 92, 143–44, 290; psychological link to Revolution, 89–90; American Revolution and male roles, 95–96, 107–8; republican ideology and, 102, 106–7, 128–29, 143, 262, 263–64; patriarchy in marriage, 108, 264–67, 290, 294, 295, 297; "separate spheres" and, 161–62, 164, 165, 168, 171, 188, 195; women and social advancement of, 180; and individualism, 201–2, 212, 215, 217, 221–23; "self-made man," 212–14, 215; and gender relations, 305, 306, 312

Mendoza, Daniel, 34n

Meredith, Gertrude, 24, 32, 111n

Mesier, Peter, 81, 104

Methodism, 121–22, 206–7

Meyer, Annie Nathan, 219, 248, 249

Meyerowitz, Joanne, 195

Meyers, Marvin, 175

Michigan, 177

Middle class, 149, 153, 181–82, 218

Middle-class women, 195; and "republican motherhood," 16–17, 96; and literacy, 18, 236; in Revolutionary War, 76, 84; and "separate spheres," 160, 164, 167–68, 181–82; and class distinctions, 164n; paid employment, 180; organizations of, 189

Middlekauff, Robert: *The Glorious Cause*, 68–69

Military service: women and, 70–74, 78–79, 88, 90, 143–44; training for, 78; and citizenship rights, 87–88, 90, 91–92, 97, 143–44, 148n, 290

Militias, 78

Milkman, Ruth, 187

Mill, John Stuart, 147

Miller, Alice Duer, 251

Miller, Perry, 203; *The New England Mind*, 227

Mills, C. Wright, 14

Milton, John: *Paradise Lost*, 246

Minor, Virginia, 134

Minow, Martha, 315–16

Misogyny, 215

Mississippi State College for Women, 249

Mitchell, Juliet: *Woman's Estate*, 165

Modernism, 221

Monaghan, E. Jennifer, 236

Monarchy, 43–44, 142, 263

Monmouth, Battle of, 72

Montagu, Lady Mary Wortley, 28

Montesquieu, Charles Louis de Secondat, Baron de, 41, 136–37; on women and government, 45–46, 55, 58–59, 142, 144; *The Persian Letters*, 142, 205; *The Spirit of the Laws*, 142, 205

Montgomery, Janet, 69

Moravians, 239

More, Hannah, 28

Morgan, Edmund S., 135–36; "The American Revolution," 135

Morris, Gouverneur, 133

Morris, Richard B., 6

Morton, Sarah, 116

Mothers, 43, 44, 61, 94. *See also* "Republican motherhood"

Mott, Lucretia, 130

Motz, Marilyn Ferris, 177–78

Murray, John, 115, 116, 121, 124

Murray, Judith Sargent, 40, 216; on women's history, 15, 23, 75n, 118; on women's education, 26, 28, 29, 30, 38, 118, 242, 257–58; on women's independence, 26, 58, 117, 129, 130, 148; periodical essays, 26, 110–11, 115, 116–17; *The Gleaner*, 26, 115, 116–19, 120, 241; on women's citizenship, 60, 92; and republican womanhood, 96, 118, 120–21, 148, 211; marriages, 115, 116; and Universalist Church, 115–16, 121; on politics, 119; "The Gleaner Unmasked," 119–20, 241; on female authors, 120, 241; on female ambition, 121, 211, 241–42; on Patience Lovell Wright, 125

Murray, Mrs. Robert, 66

Murrin, John G., 138, 154

Myrdal, Gunnar, 305n, 313–14
Mysticism, 207, 216

Nash, Gary B., 72n, 76, 147–48
Nathan, Annie. *See* Meyer, Annie Nathan
Nationalism, 131
Natural law, 42, 292–93, 295
New Deal, 220
New-England Palladium, 35
New Hampshire, 272, 277
New Jersey, 37, 273, 276
Newspapers, 33, 110n, 111, 112
New York (state), 177, 276
New York, Battle of, 66
New York, N.Y., 24, 81, 238–39
New York Press Club, 189
New York University Law School, 303
Nicols, Jeannette, 11
North Carolina, 273, 277
Northwest Ordinance (1787), 262
Norton, Mary Beth, 144–45n, 173–74
Nuclear family, 164–65

Oaths of allegiance, 273, 274, 289
Oberlin College, 229, 230, 243
Odiorne, Hetty, 282
Okin, Susan Moller, 172
Oliver, Peter, 76, 77, 80
Olmsted, Frederick Law, 254
Oppression, 91
Osborn, Sarah, 74
Otis, James: *The Rights of the British Colonies Asserted and Proved*, 54; on women's citizenship, 54–55, 267, 269
Ozick, Cynthia, 218

Pacifism, 123–24, 130
Paine, Robert Treat, 174n
Paine, Thomas: *Common Sense*, 70, 89–90, 105, 107n, 148, 266, 287n; and self-government of men, 89–90, 105, 106–7, 128, 129, 130, 263; *The American Crisis*, 105
Palm, Etta, 174
Paris, France, 103
Parsons, Elsie Clews, 182

Parsons, Theophilus, 280–81, 288
Partisan Review, 229
Pateman, Carole, 314–15
Patriarchalism: American Revolution and, 102, 262, 263–64, 265–66; republican ideology and, 107–8, 111, 128–29, 263–64, 265; family, 160, 179, 265–66, 297; and "separate spheres," 174, 176; economic development and, 175, 176, 179; and married women's property laws, 176, 264–65, 266–67
Patriotism, 76, 79, 263
Pattison, James, 270–71
Paul, Saint, 56, 163
Pennsylvania, 277
Pennsylvania Evening Post, 78–79
Pennsylvania Supreme Court, 296n
Pessen, Edward, 160–61n
Petersburg, Va., 179
Petit treason, 265, 269
Philadelphia, Pa., 24, 103, 109
Philadelphia Institute for Colored Youth, 239
Philanthropy, 57–58
Philosophes, 41, 42, 43. *See also* Enlightenment
Pierce, Sarah, 239
Pierrepont, Sarah, 205
Pierson, George Wilson, 160–61n
Pisan, Christine de: *City of Ladies*, 117
Pitcher, Molly (Mary Hays), 70, 72, 74
Pitkin, Hanna Fenichel, 143
Plato, 240; *The Republic*, 51
Plato, Ann, 227
Platt, Gerald M., 52
Pocock, J. G. A., 143; on republican theory, 132, 137, 138, 139, 146, 148n; *The Machiavellian Moment*, 137
Political parties, 119, 155
Political power, 305, 318
Political rights: Wollstonecraft on, 35, 91; denied to women, 36–37, 42–43, 58, 88, 91, 143–44; Enlightenment authors and, 42, 43–45, 46, 52, 55, 147; "republican motherhood" and, 43, 47, 58, 60–62, 144, 268; revolutionary republicanism

and, 43, 84, 87–88, 90–91, 92, 95, 96–99, 143–44, 174–75, 268; James Otis on, 54–55; French Revolution and, 98, 102, 103, 119, 147, 175; coverture law and, 300
Political socialization, 59, 61
Polygamy, 133
Pope, Alexander, 242
Pope's Day, 80
Port Folio, 24, 32
Poststructuralism, 314
Potter, David M., 213n, 310; "American Women and the National Character," 168n, 202
Poverty, feminization of, 109, 198
Prescott, Job, 65
Price, Richard, 75
Progressive Era, 61–62, 135, 140, 182, 184, 223
Property ownership: and qualification for voting, 88–89; married women's restricted rights of, 108, 176, 215–16, 264–65, 271–72, 297–98; married women's reform laws, 176, 177, 179; confiscation statutes, 273, 274–79, 289, 297–98
Prostitution, 89, 307–8
Protestantism, 121, 124, 147, 149, 238
"Public female sphere" (Freedman) 189
Public/private dichotomy, 164–65, 166, 171–72, 189, 314
"Public sphere" (Habermas), 110
Puritan society, 188–89, 203, 204, 205n

Quakers, 104, 124, 130, 189, 210, 239
Quartering Act, 81n
Quincy, Samuel, 174n

Race relations, 170, 305, 313–14
Racism, 64, 215
Radway, Jan, 18
Rand, Isaac, 272n
Randolph, John, 139
Randolph-Macon College, 230
Rape, 308
Rawle, Anna, 57, 81
Read, Eleanor, 209–11
Reading, 17–18, 235, 236, 238, 245–46

Rebel, Hermann, 67–68
Reed, Esther de Berdt, 57, 81, 83 (ill.), 91
Refugees, 317–18
Reinier, Jacqueline: "Raising the Republican Child," 141–42
Religion, 280; and Revolutionary War, 76, 85, 123–24, 147; and women's civic obligations, 85–87, 122–23, 124–25; Second Great Awakening, 86–87, 125, 206–7; women's church membership, 121–22; and women's education and literacy, 122, 203; and "separate spheres," 182; and women's individualism, 206–7, 209–11
Renaissance, 132, 263, 268, 311
Republicanism, 104, 130; and women's education, 27, 28, 38–40, 238; and women's political role, 43, 84, 87–88, 92, 95, 96–99, 143–44, 174–75, 268; Montesquieu on, 45–46, 136–37, 142; and citizenship rights, 87–88, 90, 92, 128, 263, 269; and patriarchalism, 102, 107–8, 111, 128–29, 263–64, 265; and women's independence, 108, 111; and individualism, 128, 264; and coverture law, 129, 265; historians and, 131–32, 135–36, 139–40; Constitution on, 132–33; Federalists and, 133, 146, 155; Madison on, 133–34; definitions of, 134–38, 139–40; Florentine, 137, 141, 143, 145, 147, 155; Court and Country factions and, 138–39, 146, 155; humanism and, 139, 141, 147, 148, 155; as cultural phenomenon, 141–42, 143, 144–45; Jeffersonians and, 142–43, 150–51; Roman, 143, 147; and deference to elites, 146–47; and slavery, 147; economic development and, 148–49, 150–51, 152; political party system and, 153–54, 155, 156
"Republican motherhood," 16–17, 154, 223; and women's political role, 43, 47, 58, 60–62, 144, 268; family obligations of, 58–59, 94, 121, 148, 211, 238, 268; Judith Sargent Murray on, 120–21, 148, 211; and individualism, 144, 148, 174, 211
Revolutionary War, 74–75; women in, 65–67, 69, 70–74, 78–79; war bonds, 100. *See also* American Revolution

Rhode Island, 133, 134, 276

Rich, Adrienne, 257

Riesman, David, 213n, 257–58; *The Lonely Crowd*, 221–22

Robespierre, Maximilien, 119

Roeber, A. G., 138

Role models, 28

Roman Catholic Church, 103, 104, 124

Roman republicanism, 143, 147

Romanticism, 68

Roosevelt, Eleanor, 5, 184

Rosaldo, Michelle Zimbalist, 196; *Woman, Culture, and Society*, 188

Rose, Willie Lee, 9, 10

Rosenberg, Ethel, 2

Rosenberg, Rosalind: *Beyond Separate Spheres*, 182

Ross, Betsy, 15

Ross, Dorothy, 139, 141

Rossiter, Margaret W.: *Women Scientists in America*, 183

Roubin, Lucienne, 188

Rousseau, Henri: *Sleeping Gypsy*, 97

Rousseau, Jean-Jacques: Wollstonecraft's attack on, 35, 53, 113; on education, 41, 49, 50; on mental capacity of women, 41, 56, 120; on women's political role, 42, 48–51, 52; *Émile*, 48, 49–50, 51, 60; *The Social Contract*, 48–49, 200; *La Nouvelle Héloïse*, 51; *Confessions*, 205

Rowland, Eleanor Harris, 256n

Rowson, Susanna, 116; on women's education, 58, 241; *Charlotte Temple*, 73–74, 234. *See also* Young Ladies' Academy, Susanna Rowson's

Royster, Charles, 88, 90; *A Revolutionary People at War*, 69

Rush, Benjamin: on American Revolution, 23, 69, 74–75; on women's education, 24, 25, 29, 30–31, 32, 38, 40, 58; and "republican womanhood," 38, 40, 96

Rutgers, Elizabeth, 298n

Rutgers v. Waddington (1784), 298n

Ryan, Mary P., 195; *Cradle of the Middle Class*, 179–80, 213

St. Louis, Mo., 244

Salinger, Sharon, 109n

Sampson, Deborah, 74

Saturday Evening Post, 220

Schools: women's colleges, 10, 191, 230, 248–49; women's academies, 29, 238, 239, 243, 244; coeducational, 238–39, 244. *See also* Education

Schorske, Carl, 9

Scott, Anne Firor, 8

Scott, Joan Wallach, 1, 104

Secker, William: *A Wedding Ring Fit for the Finger*, 204–5

Secularization, 182

Sedgwick, Catharine Maria, 297

Sedgwick, Theodore, 279, 288, 293–95

Seider, Christopher, 80

"Self-made man," 212–14, 215

Self-reliance, 23, 26, 27, 58, 94, 220–21

Sen, Amartya, 308, 310

Seneca Falls Declaration of Sentiments (1848), 201, 300

"Separate spheres": historians and, 18, 161, 162, 165–66, 169–70, 187, 188, 196; feminism and, 18, 163, 168, 197–98; sexual division of labor, 98, 180–82, 183, 190; Tocqueville on, 160–61, 163, 171, 175, 196, 198; development as metaphor, 161–63, 165–66, 169–71, 175, 183, 184, 187, 196–99; Industrial Revolution and, 163–64, 168; Marxist analysis and, 164, 166, 185; women's employment and, 164, 168, 178, 184, 185–87; public/private dichotomy and, 164–65, 171–72, 189; "women's culture" and, 169–71, 178; American Indians and, 173; republican ideology and, 174; capitalism and, 176, 179–80, 184; blacks and, 180–82; religion and, 182; embodiment in physical spaces, 188–90, 195–96. *See also* "Women's sphere"

Seven Wise Women, 248

Seven Years' War, 70

Sexual autonomy, 169, 234

Sexual contract, 315

Sexual violence, 308

Shadd, Mary Ann, 243

Shakers, 122
Shalhope, Robert: "Toward a Republican Synthesis," 132
Shammas, Carole, 267
Shanks, Ann Scott, 299
Shanks, Joseph, 299
Shanks v. Dupont (1830), 298–300
Shattuck, Job, 65n
Shattuck, Sarah, 65n
Shays, Daniel, 285
Shays's Rebellion, 134
Sheppard-Towner Act, 184
Shiels, Richard D., 121
Shy, John, 74, 78
Sicherman, Barbara, 18, 184
Signs, 185
Silliman, Benjamin: *Letters of Shahcoolen*, 35–36
Sklar, Kathryn Kish, 167, 192, 287–88
Slavery, 47, 60, 134, 147, 286
Slocumb, Mary, 67
Smelser, Marshall, 136
Smith, Adam, 149, 175; on women's education, 50n, 219, 235–36, 256–57; *The Wealth of Nations*, 50n, 235–36
Smith, Billy G., 71n
Smith, Daniel Scott, 169
Smith, Elizabeth Oakes, 217, 219
Smith, Henry Nash: *Virgin Land*, 4, 136
Smith, Page, 9
Smith, Samuel Harrison, 29, 29–30n
Smith College, 230, 248
Smith-Rosenberg, Carroll, 166–67, 170, 215; "The Female World of Love and Ritual," 166
Social contract theory, 48–49, 54, 262, 314–15
Social hierarchies, 69–70
Social theory, 44, 166
Society of Revolutionary Republican Women, 102
Soldiers, 57, 70, 72, 81n, 90, 113
Solemn League and Covenant, 77, 274
Solomon, Barbara Miller, 231
Sorosis Club, 189
South Carolina, 276

Soviet Union, 305, 307
"Spartan Mother," 43
Spelman College, 230, 248
Spencer, Anna Garlin: *Women's Share in Social Culture*, 224
Spooner, Hertha, 254
Stack, Carol B., 178
Staël, Anne-Louise-Germaine de: *Corrine*, 246
Stanford University, 231
Stansell, Christine: *City of Women*, 193, 195
Stanton, Elizabeth Cady, 7, 91, 148, 268; "The Solitude of Self," 201
Statelessness, 306, 309
"State of nature," 105–6
Steddiford, Catharine, 239n
Sterling, Dorothy, 180
Stevens, John, 115, 116, 118
Stevenson, Adlai E., 222, 257n
Stevenson, Molly, 42
Stone, Lucy, 159, 220n, 243–44n
Stoppard, Tom: *Rosenkrantz and Guildenstern Are Dead*, 102
Storing, Herbert, 133n
Story, Joseph, 298–300
Strasser, Susan, 190
Strober, Myra H., 187
Strong, Caleb, 281, 299
Strong, Simeon, 279, 293n, 295
"Subjugated knowledge," 226, 312
Sullivan, Daniel, 284
Sullivan, James, 281–88, 283 (ill.), 291–92, 297–98; *The Path to Riches*, 285
Sullivan, John, 282, 284
Sydnor, Charles, 59–60

Taft, Jessie, 182
Talbot, Marion, 252
Taxation, 137, 149, 152, 263, 264
Taylor, Alan, 285
Taylor, John, 139
Taylor, Peter, 67–68
Tentler, Leslie Woodcock, 178n
Terrell, Ebenezer, 233
Terrell, Jane Colman. *See* Colman, Jane
Terrell, Mary Church, 250

Thackara, James, 113
Thatcher, George, 279, 293
Thomas, Clarence, 318
Thomas, Isaiah, 117
Thomas, W. I., 182
Thompson, E. P., 168, 178
Thompson, Helen, 182
Tobias, Sheila, 187
Tocqueville, Alexis de: *Democracy in America*, 159–60, 211–12; on "separate spheres," 160–61, 163, 171, 175, 196, 198; on individualism, 201, 211–12, 213
Treason, 273–74, 289, 296n; *petit treason*, 265, 269
Trenchard, John, 53, 138
Trilling, Lionel, 6
Trinity College, 249, 252, 253
Troen, Selwyn K., 244
Trojan War, 85
Trumbull, John, 18, 97, 232
Tucker, Ellen, 214
Tucker, St. George, 37, 57
Turner, Frederick Jackson, 18
Twain, Mark, 202, 221

Ulrich, Laurel Thatcher, 124, 173n
UNICEF, 309n
United Nations, 307, 309–10, 312; Commission on the Status of Women, 304; Convention on the Elimination of All Forms of Discrimination Against Women (CEDAW), 307, 309
United States, 309, 317
U.S. Congress, 262, 318
U.S. Constitution, 85, 119, 156, 265, 284; Fourteenth Amendment, 12, 304; on republican government, 132–33
U.S. Supreme Court, 12, 134, 300, 305
Universal Asylum, 28
Universalist Church, 121, 286
University of Chicago, 231, 252
University of Iowa, 230
University of Michigan, 197 (ill.), 249
University of Missouri, 249
University of North Carolina, 231
University of South Carolina, 231

University of Virginia, 232
University of Wisconsin, 231, 249
Utah, 133

Vagrancy, 109
Vallance, John, 113
Van Blarenberghe, Louis, 71n
Van Schaack, Henry, 293n
Vassar College, 248
Venetian Republic, 137
Verba, Sidney, 59n
Versailles, women's march on, 103
Victorian culture, 166
Vietnam War, 6, 131
Violence, 81, 305; domestic, 129; sexual, 308
Virginia, 60, 277
Virtue, 129–30, 143, 156
Vocational education, 26
Volland, Sophie, 42
Voting rights, 37, 60, 88, 183n, 286–87, 318

Waddington, Joshua, 298n
Walker, Quock, 96, 286
Wallace, Michael, 53, 105, 107
Walters, Ronald G., 140–41
War, 84–85, 86, 123–24
Ward, John William, 202–3n, 213; *Andrew Jackson*, 4, 136
War of 1812, 6
Warren, James, 55
Warren, Mercy Otis, 55, 64, 73, 93–94, 131; *The Adulateur*, 80; *The Ladies of Castile*, 99; and republicanism, 142, 144, 147
Warsaw Pact, 307
Washington, George, 116, 119; and women in the army, 71, 72–73, 74; as "father of his country," 128n, 264
Washington, Martha, 64, 71, 116
Watts, Steven: *The Republic Reborn*, 151
Webster, Noah, 24, 29, 30, 33
Weekly Magazine, 30
Weinstein, Fred, 52
Wellesley College, 230, 248
Wells, Rachel Lovell, 15, 100–103, 125–26, 127, 128, 129

Welter, Barbara, 166; "The Cult of True Womanhood," 162–63, 164
Wesley, John, 115
Wesley, Susannah, 121–22, 207
Wharton, Edith, 3
Wheatley, Phillis: *Poems on Various Subjects*, 226
Whigs: and women's political capacity, 42, 53, 54; and republicanism, 139, 154, 263, 268
White, Deborah Gray, 180
White, Hayden, 187–88n
Whitman, Walt, 4
Widows, 109, 147–48, 178, 275
Wilberforce University, 230
Wilder, Laura Ingalls: *Little House* books, 220–21
Wilentz, Sean, 153–54; *Chants Democratic*, 153
Wilkinson, Jemima, 122, 206–7
Willard, Emma, 219, 239, 242
Willard, Samuel, 172–73
Williams, Samuel, 75
Winthrop, John, 200–201, 203
Witchcraft, 173
Wollstonecraft, Mary, 28, 42, 117; *A Vindication of the Rights of Woman*, 34–35, 53, 91, 112–15; on capabilities of women, 34–35, 91, 92, 113–15, 174, 198, 240, 293; attack on Rousseau, 35, 53, 113; critics of, 35–36
Woman's Christian Temperance Union (WCTU), 184
Women Invited to War (pamphlet), 85, 122–23, 129
"Women's culture," 166–67, 169, 170–71, 178

Women's history, 1–2, 13–14, 17, 242–43; feminist movement and, 7, 12–13, 242; Kames on, 51–52; and "separate spheres," 64, 162, 165–66; Tocqueville and, 160; and gender relations, 311
Women's organizations, 184, 189–90
"Women's sphere," 174, 184, 190; Rousseau on, 35; Revolutionary War and, 64, 95, 97; republican ideology and, 94, 96–97; Tocqueville on, 160–61; historians and, 161, 163, 170–71; and feminism, 163, 168; Industrial Revolution and, 163–64, 168; Marxist analysis and, 164–65; Catharine Beecher and, 167; paid employment and, 178–79, 180. *See also* "Separate spheres"
Women's Trade Union League, 185
Wood, Gordon S., 52, 136, 147, 153
Woodhull, Victoria, 134
Woolf, Virginia, 207, 227
Working class, 153, 154–55; women, 18, 80, 108–9, 164n, 185, 195; Marxist analysis and, 185. *See also* Employment, women's
World Conferences on Women, 307
World's Columbian Exposition (1892), 189
World War I, 79, 184
World War II, 187, 221, 232
Wright, Patience Lovell, 125–27, 126 (ill.)
Wright, Prudence, 65n

Yeshiva University, 6
Yorktown, Battle of, 74
Young, Alfred F., 80
Young Ladies' Academy, Susanna Rowson's, 24, 29, 38
Young Ladies' Academy of Philadelphia, 24, 29, 30–31
Yugoslavia, 308, 309

PERMISSIONS

GENDER AND AMERICAN CULTURE

Toward an Intellectual History of Women: Essays by Linda K. Kerber (1997)

Gender and Jim Crow: Women and the Politics of White Supremacy in North Carolina, 1896–1920, by Glenda Elizabeth Gilmore (1996)

Delinquent Daughters: Protecting and Policing Adolescent Female Sexuality in the United States, 1885–1920, by Mary E. Odem (1995)

U.S. History as Women's History: New Feminist Essays, edited by Linda K. Kerber, Alice Kessler-Harris, and Kathryn Kish Sklar (1995)

Common Sense and a Little Fire: Women and Working-Class Politics in the United States, 1900–1965, by Annelise Orleck (1995)

How Am I to Be Heard?: Letters of Lillian Smith, edited by Margaret Rose Gladney (1993)

Entitled to Power: Farm Women and Technology, 1913–1963, by Katherine Jellison (1993)

Revising Life: Sylvia Plath's Ariel Poems, by Susan R. Van Dyne (1993)

Made From This Earth: American Women and Nature, by Vera Norwood (1993)

Unruly Women: The Politics of Social and Sexual Control in the Old South, by Victoria E. Bynum (1992)

The Work of Self-Representation: Lyric Poetry in Colonial New England, by Ivy Schweitzer (1991)

Labor and Desire: Women's Revolutionary Fiction in Depression America, by Paula Rabinowitz (1991)

Community of Suffering and Struggle: Women, Men, and the Labor Movement in Minneapolis, 1915–1945, by Elizabeth Faue (1991)

All That Hollywood Allows: Re-reading Gender in 1950s Melodrama, by Jackie Byars (1991)

Doing Literary Business: American Women Writers in the Nineteenth Century, by Susan Coultrap-McQuin (1990)

Ladies, Women, and Wenches: Choice and Constraint in Antebellum Charleston and Boston, by Jane H. Pease and William H. Pease (1990)

The Secret Eye: The Journal of Ella Gertrude Clanton Thomas, 1848–1889, edited by Virginia Ingraham Burr, with an introduction by Nell Irvin Painter (1990)

Second Stories: The Politics of Language, Form, and Gender in Early American Fictions, by Cynthia S. Jordan (1989)

Within the Plantation Household: Black and White Women of the Old South, by Elizabeth Fox-Genovese (1988)

The Limits of Sisterhood: The Beecher Sisters on Women's Rights and Woman's Sphere, by Jeanne Boydston, Mary Kelley, and Anne Margolis (1988)